GRANDEUR AN

For my mother

GRANDEUR AND MISERY

France's bid for power
in Europe 1914–1940

ANTHONY ADAMTHWAITE

Professor of History, University of California, Berkeley

A member of the Hodder Headline Group
LONDON • NEW YORK • SYDNEY • AUCKLAND

First published in Great Britain in 1995 by
Arnold, a division of Hodder Headline PLC
338 Euston Road, London NW1 3BH
175 Fifth Avenue, New York, NY 10010

Distributed exclusively in the USA by
St Martin's Press Inc.,
175 Fifth Avenue,
New York, NY 10010

British Library Cataloguing in Publication Data
A catalogue entry for this book is available from the British Library

Library of Congress Cataloging-in-Publication Data
A catalogue entry for this book is available from the Library of Congress

ISBN 0 7131 6576 6 (Pb)
ISBN 0 340 64530 X (Hb)

1   2   3   4   5   95   96   97   98   99

Composition by York House Typographic Ltd, London
Printed and bound in Great Britain by J. W. Arrowsmith Ltd, Bristol

Contents

Illustrations, maps and tables

Illustrations

Maps

Tables

Preface

W hy study French policy? Of course, the sub-plot of scandal and sleaze has a racy readability, half Feydeau farce, half Chevalier's *Clochemerle*: a senior politician duelling with an electoral rival; his wife shooting a newspaper editor in order to prevent publication of her love letters; a war minister trying to throttle a colleague in cabinet; a former finance minister, who condemned Germany for non-payment of reparations, arrested for fraud when his cheques bounced; a president of the republic streaking into a lake and alighting from trains in pyjamas. 'Publishers know they can sell any amount of books about France', wrote Nancy Mitford, 'in fact, France, like Love, is a certain winner on a title page.'*

More seriously, the fall of France in 1940, along with Germany's two bids at continental hegemony, is one of the defining events in twentieth-century world politics. It proved decisive in shaping the pattern of international politics after the Second World War. 1940 was much more than a French humiliation; it ended four centuries of European primacy. The Japanese conquest of European colonial empires in Asia began the process of decolonization. Breaking Nazi Germany's hegemony required the intervention of the two great flanking powers, the United States and the Soviet Union. Thus France's eclipse accelerated the rise of the superpowers and contributed to global Cold War rivalry. German occupation of western Europe provided an impetus for European integration. France's disappearance as an independent great power shaped British policy for the next twenty years, both underlining the necessity of a close Anglo-American alliance and demonstrating the unreliability of continental European allies.

Don't Tell Alfred (London, 1980), p. 63.

France's fall was indeed, as David Reynolds argues, 'the fulcrum of the twentieth century'.*

The debacle of 1940 cast a long shadow over French society. The defeat swept away the seventy-year-old Third Republic, unleashing a civil war of resisters v. collaborators; a renewal of the 'Franco-French War' of 1789. Hitler's vassal, the authoritarian Vichy regime headed by Marshal Philippe Pétain, collaborated even to the extent of rounding up and deporting French Jews. In the settling of accounts that followed liberation in 1944, Pétain received life imprisonment and his chief minister, Pierre Laval, was shot. Ten thousand collaborators were summarily executed. Even in the 1990s the French are still coming to terms with the Vichy past, particularly its anti-Semitism. As late as 1971 the persistence of the Resistance myth prevented the screening on French state TV of Marcel Orphuls' film *The Sorrow and the Pity*, depicting the extent of collaboration.

How did the victorious great power of 1918 come to grief in less than a generation? In the post-mortems that followed 1940, guilty men abounded. France had been sold, betrayed and corrupted. The classic statement was Pertinax's (André Géraud) *The Gravediggers of France* (New York, 1944). As events receded, analysts tended to explain the collapse as the inexorable outcome of a cumulative moral and political disintegration, stemming from structural weaknesses: an ageing population, a diseased body politic, the blood-bath of 1914–18, social strife, the profound pacifism of the peasantry. William L. Shirer's *The Collapse of the Third Republic* (London, 1970) encapsulated this interpretation of the defeat. The consensus was that France had been an overambitious second-class power without the resources to stay in the race. Recently, however, a reappraisal has taken place. Analyses of 1940 now argue against determinism, stressing the contingency and chanciness of events. First and foremost, the defeat was a military defeat, largely explicable for military reasons.

Contingency is the theme of this book. The argument is that there was nothing preordained or inevitable about France's performance as a great power in the years 1914–40. These years were not one long slide to disaster. Interwar France was not as shabby and stagnant as traditionally portrayed. If the Third Republic had ended in 1931, it would have been celebrated as a success. Many sections of French society were creative, adaptable and enterprising. In the 1920s the economy made a remarkable recovery from the war. Post-1945 renewal had its antecedents in the interwar years. Intellectual and cultural life flourished, as evidenced in the writings of Jean-Paul Sartre, André Malraux, Roger Martin du Gard, Georges Bernanos and Louis-Ferdinand Céline. The *Annales* school, the most influential of

*'1940: Fulcrum of the Twentieth Century', *International Affairs* 66, 2 (1990), p. 350.

twentieth-century historiography, dates from 1929 when Lucien Febvre and Marc Bloch founded the journal *Annales*.

A new assessment of French policy is long overdue. The opening up of archives in the 1970s breathed new life into the study of France's role, illuminating controversial episodes such as reparations, France's Rhineland policy, disarmament and appeasement. This book provides an overview for the student and general reader. In addressing the debates, themes and problems of the period I have sought to integrate the latest research, while at the same time presenting the material in a clear and ordered way so that it can be read by those coming fresh to the subject. Secondary sources have been supplemented by my own archival research. The focus is on the years 1914–31 because this period shaped the options for the 1930s. In David Lodge's novel, *Changing Places*, Professor Morris Zapp has the ambition to kill Jane Austen forever as a subject of criticism and research by dealing with each and every subject that could possibly arise out of reading her novels. I have no such ambition. This is not an exhaustive blow-by-blow account of all aspects of French policy.

The book's central theme is the fluidity and open-endedness of French policy. I have highlighted four features often overlooked or minimized: the role of statecraft, the attitudes and assumptions of the political elite, the deficiencies of the government machine, the failure to sell France. The mindsets and methods of movers and shakers like 'Tiger' Georges Clemenceau, Raymond Poincaré and Edouard Herriot influenced France's performance as a great power much more than supposed. The key question addressed is whether France could have translated the treaty predominance of 1919 into a real hegemony? The crucial years for France were not the 1930s but 1919–24, when it had an opportunity to shape Europe's future.

Questions are one thing, answers another. The record has important gaps. We have no French record of Poincaré's talks with Tsar Nicholas II in July 1914; no French account of the Munich Conference of 1938; little documentation on the decision to devalue the French franc in 1936. For British policy after 1916 there is a plethora of sources, official and private. By comparison French governmental and private archives are meagre. Many foreign-ministry papers were lost or destroyed in World War II. British foreign office files are extensively minuted, French papers hardly at all. Third Republic cabinets did not keep a record of their deliberations. Moreover, politicians had no scruples about pocketing or destroying official files. Clemenceau warned historians to beware of documents and helped by leaving as few as possible. Aristide Briand as interior minister sent for his own police file and burnt it. Ex-premier Joseph Caillaux made off with Briand's tax records. Poincaré conducted correspondence by hand, often keeping no copies of his letters. Memoirs only partly compensate for the lacunae. They are always tendentious and frequently mendacious. Pétain wrote nothing, explaining that he had nothing to hide.

Acknowledgements

I am indebted to many people for help, advice and encouragement while writing this book, especially Diane Clemens, Gerald Feldman, Nicole Jordan, David Marquand, Yvon Lacaze, Alistair Parker, Maurice Vaïsse and Donald Cameron Watt. Christopher Wheeler of Edward Arnold has been a model of kindness, patience and courtesy. I have benefited greatly from the friendly efficiency of staff at the French foreign ministry, the Archives Nationales, the Bibliothèque Nationale, the Fondation Nationale des Sciences Politiques and the Service des Archives of the French parliament. A special word of thanks is due to Nadine Ghammaché for her careful and accurate typing of the manuscript. The good cheer of friends has sustained me, particularly Robert Coleman, Robert Finnigan, Yoichi Kibata, Koji Miura, Michael Moorey, Tobias Reich and Wesley Wark. Above all I am grateful to my daughter Anne-Marie for tracking down books and material. Without the love and support of my wife, Geraldine and my family this book could not have been written.

Grateful acknowledgement is also made to the following archives for permission to quote material: Archives Nationales, Bibliothèque Nationale, Fondation Nationale des Sciences Politiques, the Archives Diplomatiques of the French foreign ministry, Service des Archives of the French parliament, Bodleian Library Oxford, Birmingham University Library, Cambridge University Library, Churchill College Cambridge, British Library London, Public Record Office London and also to the French publisher, Masson, for their kind permission to reproduce some of the material that appears in the tables.

Chronology

1914

28 June	Assassination at Sarajevo of Archduke Francis-Ferdinand, heir to the Austro-Hungarian empire
16–29 July	Poincaré and Viviani visit Russia
23 July	Austrian ultimatum to Serbia
28 July	Austria declares war on Serbia
31 July	Assassination of Jean Jaurès
3 August	Germany declares war on France
4 August	Britain declares war on Germany
29 August	Government leaves Paris for Bordeaux
6–9 September	Battle of the Marne

1915

25 April	Dardanelles expedition
26 April	Treaty of London between Italy and the Allies
23 May	Italy enters the war against Austria–Hungary
5 October	Bulgaria enters the war with Germany and Austria
6 October	Franco-British landing at Salonika

1916

21 February	Battle of Verdun begins
31 May	Naval battle of Jutland

1 July	Franco-British Somme offensive
28 August	Romania joins the Allies
6 December	Defeat of Romania
12 December	German peace proposals

1917

31 January	Germany launches all-out submarine warfare
8–15 March	First Russian revolution; fall of Tsar Nicholas II
3 April	The United States enters the war
June	Mutinies in the French army
24 October	Italian defeat at Caporetto
6 November	Bolshevik revolution
15 December	Bolsheviks ask Germany for an armistice

1918

8 January	President Woodrow Wilson's Fourteen Points
3 March	German–Soviet Treaty of Brest-Litovsk
21 March	German offensive in the west
18 July	Start of Allies' counter-offensive
29 September	Bulgaria signs armistice

31 October	Turkey signs armistice
3 November	Austria–Hungary signs armistice
11 November	German armistice
13 December	President Wilson arrives in France

1919

18 January	Paris Peace Conference opens
4 March	Comintern founded in Moscow
19 April	Mutiny in French Black Sea fleet
28 June	Signing of Treaty of Versailles
16 November	Bloc National wins French elections

1920

16 March	Allies occupy Constantinople
19 March	US Senate rejects Versailles Treaty
4 April	France occupies Frankfurt
18–26 April	San Remo Conference
10 August	Treaty of Sèvres with Turkey
14–16 August	Poles defeat Russians at Warsaw
20–26 December	Socialist Party Congress at Tours – majority form French Communist Party

1921

8 March	Occupation of Dusseldorf, Ruhrort, Duisburg
5 May	Reparations bill finalized – London Schedule of Payments
12 November	Washington Naval Conference opens
26 December	French trade union movement splits

1922

5–12 January	Cannes Conference
6 February	Washington Naval Treaty
10 April	Genoa Conference opens
16 April	Germany and Soviet Union sign Treaty of Rapallo
12 July	Germany asks for moratorium on reparations

1923

11 January	French and Belgian troops occupy Ruhr
14 July	Treaty of Lausanne with Turkey
26 September	German passive resistance ends
29 November	German currency stabilized

1924

9 April	Dawes Plan
18 April	France accepts Dawes Plan
5 July	Britain rejects draft treaty of mutual assistance
16 July–16 August	London Reparations Conference
2 October	Geneva Protocol for Peaceful Settlement of International Disputes
29 October	France recognizes Soviet Union

1925

10 March	Britain rejects Geneva Protocol
April	Abd-al-Krim attacks French posts in Morocco
27 August	Last French troops leave Ruhr
16 October	Treaty of Locarno

1926

April–May	Currency crisis
24 April	German–Soviet Treaty of Berlin
29 April	Franco-American debt agreement
12 July	Franco-British war debt agreement
10 September	Germany enters the League

17 September	Briand–Stresemann lunch at Thoiry
26 September	International Steel Agreement
November	*De facto* stabilization of franc

1927

March	France evacuates the Saar
2–23 May	World Economic Conference
20 June	Geneva Naval Conference

1928

12 January	Arrest of communist deputies
25 June	Franc officially stabilized at one-fifth of 1913 value
27 August	Briand–Kellogg pact

1929

7 June	Young Plan on reparations
August	First Hague Conference decides on evacuation of Rhineland
5 September	Briand proposes United States of Europe
29 October	New York Stock Exchange collapse

29 December	Parliament votes for construction of Maginot Line

1930

3–20 January	Second Hague Conference
22 April	London Naval Treaty
17 May	Young Plan replaces Dawes Plan
17 June	Briand memorandum on United States of Europe
30 June	French troops evacuate last Rhineland zone
14 September	German elections (107 Nazis elected)

1931

21 March	Austro-German customs union announcement
6 May	Colonial Exhibition opens in Paris
11 May	Austrian Credit-Anstalt fails
20 June	Hoover moratorium
3 September	Germany abandons customs union plan
18 September	Japan begins occupation of Manchuria
21 September	Britain leaves gold standard

1932

2 February	World Disarmament Conference opens in Geneva
9 March	Manchukuo proclaimed
11 March	League adopts non-recognition
1–8 May	Elections: victory of left
16 June	Lausanne Conference on reparations

1933

30 January	Hitler becomes chancellor of Germany
4 March	Roosevelt's inauguration
27 March	Japan leaves the League
31 May	Sino-Japanese truce
7 June	Four-Power Pact initialled in Rome
7 June–27 July	World Economic Conference, London
14 October	Germany leaves the League and Disarmament Conference

1934

26 January	German-Polish non-aggression pact
6 February	Anti-parliamentary riots in Paris
12 February	General strike and left-wing demonstrations
25 July	Abortive Nazi *putsch* in Vienna
18 September	Soviet Union joins the League

1935

7 January	Franco-Italian Rome Agreements
13 January	Saar plebiscite favours return to Germany
16 March	Reintroduction of conscription and military air force in Germany
14 April	Stresa Agreements between France, Britain and Italy on German rearmament and central Europe
2 May	Signature of Franco-Soviet pact
16 May	Czech-Soviet pact
18 June	Anglo-German Naval Agreement
27 June	Franco-Italian military convention
3 October	Italy invades Abyssinia
8 December	Hoare–Laval Plan

1936

16 February	Spanish Popular

	Front electoral victory
7 March	Hitler remilitarizes Rhineland and denounces Locarno pacts
26 April–3 May	Elections: Popular Front victory
5 May	Italy annexes Abyssinia
18 July	Spanish Civil War begins
2 August	France proposes non-intervention agreement
27 September	25 per cent devaluation of franc
1 November	Rome–Berlin Axis announced
25 November	Germany and Japan sign Anti-Comintern Pact
14 October	Belgium announces new policy of neutrality

1937

16 March	Clichy riots between communists and right wing
31 May	Neville Chamberlain becomes prime minister of Great Britain
30 June	New devaluation of franc
7 July	Sino-Japanese war begins
24–29 September	Mussolini visits Germany
5 November	Secret Hossbach Conference on German military strategy
6 November	Italy joins Anti-Comintern Pact
11 December	Italy leaves the League

1938

12 March	Germany occupies Austria
28–29 April	Anglo-French conference, London
4 May	Third devaluation of franc
3–9 May	Hitler visits Mussolini
12 August	French financial crisis
21 August	Daladier announces changes in forty-hour week: two ministers resign
19 September	Anglo-French plan for cession of Sudetenland to Germany
22–23 September	Chamberlain–Hitler meeting at Godesberg
24 September	France recalls reservists
25–26 September	Anglo-French Conference, London
29–30 September	Munich Conference and Agreement
30 November	Collapse of general strike in France
6 December	Franco-German Declaration
22 December	Italy denounces Rome Agreements of 1935

1939

27 February	France recognizes Franco government of Spain
15 March	Germany occupies Bohemia and Moravia
	Hungary occupies Carpatho-Ukraine
23 March	Lithuania cedes Memel to Germany
31 March	Anglo-French guarantee to Poland
7 April	Italy invades Albania
13 April	Anglo-French guarantees to Greece and Romania
22 May	German–Italian Pact of Steel
12 August	Anglo-Franco-Soviet military talks begin in Moscow
23 August	German–Soviet Non-Aggression Pact
1 September	Germany invades Poland
3 September	France and Britain declare war on Germany
26 September	French Communist Party dissolved
6 October	Hitler offers peace terms
30 November	Soviet Union invades Finland

1940

28 March	Franco-British accord not to conclude separate peace or armistice
9 April	Germany invades Denmark and Norway
10 May	Germany invades Belgium, Holland and Luxemburg
	Churchill becomes prime minister of Great Britain
13 May	German breakthrough in the Ardennes
28 May	Dunkirk operation begins
10 June	Italy declares war on France and Britain
	Government leaves Paris for Tours
16 June	British offer of Anglo-French union
22 June	Franco-German armistice
30 June	French government established at Vichy
10 July	Parliament votes Pétain full powers as chief of Vichy state. End of Third Republic

Presidents and ministers of France (1914–1940)

Presidents of the republic

Raymond Poincaré	January 1913–January 1920
Paul Deschanel	February–September 1920
Alexandre Millerand	September 1920–June 1924
Gaston Doumergue	June 1924–June 1931
Paul Doumer	June 1931–May 1932 (assassinated)
Albert Lebrun	May 1932–July 1940

Prime ministers

René Viviani	June 1914–October 1915
Aristide Briand	October 1915–March 1917
Alexandre Ribot	March 1917–September 1917
Paul Painlevé	September–November 1917
Georges Clemenceau	November 1917–January 1920
Alexandre Millerand	January–September 1920
Georges Leygues	September 1920–January 1921
Aristide Briand	January 1921–January 1922
Raymond Poincaré	January 1922–June 1924
François Marsal	9–13 June 1924
Edouard Herriot	June 1924–April 1925
Paul Painlevé	April–November 1925

Aristide Briand	November 1925–July 1926
Edouard Herriot	19–22 July 1926
Raymond Poincaré	July 1926–July 1929
Aristide Briand	July–November 1929
André Tardieu	November 1929–February 1930
Camille Chautemps	February–March 1930
André Tardieu	March–December 1930
Theodore Steeg	December 1930–January 1931
Pierre Laval	January 1931–February 1932
André Tardieu	February–June 1932
Edouard Herriot	June–December 1932
Joseph Paul-Boncour	December 1932–January 1933
Edouard Daladier	January–October 1933
Albert Sarraut	October–November 1933
Camille Chautemps	November 1933–January 1934
Edouard Daladier	January–February 1934
Gaston Doumergue	February–November 1934
Pierre-Etienne Flandin	November 1934–May 1935
Fernand Bouisson	June 1935
Pierre Laval	June 1935–January 1936
Albert Sarraut	January–June 1936
Léon Blum	June 1936–June 1937
Camille Chautemps	June 1937–March 1938
Léon Blum	March–April 1938
Edouard Daladier	April 1938–March 1940
Paul Reynaud	March–June 1940
Philippe Pétain	June–July 1940

Foreign ministers

René Viviani	June 1914–August 1914
Théophile Delcassé	August 1914–October 1915
Aristide Briand	October 1915–March 1917
Alexandre Ribot	March–November 1917
Stephen Pichon	November 1917–January 1920
Alexandre Millerand	January–September 1920
Georges Leygues	September 1920–January 1921
Aristide Briand	January 1921–January 1922
Raymond Poincaré	January 1922–June 1924
Edouard Herriot	June 1924–April 1925
Aristide Briand	April 1925–January 1932
Pierre Laval	January–February 1932

André Tardieu	February–May 1932
Edouard Herriot	June–December 1932
Joseph Paul-Boncour	December 1932–January 1934
Edouard Daladier	January–February 1934
Louis Barthou	February–October 1934
Pierre Laval	October 1934–January 1936
Pierre-Etienne Flandin	January–June 1936
Yvon Delbos	June 1936–March 1938
Joseph Paul-Boncour	March–April 1938
Georges Bonnet	April 1938–September 1939
Edouard Daladier	September 1939–March 1940
Paul Reynaud	March–May 1940
Edouard Daladier	May–June 1940
Paul Reynaud	5–16 June 1940
Paul Baudouin	June–July 1940

1

France and the world

'To tell the truth', he continued, 'I have no curiosity at all about other countries. None. After all, what can I find in other countries that I can't find better in France.'
Monsieur Bernadet in Jean Rhys, *Quartet* (London, 1969), p. 174

The French have always been known as builders of enclosures, lovers of walls, and we too had this jealous sense of privacy, a hankering after locks and a desire for security even illusory, this characteristic which people of other countries sometimes deride.
Georges Duhamel, *Caged Beasts* (London, 1937), p. 34

When all is said and done, Great Britain is an island; France the cape of a continent; America another world.
Charles de Gaulle, *War Memoirs*, I, *The Call to Honour 1940–1942* (Collins, London, 1955), p. 109

Strengths and weaknesses of a great power

Good fences make good neighbours. The Pyrenees and the Alps shield France to the south and south west, but the 300 kilometres of frontier with Germany west of the Rhine have no natural protection. In 1914 the greatest single external threat was Germany. Paris and the rich agricultural and industrial departments to the north and north east lay within easy striking distance of the Belgian and German frontiers. The lack of a good hedge round the estate made the quest for security the driving force of France's foreign policy. In 1913 the war of 1870 and the loss of Alsace-Lorraine still rankled. 'The generations born since the war still bear the weight of that war', declared right-wing politician André Tardieu. 'In everything we do, in everything we undertake we sense our defeat hovering over us.'[1]

Prussia's victory in 1871 broke the continental predominance France had exercised since the seventeenth century. The new German empire rapidly overtook France in population and industrial muscle. By 1914, sixty-eight million Germans produced four times as much steel and seven times as much coal as forty million French. From second naval power in the 1870s, France slipped to fourth place in 1914. That said, France was indisputably a great power, ranking third after Germany and Britain, her army of 524,000 the second largest in western Europe.

The republic was a major exporter of capital and entrepreneurial skills. Foreign investments of $9 billion were second only to Britain. The strength of the Paris bourse gave French diplomacy powerful leverage in Russia, Turkey and the Balkans. Moreover, France had the second largest colonial empire. The Franco-Russian alliance of 1894 had ended the diplomatic isolation of the 1870s and 1880s. In 1912 a naval agreement strengthened the Russian connection. Although the Franco-British *entente* of 1904 was not a military alliance, regular staff talks from 1906 gave tacit assurance of British intervention in the event of war with Germany. In 1913 a Franco-British naval accord allowed the French navy to concentrate in the Mediterranean. Above all, France's morale was much higher in 1914 than at any time since 1870. In the first Moroccan crisis of 1905 the leadership had looked for a compromise because they feared that war with Germany would be a repeat of 1870; by 1914 leaders and led were confident of victory. The reinforcement of alliances offers only a partial explanation of this new-found confidence. Primarily, the optimism sprang from the illusion that the next war would be a short one in which the *élan* of the offensive would, at all cost, knock out Germany within weeks, before the enemy's superior economic strength prevailed.

Domestic stability gave France added strength. The Third Republic did not have an Irish problem nor the internal tensions of the authoritarian empires of Austria–Hungary, Germany and Russia. The Republic had survived since 1870 because its constitution divided the French least. Naturally, it had enemies on the far left and far right. The writer Henry de Montherlant was raised in a family so reactionary that it regarded the defeats of the French army in August 1914 as divine punishment for the sins of the Republic. But the extremists, although noisy, were not powerful enough to destabilize the regime.

Ideology and culture fuelled self-confidence. Socialists world-wide acknowledged France as the standard-bearer of the revolutionary tradition, championing liberalism against autocracy and authoritarianism. Before the Russian revolutions of 1917, the French revolutions of 1789 and 1848 were the only examples of successful European revolution. France had no schools for revolutionaries but boasted a 'civilizing mission' – the projection of language and culture. The Republic was the first state to recognize the importance of cultural diplomacy. By the 1900s French clergy had founded schools and institutions throughout the eastern Mediterranean. In 1900 the foreign ministry funded an agency to oversee cultural expansion, allocating 20 million francs to preserve 'our moral influence in the Near East and to extend it to the Far East'.[2] Surprisingly, the confident self-assertion of the nationalist revival that began about 1911 did not extend to sabre rattling. The desire to recover Alsace-Lorraine persisted but there were no plans for reconquest.

What was the downside of enhanced prestige and confidence? Keeping up with the Germans imposed severe strains. Defence spending surged from 25 per cent of the budget in 1872 to 36 per cent in 1913. In an age of conscript armies the litmus test of a great power was the number of men that could be mobilized. Manpower was stretched to the limit with 83 per cent of conscripts called up, while Germany got by with 53 per cent. In 1913 the German army rose to over 800,000; Paris kept in step by lowering the recruiting age and introducing a three-year service law. Given a young and growing population there would have been no cause for alarm. However, France, the most populous west European state in 1850, had dropped to fourth place by 1900. Between 1880 and 1910 the population grew by a mere 5 per cent compared with Germany's 43 per cent. The low birthrate coupled with an ageing population, bred deep anxiety for the future.

There were other weaknesses. The army, although committed to a doctrine of the offensive at all cost, was ill-prepared for a general war. In August 1914 soldiers fought in Second Empire uniforms, without heavy artillery. The quality of the officer corps had declined since 1900; poor pay and low prestige discouraged the very able from military careers. In 1912 little more than a fifth of a group of ninety officers at the Ecole de Guerre, the French staff college, could write correctly. Manoeuvres were infrequent and staff training camps few – Germany had twenty-six, France seven. German staff officers returned to the Kriegsacademie for refresher courses, the French had none.

In the pre-1914 industrialization race France lagged behind her chief rivals, Britain and Germany. In 1850 France and Britain were the only industrial powers of any consequence; by 1900 Germany had outstripped France in coal, iron and steel production. France produced 41 million tons of coal, Germany 279, Britain 292, the United States 474. Why did France fall behind? Economic historians have reached conflicting conclusions about France's slower rate of industrialization. Generalizations are risky since the debate continues. However, to describe the economy as retarded because it did not equal its rivals would be a distortion of the evidence. The economy,

far from stagnating, flourished. Technological innovation showed itself in
the automobile industry. Indeed, it is claimed that by the early twentieth
century in the textile and clothing industry, French labour produced more
per head than British workers.[3]

France's large overseas investments concealed two weaknesses. First,
public finances were approaching crisis point. An archaic fiscal system,
practically unchanged since 1789, could not sustain the surge in armament
expenditure. The Republic, unlike Britain and Germany which had adopted
a modern system of direct taxation, did not introduce an income tax law
until 1914 and then war delayed its implementation until 1920. Second,
continental rather than overseas investment had priority. In 1914, for
instance, Russia accounted for 25 per cent of the external portfolio, the
colonies only 9 per cent. This European bias prevented the consolidation of
overseas and colonial markets. With a few exceptions, like the Lyons silk
industry, overseas trade links were weak. Yet France's economic
vulnerability should not be overstated. To conclude that France no longer
possessed 'the dominant economic and financial means, nor even the will to
maintain a dominant world political influence' is too sweeping and
pessimistic.[4]

France's self-image

What was France's self-image? The French saw themselves as a fixed
Middle Kingdom, heir to Greece and Rome, epitome of western
civilization. 'France has throughout the world stood for the ideals of liberty,
justice and humanity', proclaimed the popular history text, *Petit Lavisse*.[5] A
geography text depicted Paris 'radiating its economic influence and
intellectual prestige across all continents; everywhere people appreciate the
luxury goods sold by the department stores, the works of art produced by its
painters and sculptors and the literary output of its writers'.[6] French
language and culture were regarded as the gold standard of civilized society.
This was not mere wishful thinking. French had to a certain extent succeeded
Latin as the universal language: it was the language of diplomacy and the
second language of cultured elites everywhere. Indeed the Russian
aristocracy spoke French more often than Russian.

However, the expansion of the English language alarmed many: 'Are we',
demanded the revolutionary Auguste Blanqui, 'going to substitute for the
pure, simple accents of our lucid language the mewings of the English?'[7]
Needless to say, the assumption that French values were absolute and self-
evident did not always make for international understanding. 'When will the
foreign ministry stop accusing people of bad faith simply because they don't
think like us', complained one envoy.[8] Nineteenth-century revolutionaries,

like Louis Blanc and August Blanqui, preached international solidarity while affirming their country 'an inspired nation. ... The principle of egoism is incarnate in the English people, the principle of devotion in the French people. England has set foot in no country without setting up her counting houses. France has nowhere passed without leaving the perfume of her spirituality.'[9]

The claim to be the home of the Enlightenment and a haven for the oppressed had substance. France was the first European nation to extend full civil rights to Jews in the 1790s. Polish refugees arrived in the 1830s and 1860s, followed by Russian exiles after 1917 and Germans after 1933. The fusion of patriotism and socialism ensured national cohesion in 1914: 'International socialists like us know only one duty; to defend the birthplace of liberty', proclaimed Gustave Hervé in 1914, 'Long live Republican and Socialist France.'[10] Liberty, Equality, Fraternity, the shibboleth of 1789 commemorated on the Republic's coinage, still rallied the faithful. The other side of the coin was a world of deep and sharp class differences. In 1932 the thinker and essayist Simone Weil, then teaching philosophy in a *lycée* at Le Puy, shook hands with unemployed workers in a public square and accompanied their delegation to the town council. The school administration threatened her with disciplinary action. In Rouen the philosopher Jean-Paul Sartre witnessed a docker dressed in his blue overall being ejected from a café after sitting down on the terrace. Religion validated national identity. France, 'eldest daughter' of the Roman Catholic church, protected Catholic interests world-wide, especially the 'Holy Places' in Palestine. This external mission weathered anti-clerical storms and the 1905 church–state separation.

However, cultural expansion mobilized only missionaries, academics and officials. The public, save for occasional outbursts like Fashoda in 1898 and Morocco in 1911, did not follow international affairs closely. There were several reasons for this neglect. An understanding of international politics was widely assumed to be the preserve of a leisured elite with time and money to follow events. Understandably, domestic issues like the Panama scandal, the Dreyfus affair, the three-year service law and the trial of Madame Caillaux in 1914 held centre stage. Local and regional loyalties were strong. Opportunities for travel were few and far between. For many in the provinces a visit to Paris was a rare treat. Cost confined tourism to the rich. The European continent existed in relative isolation; extra-European wars, revolutions and natural disasters were too remote to be more than a nine days' wonder. The relative slowness of travel even within Europe helped to distance international issues. The sea voyage of French leaders to St Petersburg in July 1914 took four days. Above all, however, the French were convinced of their own superiority and were not therefore curious about other cultures. What did a chosen people need to know about others? The lure of sex, food and culture, it was assumed, would sooner or later draw everyone to Paris.

Even empire evoked little popular interest. For Britain empire was strategically and economically of first importance, accounting for 45 per cent of pre-1914 investment. In August 1914 Britain already had a quarter of a million Indian subjects under arms. By contrast, France perceived herself as a continental rather than world power; Europe and the Mediterranean came first, global and imperial interests second. Although French colonialists had 'an almost mystical vision of a greater France embracing the northern, southern and eastern shores of the Mediterranean' their enthusiasm was not widely shared. 'All that interests the French public about the empire is the belly dance', wryly observed one politician.[11] Despite calls for an African army of 100,000, France had only 75,000 colonial troops in 1914. Colonial investments were a mere 9 per cent of the total portfolio. But the idea of a civilizing mission was taken for granted. Even anti-colonialists were 'more concerned to humanize the colonial regime than to reject it'.[12] The civilizing mission did not include the extension of parliamentary democracy to the empire.

Expansionist pressures in the late nineteenth and early twentieth centuries came from soldiers, businessmen and missionaries rather than governments and the public. The main pressure group, the Paris-based *parti colonial*, an association of fifty societies representing all aspects of colonization, had fewer than 5,000 members in 1914. The cabinet played little part in the main pre-1914 imperial initiatives – the Fashoda strategy of the 1890s, the *entente cordiale* of 1904, the Fez expedition of 1911. Public indifference reflected the belief that greatness and security were to be found in Europe, not overseas. Colonies were no substitute for Alsace-Lorraine. The nationalist Paul Déroulède told a colonialist: 'I have lost two sisters and you offer me twenty chambermaids.'[13]

This continental vision bounded by Europe and the Mediterranean assumed that Europe would remain the centre of world politics. To be sure, the foreign ministry recognized that international affairs had acquired a global dimension. President Theodore Roosevelt's offer to mediate in the Russo-Japanese war of 1904–5 provoked the comment: '[S]omething new and unexpected has happened ... for the first time in its history the USA is intervening in the affairs of Europe.'[14] 1890 atlases in the *Annuaire consulaire et diplomatique* showed mostly the European continent, with only a single map of North America and another of Asia and Africa; after 1890 the extra-European maps became numerous and detailed. However, only a handful of individuals anticipated Europe's eclipse. In 1900 socialist leader Jean Jaurès envisaged 'a movement developing throughout Asia against Europe'.[15] More prescient were the Cambon brothers, Paul and Jules. In March 1901 Paul, ambassador in London, congratulated a colleague on moving to Washington: 'The United States are going to dominate the world fifty years from now and the history of their interference in European affairs will be the politics of the next century.'[16] From Washington Paul's brother Jules wrote 'The Quai d'Orsay has got into the habit of underestimating these people [the Americans] ... I do not believe that Constantinople holds the key to the future ... it is here and in the Pacific that the future games will be played which will interest the universe.'[17]

Decision-makers

T he citizens called to arms in the chorus of the *Marseillaise: enfants de la patrie*, were not called to participate in the making of the Republic's foreign policy. The 1789 Declaration of the Rights of Man and Citizens was conveniently couched in general terms. A small wealthy political class monopolized decision-making, keeping control of the levers of power. Between 1866 and 1940, 67 per cent of ministers came from the upper middle class; 17 per cent from the lower middle class of shopkeepers, artisans and peasantry; 7 per cent had working-class origins. The 1936 Popular Front victory of the left did not change this profile – of 600 deputies in the National Assembly fifty-one were working men. Between 1871 and 1914 one-third of ministers died with over a million francs; 80 per cent were drawn from the richest 2 per cent of the population.

Governments came and went with bewildering frequency – an average life of nine months – but ministerial musical chairs concealed substantial political stability. By 1914 the Third Republic had lasted longer than any regime since 1789. Its anchor was a core group of about 129 deputies, 'the ministrables', who controlled office. In some pivotal posts, like foreign affairs, continuity was impressive. Foreign ministers averaged five years in office – Theophile Delcassé (1898–1905) managed seven. The main stable of the governing class was a private university, the Ecole libre des Sciences politiques, familiarly known as 'Sciences Po', founded in 1872 to combat 'democratic excesses'. High fees confined entry to the rich, and its graduates dominated the civil service: of 286 foreign ministry recruits in the years 1891–1935, 246 were Sciences Po alumni. Despite its oligarchical character – 'the Republic of old pals' one critic called it – the Third Republic was a tolerant society in which individuals enjoyed greater liberty than in most European states.

How did the governing class meet and make connections? The French equivalents of the British club and country house circuit were the salons and literary clubs.[18] Salons were weekly gatherings in a private house hosted by a prominent society woman. They enabled women to wield influence in a male-dominated world. One of the most prestigious was the salon of the Comtesse Greffulhe whom Marcel Proust used as a model for the Duchess of Guermantes in *Remembrance of Things Past*. In 1918 Joseph Caillaux was arrested at the Comtesse's salon for alleged treasonable contacts with Germany. The Comtesse was said to have great influence with the radical politician Paul Painlevé. Poet and diplomat Alexis Léger (Saint John Perse), secretary general of the foreign ministry (1932–40), was rumoured to have met his patron, foreign minister Aristide Briand, in Madame de Vilmorin's salon. Membership of the literary club, Déjeuner Paul Hervieu, included politician Louis Barthou, poet Paul Valéry and the hero of Verdun, Marshal Philippe Pétain. Every year down to 1939 intellectuals, politicians, and officials assembled at the *décades* Pontigny, a kind of ten-day seminar/retreat/house party initiated by the philosopher Paul Desjardins at his home, the former Cistercian abbey of Pontigny in Burgundy. Pierre Brisson, director of the mass circulation newspaper *Le Figaro*, organized monthly lunches for twelve, mostly writers and politicians, and each had the right to bring one guest.

Cultivation of a parliamentary camaraderie softened ideological divisions. Robert de Jouvenel believed that 'there is less difference between two deputies one of whom is a revolutionary than between two revolutionaries one of whom is a deputy'.[19] Tardieu, on entering parliament in 1914, was ticked off for refusing to meet the socialist leader Jean Jaurès: 'You are wrong, you are a deputy and must adopt the manners of one'.[20] But politics were pivoted much more on personalities and their followings than on parties and ideologies. The ceaseless infighting imposed by transitory cabinets envenomed personality conflicts. No amount of camaraderie could mitigate the animosity some senior politicians felt for each other. Hostility even erupted in physical violence – at a cabinet meeting in August 1914 the war minister tried to throttle a colleague. The great feud of French politics was Georges Clemenceau v. Raymond Poincaré. The mere sight of Poincaré's handwriting threw Clemenceau into a rage: 'Do you know what the word Poincaré means? Point: not; carré: square.' 'Can you lend me George V for a while', the Tiger asked British premier David Lloyd George. Waylaid by favour seekers, Clemenceau would shout without stopping: 'You wish to sleep with Madame Poincaré? OK, my friend, it's fixed.' Novelist Romain Rolland claimed that during World War I politicians were 'more concerned to pursue their ferocious rivalries than to fight Germany'.[21] France's leaders undermined their country's reputation by exporting feuds: 'Barthou would murder his own mother', Clemenceau confided to Lloyd George, 'Briand would not murder his own mother but he would murder someone else's mother.' Internecine strife was the norm; departments eavesdropped on each other and ministers used intelligence decrypts to discredit rivals. Such goings-on engendered profound mistrust. The Cambon brothers corresponded via the British diplomatic bag because they distrusted both the foreign ministry and the national post office. Yet the infighting did not encourage early retirement. Perhaps it was a kind of elixir for longevity. Aristide Briand packed so many old crocks into his 1914 administration that it was called the Ministry of the Pyramids. The seventy-four-year-old Clemenceau, on being offered a job, joked: 'What are you thinking of? I'm much too young.' But not all septuagenarians and octogenarians were geriatric. In 1917, seventy-five-year-old prime minister Alexandre Ribot had a wartime schedule that would have taxed a much younger man; he left Paris at 7.00 a.m., crossed a stormy Channel, spent all day talking to the British at Folkestone and was back at his desk by 8.00 a.m. next day.

Two features of the elite's mindset had serious implications for France's international position: insularity and a propensity for abstraction. Insularity sprang partly from the assumption of cultural superiority, partly from the primacy of local interests. Politicians had to protect their local power base by bringing home from Paris contracts for schools, bridges, railways and roads. They had international connections but close and intimate overseas friendships were rare. Premier and foreign minister Alexandre Ribot had an English wife and premier Edouard Daladier an English brother-in-law but neither had ties with the British establishment. Language was a barrier – only Clemenceau spoke fluent English and France's best-known foreign minister, Aristide Briand, had no English. The British elite knew France much better than their French counterparts knew Britain. Ignorance of continental Europe was often abysmal. During the 1914 state visit to Russia, president Poincaré spent the voyage trying to remedy foreign minister René Viviani's 'black ignorance of foreign policy'.[22] In cabinet Viviani referred to the Ballhausplatz, the Austrian foreign ministry, either as the Boliplatz or the Baloplatz.

The education of the political elite, with its emphasis on philosophy and rhetoric, fostered a preoccupation with logic and verbalism: 'A malady peculiar to Latins', wrote Alexis Léger, 'who are grammarians and rhetoricians, dialecticians and jurists.'[23] The system inculcated a belief that a problem dealt with oratorically was a problem solved. Prolix speeches acted as powerful sedatives, encouraging both speakers and audience to take words for action. The careful cultivation of the written and spoken word became an end in itself. Occasionally this had tragi-comic effects. Viviani, for example, took lessons at the Comédie-Française (his mistress worked there) and learnt the great speeches of the past, but made no distinction between a London dinner party and the League of Nations. Offstage he could not finish a sentence without a *merde*. Unsurprisingly, a nervous breakdown terminated his career. Long abstract speeches did not go down well with British leaders who prized spontaneity, brevity and wit. In the 1930s foreign secretary Anthony Eden complained that his counterpart Louis Barthou 'makes long speeches at one'.[24] In 1915 a minister ended a speech with the peroration, 'Justice, Liberty, Right and Victory'. Quipped a British listener: 'He must have strangely misread history if he thinks that justice, liberty and right are synonymous with victory.'[25]

As damaging as the tendency to take words for deeds was the casualness of the decision-makers. In terms of leadership styles they can be divided into three groups: Briand, Poincaré and the rest. Briand exerted himself on two or three issues, occasionally signing a telegram while husbanding his main energies for duchesses in the salons. By contrast, Poincaré was chained to his

desk, immersed in paperwork to the smallest detail. The rest were closer to
Briand's relaxed ways than to the workaholic Poincaré. This casualness
reflected the political system, not indolence. Distrust of a strong executive,
short-lived ministries, lack of an effective government machine – all
encouraged unbusinesslike methods. Those who tried to compensate for
these weaknesses, by combining the premiership and a senior portfolio like
foreign affairs or finance, soon wilted. The relaxed style of more leisurely
pre-1914 days constituted a serious liability in the new conditions of total
war. In 1915 Briand, en route to London for the first wartime allied
conference, spent the time reminiscing. In February 1917 negotiators
returned empty-handed from coal talks in London. Ambassador Paul
Cambon commented: 'it was absurd to send two members of our cabinet to
negotiate such an important matter as coal without agreement on the timing
or the programme of their visit. They began an argument in the House of
Commons, disturbing everyone and upsetting Lloyd George.'[26]

Decision-making

T he traditional picture of nineteenth- and early twentieth-century France
is of a centralized, bureaucratic Napoleonic state with government
controlling the provinces through the prefects. In principle the state was
highly centralized; in practice effective central decision-making was diluted
by a number of factors. France was a divided society and citizens had an
ambiguous attitude towards the state – distrusting it yet unable to do
without it. The prefects, far from being pliant creatures of central authority,
were much more concerned with local notables than transitory ministers in
Paris. Individual ministries were extremely bureaucratic but political,
regional and class divisions, combined with distrust of a strong executive,
ensured that there was no overall coordinating machinery. In effect an
'organized anarchy' prevailed, with key decisions reached informally in
huddles of senior ministers.

In the making of foreign policy, governments enjoyed great independence.
The constitution of 1875 authorized the executive to negotiate treaties
without the obligation to keep parliament informed and the president of the
republic was obliged to make treaties known to parliament only when the
interest and security of the state allowed. Parliament's role in the shaping of
foreign policy was hardly more than a rubber stamp on decisions made by
the administration of the day. Parliament was prorogued from August to
December 1914 and when regular sessions were resumed in 1915 deputies
and senators had an uphill struggle to free themselves from the harness of the
high command. The wartime parliamentary secret committees concentrated
on the conduct of the war and fell into disuse after 1917. To be sure, the

senate and chamber army committees had some say on economic and defence issues, but the foreign affairs committees had little influence.

In theory the cabinet was the supreme decision-making body; in practice it rarely discussed foreign policy, let alone decided it. Thus 'the terms of the Dual alliance with Russia as revised in 1899 were deliberately concealed from the cabinet, few ministers before the outbreak of war ever discovered what they were'.[27] Cabinet meetings were of two kinds: informal sessions chaired by the premier; formal deliberations at the Elysée Palace chaired by the president of the republic. Discussions of foreign affairs usually took place in formal meetings. Several constraints impaired the effectiveness of the cabinet. No official record was kept – the creation of a cabinet secretariat and an effective prime minister's office were post-1944 innovations. Consequently, without minutes it was difficult, if not impossible, to know what had been agreed. Informal record-keeping was frowned on – in 1940 premier Paul Reynaud reprimanded a colleague caught taking notes. Ministers would make notes after a meeting, thereby providing almost as many versions of a discussion as ministers present. There was no voting or counting of noses. Moreover the cabinet was not a handpicked team dedicated to a common purpose but an uneasy coalition of competing constituencies. Ministers ran their departments like satrapies, with scant regard for a premier no more than first among equals. 'I am their leader and must follow them', summed up the approach of most premiers. Crowded agendas and parliamentary pressures left no time for proper debate. Poincaré's send-up of an 1898 cabinet was not wide of the mark:

> Important business will be dealt with tomorrow, but this morning there are so many little things to settle! A certain deputy, displeased over the appointment of ... Another deputy demands for his protégé a judgeship which a senator solicits for another candidate. Grave conflict! ... The cabinet deliberates ... Ten o'clock sounds, ten-thirty, eleven o'clock. The Minister of Foreign Affairs has received some important news that he wishes to communicate to the cabinet, the Minister of Finance is the bearer of grand reforms which will require profound study. What can be done? It is late ... Another day we will talk about general public policy; another time we will attend to France.[28]

Premiers, in order to strengthen their authority, normally held one or more senior posts. Of forty-six premiers between 1914 and 1940 only five served without departmental responsibilities. The strategy was counter-productive; most premiers were hag ridden by the quotidian hassle of running a major ministry while holding together a fragile parliamentary coalition. After a few months on the treadmill they made way for challengers. Any initial pretensions of coordinating government action and translating large views into large policies were soon sacrificed to everyday survival. In war the burden crushed all but the most robust, Viviani complained in 1915:

'physically I cannot stand any more. Every day I spend 3–4 hours in parliamentary committees ... I return exhausted to the office where I am harassed by senators and deputies; I've no longer any time to work at ease.'[29]

How then was foreign policy made? The prime movers were the president of the republic, the premier and the foreign minister. This trio might consult colleagues and others but there were no conventions and no network of standing cabinet committees. Informal *ad hoc* consultation was the rule. Much depended on the personalities, preoccupations and political clout of president, premier and foreign minister. They did not function formally as a troika. The Third Republic presidency was a very different institution from that of the Fifth Republic in which the head of state controls foreign and defence policies. Under the Third Republic the presidency quickly became the target of suspicions previously focused on the monarchy and empire. The attempts of two presidents, Adolphe Thiers (1871–73) and Marshal MacMahon (1873–79), to strengthen the executive powers of the presidency backfired. Thereafter parliament tended to blackball any presidential candidate who showed signs of independence. 'Vote for the stupidest', Clemenceau's advice to parliament in 1887, became a constitutional maxim. As a result most Elysée incumbents were mediocrities. Exceptions were Raymond Poincaré (1913–20), Alexandre Millerand (1920–24) and Gaston Doumergue (1924–31). Doumergue invited the French ambassador in London to see him regularly, arranging appointments through the presidential office and bypassing the Quai d'Orsay. Poincaré made a determined bid to assert himself, promising the Austrian ambassador in 1913: 'I will see to it that a man takes my place [as foreign minister] ... who will carry out my policy. It will be as though I were still at the Quai d'Orsay.'[30] He was as good as his word. During the 1914 state visit to Russia the president led the discussions.

But Poincaré was *sui generis*; usually the premier and foreign minister had the principal say. In fact, foreign minister Theophile Delcassé enjoyed virtually a free hand – premier Emile Combes (1902–05) was so absorbed by the church question that he would remark: 'Don't let us concern ourselves with that, gentlemen, it's the business of the foreign minister and the President of the Republic.'[31] Yet premier Clemenceau was powerful enough to ignore both president and foreign minister, refusing access to the minutes of the Big Four meetings at the 1919 Paris Peace Conference. Normally, however, the strongest single influence on policy was that of the foreign minister. He had two large advantages: the benefit of expert advice and a good chance of staying in office longer than most of his ministerial colleagues. At the turn of the century the ministry, usually referred to as 'the Quai' from its address at 37 Quai d'Orsay, was small and leisurely in its ways, with a reputation for being a law unto itself. 'The minister's ideal', recalled one diplomat, 'was to have no business and that of the subordinates to go abroad as little as possible.'[32] Little was done before lunch and the day's highspot was the five o'clock tea round a log fire. Departments exchanged visits, vying for the accolade of serving the best tea and cakes. Entry was by competitive examination, though standards were none too rigorous. One candidate who waffled his way through an oral examination scored top marks because the examiner believed that it was more useful for a diplomat to know how to avoid a question than to answer it. While American diplomats typed their despatches, the French practised copperplate calligraphy by copying despatches on to gold-edged paper, bound together with blue silk ribbon. In the early 1900s this privileged world was rocked by charges of inefficiency, secret diplomacy and financial irregularities. The 1906 Clemenceau administration declared that foreign policy must become 'republican', and initiated the first big reforms since the early nineteenth century. A unified political and commercial division was set up, together with specialist geographical divisions: Europe, America, Asia, Africa. Technical counsellors for commercial, financial and legal affairs were created. Other reforms included a department for international organizations and a press office. Typewriters, telephones and duplicators appeared. In 1910 the archives department, criticized for burying itself in the sixteenth and seventeenth centuries, launched the first of the great twentieth-century diplomatic collections, the twenty-nine volume *Les Origines diplomatiques de la guerre de 1870–71* ('The Diplomatic Origins of the War of 1870–71').

Alas, reorganization spelt disorganization because it did not tackle the bureaucratic infighting between central staff and ambassadors. Permanent officials pursued their own designs regardless of others and ambassadors retaliated in kind. The resulting disarray explains France's confused handling of the 1911 Agadir crisis. Two factions battled for power, the Sciences Po and the colonial faction. The Sciences Po group, graduates of the Ecole libre des sciences politiques, dominated recruitment. Of 192 entrants between 1905 and 1927, 153 were Sciences Po. Both factions were fiercely nationalist and expansionist-minded. Senior diplomats, like the Cambon brothers, disliked the ambitious, specialist trained Sciences Po staffers and manoeuvred to place protégés in key jobs. Paris officials, annoyed by Jules Cambon's advocacy of *détente* with Berlin, challenged embassy expenses; in self-protection he sent many reports under cover of personal correspondence direct to the minister. On his return from Berlin in August 1914 scores were settled – the official car allocated to him was an old Panhard instead of one of the latest Renaults sported by junior colleagues.

Given the Quai's factionalism, a minister who knew his own mind and stayed in power could call the tune. His private office (*cabinet*) enabled him to bypass senior officials and ambassadors. The office operated as a semi-independent team, personally recruited by the minister and answerable to him. Delcassé, for instance, conducted a personal diplomacy, deciphering secret telegrams himself and short-circuiting officials. Philippe Berthelot, head of Briand's cabinet in 1915, handled the most sensitive matters, briefing

newspaper editors and drafting telegrams which senior functionaries had not
seen. The secretary general, Jules Cambon, charged with overall responsibility for the central administration, was left twiddling his thumbs.

Coordination of strategy and diplomacy

H ow were strategy and diplomacy coordinated? The short answer is
hardly at all. Machinery for harmonizing defence and external policy
was woefully inadequate. The interministerial high national defence council
(*conseil supérieur de la défense nationale*) set up in 1906 to bring together
ministers, defence chiefs and civil servants met infrequently (fifteen times in
the eight years, 1906–14) and focused on the conduct of operations. Until
1921 it had no planning section (*commission d'études*). The deliberations of
the army's own high war council (*conseil supérieur de la guerre*) were also
limited to the conduct of operations. Accordingly, integration of foreign and
defence policy did not take place. This inefficiency had expensive consequences. For seven years the army kept two corps on the Alps because the
general staff was not informed of the secret 1902 Franco-Italian convention
detaching Italy from the Triple Alliance. Why was not more done to improve
coordination? Lack of continuity in military and civilian leadership certainly
hindered liaison. Between 1874 and 1914 the army had seventeen chiefs of
staff, the German army four. And the war ministry frequently changed hands
– in 1913 alone there were four different ministers. After the Dreyfus affair
(1894–1906) the political stranglehold on the army turned it into another
government department. The army's acquiescence earned it the label 'the
great silent one' (*la grande muette*). Official surveillance of the religious and
political views of the officer corps induced extreme caution and slavish
adherence to the rules at the expense of imagination and initiative. Protective
mimicry offered the best defence against civilians and so the general staff
entrenched itself in bureaucratic routine. The result was a stalemate in which
no one ruled effectively. Many of the general staff's eighteen permanent and
one-hundred temporary committees duplicated each other. The war
ministry's fourteen departments functioned independently. 'It is quite
impossible', wrote one deputy, 'for even a talented minister to coordinate
and direct so many different sections.'[33]
  A dynamic civil service might have supplied the necessary drive for the
meshing of defence and external policies. Unfortunately, the bureaucrats,
unlike their successors of the Fourth and Fifth Republics, did not have a
reputation for efficiency and innovation. Indeed they seemed to have stepped
straight from Balzac's *Les Employés* – leisurely, lethargic, content to mind
the shop. Ministries functioned like fortresses, treating each other as

competing sovereign states. A 1916 parliamentary report lambasted the colonial ministry where 'each department ... deals with the affairs of the colonies ... from one particular point of view. The most frequent result ... is that three or four departments deal simultaneously with a question of principle whose settlement requires a single executive decision, and sometimes arrive at different solutions to it.'[34] Administrative procedures created bottlenecks throughout the government machine. At the top of the ladder the minister's office opened mail and sent down papers with instructions. Files had then to climb up by the same route before a second or third journey down the ladder in another section. Officials did not file papers together but kept them separate and locked away, like private property, in their offices. Records might easily be mislaid and if an official was away it was difficult to keep track of issues.[35] This was a Kafkaesque world of dark, ill-lit labyrinthine buildings enclosing sleepy, ramshackle structures. The war ministry, recalled a British liaison officer, was 'that dismal building where nothing was up to date'. Liaison conferences with French colleagues took place in a 'small, stuffy and gloomy room. The low ceiling was dirty and the pigeonholes lining the walls, full of dust.'[36]

The over-optimistic mood of 1914 concealed serious structural shortcomings – economic, demographic and military. Equally important, however, were leadership attitudes and the deficiencies of the government machine. A complacent, overconfident and incurious leadership employed a casual, almost careless, style of governing. The combination of incoherent informality at the top and rampant bureaucracy at lower levels discouraged systematic reflection and assessment. Like God in France (*wie Gott in Frankreich*) was how east European Jews described perfect happiness. The *belle époque* was far from perfect but nevertheless it did offer the individual, Frenchman and foreigner, more freedom and tolerance than any other major continental state. Paris until 1939 was the centre of a great international culture, home to a galaxy of expatriate writers, artists and intellectuals. The Ecole de Paris was known more for its foreigners than Frenchmen: Spaniards (Picasso), Italians (Modigliani), Russians (Chagall), Romanians (Brancusi), Dutchmen (van Dongen). The blend of overconfidence and deep sense of national identity enabled France to survive the hecatombs. The shortcomings must be seen in perspective. All the great powers had problems; none were prepared for the coming war.

2

Armageddon

I remember you telling me on the telephone 'But in the event of a European conflagration'. I still hear your voice and I find in it a prophetic note. You saw further than the diplomats and politicians and I confess that I would be very happy if you were mistaken and I did not have to deliver to you this certificate of perspicacity.

Marcel Proust to his banker Lionel Hauser, 26 July 1914. *Correspondance*, XIII, 1914 (Paris, Plon, 1985), pp. 271–2

I know enough history to realise that great crises move slowly, and such poor little chaps as ourselves can only take pride in our resignation.

Marc Bloch, 16 September 1917, in Carole Fink, *Marc Bloch: A Life in History*, (Cambridge University Press, London, 1990), p. 54

They will not be able to make us do it again another day: that would be to misconstrue the price of our effort.

French officer at Verdun in Alistair Horne, *The Price of Glory: Verdun 1916* (London, 1978), p. 326

Origins

On 1 August 1914 drumbeats and church bells carried the news of France's mobilization from street to street and village to village; three days later the first general war for a century began: the Triple Entente of France, Britain and Russia v. the Central Powers, Germany and

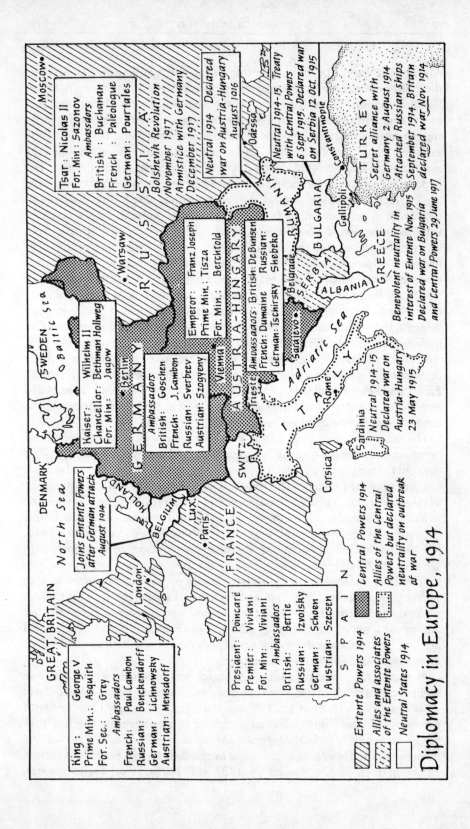

Diplomacy in Europe, 1914

GREAT BRITAIN

King : George V
Prime Min.: Asquith
For. Sec.: Grey

Ambassadors
French: Paul Cambon
Russian: Benckendorff
German: Lichnowsky
Austrian: Mensdorff

Joins Entente Powers after German attack August 1914

GERMANY

Kaiser: Wilhelm II
Chancellor: Bethman Hollweg
For. Min.: Jagow

Ambassadors
British: Goschen
French: J. Cambon
Russian: Swerbeev
Austrian: Szogyeny

RUSSIA

Tsar: Nicolas II
For. Min.: Sazonov

Ambassadors
British : Buchanan
French : Paléologue
German: Pourtalès

Bolshevik Revolution November 1917
Armistice with Germany December 1917

Neutral 1914 Declared war on Austria-Hungary August 1016

Neutral 1914-15. Treaty with Central Powers 6 Sept 1915. Declared war on Serbia 12 Oct. 1915

TURKEY

Secret alliance with Germany 2 August 1914.
Attacked Russian ships September 1914. Britain declared war Nov. 1914

AUSTRIA-HUNGARY

Emperor: Franz Joseph
Prime Min.: Tisza
For. Min.: Berchtold

Ambassadors: British: DeBunsen
Russian: Schebeko

Ambassadors: British: DeBunsen
French: Dumaine
German: Tschirsky

Benevolent neutrality in interest of Entente Nov. 1915
Declared war on Bulgaria and Central Powers 29 June 1917

FRANCE

President: Poincaré
Premier: Viviani
For. Min.: Viviani

Ambassadors
British: Bertie
Russian: Izvolsky
German: Schoen
Austrian: Szecsen

Neutral 1914-15 Declared war on Austria-Hungary 23 May 1915

Moscow

Odessa

Constantinople

Gallipoli

Belgrade

Sarajevo

SERBIA

ALBANIA

GREECE

RUMANIA

BULGARIA

Adriatic Sea

ITALY

Rome

Sardinia

Corsica

SPAIN

SWITZ.

Trieste

Vienna

Berlin

Warsaw

Baltic Sea

SWEDEN

DENMARK

North Sea

HOLLAND

BELGIUM

LUX.

Paris

London

Trento

Entente Powers 1914
Allies and associates of the Entente Powers
Neutral States 1914
Central Powers 1914
Allies of the Central Powers but declared neutrality on outbreak of war

Austria–Hungary. The immediate origins lay in the Balkan rivalry between
the multi-national Austro-Hungarian empire and Serbia, champion of South
Slav nationalism. The assassination of the Archduke Francis-Ferdinand, heir
to the Austrian throne, at Sarajevo on 28 June brought to the boil a long-
simmering quarrel between the Habsburg monarchy and Serbia. Vienna
assumed that the Serb and Croat nationalists responsible for the
assassination had been aided and abetted by the Serbian government. The
opportunity to punish Serbia and impose client state status seemed too good to
miss. Armed with pledges of support from its German ally, Austria delivered an
ultimatum to Belgrade on 23 July. Austria counted on localizing the conflict.
German insurance, it was believed, would deter Serbia's ally, Russia, from
intervention. However, the Austro-Serbian conflict ignited a general conflagration. Russian mobilization in support of Serbia on 30 July activated
Germany's war plans. German planners had long decided that the best defence
against the threat of a two-front war resulting from the Franco-Russian alliance
of 1894 was the offensive. German armies would strike first at France through
Belgium, then smash Russia in the east. The time needed by Russia to complete
mobilization allowed Germany a margin for manoeuvre. Accordingly, on 1
August, Germany declared war on Russia, followed two days later by a
declaration of war against France and an ultimatum to Belgium. The threats to
France and Belgium pulled Britain into the war. Outwardly, France appeared to
be a victim of unprovoked German aggression. Was the French government as
innocent and passive as its leaders claimed?

The debate on the causes of the conflict continues but one fundamental
point is not in dispute – all the belligerents shared some responsibility. What
part did France play in events? Two major explanations have been advanced,
one asserting the primacy of foreign policy, the other arguing the dominance
of internal policy. The traditional view was that France fought to reverse the
defeat of 1870 and to secure the return of Alsace-Lorraine. According to this
account, a nationalist revival, beginning with the Moroccan crisis of 1911,
led to the election of Raymond Poincaré as president of the republic in
January 1913 and the establishment of a three-year compulsory service law.
By contrast, the study of the domestic causes of war has produced a quite
different explanation.[1] Poincaré and the conservative right are said to have
whipped up chauvinism because they wanted war in order to defeat the left
and avoid internal reform. Allegedly this was part and parcel of a general
attempt by European establishments to preserve the status quo and ward off
unwelcome social and economic reform.

However, the interaction of foreign and domestic policies was much more
complex than either of these two explanations suggests. Revanchism did not
drive France to war. After 1871 Alsace-Lorraine increasingly identified with
Germany and only ultra-nationalists talked of reconquering the lost provinces. In February 1914 the German ambassador in Paris cabled Berlin: 'the
bellicose desire for revenge ... is now outmoded. It only exists to a certain
extent in theory. The wound of 1871 still burns in all French hearts,

but nobody is inclined to risk his or his son's bones for the question of Alsace-Lorraine.'[2]

In the run-up to war, internal questions – the introduction of income tax, electoral reform, the three-year military service law – upstaged international issues. In 1913 an increase in the size of the German army forced the introduction of a three-year service law. The law provoked a confrontation between the president of the republic, committed to strengthening both the presidency and the army, and the left centre majority in the Chamber opposed to the law. But the government of René Viviani was dependent on an anti-militarist grouping of the left and was unlikely, therefore, to pursue an aggressive foreign policy. When the crisis deepened following the assassination of the Archduke Francis-Ferdinand at Sarajevo on 28 June there were no cries of 'To Berlin'. Popular pressure did not propel France into war. In July the all-absorbing issue was the trial of the wife of the minister of finance, Joseph Caillaux. Madame Caillaux shot and killed the editor of the newspaper *Le Figaro* in a bid to prevent publication of her love-letters. Contrary to traditional accounts, even the news of mobilization failed to evoke enthusiasm for war. The public response was one of disbelief, shock and sadness. Quickly initial shock and disbelief gave way to resignation and resolution.

Did social and economic forces drive France to war? Were capitalists, politicians and generals plotting war? No evidence of collusion has been produced, though there is much that we do not know about the relations of industry, government and armed forces. Many small investors owned Russian bonds and this put a premium on the preservation of the Tsarist state and alliance. Yet investors were not an influential lobby. Although the government linked its loans to policy goals – insisting that Russia extend its strategic railways in Poland – it did not pressure St Petersburg to march against Germany and Austria.

Franco-German economic relations were a mixture of cooperation and conflict. Imperialism was not a mainspring of French policy – quite the opposite in fact. Conflicts were waning by 1914, with a series of compromises over Morocco (1909), the Congo (1910) and Ottoman railways (1914). A pressure group, the *parti colonial*, struggled to sustain interest in the empire. A section of French finance, represented by ex-premier Joseph Caillaux, advocated Franco-German financial cooperation. German and French banks invested jointly in Romania; German firms invested in France. But the reverse of the coin was that Paris reduced the flow of short-term investments in Germany between 1911 and 1914. In central Africa French business interests resented German economic penetration in the Congo; in the Balkans and South America rival arms giants Schneider and Krupp clashed. French banks blocked German efforts to raise loans on the Paris bourse for the Berlin–Baghdad railway. Yet, as economic rivalry in some areas intensified, the overall trade between the two countries also increased. In short the evidence is ambiguous. Economic tensions may have fed expectations of war but they were not a principal cause of Germany's declaration of war on France.

Was President Poincaré, as critics allege, a warmonger trying to divert attention from internal tensions? Physically he was not in the least intimidating – short and stout, pale with a small thin pointed beard and little white moustache giving his face the appearance of a Chinese mask. A Lorrainer with vivid memories of the Prussians besieging Paris in the war of 1870, he naturally feared Germany but was no warmonger. In his view the strength and cohesion of the alliances on both sides were the best guarantee of peace. Accordingly, he rebuffed moves towards *détente* with Germany and visited Russia in 1912 to tighten the alliance. For Poincaré and his colleagues, diplomacy, strategy and domestic issues were interdependent. The military reckoned that Germany's superiority could be offset by an immediate all-out attack. This doctrine of the offensive at all cost was formulated in war plan XVII. But no one was crazy enough to propose fighting single-handed; Russian help was indispensable, the more so since an advance into Belgium to meet German armies was excluded. The Russians for their own security wanted a strong France and regarded the three-year service law as the main plank of the alliance. In the summer of 1914 this scenario was jeopardized by the growing domestic opposition to the law. Leaders were in a quandary because they could not publicly avow the strategic and diplomatic considerations behind the three-year law. The doctrine of the offensive contradicted Republican orthodoxy of the nation in arms, a citizen army fighting for national frontiers. Disclosure of offensive planning would have unleashed a huge domestic and diplomatic furore. Consequently, ministers justified the law by encouraging the public to believe that Germany might launch a sudden overwhelming attack. The problem was that fears of a German descent could not be sustained for more than a few months. Moreover, a shift to the left in the elections of April 1914 threatened the three-year law once parliament reassembled in the autumn. This was the domestic context of Poincaré's state visit to St Petersburg on 16–29 July.

Controversy about France's responsibility for war has centred on this visit. Poincaré is alleged to have given Tsar Nicholas II a blank cheque for his stance over Serbia, just as Germany guaranteed its ally Austria–Hungary. The St Petersburg visit was not a response to the Serbian crisis but part of a regular series of consultations. No official French or Russian record of the talks has been found, but Poincaré's diary sheds some light on discussions. The Tsar, upset by the leftward trend in French politics, expressed anxiety about the future of the three-year law. Poincaré, worried lest Russia reconsider the alliance, overrode the misgivings of his prime minister and foreign minister René Viviani and gave unconditional pledges of loyalty. Yet it is not at all clear whether the French ministers appreciated the seriousness of the Serbian crisis. It would be unfair, therefore, to say that in pledging their support they were making a decision for war. It is true that the Russians had broken the Austrian diplomatic code and knew the Austrians were hatching some kind of ultimatum to Belgrade. However, we do not know what the French were told.

Perhaps more important than what the French said to the Russians in St Petersburg was the timing of the visit. The long absence from Paris from 16–29 July may have been crucial to the outcome of the crisis. A visit in the first half of the month would have brought the French leaders home by 20 July, allowing time to exercise some control on developments. In the event, the two-week absence seriously skewed French decision-making. During the six-day return voyage Poincaré and Viviani were at sea in more senses than one. Wireless telegraphy was still primitive and Poincaré claimed in his memoirs that 'fragmentary and incomprehensible' wireless messages from the Eiffel Tower deprived them of a clear picture of the Serbian crisis.[3] The absence of senior ministers and advisors compounded the weakness of the government machine in Paris. Acting foreign minister Jean-Baptiste Bienvenu-Martin, minister of justice, was irresolute and unequal to the job, spending barely any time at the Quai d'Orsay. His shilly-shallying encouraged the German and Austrian envoys to suppose that France would qualify her support for Russia. Interdepartmental rivalry hampered co-ordination – a Berlin telegram of 21 July reporting preliminary notice of German mobilization was not received by the war ministry until 28 July. Army commander General Joffre protested at this 'inexplicable delay' but he himself delayed passing on important information to war minister Adolphe Messimy.[4]

Without a ringmaster individuals exercised disproportionate influence on events. Two voices spoke out strongly pledging support for Russia. In St Petersburg, ambassador Maurice Paléologue reassured Russia while keeping Paris in the dark on the timing and extent of Russian mobilization on 30 July; in Paris, Joffre expressed the hope that should war come Russia would attack east Prussia as soon as possible. When Poincaré and Viviani on their return asked Russia not to provoke Germany by total or partial mobilization it was too late. By 30 July France, short of abandoning her main continental ally, could do nothing to change Russian policy. If left unsupported, Russia would be defeated, leaving France isolated and vulnerable. Russia would not have accepted another humiliation like that of the Bosnian crisis of 1908 when she had backed down in response to German pressure.

France's role in the coming of war was essentially reactive, leaving the initiative in the hands of Germany, Austria and Russia. In James Joll's words: 'the French government had not provoked or worked for war'. Norman Rich argues that France, backed by Russia and the high probability of British support, was in a very strong position: 'It strains incredulity to believe that Poincaré, native of Lorraine, passionate patriot and fierce foe of Germany, was not tempted to take advantage of this uniquely favourable opportunity if only to the extent of offering unconditional support to Russia and allowing the bungling Teutons to stumble to their doom.'[5] But there was a crucial difference between German pledges to Austria and French pledges to Russia. Germany and Austria acted aggressively to destroy Serbia, France acted defensively to preserve the status quo. To suggest, as Norman Rich does, that France's strong international position tempted Poincaré into giving pledges that he might otherwise not have given is to misunderstand Poincaré's policy. The chronology of the crisis was crucial in determining France's response. The St Petersburg visit took place *before* the Austrian ultimatum to Belgrade; the Serbian quarrel had not yet become a war-threatening crisis. Poincaré had two preoccupations. He believed that strong alliances were the best guarantee of peace and the Russian alliance was France's sole major continental alliance. Second, given the Tsar's anxiety about French domestic politics, he wanted to reassure the Russians and confirm the continuity of French policy. The government went to war not to suppress the left and social reform, nor to take advantage of a favourable international constellation, but to defend France's existence as an independent great power.

Ministers were slow to realize the seriousness of the Serbian issue. Perhaps the two-week absence from Paris contributed to this misjudgement. To be sure, everyone expected a general war sooner or later, but few believed it imminent. Even on 13 July, three weeks before the outbreak of war, Jules Cambon, French ambassador to Berlin, spoke only of the probability of a Franco-German conflict, not its imminence: 'the day will probably come when the German government will find itself facing the French government in a situation analogous to that in which the cabinets of Vienna and Belgrade now find themselves'.[6] A cabinet colleague recalled that 'when they landed at Dunkirk, neither Viviani nor Poincaré wanted to believe in war'.[7] Foreign ministry political director Pierre de Margerie, who had accompanied French ministers, looked at the Serbian file on 29 July and exclaimed: 'It's much less serious than I thought; it will certainly sort itself out.'[8] By the time the danger of general war was appreciated it was too late to offer counsels of restraint.

Mobilization elicited neither enthusiasm nor resistance. The cavalry posted to Paris as a precaution against a workers' revolt was not needed. Acceptance of mobilization and then war reflected the extreme rapidity of events. In the last days of July it was hard to know what was happening. Many were absorbed from dawn to dusk gathering the harvest and had no leisure to read the newspapers. After mobilization on 1 August information was minimal. From Brittany on 3 August physicist Irène Joliot-Curie wrote that no one knew what was happening – no newspapers or post had arrived and the wildest rumours were circulating, including a German plan to seize Brittany.[9] This atmosphere of confusion and uncertainty made it easier to accept a clear lead from above. Thereafter the growing conviction that Germany was to blame produced determination and resolution.

Above all, acceptance of war reflected confidence in a French victory. French forces were believed to be 'almost equal' to the Germans and Russia's military power appeared formidable. There was confidence also in the likelihood of British naval and military support, and it was calculated that 'the surge of the Balkan peoples has changed the ... European equilibrium by making Serbia a much more serious problem for Austria–Hungary'.[10] Of course, this confidence was misplaced. Joffre underestimated Germany in two crucial respects. He ignored evidence that Germany would utilize reserves in the front line and, second, he disregarded intelligence reports and last-minute warnings by field commanders, leaving undefended much of the Franco-German border across which German armies poured in August. But in the final analysis such misjudgements were irrelevant, since the decisive element was wishful thinking. People were confident in victory because they believed the war would be short and they wanted to win. In the words of one reservist: 'I don't know why I feel so strongly we're going to win.'[11]

Aims

In 1914 France had no expansionist ambitions in Europe. There was no French version of Germany's September programme for a *Mitteleuropa*. Naturally, the war whetted appetites for the Rhineland and Saar but it was not the product of these appetites. No full statement of war aims came until 1917 and no public debate until the relaxation of censorship in the autumn of 1916. Publicly, ministers talked only of the recovery of Alsace-Lorraine and the independence of Belgium. Ironically the restoration of Alsace-Lorraine – for which no pre-1914 government had been prepared to fight – became a key war aim. Fundamental from the outset was the desire to preserve the allied coalition; on 5 September Britain, France and Russia promised not to make a separate peace and not to define peace terms without prior agreement.

Reticence on war aims reflected a number of considerations. Waging war left scant time for discussion: 'Our time is absolutely devoured by pressing and immediate business', declared political director Pierre de Margerie. 'Nobody, except for professors ... has the leisure to study these questions.'[12] The creation of a political truce (*union sacrée*) papered over internal conflicts and the government hesitated to imperil the truce by raising contentious issues. While many on the right wanted to ensure future security by neutralizing or annexing the Rhineland, the left was suspicious of anything that hinted at territorial expansion. Rather than stir up a hornet's nest, politicians were vague and circumspect. Moreover, detailed and comprehensive declarations, it was realized, would alienate neutrals and stiffen enemy morale. Ministers wanted to discourage allies from bidding high and therefore held back from making large claims in secret. Paul

Cambon, French ambassador to London, was instructed: 'Don't make any plans for after the war, above all don't talk about any.'[13]

Active consideration of war aims began in the spring of 1915 and peaked in 1916–17. The shattering of the short war illusion stimulated informal conclaves of senior politicians and officials. Big business and other interests do not seem to have influenced debates. There was no French equivalent of the powerful German war-aims movement (*Kriegszielbewegung*) of right-wing parties and economic groups. How to provide security against Germany was the overriding issue; two approaches were envisaged: weakening Germany by detaching the Rhineland and, second, tilting economic power away from Germany. But no systematic studies were undertaken, partly for lack of time, partly because the government machine was disorganized and overloaded.

However, the Russians were not backward in coming forward. In March 1915 Petrograd requested support for its claim to Constantinople and the Bosporus. France which had its own ambitions in the Turkish empire resisted the claim. The response was a mixture of bribery and threats. The French were invited to help themselves before it was too late. 'Take Mayence, take Coblenz, go further if you like', urged Tsar Nicholas II.[14] At the same time, foreign minister Sazonov warned that he might be forced to make way for a supporter of the Three Emperors' League – a strong hint that Russia might reconsider its alliances. Foreign minister Theophile Delcassé stalled, proposing on 7 March a conference to discuss the peace treaties; two days later president Poincaré urged ambassador Paléologue to stand firm since Russian access to the Mediterranean would upset the European balance. But resistance was a lost cause. British support for Russian claims left no choice. The Constantinople Agreement of 15 March accepted Russian claims to the Turkish Straits and to Constantinople in return for recognition of British and French claims in the Turkish empire and elsewhere. Paris understood this to mean support for future claims on Germany.

In the summer of 1916 formulation of war aims quickened. Various pressures were at work: promising military prospects, possibility of an Austrian collapse, rumours of a separate Russian peace, as well as fear of a new American mediation. On 12 August Poincaré asked the military to study terms for an armistice. The high command's ambitious shopping list included the Saar coalfield, the establishment of three or four client states on the left bank of the Rhine, bridgeheads on the right bank and the redrawing of frontiers to weaken Prussia. The Rhineland states would be attached to France by a customs union and occupied for thirty-one years. Then with 'the example of French wisdom ... the people will demand union with us'.[15] In short, the German problem would be solved by dissolving Bismarck's creation into nine small states. At an Elysée dinner on 7 October Poincaré presided over a gathering of senior politicians. Some wanted immediate annexation of the left bank, others argued for prolonged occupation as security for the payment of reparations. Poincaré proposed a compromise –

full definition of aims would be postponed but the Allies would be asked to acknowledge that the Rhineland was an issue for France.

The end of the year brought fresh moves. On 12 October the Central Powers offered negotiations without specifying terms; President Woodrow Wilson of the United States responded on 20 December by asking all the belligerents to declare their war aims. The French condemned the German initiative as a 'crude snare', suspecting that Wilson's appeal had been 'concerted with Germany'.[16] The allied reply of 10 January 1917, based on a French draft, was fuller than any previous statement. Skilfully, it appealed to neutral and internal opinion, promising membership of the League of Nations and calling for the restoration of Alsace-Lorraine. More explicit than the German reply to Wilson, the allied note represented a major 'diplomatic victory, which opened the way for American war entry in the following spring'.[17]

France now had three war-aims programmes. The public version, published in the allied note of 10 January, praised the League and stressed the return of the lost provinces. But the general staff had elaborated a maximum programme calling for outright annexation of the Rhineland and the dismemberment of Germany. In negotiations with allies, Paris adopted a minimum menu insisting on the return of Alsace-Lorraine, the French frontier of 1790 (including the Saar), detachment and neutralization of the Rhineland and the preservation of Austria–Hungary. This minimum list was adopted by the cabinet and submitted to the Russians in the spring of 1917. The British were kept in the dark for several months until the Germans leaked the news of a Franco-Russian accord. Poincaré seems to have believed that prior agreement with Russia would help negotiations with Britain. He also wanted to strengthen a weakening Tsarist regime. On 3 February the Tsar conceded a combination of France's minimum and maximum demands: the establishment of autonomous states on the left bank of the Rhine under French occupation pending full execution of a peace treaty. All seemed set for a formal agreement. Suddenly Russia demanded a free hand for her western frontier. The French, who in 1915 had accepted Russian claims to Constantinople and the Straits, were flabbergasted at what seemed like a request to be paid twice. At a cabinet meeting on 8 March Poincaré objected to the request. Accepting Russian claims in the west would leave France without anything to tempt Austria from the German alliance. Yet two days later prime minister Aristide Briand conceded Russia a free hand to fix her western frontiers. The episode exemplifies the muddle and confusion at the heart of France's wartime government. The negotiator in Petrograd, former premier Gaston Doumergue, had been given no written instructions and Briand allowed his secretary Philippe Berthelot to draft and send instructions which he had not seen. In fact, only two months after Briand's departure from office, the foreign ministry 'could not reconstruct exactly what happened'.[18] Not that it mattered. Within days the first Russian revolution destroyed the Tsarist regime and rendered the agreement irrelevant.

Before 1914 France's economic inferiority to Germany had seemed a given, to be accepted like the Rhine. The war offered an opportunity to redress the balance. Two strategies, one short-term, the other medium, were pursued. The immediate action was to oust Germany from markets. Reports from consuls and overseas chambers of commerce identifying the most promising markets were circulated to industry. General Sarrail, commander in chief at Salonika, promoted French commerce in the Balkans. The results of this trade drive were disappointing – industry did not have the capacity to take advantage of openings. The second strategy was a full economic war-aims programme. The initiative came from government, not industrialists. Business leaders were divided on the economic value of Alsace-Lorraine, the Saar and the left bank. For patriotic and strategic reasons the restoration of Alsace-Lorraine was welcomed; Germany would be deprived of most of its iron ore and annexation of the Saar made sense since it would relieve France's coal deficit. The downside was that the lost provinces and the Saar would double steel production without providing adequate supplies of coking coal. Industrialists were preoccupied by the problem of overproduction and were not a monolithic group shaping economic and political war aims. The steel producers (*comité des forges*) moved cautiously and aims were modest compared to the plans of German industrialists for annexations in Briey and domination of Belgium. Only a handful of iron masters like Camille Cavallier of Pont à Mousson coveted the left bank. The steel producers' association waited until February 1917 before officially endorsing Alsace-Lorraine, Saar coal deliveries and further territorial annexations.

The architect of France's economic programme was minister of commerce Etienne Clementel. Five years of office (1915–19) enabled him to exercise a decisive influence on economic policy. He was a man of many parts – an artist, friend of Rodin and Monet, amateur playwright, opera librettist. In late 1915, alarmed by German discussion of a *Mitteleuropa*, he drew up a programme of economic war aims which was endorsed at an allied economic conference in Paris in June 1916 and partly implemented by the Treaty of Versailles in 1919. Clementel had two objectives: first, to exert economic pressure to liberalize the German government and to establish discrimination against Germany in favour of French industry; second, a permanent interallied system for pooling raw materials. The objectives were partly realized. By spring 1918 the Allies had achieved considerable economic unity and the Treaty of Versailles gave France economic advantages until 1927.

Neutrals: Greece and the United States

By December 1914 a line of trenches stretched from the Swiss frontier to the North Sea. As the armies ground to a halt the civilians grew busier – devising war aims, encouraging allies, wooing neutrals, canvassing diversionary operations. There was little to show for these exertions. War may be too important to be left to the generals but politicians and officials are not noticeably more successful. Italy's adhesion to the allies in 1915 brought no direct military relief; Serbia surrendered in 1915; the Gallipoli campaign against Turkey was a fiasco; Romania joined the Allies in 1916 only to be quickly crushed; in Greece there was nothing to show for the Salonika operation which swallowed up a Franco-British force of half a million; efforts to prop up the ailing Tsarist regime came to naught. Ironically, American intervention which contributed most to France's victory owed nothing to French diplomacy.

Allied propaganda presented the war as a crusade for the independence of small states such as Belgium and Serbia. However, in the Balkans the Allies had little cause for congratulation. French diplomacy was too inept to save Serbia, and Greece suffered more from the Entente than from the Central Powers. Two factors account for the failure of France's Balkan policy – excessive ambitions and the disarray of decision-making. The French regarded the eastern Mediterranean as their sphere of influence and did not trust their partners. The main reason for participation in the British-inspired Dardanelles and Gallipoli campaigns was to protect huge political and financial interests in the Turkish empire – investments estimated at 3,000 million francs. The objective was to break the deadlock on the western front by forcing the Straits and so eliminating Germany's ally, Turkey. Turkey's collapse, it was argued, would enable allied supplies to reach Russia as well as persuading Balkan powers to join the Entente. British advocates of a campaign against Turkey, the 'easterners', claimed that Britain would be helping France as well as Russia: 'an offensive was necessary for the morale of the French army' amongst whom there was 'a good deal of discussion about peace'; relief for Russia by boosting trade would help interest payments on French loans and so raise French morale.[19] The French suppressed their misgivings about British plans because they feared British control of Asia Minor would block their designs on Syria.

Second, there were too many cooks. From August 1914 the general staff exercised a quasi-dictatorial control of the war. When government and parliament returned to Paris in December a battle royal developed for supremacy. The atmosphere of intrigue and confusion which bedevilled policy-making was such that in January 1915 the minister of marine secretly committed his country to the Dardanelles expedition without telling the cabinet and commander in chief in the Mediterranean. Despite the failure of the Dardanelles naval expedition to force the Straits, the French joined the British in a second attempt to defeat Turkey in landings at Gallipoli in April. An additional reason for participation was to provide a job for General Maurice Sarrail. Left-wing opinion was critical of the French commander in chief General Joffre and idolized Sarrail. When Joffre struck back by sacking the general, his fans urged that he be given a new command at Gallipoli. Sarrail got the job but Joffre had the last word and stopped reinforcements going to Turkey. Yet even with more troops it is unlikely that the Allies would have defeated Turkey.

By September 1915 the Balkan front had rapidly deteriorated – Gallipoli was a mess and Bulgaria was poised to strike Serbia. The Greek port of Salonika appeared to offer a solution – landing an allied force would help Serbia and encourage Greece and Romania to join the Entente. Not least it offered a chance of saving the Viviani government from angry critics of the Dardanelles and Gallipoli fiascos. But the Salonika force was too small and too late to save Serbia and the Viviani administration fell on 25 October 1915. Foreign minister Delcassé's policy was ill-conceived and ineptly executed. Delcassé himself was in failing health and overwhelmed by the fate of his son who had been captured by the Germans. 'I am truly staggered', confided André Tardieu, 'by the ineptitude of our governments. The Dardanelles have been badly managed and the Balkan negotiations also.'[20] The hope of enlisting Greeks, Serbs and Bulgars in the allied camp was unrealistic. Fierce ethnic hatreds divided them. The Greeks were fired by the 'Great Idea', a project of a new Byzantine empire ruling over Constantinople and the Straits. But the Straits were already promised to Russia. Bulgaria claimed territory from both Greece and Serbia. By the end of October common sense dictated withdrawal from Salonika but premier Briand stayed and an army of half a million, predominantly Franco-British, seasoned with Serbs, Russians and Italians, virtually marked time until September 1918.

Why were the 'gardeners of Salonika' as Clemenceau contemptuously called them, left to vegetate for nearly three years? At the time, an allied presence was defended on the grounds that a watch had to be kept on Greece. King Constantine of Greece, the Kaiser's brother-in-law, was said to be Germanophile. The Allies claimed to have acted within their rights in engineering his abdication and the return of the pro-Allied statesman Venizelos as prime minister. In fact, King Constantine never seriously considered joining Germany and the Greek army was too weak to pose a real threat to the Salonika force. Salonika, in reality, was a springboard for French domination of the Balkans and Turkish empire. France 'repeatedly and often unnecessarily employed force against Greece, completely ignoring her rights as a neutral state and causing considerable suffering to her people'.[21] Britain cooperated because Briand's career depended on staying at Salonika: 'If Briand went then General Joffre would go too and then General Sarrail would command in France.'[22] But the British were reluctant in the extreme and the episode sowed deep mistrust. 'The French are playing a very crooked game over Greece', wrote British cabinet secretary Maurice Hankey.[23] A French parliamentary report of June 1917 on Salonika concluded: 'If we re-embark we lose for ever our strength in the east. The abandonment of Salonika would be the end of France in the eastern Mediterranean.'[24]

The French stayed but by March 1917 their brief pre-eminence in Greece was over. Britain, Italy and Russia opposed French designs; royalists and

Venizelists united to avert the threat. The bid for power was badly bungled. French representatives on the spot were inept, policy-making in Paris confused and contradictory. Briand's policy was 'so complex and devious and the instructions ... so unclear and contradictory that they led to confusion and, inevitably, mistakes'.[25] The premier's fondness for the Greek royal princesses was a joke in London. Not least of France's liabilities was her overzealous man in Athens, Commandant de Roquefeuil, head of the naval mission and French intelligence. He ran a private army, kept 25,000 files on Greek leaders, stage-managed an attack on his own legation and discovered German spies everywhere. Since much of the intelligence supplied to Paris was fabricated, policy was seriously flawed. Indeed, his activities 'were the major reason for the appeal of German propaganda and the growth of anti-French sentiment'.[26]

Ambivalence marked France's attitude towards the principal neutral, the United States. Supplies and dollars were required, not intervention. In fact, the French were almost as keen to keep the Americans out of the war as the Americans were to stay out. Three aims were pursued: to tighten the economic blockade of Germany without alienating the United States; to ensure that American mediation insisted on the lost provinces; and to secure American money. In 1915–16 Wilson's emissary, Colonel House, failed to persuade France and Britain to accept American mediation. Paris–Washington relations were dominated by negotiations for supplies and credit. The United States became France's chief supplier of wheat, sugar, steel and explosives. American imports which had been 10 per cent of the total in 1913 reached 30 per cent by 1916, opening up an enormous deficit in France's balance of payments. Until 1916 the government struggled to maintain payments and to limit the depreciation of the franc. But raising money grew more difficult, with American banks demanding high commission and insisting on the surrender of investments as collateral. France's imminent bankruptcy gave Wilson powerful leverage. Washington considered refusing further loans in order to secure acceptance of its peace proposals. America's entry into the war in April 1917, following Germany's resumption of all-out submarine warfare, rescued France from financial and economic collapse.

Without Uncle Sam, France and the Allies would have had to seek a negotiated peace. American dollars and doughboys were decisive – France bought all she needed and the value of the franc was maintained. Wilson's new diplomacy recharged the Entente's moral armoury. The prospect of American troops in Europe within a year sustained morale through the worst year of the war. Of course, acceptance of American aid inevitably meant some loss of independence but French misperceptions ensured that the damage was greater than it might have been. Assuming the Americans to be naive, inexperienced and generous to a fault, the French pitched their demands high and sought to direct their ally's contribution. This approach reinforced America's sense of superiority and suspicion of Old World diplomacy. By projecting President Wilson as the world's number one hero, Paris enhanced his influence at the peace-making. Finally, France underestimated American economic imperialism.

Economic cooperation

For the public, great battles like the Marne, Somme and Verdun were the war. But what really counted were the sinews – money, ships and supplies. French leaders, assuming a short war, had not prepared for economic mobilization and allied coordination. Strategic coordination consisted of sporadic allied summits, more cosmetic than constructive. The only interallied economic organization, the International Food Commission, was purely advisory and concerned with military supplies. For civilian needs France and Britain competed on the open market. Full economic and strategic unity was only realized in the spring of 1918. 'Had we really worked as one Government and one General Staff', declared British premier David Lloyd George in April 1917, 'we should already have won the war.'[27]

This was hyperbole, but undoubtedly the delays in achieving unity prolonged the conflict. In the end the superior organization of the French and British war economies, by keeping armies and peoples supplied, made a critical contribution to victory. Yet it was 'a damned nice thing', realized at the eleventh hour. Arguably, greater unity in 1916–17 would have shortened the war and limited American influence on the peace-making.

The war greatly increased France's economic dependence on Britain. The Republic did not have the resources to sustain a major war single-handed. The tanker fleet 'consisted of three small vessels which together were capable of transporting only one-twentieth' of imported oil.[28] The merchant fleet was 1.9 million tons compared with Britain's 21 million (45 per cent of world total tonnage) and coal, rubber, iron and steel had to be imported. German occupation of much of northern France deprived the economy of 83 per cent of its iron ore, 74 per cent of its coal and 63 per cent of its steel. Forced to import wheat, sugar and coal, France had to borrow ships and money – by November 1916, 47 per cent of imports were carried in British freighters. Gradually, a series of agreements established economic cooperation: the Clementel–McKenna accord of February 1916 made the Royal Sugar Commission the sole allied purchasing body; the Runciman–Sembat agreement of May 1916 provided for coal needs. The British made up losses of productive capacity but 'demanded correspondingly greater internal controls within France' leading to the 'increased intervention of the French state in the private sector of the economy'.[29] France entered the war with substantial gold stocks and a large overseas portfolio. It was assumed that the cost of a short war would be met from reserves and short-term loans. In February 1915 Paris appealed for allied help. A 'gold pool' organized financial cooperation – Britain as banker made loans to France and negotiated American loans for the benefit of France and Russia. In return, the Bank of France either sold gold or lent it to the Bank of England as a guarantee.

France's *annus terribilis* came in 1917. Everything seemed to go wrong: the collapse of the Tsarist regime; failure of the spring offensive; mutinies; food shortages; imminent bankruptcy. America's entry into the war in April averted financial collapse but the mutinies of May–June were followed by a poor harvest with Paris down to one day's flour reserve and the army only one to three days. Germany's submarine warfare created a severe shipping shortage. Britain prohibited French luxury imports and asked for the return of 500,000 tons of shipping on loan. Between January and September France imported only 20 per cent of its needs. Worse was to come. The harsh winter of 1917–18, combined with the diversion of shipping for American troop transports, left the country short of wheat, steel, nitrates and coal.

Salvation came through a long overdue breakthrough in strategic economic planning. The first phase was the creation of the Supreme War Council in December 1917 and an international shipping pool. Military unity on the western front had existed only briefly during General Nivelle's 1917 spring offensive. Full unity was finally achieved in April 1918 with General Ferdinand Foch's appointment as commander in chief. Economic unity was realized in March 1918 with the first meeting of the interallied maritime transport council. By the summer a network of commissions controlled shipping, food and raw materials. The coordination enabled two million American troops to be ferried to Europe, a million more than originally estimated.

The architect of allied economic unity was commerce minister, Etienne Clementel, aided by his London representative, Jean Monnet. Dependence on London bred resentment compounded by fear of a British postwar economic ascendancy. Clementel's initiatives were intended to free France from postwar dependence. The minister believed that successful wartime cooperation would be a framework for postwar reconstruction. He insisted on a shipping pool, opposing British wishes for prior agreement with Washington: 'We should be able to present a united front ... We have reached a decisive turning point in the war.'[30] Premier Paul Painlevé supported Clementel: 'It is a matter of life and death for France'.[31] The long delay in realizing full economic cooperation had two consequences. First, the public did not fully recognize that victory was an *allied* victory. They took pride in equipping General Pershing's army, forgetting that the steel came from the United States, paid for in American loans. Second, Clementel's success in cementing allied unity encouraged false hopes that continuing international cooperation would enable France to exercise postwar leadership.

Clementel's power over the economy in 1918 can largely be attributed to measures initially forced on the French government by the British in 1917 and 1918. British influence included the organization of allied decision-making. One of the fundamental weaknesses of the French state before, during and after World War I was the failure to modernize the government machine. The organized anarchy that prevailed in 1914 persisted. Although the war widened the scope and activity of the state, the machine did not keep pace. Indeed, total war brought almost total anarchy. Ambassador Paul Cambon condemned 'the shambles of government and high command'.[32] Even in the war ministry peacetime routine changed little; almost everything was done by correspondence which took two days to travel from one floor to the next. Much of the paper mountain built by the growing army of bureaucrats was unreliable.[33] Standard accounting methods did not exist and the resulting confusion meant 'that there was a difference in the effective price for each shell of 78 per cent between two companies'.[34] As late as December 1917 André Tardieu, high commissioner in the United States, complained to Poincaré 'of the anarchy in our bureaux and of the complete lack of system in the orders that they place in America. No programme, priorities perpetually changing'.[35]

Allied decision-making

Poor organization seriously disadvantaged French negotiators. On the eve of the October 1916 Boulogne conference Cambon vented his frustration:

> The English have set off well briefed on all points; papers, statistics, state of their forces and transport resources. They have all that is needed for a serious discussion and will find themselves, as last time, in the presence of people without precise ideas on anything. At the last conference in London Briand and Joffre came to ask as always for men for Salonika. They were told with chapter and verse of the transport difficulties. Our representatives had nothing to counter these figures. It was deplorable.[36]

The war accentuated the tendency to take words for deeds. Cambon castigated 'our oratorical diplomacy', citing a top-heavy allied conference in Paris, much too large to achieve anything useful: 'Parisians gather at the railway stations to welcome foreign envoys. These events give pleasure and the government is as proud as if it had done something.'[37] French speechifying amused their allies. In 1915 octogenarian ex-premier Emile Combes accompanied British visitors to their train. When they were about to leave, Combes launched into a big speech on 'Progress, citing Michelet ...

and all the men of his time'. 'Very funny', remarked British premier Herbert Asquith.[38]

Defective organization and rhetorical indulgence allowed London to dominate the management of allied decision-making. War cabinet secretary Maurice Hankey took the lead in servicing allied summits. At the February 1917 Calais conference the French did not bring a secretary and left arrangements to Hankey. Disappointed by long inconclusive meetings, premier Lloyd George came to conferences with resolutions already drafted. At the November 1917 Rapallo conference which created the supreme war council the French and Italians accepted Hankey's versions of minutes as official and allowed him to draft all agreements. The British war cabinet secretariat of 1916 served as the model for the supreme war council. General Maxime Weygand, the French military representative, 'was a little worried at the way I [Hankey] and my secretariat took charge but I said we had only done it to suit our convenience, and that as they were not so highly organised yet, we should put all our arrangements at his disposal. Of course, my real objects ... were to get the thing run on our lines.'[39] The British even drafted Clemenceau's opening address to the council on 1 December 1917.

Propaganda

As a war of peoples, World War I brought a new awareness of the power of opinion. Afterwards it was widely assumed that propaganda had made an important contribution to Germany's defeat. Indeed, Adolf Hitler in *Mein Kampf* praised the skill of British propaganda. But Hitler and opponents of the Weimar Republic were committed to the stab in the back legend. They claimed that German civilian and military morale had been undermined by allied and red propaganda rather than by military defeat at the front. Equally it suited the Allies to believe that large amounts of time and money had been well spent. In fact French propaganda does not seem to have been very successful. The pattern for the first year or so of war was one of extreme decentralization. Ministries had their own press offices and several private organizations were involved in propaganda work – the Alliance Française, chambers of commerce, church committees (*comités catholiques*), Touring Club de France. Alongside the mainline agencies unofficial propaganda groups mushroomed. In January 1916 prime minister Briand created a central organization, the Maison de la Presse, directed by the head of his private office, Philippe Berthelot. The new agency soon became a political football, attacked as a nest of draft-dodgers and anti-republicanism. After further restructurings premier Clemenceau created a commissariat general for propaganda in May 1918, but no complete centralization was realized and interdepartmental rivalries flourished. Effectively there were two propaganda agencies: the Maison de la Presse, responsible for allied and neutral countries, and the centre for enemy propaganda under military control. Allied cooperation seems to have been largely nominal. A member of American military intelligence reported in August 1918:

> We expected to find three organised and working interallied propaganda Boards, one in Paris, one in London and one in Padua, which would be landmarks in the field, with which we would have to deal and to which we could immediately designate liaison officers. These boards are ghosts. This afternoon we sat in at a session of the so-called Board here. It is essentially the old French Army Board for Propaganda into enemy countries ... and international only by virtue of the fact that an Italian, an Englishman, three Belgians and three Americans ... were present to hear what the French had done and were planning.[40]

What difference did French propaganda make? Perhaps very little. After all Germany occupied Belgium, much of northern France and large areas of Russia. Twice Paris came within Germany's grasp. No propaganda could alter the fact that Germany seemed to be winning. There is no evidence that German civilian and military morale dipped significantly until after the failure of the March 1918 offensive. 'The French', it is said, 'were not effective producers of the type of propaganda needed for an attack upon the morale of the enemy. It was difficult for them to get away from the propaganda of hate – the atrocity story type of material.'[41] Propaganda towards neutrals drew heavy criticism. The French envoy in Berne criticized his country's efforts in Switzerland. Berthelot was alleged to have compromised French propaganda in Spain by getting involved in attempts to secure the downfall of King Alfonso XIII. In Romania every nightclub dancer claimed to be working for France and Berthelot joked that when a third-rate dancer asked for a passport he replied: 'Mademoiselle you are too beautiful for a passport. I'm sending you on a mission.' In neutral countries London, not Paris, was usually first with the news, partly because the British cable network was cheaper and better organized, partly because the French censorship delayed important news for as much as twenty-four hours until the arrival of British and Swiss papers made further concealment impossible. Given Germany's military ascendancy, it is difficult to imagine how any kind of propaganda could have undermined enemy morale. Yet there was a missed opportunity for French propaganda – not during the war but in the early postwar years. The revitalized and revamped service of 1918 might have projected a French peace. Alas, within two months of the signature of the Versailles treaty wartime services were axed on grounds of economy.

Peace feelers

Forain's famous war cartoon depicts two French soldiers talking gloomily in the trenches: one says, 'if only they hold out' ...'. 'Who?' asks his companion. 'The civilians' comes the reply. In 1917 war weariness provoked peace feelers. All news seemed bad: civilians on two meatless days a week began to feel the strain – shops were looted and demonstrators protested shortages and the high cost of living. The February revolution in Russia disabled a leading ally; American intervention offered no immediate relief since substantial forces would not reach Europe until early 1918. The collapse of the spring offensive was followed by mutinies in May and June. As a result, leaders welcomed peace soundings with Germany and Austria. There were also two international initiatives: the Stockholm conference of international socialists and Pope Benedict XV's mediation.

In March 1917 Emperor Charles of Austria–Hungary, apprehensive that Germany's unconditional submarine warfare would trigger American intervention, approached Paris through his brother-in-law Prince Sixte of Bourbon-Parma. The prince had several meetings with Poincaré. Austria offered the return of Alsace-Lorraine and restoration of Belgium but was cagey about Italian claims to Austrian territory. Both Poincaré and premier Ribot believed that Austria was on the verge of concluding a separate peace. This was a serious error. The emperor may have toyed with the idea but his advisors envisaged only a general settlement. And the conditions for a general peace were lacking since Germany had no intention of disgorging Alsace-Lorraine or Belgium. Indeed, the success of the submarine offensive and the eclipse of Russia reassured Berlin that the war was winnable. Austria, in order to buy a separate peace, would have had to make substantial concessions to Italy. At a final meeting with Sixte on 20 May Ribot insisted that the Allies could not desert Italy. Ribot and British premier Lloyd George were afraid that pressuring Italy to abandon Austrian claims would force her out of the conflict. Another problem was Russia. In the spring France and Britain wanted to keep Russia in the war, yet the Austrians did not include Russia in their offer. Paris and London feared that a separate peace would release Austrian troops for the Russian front, while freeing German troops for an offensive in the west.

Next it was the turn of war minister Paul Painlevé. Painlevé, through his mistress, was in touch with Germany but his main interest was Austria–Hungary. The go-between was Commandant Armand of French army intelligence. Armand had several meetings with Austrian Count Revertera. The general staff considered Austria the weak point of the enemy coalition and urged every effort to encourage a separate peace. At a first meeting on 7 August Armand, speaking for Painlevé, armaments minister Albert Thomas and prime minister Ribot, offered Austria Prussian Silesia, Austrian Poland of 1772 and even Bavaria. On 22 August Armand presented a general peace plan, asking for Alsace-Lorraine with the frontiers of 1814 and demilitarization of the left bank of the Rhine. In exchange, Germany would receive Madagascar and the Belgian Congo. Austria would be rewarded with Poland. The Armand-Revertera discussion, like the Poincaré-Sixte contacts, came to naught. Austria would not make a separate peace and Germany was not ready for a general settlement.

Then Briand tried his hand. The idea for a meeting between the ex-premier and the German official Baron Lancken came from prominent Belgians. Briand insisted on the return of the lost provinces as a *sine qua non*; Lancken mistakenly believed Alsace-Lorraine to be negotiable. Briand, he assumed, would ask for the provinces but accept less, say neutralization. To be sure, Lancken had warned his Belgian friends that Germany considered the return of the lost provinces as 'completely out of the question'.[42] This warning was not passed on. Painlevé, who was now premier, encouraged Briand to meet Lancken in Switzerland on 22 September. However, Poincare and Ribot warned Briand that he would commit 'a grave imprudence' by going to Switzerland.[43] They dismissed the Lancken feeler as a 'German trap' and asked for Briand to be kept under surveillance.[44] Briand never met Lancken and the contact petered out. Nothing could have come of it since Germany would not surrender Alsace-Lorraine.

The proposal for an international socialist conference at Stockholm came from the Russian provisional government in May 1917. Pressured by both the Petrograd Soviet and the Bolsheviks, the provisional government cancelled its declaration of 20 March to continue the war and called for a peace without annexations. Socialist leader Albert Thomas, armaments minister, met Russian socialists and urged that French socialists be allowed to go to Stockholm rather than leave the Russians alone with German socialists: 'The impression on the Russian socialists would be detestable if French or English socialists were absent.'[45] But prime minister Ribot refused passports. Army commander in chief in the north east, General Philippe Pétain, warned the government on 31 May against allowing French socialists to go to Stockholm. Pétain blamed pacifist propaganda for the mutinies and claimed that troops were saying, 'It's the government which has refused to make the peace Germany offered.'[46] Further peace talks risked demoralizing the army. Even the threat of seventy-five fresh German divisions in the west 'was appreciably less serious than the demoralization of our army'. On 14 June Thomas brought back from Petrograd a provisional government proposal for an interallied conference on war aims. The rapid decline of the provisional government's authority soon rendered the proposal irrelevant.

On 1 August Pope Benedict XV weighed in with a note setting out the principles of a just and lasting peace: arbitration, disarmament and freedom of the seas. The pope called for the restoration of Belgium but talked of a reasonable compromise on Franco-German and Italian-Austrian claims –

thus excluding the complete restoration of Alsace-Lorraine. War damages should be renounced. On Russia, the pope was silent, a hint perhaps that Germany might be compensated in the east. The French press lambasted the papal note as a German-inspired manoeuvre. Ribot declined to reply and requested the Allies not to do so without consultation. This cold-shouldering reflected long-standing church–state antipathy following the 1905 separation. Also, there were deep-seated fears that a Roman Catholic block from Madrid to Vienna would influence French Catholics. To Ribot's annoyance, British foreign secretary A. J. Balfour replied without consulting Paris and without mentioning Alsace-Lorraine. Ribot, in order to keep an eye on discussions, insisted on being associated with the British reply. Then Berlin torpedoed the initiative by refusing to discuss Belgium.

All initiatives fizzled out. Yet the soundings confirmed the leadership's desperate desire for peace as well as the strength of Anglophobia. A general staff paper of July 1917 urged a general peace settlement in order to avoid 'revolution in France'.[47] France should trade colonies for Alsace-Lorraine; there was no point in weakening Germany unduly because it offered a necessary counterweight to Britain and an Austria strengthened by the annexation of Poland would help to offset a strong Germany. Europe had to be reconstructed on three pillars – France, Austria and Germany:

Economically, all European peoples are being ruined to the profit of Japan, North America and new peoples . . . Socially, Europe is approaching revolution . . . If Germany is reduced to nothing by the peace treaty . . . England will be mistress of the seas and our economic life, like our colonial, will depend on her favour.[48]

Painlevé seems to have been the strongest advocate of a negotiated peace – he was said to be ready 'to conclude peace at once in return for Alsace-Lorraine'.[49]

That the peace soundings petered out was not due to any lack of goodwill on France's part. Germany might have had peace in 1917 if it had been willing to offer Alsace-Lorraine. Certainly the French doubted whether the Germans wanted to return the two provinces but they could not afford to reject what might be genuine overtures. The arguments for a negotiated peace were powerful. Russia's collapse and the failure of Nivelle's offensive eliminated hope of France imposing her own peace. Within a year the build-up of American forces in Europe would make Anglo-Saxon influence dominant. In the meantime, defeat remained a real danger since Germany could transfer troops from the eastern front before Americans arrived in strength. Lastly, a negotiated peace would spare Europe economic ruin and social revolution. The exhaustion of the continental powers would only benefit extra-European nations. Why, then, given such arguments, did the government not intensify the peace offensive? Quite simply because the case for a negotiated peace, although persuasive, was not overwhelming. France had made the return of the lost provinces her main public war aim. Without an unequivocal German offer the risk of failure was too high. A peace without Alsace-Lorraine would be tantamount to defeat; equally an abortive peace negotiation would demoralize army and people, perhaps sparking a revolution. Without a copper-bottomed German offer France had too much to lose.

Winners or losers?

On 16 November 1917 seventy-six-year-old 'Tiger' Georges Clemenceau became premier. 'I wage war', he proclaimed, and within months he was a national hero incarnating the will to win. The immediate problems of morale and discipline were vigorously tackled. Officers had hesitated to wear uniform in the streets and women feared to travel alone. When New Zealand novelist Katherine Mansfield travelled from Marseilles to Paris, soldiers commandeered the train, throwing out passengers and luggage. The Tiger's cub, interior minister Georges Mandel, purged the prefects, and created a nucleus of loyal supporters. Rigorous censorship silenced dissent; shirkers were sent back to their units; defeatism was ruthlessly suppressed – minor figures already indicted were executed and two leading politicians, Joseph Caillaux and Louis Malvy, arrested.

Nevertheless, France suffered two defeats, one internal, the other external. Outwardly, the civilian front was much firmer than supposed. Strikes took place in 1917 and 1918 but these and other disturbances did not shake the prevailing mood of *jusqu'au boutisme* – fighting to the finish. Pacifism and the idea of a negotiated peace drew little support. Yet, as Jean-Jacques Becker argues, towards the end the strong sense of nationhood that saved the Republic was tempered by feelings of resignation. This was perhaps a portent: 'the unbowed France of 1918 heralded the humbled France of 1940'.[50] The second defeat was the erosion of national power. Allies, it was realized, could be more dangerous than enemies. 'I am outraged', complained one official, 'by the disproportion between France's effort and her share in the diplomatic game . . . the English make use of us. There is no equality of sacrifice.'[51] 'How dare the Italians compare their role and ours', another functionary fulminated. 'It is wrong to give way to the Italians . . . France cedes always and everywhere; she makes sacrifices and gains nothing. The English have opposed us to the Americans.'[52] From the Washington embassy came a prophecy: 'the Americans . . . will be the real victors.'[53] The London embassy added its own warning: 'the British and the Americans have the same mentality and will always end up in agreement . . . the Americans will turn out as domineering and demanding as the English.'[54]

 Declaring 'we must be winners or losers' Clemenceau called for total war and refused to discuss peace terms. Yet the truth, as Clemenceau doubtless knew, was that France would be both winner and loser. President Wilson announced his Fourteen Points without consultation. The definition of peace terms slipped out of French control. 'We will not perhaps have the peace that you and I would like', Clemenceau confided to Poincaré. 'France will have to make sacrifices, not to Germany but to her allies.'[55]

3

Peace-making, 1919

I opened the window and it really did seem – just in those first few moments that a wonderful change happened – not in human creatures' hearts – no – but in the air ... Oh, why is the world so ugly – so corrupt and stupid? When I heard the drunks passing the house on Monday night, singing the good old pre-war drunken rubbish, I felt cold with horror. They are not changed – and then the loathsome press about Germany's cry for food.

Katherine Mansfield, 13 November 1918, *The Letters and Journals of Katherine Mansfield*, ed. C. K. Stead (London, 1977), p. 130

After expending the greatest effort, and suffering the greatest sacrifices in blood in all history, we must not compromise the results of our victory ... if the League of Nations cannot buttress its orders with military sanctions we must find this sanction elsewhere ... I beg you to understand my state of mind, just as I am trying to understand yours. America is far away and protected by the ocean. England could not be reached by Napoleon himself. You are sheltered, both of you; we are not.

Prime minister Georges Clemenceau, 27 March 1919, in Paul Mantoux, *Paris Peace Conference 1919: Proceedings of the Council of Four* (Geneva 1964), pp. 24–9

No one esteems more highly than I the offers of alliance which have been generously extended to France by the President of the United States and the Prime Minister of Great Britain. The permanent alliance of our three nations in defence of justice and liberty will be a fine and splendid thing. But the ... assistance ... in the event of German aggression cannot unfortunately ever be instantaneous. Besides it will not directly affect the security for the debt. It will thus be no substitute for occupation.

President Poincaré of France, 28 April 1919, letter to Clemenceau, in David Lloyd George, *Memoirs of the Peace Conference*, I (New Haven, 1939) 281–4

Armistice

The armistice negotiations of October–November 1918 are the essential starting point for an understanding of the peace treaties. The armistice conditioned the peace settlement in three ways. The Allies, by concluding an armistice, acknowledged Germany's survival as a great power, thereby ensuring that the settlement would sooner or later be challenged. Second, the Allies, in reaching agreement with representatives of the new democratic Germany, tied their hands because the preservation of the moderate socialist government against Bolshevism became a principal allied interest. Only a stable moderate regime could be relied upon to honour the armistice. Finally, the delay of eight months between armistice and peace treaty produced bitterness and recriminations about its enforcement. Germans fulminated because no food reached them for four months while the French denounced what they saw as efforts to evade armistice terms. Thus, both the armistice and its enforcement exacerbated the difficulties of peace-making.

'Does Daddy know that we won?'

On 5 October Germany asked President Wilson for an armistice based on the Fourteen Points of January 1918. The request surprised the Allies because they expected the war to last into the spring of 1919. However, the failure of Germany's March offensive had broken the army's offensive power and troops were in full retreat. Allied generalissimo Marshal Foch impressed on Clemenceau the significance of the armistice for a peace treaty: 'the only definitive territorial sacrifices will be those conceded by the enemy when the armistice is signed'. The general staff wanted terms that would restore France's pre-1871 position. But Wilson took sole charge of negotiations and allied consultations were delayed until the meeting of the supreme war council in Paris on 29 October. Clemenceau presented French conditions: occupation of the left bank of the Rhine; bridgeheads at Mainz, Coblenz and Cologne; a neutral zone on the right bank; special status for Alsace-Lorraine; reparations. Both Clemenceau and Lloyd George raised strong objections to the Fourteen Points. 'Have you ever been asked by President Wilson whether you accept the Fourteen Points?', enquired Clemenceau, 'I have not been asked.' 'I have not been asked either,' answered Lloyd George.[1] Wilson's representative, Colonel House, warned that unless the Fourteen Points were accepted as the basis of the armistice the United States would withdraw from the conflict.

Although defeated on the Fourteen Points, Clemenceau secured American backing for France's conditions. How did Clemenceau win support for a programme that Lloyd George and House had resisted at the start of discussions? Clemenceau and House met privately and it seems likely that the Tiger traded support for the Fourteen Points for American backing on French proposals. House assured allied leaders that from Wilson's speeches 'you could establish almost any point that anyone wished against Germany'.[2] No doubt Clemenceau decided that the vagueness of the Points would allow scope for manoeuvre at the peace conference. On 9 November Foch presented armistice conditions to the Germans. He and Clemenceau 'spoke ... of 1870, of this revenge at last obtained, the supreme object of our existence, the dream so often cherished'.[3] Two days later Clemenceau had second thoughts: 'It will all be useless.'[4]

Within a year this pessimism was widely endorsed. The Allies, it was said, should have marched on Berlin and dictated an armistice. Years later General de Gaulle asserted that the possibility of national renewal had been lost because the armistice came too soon. Marshal Pétain, then army commander in the north east, claimed to have begged Foch to delay the armistice.[5] Why, then, did French leaders not continue the war? In early October they did not know how close Germany was to collapse. There was an astonishing failure of intelligence. Clemenceau acknowledged: 'at the time of the armistice we did not know the precise state of the German armies ... If we had been better informed we would have imposed much harsher conditions.'[6] Given better intelligence France would have had two options: to demand harsher conditions or insist on marching to Berlin.

Could the French by continuing the war have imposed a French peace? At the time leaders wanted an armistice. Although a major offensive in Lorraine was planned for 14 November, Foch did not set great store by it. Only General Pershing, the American military commander, believed that allied morale and manpower justified a continuing offensive and a demand for unconditional German surrender. To be sure, the French had reservations about an armistice, suspecting a German trap of some kind, but once Foch had drawn up detailed conditions even Poincaré accepted that they were rigorous enough to enforce war aims. There were other reasons for accepting an armistice. Humanitarian feeling played a part – no one wanted to be accused of needlessly prolonging the blood-bath. Rulers were also apprehensive of national morale. Rejecting an armistice request risked demoralizing armies and peoples. Equally powerful was the fear of Bolshevism engulfing Germany and perhaps the Allies themselves. Delaying an armistice might plunge Germany into chaos. But the decisive factor was the determination to forestall an Anglo-Saxon military triumph. In November 1918 France with 102 divisions still dominated the coalition; by 1919 Pershing planned to have 100 American divisions in line. Pétain's projected Lorraine offensive in mid-November might have succeeded, but the risk of failure and a resulting Anglo-Saxon peace seemed too great. In the words of General Weygand, Foch's chief of staff: 'French soil would not have been liberated by a pre-eminently French victory: this victory would have been above all Anglo-Saxon, especially American.'[7]

Aims

'Restitutions, reparations and security', ran Clemenceau's vague statement of aims. More than this he would not disclose publicly. Secrecy characterized his whole approach. During the peace conference the Tiger sidelined cabinet, presidency and parliament, keeping his own foreign minister in the dark about Council of Four sessions. The cabinet was not consulted about the peace treaty as a whole until the end of April 1919. Even the Tiger's cub, interior minister Georges Mandel, often discovered important information from press leaks. This was carrying secrecy too far but some reticence was necessary. Unpopular compromises would probably have to be made so the less said the better. Moreover, Clemenceau counted on the Allies to continue wartime economic and financial cooperation. Given allied goodwill France could afford to be flexible on aims. It made no sense therefore to prejudice France's position in advance by declaring a large and detailed programme. Announcing claims to German territory might be counter-productive and unify German opinion. This was the last thing

Clemenceau wanted. With luck the German revolution might yet shatter Bismarck's creation without France lifting a finger.

John Maynard Keynes savagely pilloried Clemenceau as 'dry in soul and empty of hope ... cynical and almost impish ... He felt about France what Pericles felt of Athens – unique value in her, nothing else mattering.'[8] Cynical and contemptuous the Tiger may have been but his nationalism was backed by a huge parliamentary vote of confidence on 29 December 1918, 386 to 89. None of the many pressure groups, not even the powerful *comité des forges* representing heavy industry, challenged him. The armistice opened up an acrimonious internal debate on peace conditions, yet no groups or individuals called publicly for reconciliation and moderation. The peace, it was assumed, would be a *paix française*; at a minimum Germany should pay for the war, return Alsace-Lorraine and surrender the left bank of the Rhineland as a pledge of good behaviour. What provoked controversy was whether Germany should be dismembered. Although continuing wartime censorship may have kept conciliatory sentiments out of the press, postal censorship and monthly police reports indicate that hatred of Germany and desire for revenge overrode all other concerns: 'Germany must pay; on this point opinion is unanimous.'[9]

Too much a realist to suppose that paper barriers would hold Germany, Clemenceau took important initiatives. The first was to secure allied agreement on the organization and programme of a peace conference. On 27 November foreign minister Stephen Pichon outlined a timetable: a preliminary treaty covering all immediate questions would be imposed by the Allies, followed by a general peace congress. What doomed the plan was a clumsy attempt to undo the armistice. Pichon proposed a new scheme to replace the Fourteen Points. Wilson never replied. Next Clemenceau tried to win British support before Wilson arrived in Europe. France wanted prolonged occupation of the Rhineland, a strategic frontier to include part of the Saar, control of the main Luxemburg railway system, upper Silesia for Poland and the return of Alsace-Lorraine. At a meeting on 29 November Lloyd George refused to discuss territorial issues in Wilson's absence. However, Clemenceau made a major concession, promising Palestine and Mosul to Britain. There was nothing in writing and the British premier later denied a trade-off. Almost certainly however, some understanding was reached – Clemenceau receiving verbal support for Rhineland claims in return for concessions on the Middle East. Significantly, Clemenceau felt confident enough later in December to tell London that instead of prolonged occupation the Rhineland was to be an independent neutral state.

France endeavoured to tighten links with Belgium, proposing a cartel linking Franco-Belgian iron and steel industries with those of Luxemburg and the Saar. Belgian ambitions for a take-over of Luxemburg were opposed on the grounds that increasing Belgian's size would merely widen Germany's invasion corridor into northern France. France had ambitions of her own in Luxemburg. The ruling house was discredited by charges of wartime collaboration with Germany, and Paris encouraged opposition groups to stage a coup in January 1919. However, the local French commander, ignoring or misunderstanding instructions, actually helped restore order.

Revolution and war in central and eastern Europe hindered the construction of a barrier against Germany. Bolsheviks and White Russians fought for control of Russia; German troops struggled to retain territory in the east, in 1919 Polish and Bolshevik armies clashed. In December 1918 troops were sent to the Black Sea port of Odessa to protect French interests in the Ukraine. In central Europe newly proclaimed Czechoslovakia seemed endangered by a breakaway movement in the German-speaking Sudeten-land. France strengthened the new state by sending a military mission and allowing Czech veterans to return. When on 12 November the Austrian parliament voted for the union of Austria and Germany, Clemenceau declared an *Anschluss* 'absolutely inadmissible' and urged an allied march on Vienna.[10] France's traditional ally Poland, now resurrected, received military aid.

In Alsace-Lorraine, the Rhineland and Saar France wasted no time in raising the *tricolore*. Troops prepared the way for political and economic control. Alsace-Lorraine, with flagrant disregard for armistice provisions, was rapidly Gallicized. Many believed, like Jules Cambon, ex-ambassador in Berlin, that France at last had the opportunity to destroy 'the artificial work of the Vienna Congress' by excluding Prussia from the Rhineland.[11] The German revolution of 1918–19 threatened German political unity. In the autumn of 1918 separatist movements, spurred by fear of Bolshevism, sprang up in the Rhineland. General Fayolle, commander in chief, instructed his officers to conduct discreet propaganda in order to convince inhabitants of the left bank that it was in their interests to separate from the right bank: 'for the peace of the world the Rhine must be the barrier of West Europeans against Germans and Bolsheviks'.[12] Paris gave no direct political encouragement until the early summer of 1919 but from January Foch and his civilian advisor, Paul Tirard, were authorized to offer left-bank industries economic incentives 'to turn towards France'. In the Saar Paris focused on a cultural offensive, stressing the seventeenth-century origins of the French connection.[13]

Constraints

The Tiger, despite a free hand from cabinet and parliament, was reined in by powerful pressures: demands for an early peace, turmoil in central and eastern Europe, allied disagreements, social unrest and economic weakness at home. After the armistice came the reckoning – 1,364,000

deaths, 740,000 casualties. A flu pandemic killing twenty million world-
wide, together with a hard and long winter, gave life a surreal quality. The
struggle for survival dominated everything: jobs, housing, coal shortages,
strikes and the cost of living captured the headlines. Conditions in central
Europe were worse than during the war. Sigmund Freud wrote a paper for a
Hungarian periodical and asked to be paid in potatoes. Victory was a
wasting asset. Peace-making depended upon retaining sufficient power to
impose a settlement by force, if necessary. Yet soldiers and their families
wanted out. But Germany demobilized slowly and on 1 January 1919 still
had seventy-five divisions. However, delaying French and allied
demobilization would have antagonized conscripts and electorates. When
the ship carrying the British delegation to the peace conference crossed from
Dover to Calais on 2 January it was passed by a string of ships sailing from
Calais to Dover, each crammed with British soldiers wild with joy at
returning home. Men once liberated were resolved not to fight again. As a
result, demobilization schedules imposed a deadline on peace conference
discussions. On 26 March Clemenceau reminded the conference 'of the
universal desire to demobilize the armies ... on every side complaints are
heard about the Conference's slow progress.'[14]

Fear of a pandemic of Bolshevism darkened deliberations. Censorship
directives betrayed official anxieties: 'Absolutely nothing on the workers'
and soldiers' councils in Germany' (8 November); 'nothing on Bolshevism in
the German revolution' (9 November).[15] In January a rising of the extreme
left in Berlin was suppressed but Soviet republics were successfully
established in Munich and Budapest in the spring. France could not be
sealed off from this ferment. The censor's blue pencil kept news of minor
disturbances out of the press but the mutiny of the French Black Sea fleet in
April was too big to be ignored. Clemenceau, when informed that local
Soviets were organizing strikes and protests, concentrated cavalry divisions
at danger points. Violence invaded the conference – on 19 February an
anarchist wounded the Tiger. On May Day troops were used to forestall a
general strike, leaving many demonstrators injured in street battles. June
was the worst month for strikes and the government took no chances –
seven divisions were in the Paris area with two on stand-by. Despite
industrial unrest, Clemenceau's main bogey was Germany, not Bolshevism.
In November the premier reported that German representatives had 'dwelt
on the fact that Germany is on the verge of Bolshevism unless we assist them
to resist and that we ourselves will ... be invaded by the same scourge.'[16] But
Clemenceau suspected that Germany's new leaders, having used Bolshevism
as leverage for a moderate settlement, would then check the revolution and
make up with Russia.

Allied rivalries imposed a further restraint on peace-making. Old enmities
reappeared. France's programme for the Rhineland, Saar and eastern
Europe excited Anglo-American fears that the result would be 'nothing less
than the domination of Europe'. Schemes for the Rhineland were

condemned as 'short-sighted, selfish and quite impractical'.[17] Franco-British
animosities resurfaced. Clemenceau taxed Lloyd George with being an
enemy of France 'from the very day after the armistice' and got the reply:
'Was it not always our traditional policy?'[18] At dinner, on the evening of the
armistice, Lloyd George talked about the great qualities of the Germans, the
need to send food ships and the impossibility of rebuilding Europe without
them. There was no mention of succouring France. London and Washington
were told of French agents 'working deliberately and under instructions to
upset the League of Nations, to overthrow Anglo-Saxon predominance'.[19]
Britain, while supportive of claims for reparations and Alsace-Lorraine,
opposed ambitions for the Rhineland and Saar. Weakening Germany
territorially, it was reasoned, would be a recipe for Bolshevism or French
hegemony.

Clemenceau, shocked by America's railroading of the armistice talks, was
unimpressed by declarations of disinterestedness in European broils. He
feared an instinctive Anglo-American *entente* and tried hard to exclude
Wilson from the peace conference. The Tiger mocked the Fourteen Points:
'The good Lord Himself required only ten'. Americans had given offence by
boasting of coming in to finish the war. 'When the war is over', Wilson
wrote in July 1917, 'we can force them [Britain and France] to our way of
thinking because by that time they will, among other things, be financially in
our hands.'[20] Wilson never failed to remind his partners that he had 'given
his word' to Germany that the peace would be based on the Fourteen Points.
Tensions at the top were matched by ill-feeling between the French public
and Americans who were blamed for sending up the cost of living,
corrupting women and posing an economic threat with mass production
methods. American doughboys complained of overcharging. 'We pay good
rent for every inch of French soil which we occupy behind the lines; we
didn't, it seems', observed one American caustically 'actually pay rent for
our front-line trenches'.[21]

With Italy France might have made common cause; both had territorial
ambitions in Europe. Italy looked for gains in the Adriatic and Danubian
Europe, the annexation of the Alto-Adige plus colonial satisfactions
promised in the secret Treaty of London. Although Poincaré talked of a
rapprochement, Clemenceau dismissed Italy as too weak militarily and
financially to be a credible counterweight to the Anglo-Saxon powers.
Indeed Franco-Italian relations were as stormy as Franco-British. There
were colonial squabbles and in December 1918 Italy called for the cession of
the Roya valley, part of metropolitan France. Returning from a London
conference on 4 December, French and Italian delegations travelled in the
same London–Paris boat train without making contact.

The clash of different mindsets and national traditions made peace-
making both factious and flawed. The experts were as prejudiced as the
politicians. 'I had a nice time with Count Vanutelli, who is probably a
trickster, being Italian', opined Yale professor Charles Seymour. 'French

politicians and functionaries as a class', he wrote scathingly, 'are absolutely selfish in their national aims ... the influence of finance and business in politics ... is enormous and at times disgusting.'[22] British advisor Sir James Headlam-Morley targeted French experts who 'bargain like Jews and ... generally are Jews ... the French Departments of State and the inferior people seem completely defective in all sense of justice, fair play and generosity.' Camille Barrère, French ambassador to Italy, was judged 'fairly straight, thanks probably to his having been educated at Eton'.[23] A sense of historical continuity might be virtue or vice – depending on national viewpoints. 'The French of today are just the same as the French of Richelieu and Louis XIV', Headlam-Morley pontificated.[24] But Clemenceau lectured Wilson: 'for you a hundred years is a very long time; for us it does not amount to much. I knew men who had seen Napoleon with their own eyes. We have our conception of history and it cannot be the same as yours.'[25]

French leaders were oppressed by the crushing burden of war costs and reconstruction. American and British loans had saved France from bankruptcy in 1917. By 1918–19 France relied on British coal and Anglo-American support for the franc. The merchant fleet was so run down that Clemenceau begged the loan of American ships in order to supply French colonies. Allied help was urgently needed for reconstruction of the devastated north east. In January 1919 London and Washington stopped supporting the franc. While Britain was persuaded to extend assistance for a few months, it was clear by April that allied financial and economic cooperation was over. The United States treasury, reported France's Washington mission, considered that the difficulties were largely due to 'a lack of banking organization and to the ignorance and egoism of our people'.[26] The British talked of withholding financial help in order to force France to hand over colonies.

Organization

The choice of Paris as conference venue gave Clemenceau the chair, with the right to appoint a secretary general. Two leading diplomats, Philippe Berthelot and Pierre de Margerie, were passed over in favour of a nonentity, Paul Dutasta, ambassador in Berne. The Allies were each represented by five plenipotentiaries. Clemenceau ignored senior politicians and fielded a team of trusted lieutenants: Stephen Pichon, foreign minister; Lucien Klotz, finance minister; Jules Cambon, ex-secretary general of the foreign ministry; André Tardieu, high commissioner for foreign affairs. Only Tardieu enjoyed the Tiger's full confidence. At forty-three he had a distinguished record as diplomat, civil servant and journalist. His talents, which included fluent English, made him Clemenceau's right-hand man. British delegate Robert Cecil thought him 'one of the cleverest of the French'.[27] 'Little Pichon', as Clemenceau dubbed him, was a mediocrity whom the premier treated more like a major-domo than colleague. 'He looks at Clemenceau just like my Welsh terrier looks at me', joked Lloyd George.[28] His chief asset was a wonderful voice so he could always be relied on for a good speech. Klotz, ridiculed by Clemenceau as 'the only Jew who can't count', was quickly eclipsed by Louis Loucheur, minister for industrial reconstruction. Klotz's slogan 'Germany will pay' did not cover his own cheques. In the late 1920s he was disgraced when a cheque bounced – he ended up in an asylum.

On 18 January 1919 the conference opened and for the first time since the Congress of Paris in 1856 France was the world's diplomatic capital. Clemenceau was the star; posters displayed his silhouette alongside that of a tiger. But there was no physical resemblance – he was small, stout and undistinguished. Born in 1841 in the Vendée, he trained as a doctor before entering politics. Widely read, he expected those about him to be conversant with Japanese art, the Peloponnesian war and Cro-Magnon man. A healthy distrust of perfidious Albion did not extend to British products. He had a Rolls Royce, ordered clothes from London, furnished from Maples and apprenticed his cook at Claridges. He kept fit chasing British generals: 'The old boy of seventy-eight began to chase Wilson [General Sir Henry Wilson] around the room like a schoolboy.' In March 1918 at the start of the German spring offensive Winston Churchill, munitions minister, accompanied the seventy-seven-year-old to the front. After fifteen hours of driving over rough roads a 'tired out' forty-three-year-old Churchill marvelled at the Tiger's vitality. At one point a German shell burst, scattering some horses, and a wounded riderless horse trotted towards them. The Tiger sprang forward, seized the bridle and brought it under control, exclaiming 'What a marvellous moment.'[29]

A strict regime conserved energy. Getting up at 5 or 6 a.m. – he never slept well until out of office – he worked alone, fortified by a peasant dish, half stew, half porridge. At 7.30 a.m. a keep-fit instructor arrived; at 8.45 a.m. he left his flat in the rue Franklin for the war ministry, rue Saint Dominique. Press briefings were particularly important since he never looked at a newspaper. Cabinet and committees followed. Afternoons were filled with parliament and more meetings. After signing papers at the end of the day he unwound in the company of intimates. Later family and friends called, including Madame Hennessy of cognac fame. At 9 p.m. he was home for supper and sleep. His private office organized the conference, tuning the press and preparing minutes. Control of minutes became crucial from 24 March when the Council of Four replaced the Council of Ten as the supreme decision-making group. Officially no minutes were kept but the notes of the interpreter, Paul Mantoux, provided a record. The extension of wartime censorship enabled the government to suppress internal critics and orchestrate onslaughts on allied leaders.

Allied delegations were lodged in leading hotels – Americans at the Crillon, Italians at the Edouard VII, British at the Majestic and the Astoria. Special telephone links between the Crillon and the Majestic confirmed French fears of an Anglo-Saxon *entente*. For security the Majestic was staffed with British domestics, including cooks. The impression that stuck most with Keynes was the taste of Midland Railway breakfast marmalade. The Americans fared better with offices directly above Maxim's.

Traditionally, peace congresses were glittering state occasions with more dances than discussions. Although Clemenceau vetoed the glitz of the old diplomacy, Paris offered plenty of entertainment: high society dinners, soirées with Proust and Cocteau, Balliol reunions, visits to the battlefields, amateur theatricals in the basement of the Majestic, special English language shows at the *Folies Bergère*, schoolboyish humour at the Astoria – T. E. Lawrence (Lawrence of Arabia) in high spirits cascaded toilet paper down the stairwell upon Lloyd George and Balfour.

After the opening fanfares the conference seemed to go round in circles. Delegates tussled over procedural questions: equal status for the English and French languages; the number of representatives for the British Common-wealth and smaller powers; the exchange of visiting cards between delegations. Paul Cambon, sickened by the 'indescribable mess', rushed back to London.[30] The sheer scale of proceedings produced confusion. Thirty-two countries were represented, allied delegations were large – over 1,000 Americans, 400 British. There was a 600-strong press corps. But the main reason for the confusion was that no one had done their homework. Although the content of a peace settlement had been researched during the war, little thought had been given to programmes, procedure and organization. The Allies had not thrashed out in advance the purpose and organization of the conference. As late as 12 January, Clemenceau still talked as if there would be three phases: informal allied discussions, next a brief preliminary peace conference, finally a full congress of all the powers. Gradually, order appeared – the supreme war council became the Council of Ten, with two representatives from each of the Allies: France, Britain, the United States, Italy and Japan. An occasional plenary session of the conference was the only concession to open diplomacy. From the end of January much of the real business was in the hands of fifty-eight specialist committees.

Twice daily the Council of Ten gathered in Pichon's room at the Quai d'Orsay. Against an *ancien régime* décor of gilt, marble, mirrors and de Medici tapestries, plush sofas were arranged on both sides of a large regency writing table. Clemenceau, back to the fireplace, presided, flanked by Wilson, secretary of state Robert Lansing, Lloyd George, foreign secretary Arthur Balfour, prime minister Louis Botha of South Africa, Italian premier Vittorio Orlando, foreign minister Sidney Sonnino and Japanese representatives. Behind the sofas, all round the edges of the room, secretaries and experts sat on small gilded chairs, ready to prompt with maps and documents. Wilson's doctor, overcome by the overheated atmosphere, incautiously opened a window. Clemenceau and Pichon at once asked for it to be closed. Lloyd George joked that it was probably the first breath of fresh air in the foreign ministry since the time of Louis XIV.

Clemenceau with Mongol-like features, skull-cap, long walrus moustache, heavy eyebrows over half-closed eyes and grey suede gloves, played the prima donna to perfection – fluent English more than compensated for slight deafness. Neither Wilson nor Lloyd George spoke French. While Lansing doodled with pictures of hobgoblins, Wilson walked up and down to ease attacks of pins and needles. Lloyd George kept up an audible running commentary on all and sundry. During lengthy presentations by minor powers, the Tiger roused himself from somnolence induced by the overheated room and snarled insults. When Czech foreign minister Edward Benes talked for three hours, Clemenceau loudly said: 'He has been awfully long-winded.' A Czech request for extra time got the reply 'Oh we'll appoint a special commission and you can talk to them for a couple of hours.'[31] The Italians were mercilessly bullied. Sonnino tried to dodge questions and was brutally cornered: 'You must want one thing or the other ... Are you in favour of the proposal made by Monsieur Tardieu and the Commission, yes or no?' Intimates were slapped down with devastating rudeness. At one point Tardieu rose to whisper to a colleague, momentarily obscuring Clemenceau's view of the Italians. Clemenceau rapped sharply on the table, motioning Tardieu back, growling 'if you please Monsieur'. A mixture of wit and dispatch made the rudeness tolerable. Pichon pleaded for the admission of Monaco to balance British Commonwealth representation on the League of Nations – 'if nobody objects'. Clemenceau snapped: 'You know everybody objects; that's where we have lost all our money.' After speaking for ten minutes French spokesman for the League, Léon Bourgeois, unwisely stopped to look at his notes. Clemenceau rapped his gavel: 'As I hear no objection, the revised Covenant is adopted.' At the end of the afternoon came much-needed tea and macaroons.

Allied leaders, frustrated by the unwieldy Council of Ten, initiated from 24 March a Council of Four, relegating foreign ministers to the Council of Ten. The new core group usually met at Wilson's residence in the Place des Etats-Unis, sometimes at Lloyd George's flat or at Clemenceau's office. The interpreter, Paul Mantoux, took notes but no formal minutes were kept until Sir Maurice Hankey became secretary from 19 April. Informality ruled. One expert discovered the Big Four on all fours over a large map of the Adriatic spread on the carpet. All was not sweetness and light. 'You have told me seven lies this morning, this is the eighth', growled the Tiger. At which the British premier jumped up and seized Clemenceau by the scruff of his neck. Wilson separated the pair.[32] Clemenceau's cantankerousness had a saving wit: 'Wilson talked like Jesus Christ but acted like Lloyd George.'

Settlement

All too often the peace settlement is equated with the Treaty of Versailles. In fact, Versailles was the start of a process that lasted five years. However, the German treaty was by far the most important of the five treaties forming the Peace of Paris. Before looking at the peace-making process, an overview of the settlement may be helpful. Germany lost Alsace-Lorraine to France, Eupen and Malmedy to Belgium, Posen and West Prussia to Poland, the ports of Memel and Danzig to the Allies (Danzig was made a free state under League of Nations administration). Plebiscites were to decide the future of Upper Silesia, Schleswig and the Saar. The Saar was placed for fifteen years under international administration giving France the use of the coalfields. Germany lost all her colonies and was disarmed, save for a defence force of 100,000. The east bank of the Rhine was demilitarized to a depth of 50 miles. The land west of the Rhine was placed under allied administration and occupation for fifteen years. Economic and commercial clauses gave the Allies most favoured nation treatment for a decade and Alsace-Lorraine had the right to export duty free to Germany for five years. By 1921, when the territorial clauses had been fully implemented, Germany had lost 80 per cent of its 1913 iron ore output and 36 per cent of its steel-making capacity. Of the economic clauses the most contentious was the so-called 'war guilt' clause covering the payment of reparations. Germany had to accept 'responsibility ... for causing all the loss and damage ... as a consequence of the war imposed ... by the aggression of Germany and her allies'. Overarching the whole treaty was an Anglo-American guarantee of assistance for France in the event of unprovoked German aggression.

After Versailles came the treaties of the Parisian suburbs. On 10 September 1919 Austria accepted a treaty signed at St Germain. The non-German-speaking parts of pre-war Austria were distributed to claimant powers and a population of twenty-eight million was reduced to less than 8. Over three million German speakers in the Sudetenland were given to the new Czechoslovakia. A veto was placed on an *Anschluss* with Germany. By the treaty of Neuilly on 27 November 1919 Bulgaria ceded western Thrace to Greece and paid reparations. Hungary, by the treaty of Trianon on 4 June 1920, lost thirteen million of its pre-war population of twenty-one million and surrendered territory to Romania. Both Austria and Hungary had to pay reparations and had their armies reduced. The treaty of Sèvres of 10 August 1920 imposed terms on Turkey, leaving Greece in possession of Smyrna in Asia Minor.

Colonies, disarmament, the League of Nations

Between January and March the conference resolved three questions: Germany's colonies, German disarmament and the League of Nations. Although disarmament and the League generated considerable disagreement they were not sticking points for France. Clemenceau pressed home his views but avoided deadlock. His aim was to demonstrate that, since allied proposals fell short of security needs, France would expect satisfaction on her main territorial claims. On disarmament Britain and France were poles apart. Foch asked for a conscript army of 200,000; Lloyd George proposed a small volunteer force. Foch objected that voluntary enlistment would provide a nucleus for future recovery. Lloyd George suspected that Foch's proposal for a conscript force was a pretext to justify a large French standing army. In the event, Clemenceau overruled Foch and accepted the British scheme for a volunteer force of 100,000.

By mid-February two sections of the peace treaty were in place – colonies and the Covenant of the League of Nations. The disposal of colonies went smoothly, with France gaining League mandates for Togoland and the Cameroons in west Africa. The war had confirmed the empire's value as a reservoir of cannon fodder and Clemenceau insisted that the mandates should not bar France from 'raising troops in case of general war'. Wilson and Lloyd George agreed 'so long as Monsieur Clemenceau did not train big nigger armies for the purpose of aggression'.[33]

Conflicting Anglo-Saxon and French conceptions of the League of Nations provoked argument. The Fourteen Points called for a new international organization guaranteeing the integrity and independence of all states. But Anglo-American schemes envisioned the League as essentially deliberative and did not provide for military sanctions. By contrast, the French wanted an international peace-keeping force and a general staff. The League had few converts in France. 'French official and society circles', noted Lord Robert Cecil, British representative on the League of Nations commission, expressed 'complete disbelief' in the League idea. Foch took the view 'that it was a queer Anglo-Saxon fancy not likely to be of the slightest importance in practice'.[34] Léon Bourgeois, France's representative on the League commission, was a true believer who had long preached an international body. His zeal earned him the first presidency of the League and a Nobel peace prize. But the long-winded Bourgeois was shamelessly used. Clemenceau instructed him to court allied opposition to French proposals: 'Fight away, I don't mind. Your defeats will enable me to demand extra guarantees on the Rhine.'[35] Bourgeois, however, was such a windbag that the British lost patience even before the League commission got to work. 'If this old humguffin is as lengthy as this on the Commission of the League ... he will destroy the whole show', complained Cecil. 'That is no doubt why Clemenceau put him on', snapped Lloyd George.[36] By 11 February there was an impasse. The League, the French were warned, was 'their only means of getting the assistance of America and England, and if they destroyed it they would be left without an ally in the world'.[37] As a result, the French cut their losses and withdrew their plan for an international force. The Covenant, while providing for economic sanctions against aggressors, stipulated that military sanctions required a unanimous decision of the Council of the League, with implementation at the discretion of individual members.

Rhineland and Saar

After the dogfight on the League came the main battle on France's territorial demands. In early February Clemenceau abandoned delaying tactics and announced Rhineland and Saar claims. There were compelling reasons for the change. Criticism of Clemenceau's 'hide and seek' game was growing. The delay in announcing France's main claims had been counter-productive. Philip Kerr, Lloyd George's advisor, complained of 'the deliberate obstruction of the French who fill the agenda paper with small points and more or less openly admit that they want to postpone the discussion'.[38] Tardieu was apprehensive that Britain and the United States would say: 'Now you have got the League of Nations you do not need any further safeguards.'[39] Wilson's return to the United States offered a chance to win British backing. By early February hopes that London and Washington would extend wartime financial and economic support had collapsed. Further stalling served no useful purpose.

The Tiger, it is claimed, never regarded a separate Rhineland as 'feasible and desirable'.[40] The Rhineland claim was a bargaining counter to secure an Anglo-American guarantee. In fact, Clemenceau was committed to a separate Rhineland: 'We shall occupy until the country is willing to unite itself with France', he proclaimed in February. On 25 February Tardieu issued a detailed programme. The objective was an independent Rhineland under allied occupation. Deftly, Tardieu argued that his country's security was an allied interest – an independent Rhineland would bar the natural invasion route, giving allied forces time to come to the rescue. What France asked for was the same security that the destruction of the German fleet had given the Anglo-Saxon powers. By early March discussions were deadlocked. Lloyd George told the French: 'Well, now that we have disarmed Germany you don't need the Rhine.'[41] Clemenceau, convinced that in December 1918 Lloyd George had expressed support for the Rhineland claim, accused the premier of double-crossing him. Wilson's return to Paris on 14 March brought a partial breakthrough. France was offered an Anglo-American guarantee in return for withdrawing her claim. Clemenceau insisted on additional security: demilitarization and allied occupation linked to Germany's repayment of reparations. Again deadlock. Wilson and Lloyd George accepted demilitarization but baulked at occupation. On 25 March Lloyd George counter-attacked. The Fontaine-bleau Memorandum called for 'a just and far-sighted peace'. However, 'a just and far-sighted peace', as the French riposted, was also an Anglo-Saxon peace biased towards the naval powers.[42] London did not propose the return of Germany's navy and colonies. Finally, on 15 April, during Lloyd George's absence in London, Wilson and Clemenceau reached a compromise: demilitarization with allied occupation for fifteen years. Clemenceau telephoned Poincaré: 'Now I consider the peace is made.'[43]

The Saar, like the Rhineland, brought proceedings near to breaking point, with Wilson threatening to return to the United States. France proposed to annex part of the Saar and occupy the remainder. Saar coal would compensate for the devastation of France's northern coalfield and reduce dependence on imports. Allied leaders accepted the need for coal but rejected annexation. Clemenceau then proposed a fifteen-year occupation and plebiscite. In the interim France would enjoy sovereignty. Wilson objected to a transfer of sovereignty and ordered his ship to prepare to sail. The final settlement provided for a fifteen-year League of Nations admini-stration giving France the right to exploit the coal.

Reparations

Reparations raised more passion than any other single issue. Keynes' contention in *Economic Consequences of the Peace* (1919) that payments for war damages would be a millstone on Germany and delay Europe's recovery became the received wisdom. The French were pilloried for seeking Germany's ruin by extracting every gold mark. Research has produced a different interpretation. Discussion of reparations at the peace conference has to be separated from later disputes. Singling out France as the villain of the piece is quite wrong. Both Britain and Belgium wanted large payments and for a while France's policy was relatively moderate.

Reparations responded to several needs. The punitive aspect was salient. 'Squeezing the Germans till the pips squeaked' summed up the mood in London and Paris. In April over 300 French deputies called for Germany to bear the entire cost of the war. Since Germany was believed to have caused the war it seemed fair to insist that the loser should pay. But reparations were also linked to security and interallied debts. Taxation covered only one third of war costs, internal and external borrowing accounted for the rest. France ended the war with astronomical budget deficits and external debts to the United States and Britain. The preferred solution was an extension of wartime allied cooperation which would protect the franc and perhaps cancel or ease debts. In December 1918 Clémentel asked London for assurances that France would receive credit, shipping and commodities to avoid 'a situation of inferiority resulting from the war'.[44] The British waited for an American decision. But Wilson was intent on dismantling allied economic cooperation as quickly as possible. The state department opposed 'any programme that even looks like inter-Allied control of our economic resources'.[45]

In February 1919 it became clear that Britain and the United States would not continue the wartime economic partnership. Until then French claims were fairly reasonable, insisting that Germany pay only a modest proportion of war damage costs. Lloyd George's Keynes Plan attempted to bring the United States into a reparations settlement through guarantees and private investment. Faced with an American refusal to finance a settlement, France, Britain and Belgium went for as much as they could get. Wilson's efforts to win agreement on a fixed sum were defeated. France, having failed to secure her full Rhineland claim, wanted to establish linkage with reparations. Saddling Germany with an enormous bill which would take decades to pay off became an attractive reinforcement of security. Poincaré advised indefinite Rhineland occupation until all reparations had been cleared.

 The outcome was messy and unfortunate in every way and all the peace-makers were responsible for this result. The failure to agree a fixed sum poisoned postwar international relations. The most damaging part of the settlement, however, was Article 231, the war guilt clause. Nothing united German and allied opponents of the treaty more than this apparent moral condemnation. It was not intended as such. Wilson successfully resisted claims that Germany should pay the whole cost of the war and the purpose of Article 231 was to make clear Germany's liability for civilian damage only. Unsurprisingly, the clause was read as a moral indictment and at the time it expressed what most people in France and Britain believed. France won the right to prolong the Rhineland occupation if Germany reneged on its obligations. This gave Clemenceau a false sense of security: 'Germany will default and we will stay where we are.'[46] Was there an alternative to the reparations muddle, short of American involvement? France's large internal and balance of payments deficits could have been reduced by higher taxation and retrenchment. Higher domestic taxes sugared with a modest reparations package might have been sold to the electorate. Alas, the

Clemenceau government preferred to anaesthetize opinion with slogans like 'Germany will pay'.

Central and eastern Europe

For France the settlements in western and eastern Europe were interdependent. Germany had to be contained by double barriers and France had to have the means to support her allies in the east. Occupation of the Rhineland was intended not only to prevent a direct attack on France but to serve as a springboard for the defence of Czech and Polish allies. Civil war in Russia blocked a final settlement in the east. For once, Clemenceau's and Wilson's programmes harmonized. Point 13 of the Fourteen Points called for the reconstitution of an independent Poland with access to the sea. But Poland illustrated the practical difficulties of applying self-determination. Systematic Germanization of former Polish territory meant that a restored Poland was bound to include German speakers. France pressed for her protégé to have Danzig and two key railways which crossed the largely German district of Marienwerder. Lloyd George argued that the Polish Corridor should be drawn to include as few Germans as possible. It was settled that Danzig should be a free city under League administration with Polish control of customs and foreign affairs. Marienwerder's future would be decided by a plebiscite. France did better for Czechoslovakia, winning the Bohemian–German frontier of 1914. Gaining the German-speaking Sudetenland made strategic and economic sense for Prague. Clemenceau resisted Austrian chancellor Karl Renner's call for union with Germany. An *Anschluss* would have imperilled Czechoslovakia and left Germany stronger than in 1914.

Last battles

Now Clemenceau had to do battle with allied generalissimo Foch. By mid-April the draft treaty was ready and Clemenceau asked Foch to summon the German plenipotentiaries to Paris for 25 April. The general refused to do so until the draft treaty had been submitted to the cabinet. He considered it 'a capitulation, a treason' – only permanent occupation of the Rhineland would give adequate security.[47] Foch did not have a commanding appearance. A short, stocky figure, slightly bald with bandy legs and badly kept moustache, he had great difficulty in expressing himself and relied on a pantomime of gestures, explanations and movements, finishing sentences with strange little grunts. The Rhine he pronounced 'Rrrrhin', rolling his Rs like a roll of drums. To allow time for thought, he always had a cigar that would never draw and which he was for ever relighting. When words failed he fell back on gestures. An American liaison officer recalled a close encounter: 'he came up close to me, took a firm hold on my belt with his left hand and with his right fist delivered a punch at my chin, a hook under my ribs and another drive at my ear ... he then shouldered his stick and without a word marched on.'[48]

Foch urged Poincaré to take over the peace negotiations. Poincaré was sympathetic. Like Foch, he considered that only an indefinite occupation of the Rhineland would protect France since the Anglo-American guarantee 'cannot unfortunately ever be instantaneous'.[49] The feud with the Tiger isolated the president. He did not receive Council of Four minutes and depended on Clemenceau for crumbs of information. Excluded from decision-making he fretted and fumed, peppering the premier with notes and criticism, venting anger in his diary: Clemenceau was 'a fool ... losing his memory and hearing ... vain and feeble old man'.[50] On 6 April a tragi-comic slanging match took place between the two prima donnas, each menacing resignation. Clemenceau carried the day. Foch, after his initial insubordination, obeyed the order to summon the German delegates to Paris. On 25 April the cabinet, despite an impassioned plea by Foch, approved the draft treaty. At a plenary session of the peace conference on 6 May Foch reiterated: 'If we hold the Rhine solidly, France can set its mind at ease . . . anything offered in exchange is mere illusion, appearance, and vanity.'[51] Why did Foch and Poincaré not press home their challenge? Constitutional scruples deterred Poincaré but the decisive consideration was awareness that on their own they might not secure better terms. 'What will we do', asked Foch, 'if Clemenceau resigns?' Poincaré replied with another question: 'Will we do better tomorrow from Wilson and Lloyd George? ... All this has to be considered.'[52]

Two attempts were made to secure the Rhineland by stealth. On 17 May General Louis Mangin, French commander in chief, met Dr Andreas Dorten, leader of Rhineland separatists, and promised aid. He then asked General Liggett, American commander at Koblenz, for support for an impending coup. Liggett at once alerted Wilson. Clemenceau disavowed Mangin. On 19 June Dorten, with Mangin's collusion, proclaimed a republic. The coup failed miserably. Again Clemenceau apologized to allied leaders and reprimanded Mangin. Although the Tiger did not engineer the attempted coup the government gave general encouragement to the separatists. Mangin received only the mildest of reproofs and Clemenceau agreed with Poincaré that France should avoid 'a disavowal of any attempt at independence on the left bank'.[53]

Defeat or opportunity?

On 28 June 1919 the Treaty of Versailles was signed in the hall of mirrors at the chateau of Versailles where in 1871 the German empire had been proclaimed. Parisian dailies which had long since lost interest in the peace conference featured the reopening of racing at Longchamps. France's predominance was less securely based than it appeared at first sight. In a real sense Versailles was a defeat. 'This is not peace,' thundered Foch, 'it is an armistice for twenty years.'[54] People called it a Boche peace, a Wilsonian peace – anything but a French peace. The Anglo-American guarantee foundered in October 1919 when the United States Senate refused ratification. Of course, Anglo-American forces could not have landed in time to stop a German invasion but the psychological value of a commitment was incalculable. Its loss contributed to the erosion of will that undermined the Republic's post-1919 pre-eminence.

What of the rest of the treaty? The Rhineland demilitarization and disarmament were too flimsy to prevent Germany rearming and reoccupying within the foreseeable future. Clemenceau's assurance that Germany would default on payments, empowering France to prolong the Rhineland occupation, did not carry conviction. Fragile also were the anti-German barriers in east central Europe. Poland and Czechoslovakia were too weak and divided to substitute for the old Russian alliance. Indeed, the restoration of an independent Poland prejudiced a new Franco-Russian alliance, since Germany had now no common frontier with Russia. And the recasting of Poland out of German and Russian lands gave both states a common interest, a possible prize. In 1919–20 Poland had to fight for survival against Bolshevik Russia.

Versailles has been called an uneasy compromise between Anglo-Saxon moderation and French vindictiveness. This is a gross distortion of the complexities of peace-making. None of the Allies consistently pleaded reconciliation and moderation. 'Hang the Kaiser' calls came from Britain. The British Labour Party was the first to press the demand for war trials in the Coupon Election of November 1918. The idea of a punitive peace was deeply embedded in basic liberal assumptions about the problems of war and peace.[55] Lloyd George's Fontainebleau Memorandum insisted that a settlement 'do justice to the Allies by taking into account Germany's responsibility for the origins of the war and for the way in which it was fought'.[56] Allied leaders believed that Germany would accept 'stern' and 'severe' terms because they conformed to an absolute standard of justice. No allied leader advocated face-to-face negotiations with Germany because direct talks would have jeopardized 'the whole network of inter-allied compromises . . . and the almost insuperable difficulties that had emerged in

Europe's Frontiers 1918-1937

attempts to reconcile the Fourteen Points with the demands of the Allies'.[57] Versailles was flawed because peace-makers and peoples had ambivalent attitudes. The war aroused intense and excessive expectations of a new and better world that no peace could have satisfied. The public demanded speed, but speed conflicted with dispassionate and searching scrutiny of issues. Unrealistic hopes of a better world co-existed with the conviction that Germany had caused the war and should pay for it.

More can be said for the settlement than critics have conceded. In the perspective of World War II and the Cold War, Versailles was a brave attempt to deal with intractable, perhaps insoluble problems. Peace-making went on for five years after 1918; after 1945 the process continued in Europe for nine years, with Japan for eleven years and a peace treaty with Germany had to wait until 1990. Japan and Russia have yet to sign a peace treaty. The Paris peace has been compared unfavourably with the Congress of Vienna. The comparison is not a fair one. The overthrow of four empires in Europe and the Middle East confronted the Allies with problems on a scale which no previous congress had encountered. Pressures were horrendous. Europe had not known such violence and turmoil since the 1848 revolutions. Vienna statesmen safely ignored the nascent nationalism of their world; Paris peace-makers were presented with a *fait accompli* – revolution and self-determination in east central Europe were a reality. In 1815 Europe was a self-contained system; in 1919 the old balance of power had gone – Russia, a central link in the pre-1914 balance, was absent. The solution was also the problem. Peace-makers tried to square the circle, attempting 'to reconstruct some sort of balance of power in Europe, at Germany's expense and yet premised on German acceptance or on Allied readiness to maintain it, neither of which was forthcoming'.[58]

Versailles for all its flaws was not a botched or doomed peace. For France it was both defeat and opportunity. Clemenceau's handling of negotiations has provoked conflicting judgements. The nationalist right railed at Clemenceau for not securing a strategic frontier on the Rhine. Historians, however, have generally considered him France's greatest asset – tough, determined and realistic. Thanks to him a second-class power 'without the resources to control her destiny' did better than might have been the case.[59] Arguably, however, the traditional criticism has substance. The conference, in Jules Cambon's words, was an 'improvization'.[60] The lack of prior agreement on programmes and procedures enhanced the role of statecraft and personality. But Clemenceau had a major disability – by January 1919 he was burnt out. He had peaked in the struggle to hold France together in the winter of 1917–18. Age, strategy and temperament disadvantaged him. The Tiger made a crucial mistake in declaring his hand in advance of negotiations. The game plan was one of making concessions on non-essentials in order to win goodwill for essentials but Clemenceau vitiated it in advance by stating publicly on 29 December 1918 that 'nothing must happen which might separate ... the four powers. For this unity I will make every sacrifice.'[61] In January 1919 Clemenceau still believed that the wartime coalition could be continued in some form. This was a serious overestimate of allied solidarity. Delaying France's key demands only made sense if France had assurances of Anglo-American support. Clemenceau believed he had secured Lloyd George's backing for Rhineland claims but had nothing in writing.

The premier's lifestyle – dining alone and going to bed early – limited political contacts. More crucially, his vision was dangerously narrow. He had, noted Jules Cambon, 'his own ideas on two or three essential points; the rest left him indifferent'.[62] The 'rest' included imperial, economic and financial affairs. Paul Cambon was more damning than his brother: 'Clemenceau is drowning; he is quite unable to grasp the importance of questions about which he knows absolutely nothing.'[63] The Tiger's pragmatism – 'I live from day to day' – discouraged overviews.[64] Advisors operated as individuals, not as a team. Clemenceau's recognition of the underlying anarchy of government – 'there is no administration, no government, everything is collapsing' – led him to take on too much.[65] A willingness to work with cabinet, parliament and presidency would have strengthened his hand in negotiations. But, like Lloyd George, he bypassed the foreign ministry and kept an iron grip on policy. This was a mistake since experienced diplomats like Berthelot and de Margerie might have compensated for blindspots. Fatigue imposed an extra handicap. The cumulative effect of nearly two years of leadership told on the seventy-eight-year-old. Before the peace conference he was 'very tired' and looking forward to a complete rest.[66] The assassination attempt of 19 February weakened him and doctors decided not to remove the bullet. Lloyd George found the premier's failing 'very marked' and by June extreme exhaustion left him with permanent insomnia.[67]

The Tiger played a poor hand poorly. To be sure, the allied contribution to victory imposed compromises, yet a younger and cannier Clemenceau might have won better terms. A French peace in the full sense was unobtainable; the Allies would not accept the dismemberment of Germany. The Tiger contended that France had to choose between allied solidarity or isolation on the Rhine. But the choice was not necessarily as stark as presented. The danger of alienating the Allies was exaggerated. Determined pressure might have extracted more concessions. After all, Wilson and Lloyd George needed peace as much as Clemenceau. French leaders lacked confidence. Clemenceau's 'It will all be useless' response to the armistice betrayed a fatalistic streak. 'The French are still in a mortal funk over Germany', signalled British ambassador Lord Derby.[68] Poincaré, president since 1912, showed no sign of a conqueror's mentality. In 1919 his daily notes overflowed with anxiety and fear that Germany would renew the conflict by seizing Poland and Austria. However, the failure to extract greater concessions from the Allies did not mean that all was lost. The five years that followed were decisive. Versailles was the beginning, not the end of peace-making. 'The real work of making peace', observed South African General Smuts, 'will only begin after this treaty has been signed.' In Clemenceau's words: 'The treaty will be what you make it.'[69] For the first time since 1870 French leaders had an opportunity to establish a French predominance.

4

The price of victory

We must show the world the extent of our victory, and we must take up the mentality and habits of a victorious people, which once more takes its place at the head of Europe.

Clemenceau's last words to his cabinet before resigning, January 1920, in David Robin Watson, *Clemenceau: A Political Biography* (London, Eyre Methuen, 1974), p. 387

People are disquieted and discontented. They don't understand why a victorious war leaves us grappling with difficulties whose solution falls more and more short of our expectations.

Prefect of the Cantal, 5 July, 1922, in *Journal d'Alexandre Ribot et correspondances inédites 1914–1922*, published by Dr A. Ribot (Paris, Plon 1936), p. 298

What dominates everything are the awful threats that hang over France . . . She has not known such in all her history. Alone, exhausted, ruined, without government, without compass, living from day to day, haphazardly. The future is terrifying. I believe German revenge inevitable, unavoidable and close.

Marshal Lyautey, letter of 16 August 1921, in Pierre Ordioni, *Le Pouvoir Militaire en France*, 2 (Paris, 1981), p. 335

In 1919 French arms and prestige appeared supreme: an army of 900,000, 2,500 tanks, the largest air force in the world, supported by a stable of east European allies dominated a vanquished Germany. The colonial empire was second only to Britain; Poland, Romania, Czechoslovakia, Brazil and other states requested military missions; *poilus* were deployed in Europe, north

Africa and the Middle East; Paris was the world's diplomatic capital. But the reverse of the coin, as months became years, was a creeping disillusionment, a loser's psychology. After the blood-bath of the trenches came an unbloody, more refined form of death, a Chinese torture of setbacks and disappointments. The saying went that the army had won the war and Clemenceau had lost the peace.

Versailles was but the start of a lengthy process of peacemaking beset with increasing difficulties as the ex-Allies drifted apart. The Ambassador's Conference charged with completing and implementing Versailles took more than six years to determine the new frontiers. A rash of international conferences followed the Paris Peace Conference. Fighting in Europe and the Middle East raged until 1923. The Ruhr occupation of 1923 resulted in the Dawes Plan, an international reparations settlement endorsed at the London Conference in August 1924. The settlement slashed the amount of German payments and deprived France of the right to enforce sanctions unilaterally. Dawes, it is said, marked 'the end of French predominance in Europe'.[1] Why did victory turn to ashes? The reasons were many: war wounds and the pyrrhic nature of the victory; the immensity and novelty of postwar problems; lack of a major ally; flawed attitudes and assumptions; the shortcomings of leaders and institutions; lack of confidence.

Internal wounds

The slaughter exacted almost a million and half lives and over 700 000 wounded. Marianne, like Godefroy in Henri Barbusse's war novel *Le Feu* (1916), had been emptied of blood like an upturned bucket. The carnage scarred the whole of society. Nearly every family lost one or more members – politician Paul Doumer lost four of his five sons. Of the belligerents the Republic suffered most in relation to its active male population, losing over 10 per cent compared to Germany's 9.8 per cent and the British Empire's 5.1 per cent. The war cancelled forty years of demographic growth – 1921 census figures were only slightly higher than in 1876. Intellectuals were heavily hit; the elite Ecole normale supérieure lost over 40 per cent of alumni. Did the haemorrhage weaken France's ability to stay a great power? This is imponderable. Naturally, the hecatombs left a horror of war and pessimism about western civilization. But because the trauma ran deep the effects can be overstated. It is impossible to say whether the loss of human talent, by impoverishing elites, decisively influenced France's performance. The country's political and economic recovery in the 1920s suggests that the 'lost generation' was not a critical variable. Perhaps more significant was the generational conflict. Those who reached maturity after the war rejected the culture of their elders, blaming them for the massacre. This made it hard for politicians to communicate with the younger generation.

For all its physical and psychological impact the war did not bring profound social changes. Society remained deeply inegalitarian and only the upper middle class enjoyed real power. Emphasis on hierarchy and correctness in dress and manners reinforced social divisions. When a civil servant arrived five minutes late on the day his daughter was born his boss reminded him to be on time. It was a society of strong contrasts. The French prided themselves on their liberalism yet public executions by guillotine continued until 1939 (public executions ended in Great Britain in 1868). Some aspects of public health left a lot to be desired. Eric Blair (George Orwell) was traumatized by his experience as a patient at the Cochin Hospital, Paris.

The battlegrounds of northern France were a shambles. The war's brooding presence loomed everywhere: ploughed-up bodies and equipment, the sight of the maimed, widows and orphans, mile upon mile of black and white crosses in the cemeteries. Six years on, tourists 'passed great funeral pyres of sorted duds, shells, bombs, grenades and equipment'. Many, like the red-haired girl from Tennessee in F. Scott Fitzgerald's *Tender is the Night* (1934) must have despaired of ever finding their loved ones in the great sea of graves. Sixteen years on, Verdun exuded 'catastrophe and gloom'.[2] Understandably, in the context of a declining and ageing population, the megadeaths induced pessimism and anxiety. A spectacular increase in natality might have restored confidence: 'The Treaty means nothing', counselled Clemenceau in 1919, 'if France does not agree to have more children . . . if France renounces large families, we will have taken all the guns from Germany for nothing.' In the first year of peace the birthrate picked up slightly only to drop again. The fall coming after wartime losses had serious implications for future military strength. The years 1935–40 would be lean ones when the number of conscripts would decline because of the wartime slump in the birthrate. Consequently, France would not be able to mobilize the same number of men as in 1914.

The bloodletting reshaped attitudes to war. In 1914 war was taken for granted not only as an instrument of national policy but as a test of a man's worth: 'When one has not been a soldier, one is not a man', a peasant woman assured a departing son. Pacifist and socialist suspects on the government's blacklist, Carnet B, quietly rejoined their regiments. Unsurprisingly, four years of destruction bred revulsion. The rituals of private and public mourning – veteran parades, the ceremony of the 'unknown warrior', inauguration of memorials, the liturgy of the 11 November armistice commemoration – by keeping grief fresh helped to make the idea of a second European conflict an abomination. General Weygand, Foch's assistant, told how 'the young men . . . were refusing to take up a military career, as all France was fed up with war and even his own sons were becoming engineers'.[3] But outright pacifists opposed to all violence were an uninfluential minority. Most people perceived security and national defence as necessary evils. The public demanded a shorter period of conscription, not its abolition. Although reservists called up for the occupation of German towns in May 1921 sang the *Internationale* as their train passed through French and German stations, the Ruhr occupation of 1923 was popular. Only the communists protested.

After loss of life and physical injury, financial and economic damage was most in evidence. Large areas of northern France had been occupied and laid waste; retreating German armies flooded mines and carried off industrial plant. The war consumed billions of francs, leaving huge internal and external debts – to French bondholders, to Britain and the United States. 1918 opened nearly a decade of high inflation and currency instability. The franc which had been propped up by London and Washington, plummeted rapidly after the withdrawal of Anglo-American support in March 1919. Its pre-war parity of 25 to the pound sterling fell to 124 in December 1926. Real wages lagged behind inflation; by 1920 the prices of 1914 had quadrupled with the franc losing two-thirds of its pre-war value. An empty treasury, massive debts and an enormous reconstruction bill explain why reparations and interallied debts topped the international agenda for much of the postwar decade.

This picture of financial crisis is common to all accounts of the period. Most writers stress the war's financial and economic legacy as a major disabling factor in France's bid for predominance. And so it was. But it need not have been. Appearances were deceptive. In fact, the economy rapidly recovered, generating new wealth. Older economic histories pictured the French interwar economy of a piece with public finance – old fashioned, run-down, inefficient. In reality, from 1921, the economy, powered by industrial expansion, grew by leaps and bounds. The annual growth rate was 9.5 per cent and by 1924 industrial production equalled 1913 totals. Monetary depreciation, by making exports more competitive, boosted this expansion. During the 1923 Ruhr crisis British ministers looking for ways and means of exerting financial pressure on France were told: 'the whole country was in an exceedingly flourishing condition' and did not need to borrow money abroad.[4] Thus France in the early 1920s had the resources to pursue an independent foreign policy – even perhaps to the extent of imposing her own reparations and debts settlement.

Why then was there such a gap between potential and performance? One difficulty was that the economic take-off of 1921 could not be foreseen in 1919–20. The immediate aftermath of war brought a slump in 1920–21 and the outlook seemed grim. Wartime dependence on imports, especially British coal (over 50 per cent of coal was imported, 70 per cent of it from Britain) made ministers and their advisors over-pessimistic. Britain's economic policy was regarded as crucial. Ministers were told that 'It would be vain to pursue our country's economic recovery ... if Britain constructs a vast economic empire separate from the rest of the world'.[5] High British coal prices and a reduction in exports to France aggravated a coal crisis in 1919–20.

However, official and public attitudes constituted the main barrier preventing government from tapping into burgeoning economic strength. Inflation was a new and disorientating phenomenon, particularly bewildering for the French because the *franc de germinal* of 1803, like the Seine, was considered part of a fixed and unchanging natural order. The depreciation and sharp rise in living costs mesmerized the public. 'External and internal affairs, the Locarno agreements, wars in Morocco and Syria ... ministerial changes', signalled police reports, were seen as secondary to 'the agonizing financial situation'.[6] The archaic fiscal system both exacerbated the crisis and hindered its solution. The problem was how to persuade the agricultural majority in parliament to tax their electors. Resistance was strong. Unlike Britain and Germany who adopted a modern system of direct taxation in the nineteenth century, France delayed implementing the tax until 1920 and then applied it half-heartedly. In July 1922 the leading daily *Le Temps* campaigned for the suppression of income tax and a finance minister even apologized to businessmen for having to collect it. War costs had been met almost entirely by borrowing – only seven of fifty-five million francs spent in 1918 came from taxation. The lack of standard accounting procedures compounded confusion. A Frenchman was said to keep 'three sets of books: one for the tax collector, one for his wife and the other for himself which he keeps in his head'.[7] Without centralized procedures for controlling income and expenditure 'budgets were so complicated that they seemed to have been deliberately designed to conceal the real results of the government's financial mismanagement from public and parliament'.[8] War and reconstruction destroyed the ramshackle fiscal system. The enormous material and psychological cost of the victory made it natural to look to Germany and the Allies for solutions. It seemed both logical and just that Germany should foot the bill for damages and that the Allies should either cancel interallied debts or link them to the payment of reparations. External solutions appeared easier and more attractive than raising taxes and restructuring public finances. This was a snare and delusion that compromised France's independence. If the French had managed to stabilize their currency in the early 1920s, post-1918 European history might have taken a different path.

Fear of social unrest preyed on rulers. The war, as well as promoting trade union membership and militancy, sharpened social and economic distress. Economic mobilization, by creating new industrial centres, quickened migration from countryside to town. The influx set up severe strains especially in housing. The selfishness of the well-heeled threw the tax burden, in the form of indirect taxes, on those least able to pay. The urban working class had no recognized place in a Republic 'created by the aristocracy, administered by the upper and middle bourgeoisie, governed by the lower bourgeoisie and dominated by the peasantry'.[9] Social security provision was minimal compared to the system Bismarck gave Germany in the 1880s. The Bolshevik revolution of 1917 and the establishment of the Third International in March 1919 aroused millennial hopes. Dread of a red dawn stampeded employers and government into making two tardy concessions: legal recognition of trade union contracts and an eight-hour day. As danger receded the fiercely right-wing blue horizon parliament of November 1919 resisted further reforms. Trade Union leader Léon Jouhaux of the *Confédération générale du travail* believed that the bosses wanted a battle in order to exhaust union strike funds and undermine the eight-hour day. The government's brutal suppression of left-wing protest shocked an American onlooker at a Paris May Day demonstration in 1919: cavalry and police 'set on the people with ferocity . . . hammered them about the heads, got them on the ground and kicked them . . . a fairly well dressed man under our windows, after the real fighting was over, simply spoke to a serjeant and got two hard punches on the jaw which sent him sprawling.'[10] The left, demoralized by the collapse of a revolutionary strike in May 1920, then splintered at the Congress of Tours in December. A Communist Party adhering to the Comintern broke away from the main Socialist Party.

Military strength was not as impressive as it looked on paper; indeed, it was a wasting asset and the size of the army fell significantly between 1921 and 1933. Several pressures were at work. Occupation forces of 100,000 in Morocco and 70,000 in Syria reduced effectives in Europe. Risings in Morocco and Syria in 1925–26 required the transfer of substantial forces from Europe. By the mid-1920s 'the army at home was desperately struggling to maintain itself as a fighting force'.[11] Another reason for declining strength was the reduction in the length of military service from three years to eighteen months in 1923 and then twelve months in 1928. Military careers were unpopular. The pacifist climate, coupled with low pay and poor conditions of service, discouraged long-term enlistment. Financial stringency imposed an additional constraint. The battle for solvency had priority. In December 1921 war minister Louis Barthou considered 'a reduction in the budget of the War Ministry as a form of national defence'.[12] By the spring of 1924 cost-cutting forced the withdrawal of most of the French occupation troops in the Ruhr. The empire did not provide compensating reserves of manpower. General Mangin, proclaiming France to be a nation of 100 million, called for a permanent native army of 300,000 but colonial authorities were lukewarm since conscription was believed to have seriously reduced the combat efficiency of Algerian and Tunisian troops in World War I. In 1920 Marshal Louis-Hubert Lyautey, the resident general, successfully opposed conscription in Morocco, declaring that in black Africa conscription had been nothing but 'a manhunt, which produced men but not soldiers'.[13]

External constraints

A transformed and swiftly changing international environment circum-scribed France's freedom of action. The war reconstructed world politics in a number of ways. Although key political decisions continued to be made in European capitals, the United States had gained economic hegemony. The war produced a massive transfer of wealth between Europe and North America, making the United States the world's banker. The growth of the European economy had been retarded by eight years and the international economy was much weaker than in 1913. Not only was industrial output 30 per cent lower than in 1913 but the City of London was no longer the linchpin of the system. The different structure and interests of American capitalism deprived the 1920s of a stabilizing hub. World industrial production recovered but commerce languished. A protectionist fever gripped leading manufacturing countries and intra-European trade declined. The successor states created by the balkanization of Europe were economically weak and imposed high tariffs.

War and revolution expanded the scope of diplomacy. Before 1914 European diplomacy had been a self-contained system in which social, economic and ideological concerns played a subordinate part. Now the world had become much busier and, in President Coolidge's words, 'little more than a great neighbourhood' in which key issues interlocked and impacted on the home front.[14] This is why the reparations question proved so intractable. Wartime allied summits established a pattern of conference diplomacy conducted by heads of government and foreign ministers.

As a result, politicians and professionals were much more in the public eye and therefore more sensitive to popular opinion. New and competing forms of internationalism emerged – the League of Nations and the Moscow-based Third International. Both organizations inveighed against classical European diplomacy which allowed great powers to exercise a collective hegemony, disciplining small powers, creating buffer states, arranging territorial compensations for each other. The cosy, confident, pre-war world in which European elites shared common assumptions vanished. Communist and fascist ideologies exacerbated social and political conflict world-wide. The Geneva-based League of Nations, jewel of President Wilson's new diplomacy, quickly developed its own ethos and agencies, emphasizing a multilateral approach to foreign policy. The League's stress on openness and equality of states both reflected and encouraged greater public interest in foreign affairs.

What were the implications for policy-making? Before 1914 international affairs, like Napoleonic battles, could still be comprehended in the round. After 1918 rapidity of change and the multiplicity of interlocking concerns made it hard for leaders to resolve the issues. Conventional approaches were inadequate: 'The basic problem was not anyone's intransigence, but rather the poverty of traditional financial and monetary theory in an international economy which no longer functioned under the old laws of economics.'[15] The sheer intricacy and scale of affairs daunted leaders schooled in more leisurely days. Lloyd George and Clemenceau got 'hopelessly confused' about the terms of the Long-Bérenger oil agreement of May 1919.[16] An official complained of 'the swelling services, the avalanche of paper, abundance of telephone calls, flood of visitors'. Another cursed 'the press, parliamentary lobbies, activities of businessmen, ignorance of the public . . . the impatience of popular opinion insisting on knowing everything'.[17] The tangle of interdependent problems could not be unravelled one by one. Crises came like Job's messengers, each heralding disaster: 'And while he yet spake, there came another.' The rush of events crowded out careful assessment. British cabinet secretary Sir Maurice Hankey captured the frustration:

> What with our continual rows with the French; the entire withdrawal of the Americans from European affairs; the mechanical difficulties of conducting a Peace Conference with the Supreme Council under Lloyd George in London; a foreign minister's conference under Lord Curzon in London; an Ambassador's Conference under Millerand in Paris (a jealous rival of the London conference); commissions of the peace, some in London, some in Paris, with exasperated experts dashing from one to the other; a League of Nations meeting at odd times . . . international affairs are not easy to conduct.[18]

Conferences (twenty-four in three years) often met without adequate preparation; conclusions 'inevitably were inconclusive, intangible, specious, superficial and unreal'.[19] The more frequent the meetings the more the *amour propre* of participants was engaged and the greater the pressure to show results. Wartime government interventions in the economy fostered expectations that continued intervention would solve world problems. To win popular approval leaders forced issues prematurely, thereby accelerating events and generating new pressures. At fun resort conferences like Cannes, Rapallo and San Remo, ambience and incidentals acquired disproportionate importance. Sumptuous teas on sunny verandas in Italy generally eased the way to agreement. However, photographs of British premier David Lloyd George coaching his French counterpart Briand in golf at Cannes in 1922 gave the Frenchman a large domestic handicap. The political and cultural climate was not conducive to agreement. The war engendered contradictory feelings. People expected both too much and too little. The shaking of liberal values induced a cultural pessimism: 'We civilizations know that we are mortal', lamented writer Paul Valéry.[20] T. S. Eliot's *The Waste Land* (1922) expressed a widely felt disillusionment with western civilization – a 'heap of broken images'. Yet simultaneously the cataclysm nurtured hopes of universal disarmament and reconciliation. It was assumed that there were no

Table 1   Long-term external investments (US$m)

	1914	1929
United States	3,380	14,600
Great Britain	18,000	16,800
France	8,600	3,800–4,000
Germany	5,800	1,100–2,300

Source: René Girault and Robert Frank, *Turbulente Europe et nouveaux mondes, 1914–1941* (1988), p. 75

insoluble problems; conflict arose from ignorance and misunderstanding. One-to-one contacts, backed by expert scientific advice, would ensure understanding. Two initiatives – the League of Nations committee on intellectual cooperation and the *cité universitaire internationale* in Paris (1925) – expressed faith in international harmony. An informed public opinion, it was believed, would insist on openness and accountability and so help prevent conflict. University chairs and research institutes for the scientific study of international relations burgeoned: the Royal Institute of International Affairs, London, the American Council for Foreign Relations, the Carnegie Endowment, and the Institut für Auswärtige Politik, Berlin.

The sea change in international politics made France's future as a great power problematical. One indicator of diminished power was the loss of overseas investments (see Table 1). Half of the portfolio was sold to pay for the war. External assets of US$8,686 million in 1914 had shrunk by 1938 to US$3,859 million. Postwar indebtedness of 30 billion francs to Britain and the United States gave London and Washington leverage on French policy. France had the humiliation of having to borrow from Argentina, Spain and Uruguay. In 1923 Argentina requested Paris to pay interest on the debt. Another indicator of change was diplomatic isolation. Without powerful allies France was weaker internationally than in 1914. The new east European allies could not replace Russia, Britain or the United States. Empire aroused anxiety as well as pride. Nationalist insurrections in Syria, Morocco and Indo-China drained troops from Europe. In 1926 France and Spain mounted a joint expedition to crush Abd-al-Krim's rebellion in Morocco.

Financial and strategic vulnerabilities, however, did not lead to questioning of great-power status. On the contrary. In 1919 the French were said 'perhaps for the first time for 50 years' to be 'taking themselves seriously as a first-class power'.[21] Yet British foreign secretary A.J. Balfour believed that 'no manipulation of the Rhine frontier is going to make France anything more than a second-rate Power trembling at the nod of its great neighbour on the East'.[22] Was Balfour expressing a British consensus? Without more evidence it is impossible to say. One memorialist recalled diplomat Jules Cambon saying in 1921: 'In the immediate future the difficulty will be to slide France reasonably smoothly into the ranks of the second-rate powers to which she belongs.'[23] Yet there is no contemporary evidence of Cambon's opinion and no traces of policy-makers reassessing their country's ranking. Pluses outweighed minuses, discouraging reappraisal. French military might *was* overwhelming. Moreover until 1924 Britain and the United States hesitated to use direct financial pressure on France. Of course, bankers like T.W. Lamont of Morgan and Co., dropped broad hints that until French foreign policy became less aggressive in character there would be no American help for the franc. In May 1923 Montagu Norman, governor of the Bank of England, advised British ministers that France had managed to raise all the loans she needed and current economic prosperity made governmental pressure an unrealistic option. In the winter of 1923–24 the franc fell sharply because of the uncertainties of the Ruhr occupation and this enabled Anglo-American finance to call the tune by making short-term credits conditional upon acceptance of the Dawes reparations settlement. Nevertheless, sustained economic growth from 1921 reassured French leaders that despite internal and external deficits the economy was sound.

Mésentente cordiale

The ending of the wartime Franco-British alliance was a major disability for which the small east European allies in no way compensated. Although London and Paris paid lip-service to the *entente* they agreed on one point only: the extent of their disagreement. 'In every quarter of the globe', complained foreign secretary Lord Curzon, 'the representatives of France are pursuing a policy ... unfriendly to British interests.' 'Everywhere, on every point, there is disagreement', echoed ambassador Paul Cambon.[24] The sharp variance of aims and outlook between the ex-Allies allowed Germany to undermine French predominance.

Centuries of rivalry from Joan of Arc to Napoleon I left deep distrust. 'In my day we were content to hate 'em and lick 'em', declares Squire Hamley in Mrs Gaskell's *Wives and Daughters* (1866).[25] In 1898 the Fashoda crisis in the Sudan pushed both countries to the edge of war. Doubts about France's reliability as an ally helped to kill the Channel tunnel project in 1924. The wartime partnership was not all roses. 'Anti-French feeling among ex-soldiers amounted almost to an obsession', observed writer Robert Graves.[26] Younger generations inherited traditional animosities through war games. In the interwar years British and French children replayed old Franco-British battles in the military board game *L'Attaque*.

But the main source of post-1918 dissension was simply the fact that Germany's defeat and Russia's eclipse made London and Paris once again leading contenders for international influence. The French suspected perfidious Albion of a policy of divide and rule on the continent in order to further the pursuit of global imperial ambitions. The French resented Britain's dominance, especially control of international cable networks: 'France suffers a real economic yoke from the convergence of cables on Great Britain.'[27] Getting information much sooner gave the City a head start on Paris in business dealings. 'In reality we are alone', declared Marshal Lyautey, pro-consul in Morocco, 'because England, mistress of the seas, mistress of our communications ... thinks she has us at her mercy ... treating us more or less like a Portugal ... we undergo periodically ... new Fashodas.'[28] By contrast, the British felt intimidated by French military might. In 1922 British air staff considered war with France 'the greatest menace to this country' and believed France capable of delivering 'a tremendous air attack'. The foreign office objected to the construction of a Channel tunnel because relations 'never have been, are not, and probably never will be sufficiently stable and friendly to justify the construction ... it is almost certain that we shall have conflicts with France in the future.'[29] 'The brutal fact', wrote H.G. Wells, 'is that France maintains a vast army in a disarmed world ... and is energetically preparing new aggressive operations in Europe, including a submarine war against England.'[30]

Rows over Germany, the Middle East, economic reconstruction and almost everything poisoned the early 1920s. Even Tangier excited strong feelings. Britain viewed the port as the key to imperial communications with India and preferred to maintain the international regime; France, controlling most of Morocco, wanted possession. But Germany was the big bone of contention. 'The fact is that they [the French] wanted a stiffer treaty', recorded Hankey, 'and we wanted an easier one.'[31] Britain's conciliatory approach to Germany sprang from political and economic anxieties. War weariness induced a 'never again' mood towards continental conflicts. The economic slump of 1921 seemed confirmation of John Maynard Keynes's argument in *Economic Consequences of the Peace* (1919) that European economic recovery depended on German recovery. 'Great Britain's real desire', Lloyd George assured Briand, 'was to get on with business.'[32] Eastern Europe was a further source of discord. French requests for a British guarantee for the settlement in eastern Europe got a dusty answer from Lloyd George: 'The British people were not very much interested in what happened on the eastern frontier.'[33]

Different outlooks made for a dialogue of the deaf. When two peoples believe they have unique values and a divinely appointed place among the nations it is difficult to find common ground. 'There is in the Englishman a combination of qualities, a modesty, an independence, a responsibility, a repose', boasted Mr Podsnap to his French guest, 'which one would seek in vain among the Nations of the Earth.'[34] 'The Latin mind', foreign secretary Austen Chamberlain pontificated, 'was more logical than ours and was always inclined to try and press arguments ... to their logical conclusions. It was our nature to shun these logical conclusions.' The British preference for a middle course explained 'the peaceful evolution of our national history and the strength of our institutions'.[35] Curzon became quite insulting about the 'fundamental' difference in method and outlook, inveighing against 'the French practice of subordinating even the most trivial issues to general considerations of expediency, based on far-reaching plans . . . and the gratification of private, generally monetary and often sordid, interests or ambitions, only too frequently pursued with a disregard of the ordinary rules of straightforward and loyal dealing which is repugnant and offensive to normal British instincts.'[36]

Gallic attitudes, although free from British self-righteousness, displayed intellectual arrogance and deep distrust of others. 'It is a very stupid mistake to think that the English are less intelligent than us', warned Anglophile novelist André Maurois.[37] 'The secret of getting the English to accept you', counselled Paul Cambon, 'is never to give the impression of doubting their good faith but unfortunately we spend our time in showing them our mistrust.'[38] If France wished to lead Europe, advised Seydoux, she had to dispel mistrust of her 'which derives from the mistrust that she herself feels towards others'.[39] At the end of a twenty-year ambassadorship in London Paul Cambon finally came to terms with British pragmatism: 'It is childish to make long-range policy with people who dislike hypotheses and live only for the present; we must concentrate like them on current problems.'[40]

Interwar summits brought out the worst in both leaderships. In 1922 Poincaré 'lost all command of his temper and for a quarter of an hour shouted and raved at the top of his voice'. Curzon collapsed in tears, panting: 'I can't bear him.'[41] On another occasion Poincaré 'declared that Lord Curzon was laughing at him, and, as he tolerated no criticism he would tolerate no smiles'. Encounters with Poincaré were singularly stressful. As premier Andrew Bonar Law's train was waiting to leave the Gare du Nord the premier mouthed to Poincaré through the closed window: 'And you can go to Hell', smiling the while. When Stanley Baldwin and Poincaré parted after discussions in September 1923 the Frenchman embraced Baldwin, kissing him on both cheeks. But it was kiss and fall out. Baldwin felt betrayed. 'Poincaré has lied', he said. 'I was led to believe that when passive resistance ceased he'd negotiate with the Germans.' In 1937 Baldwin welcomed retirement because he would not have to meet French statesmen.

In this climate alliance projects got nowhere. 'We cannot remain at peace in Europe if we are not in agreement with England', declared senior foreign ministry official Jacques Seydoux in November 1921. 'We must resolve our differences as soon as possible.' Without an alliance Seydoux foresaw 'an Anglo-German *entente*', giving London and Berlin an economic condominium in eastern Europe. 'In this case France would have no alternative than to use force against Germany.'[42] A colleague highlighted the obstacles to an alliance: 'England's desire for hegemony and wish to be the arbiter of Europe; a fear of being ensnared by France in eastern Europe; anxiety lest a pact drive Germany into Russia's arms.'[43] The stumbling block was that the French wanted a general alliance guaranteeing each other's interests in all parts of the world while the British would guarantee only France and insisted on a quid pro quo. Lloyd George's January 1922 defensive pact offer was conditional upon a settlement of Middle East disputes. Once it became clear that a pact was no longer feasible, both sides tried to scapegoat each other. In March 1922 ambassador Saint-Aulaire pressed Paris for a new initiative which even if it failed would do 'what I consider to be essential, to throw the responsibility for failure on England'.[44]

5

A flawed response

In five years from a country which represented the liberty of the world, we have become a personification of reaction.
Jean Giraudoux, head of Quai d'Orsay's cultural diplomacy section, 1923, in Jacques Body, *Giraudoux et l'Allemagne* (Paris, 1975), p. 269

[Quai] is in a most desperate state of disorganisation and disorder ... it is almost impossible to extract an answer to the simplest question which we address to it.
British embassy in Paris, 16 February 1925, *Phipps Papers* 2/5 (Churchill College, Cambridge)

There is no one like Poincaré for getting up steam in the engine but he can't stop at the platform.
Jacques Seydoux, Poincaré's advisor, in Sir Arthur Salter, *Personality in Politics* (London 1947), p. 198

Attitudes and assumptions

The war's shaking of values did not shake France's insularity and assumption of cultural superiority. Understandably, the strategic vision remained continental rather than global. Large colonial gains reinforced European priorities. Mandates in the Middle East and ex-German colonies had been won by French negotiators in London and Paris, not by overseas armies. 'The position of France in Europe', explained a French envoy, 'made it a primary object of French policy to avoid, if possible, entanglements and commitments elsewhere.'[1] Yet France's vulnerability in Europe made it necessary to have friends and influence world-wide. Unfortunately, parading cultural superiority tended to irritate and alienate potential allies. 'They [the French] lack tolerance', reproved British diplomat Harold Nicolson, 'so convinced is the average Frenchman of his own intellectual pre-eminence, so conscious is he of the superiority of his own culture, that he finds it difficult at times to conceal his impatience with the barbarians who inhabit other countries. This causes offence.' Equally offensive was the assumption of always being in the right. Socialist deputy Vincent Auriol, later president of the Fourth Republic (1947–1954), promised to defend 'the interests of France ... identical with the ideas of international justice'. One critical voice was Marcel Proust. In 1919 he deplored his friend Daniel Halévy's participation in a group letter to *Le Figaro*, ending with the words 'victorious France, guardian of all civilization'. Proust chided: 'One could weep tears of joy to learn that among all the nations of the world, France has been chosen to watch over the world's literatures; but it's a bit shocking to see us *assuming* that role ourselves.'[2]

Confidence in their own superiority kept the elites relatively incurious about the rest of the world. Establishment figures like Bank of France governor Emile Moreau and Pierre Brisson, director of *Le Figaro*, had no English and travelled little. Before World War II no French newspaper had a permanent representative in Moscow and only one paper had a special correspondent in the United States. The foreign ministry's American section had a staff of three while the European had ten. Although the tempo of affairs quickened, the slowness of intercontinental travel and communication helped preserve a self-image of separateness and specialness. A four to five day sea voyage made America another world – there was no regular air service until 1939. By 1938 Air France flew Paris-Hanoi-Hong Kong but it took six days. Even Paris–Berlin by air took five hours in 1930. Europe was not linked to the United States by radio telephone until the late 1920s and then telephoning was an exercise in masochism. To place a call normally required waiting between one and ten hours while few calls were completed without being interrupted by 'atmospherics'.

Two examples evoke this culture of superiority and insularity. In the 1920s Paul Gore Booth, a British foreign service candidate, lived with German and French families. The Germans were anxious to sell their country and were tolerant towards 'one's stammering efforts to speak German'. However, the French took the view that their culture sold itself and were bored stiff 'unless you could speak French the way they did'.[3] When a French student went to Berlin university for three months it was treated as something quite exceptional. Her German professor was invited to give 'the warmest encouragement' to a 'most praiseworthy initiative'. As the student remarked, 'You'd think I'd flown over the North Pole.'[4]

The war had two special effects: it confirmed the notion of a civilizing mission – Latin Catholic civilization had triumphed over the invader, a triumph symbolized in the canonization of Joan of Arc in 1920; secondly the war deepened xenophobia. The French congratulated themselves on being more successful and enlightened colonial rulers than Anglo-Saxon rivals. 'The mass of peasants ... are full of admiration for France and gratitude for the fraternal welcome received in our rural areas', the governor general of Indo-China assured deputies. 'The Yellow People ... have noticed the contrast between our attitude and the indifference of Anglo-Saxons towards other races. The Indo-Chinese elites have observed with great satisfaction that France has affirmed the equality of races. England and America, however, have refused Japan ... the victory of this principle.' In China, notwithstanding Anglo-American influence, Chinese intellectuals were turning to France, 'the country of tolerance.'[5]

Alarmed by the fall of the franc, unemployment and the influx of immigrants, elite and popular opinion demonized foreigners. People, events and crises were perceived in simplistic conspiratorial categories – bankers' plots, machinations of international speculators, malevolent foreign leaders. Wartime experience reinforced traditional stereotypes. Captain Charles de Gaulle, shocked by 'the insolence and uselessness of allied officers', finished the war 'overwhelmed by general feelings of xenophobia'. British academic Harold Laski meeting French socialists in the late 1920s was 'amazed at the intensity of their dislike of America' but ascribed it to 'sheer ignorance. The America they know is tourist America – rich, careless, dominating ... The insularity of the French is ... a danger to the world'.[6] Distrust towards foreigners fluctuated according to the economic and political climate and the rate of immigration. By 1921 France had 1,550,000 foreign residents – 400,000 more than in 1911 (3.9 per cent of the total population). This figure jumped to 2,498,000 in 1926 (6.1 per cent). In the 1926 financial crisis a coachload of tourists was attacked in Paris and Poincaré protested publicly that when the franc fell British unemployed came to sun themselves on Normandy beaches. Sennep's popular cartoon depicted a Parisian urchin calling to a tourist bus driver: 'Give me your megaphone so that I can shout merde to them.'

Germanophobia infected intellectuals, officials and politicians alike. Seydoux's bêtes noires were German industrialists who had 'decided to do everything to avoid paying reparations ... it must not be forgotten that they decided on the war.'[7] The International Research Council established in July 1919 in order to break Germany's scientific hegemony, excluded ex-enemy institutions from membership. In 1921 France boycotted the first postwar International Red Cross conference because Germans would be present. Germany was banned from the Paris 1924 Olympics. A handful of academics like historians Elie Halévy and Pierre Renouvin resisted the tide. Halévy contended that critical analysis of contemporary history would break the stranglehold of prejudice and ideology. At the Sorbonne the newly-founded Society for the History of the War initiated a new course on the sources of

'List me the English colonies, – India . . . Gibraltar . . . Paris . . .'
L'Œuvre, 7 August 1925

'Your roast beef is overdone, – the English prefer it like that!'
L'Œuvre, 7 August 1926

World War I history. But Germanophobia persisted, forcing Renouvin to concede in 1928 that the 'war spirit' still dominated the study of war origins.[8]

War and its aftermath gave the French a persecution complex. Marshal Lyautey, for example, believed that from the armistice of 1918 there was a British plot 'against the existence of France . . . coldly organized and implacably executed by the most perfidious of our enemies'. In April 1919 Americans were reported 'advising the Germans to resist Allied demands and to be infiltrating German industry and finance'.[9] Anglo-Saxons were arraigned for Europe's economic ills: 'The two countries which complain most about the European economic situation, England and the United States, carry the most responsibility.' Prolonging wartime cooperation, argued the French, would have ensured recovery:

> Under Anglo-American pressure this organisation collapsed; extremely strong pressure was exerted by American and British exporters who saw the peace as an opportunity to get rid of trade restrictions and to dump on the empty European market the products they were making in great quantities for the armies.[10]

Elder statesman Léon Bourgeois warned: 'England whose vital interests . . . depend above all on the United States will always tend to model its policy on American policy . . . England . . . will find in American attitudes a pretext for slowing down cooperation with us in the application of the treaty.'[11] German–American financiers were rumoured to be plotting against reparations, supported by a 'mischievous or insufficiently informed press intent on exciting the naive pity of Americans for poor Germany'.[12] Anglo-American affinity and cooperation, however, was one thing, ganging up against France another. Because of their isolation the French greatly exaggerated Anglo-Saxon solidarity, scenting collusion and antipathy everywhere. It was mid-decade before an informal Anglo-American economic *entente* emerged.

Opinion after 1918 showed greater interest in international affairs but no sustained engagement. Even the November 1918 general election manifestos said little about foreign policy. The *détente* that followed the Locarno treaties of 1925 did not stir the electorate. 'The question of electoral reform will prove more dangerous to the life of the Ministry than the vital question of foreign policy', signalled one observer. There were several reasons for this relative indifference. The old assumption that foreign policy-making had its own mystique and autonomy persisted. The war in discrediting traditional diplomacy spawned a new breed of specialists. Cataclysmic upheaval and postwar complexities encouraged the public to leave foreign policy to the experts. More importantly, the franc's slide and the cost of living blotted out almost everything else. 'Foreign policy questions leave people indifferent', concluded an opinion report, 'even Germany's joining the League of Nations [and] the Thoiry conversation . . . have not captured public attention.

Economic difficulties dominate thinking.' Moreover, the postwar generation was much more private than the pre-war. The general disillusion with traditional ideals of honour and duty plus the conviction that another war was unthinkable led students to seek a life that was good in itself rather than one shaped by public service. In 1923 the rector of the Sorbonne claimed that 'practically all young students disapprove of the militarist policy pursued by the Quai d'Orsay' in the Ruhr. Other evidence, however, suggests that most students were apolitical. 'Public affairs bored us', recalled Simone de Beauvoir. Future communist heavyweights like Paul Nizan and Louis Aragon flirted with the idea of withdrawing into a religious order. And there was a gulf between intellectuals and the wider public. Historian Marc Bloch acknowledged that academics were 'too absorbed in day-to-day tasks' to be good citizens. Academics by sealing themselves off left the public 'woefully ignorant of history and of the wider world'.[13]

Statecraft

Internal and external constraints left France only a narrow margin for manoeuvre. As a result, statesmanship was at a premium. Poincaré's flawed leadership crippled his country's chances of hegemony. He was one of the Republic's movers and shakers: president, 1913–20; premier and foreign minister 1922–24; premier, 1926–29. Saving Pierre Laval, no one had a worse press. The left dubbed him *Poincaré la guerre*, blaming him for the 1914 war. Parisian café songs praised his square fists (*poings carrés*); Anglo-Saxon opinion outraged by the Ruhr occupation labelled him vindictive, legalistic and intransigent. In Jean Giraudoux's novel *Bella* (1926) Poincaré is caricatured as Rebendart, a dry peevish lawyer, imprisoned in the past who spends weekends inaugurating war memorials.

Born in 1860, at Bar-le-Duc in Lorraine, Poincaré came of a distinguished family. A cousin, Henri Poincaré, was a world-famous mathematician. As a Lorrainer with memories of the war of 1870, Poincaré feared and distrusted Germany. Such distrust might have fired a successful foreign policy but Poincaré lacked the necessary drive and skill. He was a kind of twentieth-century Philip II of Spain refusing to delegate, trying to oversee everything. Leaving home in the rue Marcheau at 8 a.m. he rarely returned before 9 p.m. All staff down to the chauffeur received handwritten orders for the day. Scorning typists and secretaries he conducted affairs in his own hand – even copying out letters. Visitors could arrive in Paris, ask for an interview and get back a handwritten reply the following morning, usually fixing an interview for that same afternoon. He was an utter workaholic, whenever possible travelling by train so that work could continue, even reading papers during a daily massage. A heavy week in Paris would be followed by weekends in his constituency, driving over bad roads and delivering long speeches at each stopping place. Gifted with a computer-like memory he wrote in one day, without consulting files, a 1300-word answer to a British note which had taken several weeks' preparation. 'He was the only man I have ever known', recalled a British colleague on the Reparations Commission, 'who at any moment, on any subject within his wide range, could make a speech, logically developed, exact in phrasing, fortified with every fact and figure, which could be taken down and printed without revisions.'[14] Quiet, honest, non-smoking, abstemious, he shunned the salons. When the manuscript of his memoirs went to the publisher he paid from his own pocket the expenses of the civil service messenger boy.

Poincaré had three defects: a cold, shy, withdrawn manner; an inability to delegate and to listen to advice; and a lack of judgement. Even the foreign ministry's director of political affairs dreaded asking him for a signature. One of the warmest expressions of emotion in the memoirs is reserved for the death of his sixteen-year-old cat Grisgris. 'I have just received my nine-hundredth telegram this morning from Poincaré', Louis Barthou, France's representative at the 1922 Genoa Conference, told Lloyd George.[15] Energies were frittered away in obsessive attention to detail. Incredibly, at the height of the Ruhr occupation, the premier wrote personally to France's envoy at the Hague challenging a claim for expenses on an official car. Unwelcome advice brought out a mean streak. When Berlin ambassador Pierre de Margerie sent a long telegram on 20 January 1924 stressing German readiness for talks, Poincaré charged the cost to the envoy's salary. Most damaging was a lack of judgement. As a lawyer he knew how to plead a case but he lacked the statesman's ability to make decisions quickly and effectively. Poincaré could not see the wood for the trees. Policy implications and coordination were neglected. 'Poincaré's failure to work out with any care even the direct implications of his policy', writes Marc Trachtenberg, 'seems virtually incomprehensible'.[16] Having occupied the Ruhr he did not know when to stop and bargain. In Seydoux's words: 'There is no one like Poincaré for getting up steam in the engine but he can't stop at the platform.'[17]

The government machine

Before 1945 France did not have a unified civil service. Individual ministries handled their own recruitment and examinations. The wartime expansion of government overloaded a run-down bureaucracy. Salaries lagged behind inflation, the high-powered deserted to industry and commerce, able candidates were hard to recruit. Much clerical work was done laboriously by hand. In 1923 a government report found it necessary to argue the advantages of typewriters. Few officials were capable of dictating a letter – as late as 1940 war ministry staff were urged to get used to dictation. In the 1920s ministries were not yet connected by direct line and had to rely on the slow-moving and leaky public telephone system. A plethora of *ad hoc* committees served only to obfuscate issues and provided 'a convenient way of temporarily burying delicate questions'.[18] The upshot of endemic inefficiency was that policy-makers were blind men in a fog, lacking up-to-date and accurate statistical tools, yearbooks and the like. When, for example, in 1932 the government ordered an investigation into communist strength in France, the police simply recopied the results of previous enquiries. In 1919 the young Captain Charles de Gaulle, exasperated at interminable delays in securing appointment to the French military mission in Poland, expostulated: 'The simplest things become ridiculously complicated. And nobody, at whatever level of the hierarchy he is, takes responsibility. We greatly need a Richelieu or a Louvois.'[19]

The doyen of French interwar diplomats, André François-Poncet, remarked that to be a French ambassador required a superb intelligence because the foreign ministry was so woefully chaotic. Discounting the hyperbole, the record does reveal weaknesses. The *comité d'études*, a wartime think-tank researching peace conference proposals, refused to work at the ministry because of inadequate library and technical services. Political director Philippe Berthelot claimed that during the Paris Peace Conference the ministry 'had had to prepare highly technical clauses without any expert knowledge'.[20] The ministry was ill-prepared for postwar multilateral diplomacy.

Some modernization took place: sections for the League of Nations, economic and financial affairs, cultural diplomacy and the press, appointment of specialist commercial, military and financial attachés. Thanks to Berthelot, the Quai which had been eclipsed during the peace conference recovered influence. Poincaré and Briand worked closely with the foreign ministry. Berthelot, unlike British counterparts, participated regularly in international conferences between 1919 and 1921. However, change was piecemeal, with no root and branch reform attempted. The Foreign service remained a gentleman's club drawn from a wealthy upper crust in which family dynasties like the Cambons and de Margeries flourished. Ambassadors moved in rarefied circles. In 1924 ambassador Count Saint Aulaire discovered that he knew almost none of Ramsay McDonald's new labour government.

Lack of thoroughgoing modernization was exacerbated by the temporary disgrace and removal of secretary general Philippe Berthelot in 1922. By 1925 the Quai was 'in a most desperate state of disorganization and disorder'. 'It is almost impossible', complained the British embassy, 'to extract an answer to the simplest question which we address to it.'[21] The ministry did not have total control of external relations. The invasion of international affairs by economic and financial considerations fragmented policy-making between different ministries. The finance ministry handled interallied debts. Coordinating the inputs of several ministries through interministerial committees was lengthy and laborious.

Interdepartmental jealousies and suspicions hindered cooperation. The foreign ministry and war ministry waged a private war, often over trivialities. Thus the war ministry flatly refused to send a copy of its annual budget statement to the Quai because 'it was an extremely detailed and candid document'. The foreign ministry needed to be very efficient to be an effective ringmaster. This was not the case and national interests suffered accordingly. In preparing plans for the reconstruction of Russia for the 1922 Genoa Conference 'French attempts to combine multilateral negotiations with bilateral deals were poorly coordinated and hesitatingly implemented'. No lessons were learnt from wartime experience of Hankey's Rolls Royce organization. At San Remo in April 1920 premier Alexandre Millerand, recorded Hankey, urged that 'it was quite unnecessary for Germany to know her total indebtedness in order to raise a sum on account, in which he was obviously quite wrong. He had never heard of the Protocol (to the Peace Treaty) ... but luckily I had it in my box.' Control of information is a source of power and the British scored a first with conference minutes: 'soon we were days ahead of the Italians, and the French and the other delegations accepted ours as authoritative ... Foch told me that he regarded me as the Chancellor of the Conference.'[22] Poincaré arrived in London in June 1922 without a secretary and Hankey minuted the talks.

Selling France

French culture provided a rationale for predominance but unlike vintage champagne its superiority was not self-evident; it had to be marketed. Sadly, prestige and influence were squandered. 'In five years', lamented novelist and playwright Jean Giraudoux in 1923, 'from a country which represented the liberty of the world, we have become a personification of reaction.'[23] History is sometimes the propaganda of the losing side; Germany won the war of words hands down. How did this happen? Certainly the need to sell France vigorously was recognized. A 1920 parliamentary report stressed the urgency of projecting a civilizing mission:

> Our letters, our arts, our intellectual civilization, our ideas have always had a powerful attraction for foreign nations ... the ministry of foreign affairs and its agents abroad must direct and control efforts, inspire and encourage at any price French intellectual penetration.[24]

France, pioneer of cultural diplomacy, was on the defensive. At the Paris Peace Conference Clemenceau under protest recognized English as an official diplomatic language. Following the disbandment of wartime propaganda services new agencies were set up: a news department, a sports and tourism section. 'It is absolutely indispensable that France does not lose in the eyes of the athletic world . . . the prestige gained in the supreme sport: war.'[25] Foreign ministry services liaised with private and semi-official bodies like the Alliance Française, church organisations and the Franco-German Committee, sponsoring lectures, exchanges, exhibitions, academic institutes and the endowment of chairs for French literature and language like the Marshal Foch Chair at Oxford University. Publishers plugged French science and culture.

It was not enough. Germany, Italy and the Soviet Union competed fiercely for influence. For a number of reasons the advertising of France fell short. Suspicion lingered that propaganda was not quite respectable. Jules Cambon's classic study Le Diplomate (1926) did not discuss propaganda or cultural diplomacy. There was no overall theme, no coordination of effort. Propaganda towards Germany lacked coherence, dithering between severity and compromise. The 1921–22 Washington Conference witnessed a major public relations disaster. Ambassador Jules Jusserand's 'lackadaisical supervision' was no match for Lloyd George's propaganda chief, Lord Riddell, whose 'exquisitely timed leaks of confidential information . . . to his carefully cultivated contacts in the Washington press corps' strengthened the British case.[26]

Jean Giraudoux, head of the foreign ministry's cultural diplomacy (1922–24) and press departments (1924–26), shared responsibility for the feebleness of French propaganda. He was a square peg in a round hole – a brilliant writer and excellent athlete (national 400 metres champion) but no organizer. Admittedly, resources were inadequate. Daily press briefings relied largely on agency releases. There was no interministerial liaison. After press conferences Giraudoux organized games of football in the office, followed by writing workshops, with readings from work in progress. His deputy kept callers at bay when – as frequently happened – the playwright did not turn up or came late.

Germany's propaganda was vastly better resourced and managed. The foreign ministry's string of freelances – each contributing three or four pieces monthly – focused on exonerating Germany from war guilt. In August 1922 the Süddeutsche Monaftshefte claimed that French artillery had destroyed the town of Lens and published photos of towns Germany had entered without causing damage. It was a broadside demanding an immediate riposte. Incredibly, Giraudoux took nearly three years to respond. The ministry funded a weekly periodical Pariser Correspondenz-blatt profiling French personalities. It was hard to know who read it since it was crudely propagandist and did not invite dialogue with German opinion. During the 1923 Ruhr crisis the ambassador in Berlin begged Paris to be more skilful in news management: 'You cannot believe the number of enemies in all countries the press makes for France.'[27]

Above all, France lost the battle of war documentation. Astonishingly in four years (1922–26) the Weimar Republic published forty volumes of *Die Grosse Politik*, a collection of German diplomatic documents on the origins of 1914. The French were not in the race – the first volume of the rival series *Documents Diplomatiques Français* appeared in 1929, the last in 1959. Ironically, France made better progress translating *Die Grosse Politik*, so publicizing the German case against war guilt. The amazingly rapid publication of German documents helped win Anglo-American sympathy for German revisionism.

External publicity defeats were paralleled by the government's failure to mobilize domestic support. Not that ministers neglected opinion. Poincaré obsessively monitored the press – reading, annotating, summoning authors of critical pieces. But the focus was on censorship and repression. Little or no attempt appears to have been made to sell a French ascendency. All demonstrations were treated as potential insurrections. Organizers who gave advance notice were liable to preventive arrest. The police were notorious for their brutality. In 1930 truncheons were used to break up a peaceful gathering of pacifists welcoming Briand's return from Geneva. Nor did the authorities seek to overcome traditional indifference to foreign affairs by promoting an informed community. A counterpart to the British Royal Institute of International Affairs (1920), the Centre d'Etudes de politique etrangère, was only established in 1935.

Incoherence?

L eadership faults and deficiencies in decision-making machinery pose the wider question of institutional incoherence. Some scholars stress 'governmental anarchy', the incoherence of policy formulation and execution.[28] Certainly, considerable incoherence existed. Poincaré was told of 'ministers acting without the knowledge of their departments, departments repudiating their ministers, varying systems adopted and then rejected by turns, no clearly defined line of conduct; in short absolute incoherence'.[29] How significant was lack of coordination? Did it frustrate ambitions for predominance? Incoherence did not spring from uncertainty about France's external role. The Republic, it was assumed, would remain a leading great power in Europe. The nub of the problem was the incompatibility of policy options. While individual options were defensible, the mix adopted had conflicting elements. There was a case for conciliating or coercing the ex-enemy but juggling both invited confusion and misunderstanding. Keeping Germany weak, with a special status for the Rhineland, clashed with the desire to maintain allied unity and pursuit of a Franco-German *entente*.

Some integration took place: 'French reparations policy, security policy and industrial policy', it is argued, 'had a coherent structure ... and were regarded by policy planners as a package of interrelated demands.'[30] Interministerial discussions produced the April 1923 plan, a general statement of aims, calling for an autonomous Rhineland within the Reich, evacuation of the Ruhr conditional upon payment of reparations, cancellation of French war debts, permanent cession of the Saar coal mines and cancellation of the 1935 Saar plebiscite. The crux of the matter was that Poincaré did not integrate his Ruhr policy with the April plan. His initial goal in occupying the Ruhr was simply to secure a pledge for an international reparations and debts settlement. The crucial failure was one of leadership. Foch diagnosed a 'total inability to implement and follow through ... we have no overall plan.'[31] In 1922–23 Poincaré failed to give clear policy guidelines. At a meeting in December 1922 proposals from two ministries were criticized as 'deplorably vague – they do not know what they want'.[32] Poincaré gave them eight days to get their act together but gave no specific instructions on what he wanted. Missing was a net assessment of aims and resources. Lack of direction and coordination from the top thickened institutional incoherence. The Renault was running on one cylinder. Missing also was confidence. Clemenceau's call for the 'mentality and habits of a victorious people' went unanswered. The ambivalent mood of 1919, half confident, half fearful, turned to disillusionment. No attempt was made to harness the sentiments of 1918–19 for the construction of a new national consensus underpinning French hegemony. Conservative Bloc National leaders were unwilling to pay the domestic price in terms of social and political compromise.

6
Predominance, 1919–1924

It is a violent solution [Ruhr occupation], *but it will settle everything. We will become the masters of Germany, independent of England, and an industrial power of the first rank. There are many in France who consider it the only solution but it is full of risks internal and external. Before it is turned to, all avenues of conciliation must first be exhausted.*

    Jacques Seydoux, letter of 25 October 1920, in Walter A. McDougall, *France's Rhineland Diplomacy 1914–1924: The Last Bid for a Balance of Power in Europe* (Princeton, New Jersey 1978), p. 136

One should not forget that if we are today the strongest and [remain so] for another decade or so, the weight of 70 million organised and industrious men will end up heavier than that of 38 million French within 20 to 50 years. If then we don't succeed in helping to create a German Republic hostile to war, we are condemned. Far from gaining ground with German democratic opinion we will stir up its hatred. Even admitting that we manage to make Germany give way by our pressure on the Ruhr, the policy which immediately follows ought to be very generous ... I do not believe that any German government can surrender now that the Anglo-Saxon world has separated itself from us ... What is dramatic is that the slightest retreat today will throw everybody on our back. If we are not complete victors, the situation will be settled in a manner both ruinous financially and destructive of our prestige in the world.

    Philippe Berthelot, letter of 29 January 1923 to Aristide Briand, in Georges Suarez, *Briand: Sa Vie, Son Oeuvre, V, 1918–1923* (Paris 1941), p. 429

My country has a dagger pointed at its breast ... Common efforts, sacrifices, deaths in the war, all that will have been useless if Germany can once more

have recourse to violence ... France cannot count only on an international
conference and the United States are a long way off... Can we not try to find
a formula of guarantee against a danger of such a sort that it would render
the Dawes Report useless. I speak to you from the bottom of my heart.
  Edouard Herriot to Ramsay MacDonald, Chequers Conversations,
  21–22 June 1924, in David Marquand, *Ramsay MacDonald* (London
  1977) p. 340

Traditionally, Marianne was pilloried as a greedy militarist shuffling off
war debts while vindictively squeezing mammoth reparations from a
down-and-out foe. By contrast, John Bull and Uncle Sam played benevolent
uncles, striving for European recovery and harmony. Why did French
governments get such a bad name? Anglo-Saxon historiography followed
Keynes in condemning the economic clauses of Versailles as vengeful and
unfair. From this standpoint French efforts to secure their treaty rights were
judged inopportune and unreasonable. As treaty revisionism gained ground
in Britain and the United States in the 1920s and 1930s, the whole settlement
came to be seen as a disaster. Etienne Mantoux's rebuttal of Keynes, *The
Carthaginian Peace or the Economic Consequences of Mr Keynes*, did not
appear until 1946. By then it was much too late in the day to overturn the
ruling orthodoxy that Versailles had been a bad peace made worse by French
folly in seeking to implement it lock, stock and barrel. French historians
wrote superb syntheses of interwar international history but, lacking access
to archives, they could not reassess their country's policies.[1] The old image of
France's international persona has now been effectively demolished. The
opening-up of archives in the 1970s yielded more sympathetic
interpretations.[2]

  Reassessments emphasized several features: France's post-1918 strategic
and financial vulnerability; the reasonableness of much of French policy,
especially on reparations; the cautiousness of the Ruhr occupation, only
undertaken after long and fruitless parleys with London and Berlin; the
absence of a coherent bid for hegemony – bureaucratic, military, industrial
and political elites generated a diversity of projects and gave conflicting
advice on key issues. Revisionists contended that the French, far from being
wreckers, responded rationally to an Anglo-Saxon attempt to impose
economic leadership on the continent: 'The French rejected British and
American notions of theoretical orthodoxy and *laissez-faire* not out of
ignorance, but in accordance with a well-founded belief that Anglo-
American theories and institutions did not operate in France's best national
interests.'[3] Reparations did not profit France, On the contrary, the net capital
flow 'ran toward Germany during both the inflation and stabilization phases'
of the Weimar Republic and 'not only did the Reich entirely avoid paying net
reparations to its wartime opponents; it actually extracted the equivalent of

reparations from the Allied powers, and principally from the United States'.[4] The Anglo-Saxons, it seems, not the French, were chiefly responsible for international instability: 'the Anglo-Americans spent the interwar years looking for excuses to do nothing'.[5] Reappraisals highlighted the moderation of French leaders who, rather than itching to crush Germany, wanted German and allied economic cooperation in a new international order. The Anglo-American refusal to continue wartime economic cooperation prompted Paris to offer Berlin economic partnership in the Seydoux Plan of 1920. Anglo-Saxon obstructionism and German footdragging, it is said, forced the adoption of a revisionist strategy aimed at destabilising Germany by encouraging separatism and by imposing limits on German sovereignty in the Ruhr and Rhineland. The objective was not predominance but 'to make Europe safe from Germany'.[6] Stabilization on France's terms, it is implied, might have spared Europe World War II. Revisionism, however, while discrediting traditional stereotypes has not yet produced a consensus and it seems unlikely that one will emerge. The ambiguities, complexities and confusions of French policy mean that more than one interpretation is possible and plausible.

Goals

What did French leaders want? In a word, security but the problem was how to achieve it. Predominance in 1919 rested on a pyrrhic victory. The costs of the conflict were staggering. Peace brought immense disappointments: collapse of the Anglo-American treaty of guarantee, dissolution of the allied coalition. For the French, security and hegemony were synonymous. Treaty predominance had to be translated into a real hegemony. Only hegemony would ensure permanent security.

The bid for predominance had six elements. First, policy towards Germany oscillated between strict execution of the treaties, economic collaboration and a revisionist strategy aimed at Germany's dissolution. Second, Paris planned military and political alliances in central and eastern Europe to serve as a *cordon sanitaire* against Bolshevism and German revanchism. Third, a powerful steel industry was projected which would supplant Ruhr firms in European markets. French industry would exploit substantial treaty advantages: sequestration of German enterprises in Lorraine, Saar coal mines, German coal deliveries and most favoured nation status for five years. Fourth, economic ambitions in central Europe: the collapse of the Habsburg empire and the enforced liquidation of German and Austrian enterprises in the successor states offered French capital an

unprecedented opening. A fifth goal was to free France from dependence on
Anglo-Saxon oil interests. Finally came colonial ambitions. Ex-German and
ex-Turkish territories had swelled the empire to its greatest extent. In the
flush of victory ambitious schemes for colonial development captured
attention. For the first time in France's colonial history the empire aroused
popular enthusiasm. 'Everything has changed', announced Maurice Barrès,
one of the architects of the Bloc National. 'Colonial policy has become part
of our general policy'. Interest was fired by two considerations: the value of
black troops who had demonstrated their military worth; and the Empire's
potential contribution to postwar recovery. Investment and modernization,
it was believed, would attract capital from its preferred European outlets. In
1921, colonial minister Albert Sarraut announced a ten to fifteen year
investment programme, including the setting up of a world-wide
telecommunications network connecting metropolitan France and the
empire. Next came a scheme for a Trans-Saharan railway to create one
France 'from the North Sea to the Congo'.[8]

These goals did not form a unified design or master plan. Institutional
incoherence, as usual, hindered coordination. More to the point there was no
consensus on how to handle Germany. It seemed axiomatic that the former
enemy would challenge Versailles within the next ten to twenty years. Too
much of the stick would isolate France and mean facing the foe alone; too
little would infuriate the Bloc National parliamentary majority, speed
German recovery and probably still mean single combat. The seemingly
insoluble dilemma produced a confused, shifting and uneasy mix of firmness
and conciliation. And this is why the record has provoked such different and
divergent readings. Officials had great difficulty in formulating clear and
consistent guidelines. In 1920 Jacques Seydoux, the foreign ministry's
leading economic advisor, urged a blend of coercion and conciliation, while
excluding for the time being 'the necessary solution' – occupation of the
Ruhr.[9] But in 1923 with the Ruhr occupied and Germany apparently going
downhill fast, Jules Laroche, a high official at the Quai d'Orsay, voiced
serious doubts: 'Is it wise to destroy German unity? Who knows what will
happen in twenty years ... After a crisis Germany will pick herself up again
and a reconstitution of her unity in a spirit of revenge might be the
programme of a Reich more dangerous to us than that whose ruin we have
sought.'[10] 'If we don't manage to create a German Republic hostile to war we
are condemned', advised Berthelot, former secretary general of the Quai
d'Orsay. 'Even if our pressure on the Ruhr forces Germany to give way, the
policy that immediately follows should be very generous and very probably
sacrifice the goal itself of our action'.[11] Moreover, the French lacked one
essential ingredient for success – a conqueror's mentality. 'We are lacking in
confidence and boldness', recognized Seydoux, 'these alone ... will enable us
to exercise the ascendancy that the peoples of Europe are ready to accept as
in the great centuries of our history.'[12]

Turkish delight

The settlement of Turkey and its empire illustrates the fundamental difficulties of peacemaking and peacekeeping. The German peace took six months to negotiate, the Turkish settlement took four years. Allied occupation of Constantinople lasted longer than the war itself. The problems were huge: conflicting wartime agreements, Arab and Turkish nationalism, Zionism and great-power conflicts of interest. France fell between two stools. The effort to preserve Turkish and Middle Eastern interests led to estrangement from Britain, preventing a concerted approach to Germany.

During and after the war Britain and France jousted for hegemony in the Near and Middle East. Paris heard of 'intensive propaganda by British intelligence officers in Anatolia ... anyone with a reputation for French sympathies was regarded with great suspicion'.[13] France's historical and cultural links with the Turkish empire dating from the Crusades, were buttressed by extensive financial interests. The 1916 Sykes-Picot agreement allowed France substantial ill-defined territory in Syria and the Levant. But British policy was a tangle of conflicting promises – to France, the Arabs, the Jews and Italy. The St Jean de Maurienne treaty of April 1917 offered Italy a large slice of south and west Anatolia, including the province of Smyrna – which Greece coveted because of its large and prosperous Greek community. Moreover, King Faisal and the Arabs wanted a united Arab empire and opposed French control of Syria. Before the war ended, London and Paris had quarrelled over everything to do with Turkey and the Middle East. British leaders, arguing that France had not contributed militarily to Turkey's defeat, set about whittling away her share of the Sykes-Picot agreement. In December 1918 Clemenceau surrendered oil-rich Mosul and Palestine.

At the Paris Peace Conference two developments occurred. First, France sided with Britain in opposing far-reaching Italian claims in Asia Minor, while encouraging Greek demands. Italy, with great-power pretensions, was regarded as a potential threat, whereas Greece, it was believed, would be a useful client state. Wilson, Lloyd George and Clemenceau authorized a Greek landing at Smyrna in May 1919. The decision had momentous consequences: it brought war between Greece and Turkey, incited Turkish nationalism under Mustafa Kemal and divided the Allies. The second development at Paris was Clemenceau's growing conviction that Lloyd George had not honoured their private pact of December 1918. The Tiger had traded concessions on Mosul and Palestine for support on Rhineland claims. In retaliation, Clemenceau dug his heels in over the Middle East and the resulting acrimony delayed a settlement.

In 1919–20 Turkey and its former empire was in turmoil. Traditional

Greek-Turkish antipathies, inflamed by Greek treatment of Turks in Anatolia, provoked a Turkish revival led by the nationalist Kemal. His forces attacked Greek, Italian and French forces occupying Asia Minor. To the South, Britain and France disputed Syria and Palestine. Gradually, a settlement was cobbled together. Clemenceau, in need of British support on Germany, wanted a Turkish settlement. In February 1920, two weeks of fighting with Kemal's nationalists claimed over 500 French lives. Demobilization demands deterred Alexandre Millerand, Clemenceau's successor, from sending reinforcements. Above all, the threat of Arab nationalism in Syria made peace with Turkey imperative. Yet making peace was nearly as painful as fighting. France, after insisting that peace negotiations should be held in Paris, climbed down in the face of British threats to conclude a separate peace. Only the formal signing ceremony of the Treaty of Sèvres in August 1920 took place in Paris. Sèvres outraged both the Turks and the French. Turkey ceded sovereignty over Smyrna to Greece for five years pending a plebiscite. An international commission to supervise the Straits and Turkish finances would be controlled by a Three-Power Financial Commission. French and Italian zones of influence in Anatolia were confirmed and Turkey lost all her Arab territory.

Sèvres disappointed France almost as much as it did Turkey. Opinion, egged on by colonial pressure groups, denounced the treaty as a sell-out. 'Nothing would induce the French government to ratify the treaty', warned premier Georges Leygues.[14] With Turkish armies harassing French troops in Cilicia, France sought a separate settlement. Keeping 80,000 troops in the region cost 500 million francs a year. Fears that Bolshevik Russia, in order to gain the Straits, would reach agreement with Turkey strengthened the case for withdrawal. In June 1921 premier Briand sent a Turkophile emissary, Franklin Bouillon – 'Boiling Frankie' as the British called him – to prepare the ground. The Ankara agreement of October 1920 allowed France to withdraw from Cilicia. The French foreign ministry was over the moon about the treaty. 'The signing of the treaty', enthused Emmanuel Peretti de la Rocca, director of political affairs, 'has given us ... popularity not only in Turkey but throughout North Africa ... The letters I get from Morocco, Tunisia and Egypt are enthusiastic ... today the Islamic world is for us. We have returned to the traditional policy of France, that of our kings, of the empire, of the Republic.'[15]

London was not pleased, condemning the Ankara agreement as a betrayal, since Paris had promised consultation before signing an agreement. France's withdrawal increased Turkish military pressure on the Greeks and their British minders. The indignation of Curzon and officials was fuelled by the interception of French diplomatic communications disclosing the full story of the Paris-Ankara negotiations, including offers of arms to the Kemalists. Ambassador Lord Hardinge believed Briand was 'the victim of treachery' by an Anglophobe foreign ministry.[16] Franco-British relations touched bottom. Poincaré who succeeded Briand in January 1922, told Curzon 'there was no sympathy anywhere in France for Greece' and promptly withdrew French troops from Chanak in the Dardanelles, leaving 300 British soldiers facing the Turks.[17]

The fall of Lloyd George's government because of the Chanak crisis cleared the way for the longest and most successful of the peace conferences – Lausanne 1922–23. Prime minister Bonar Law was determined to prevent any further deterioration in relations with France, insisting that 'if the French . . . will not join us, we shall not by ourselves fight the Turks to enforce what is left of the Treaty of Sèvres'.[18] The Treaty of Lausanne in July 1923 concluded a final and definitive peace with Turkey. It cancelled reparations and restored to Turkey eastern Thrace, Smyrna and some of the Aegean islands. A republic with its capital at Ankara replaced the sultanate. There were losses for France. Lausanne, as well as abolishing capitulations, the preferential legal and economic status accorded foreigners and the mainstay of French influence, allowed Turkey to pay interest on the Ottoman debt (mainly held by France) in francs rather than gold. However, in the thick of the Ruhr crisis, France was in no position to drive a hard bargain.

The Turkish settlement illustrated the precariousness of France's predominance. By 1924 the final score was more negative than positive. The empire grew with the addition of the Syrian and Lebanese mandates, but at a price. Mosul with its oil had gone to Britain. Syria was expensive – in November 1920 security and administration swallowed 1,200 million francs. French leaders seriously misjudged the strength of Arab, Turkish and Jewish nationalism – in December 1919 Berthelot dismissed the Kemalist movement as 'largely bluff'.[19] Much more significant, however, was the impact of Middle East rivalries on security in Europe. Franco-British bickering culminating in the 1921 Ankara agreement queered the pitch for an alliance in Europe. Lloyd George's January 1922 offer of a British guarantee 'in the event of direct and unprovoked aggression against the soil of France' was conditional upon a settlement of Middle East disputes. Poincaré's refusal to support Britain in the Chanak crisis left Curzon determined not to have 'any more abortive conferences, particularly with the French'.[20] Berthelot was convinced that 'if we had not deserted England in the Middle East she would not have abandoned us in Europe whatever the difficulties and differences of views'.[21]

Franco-German duel

Germany, not Turkey, mattered most. Could Germany's resurgence be delayed or controlled? 'Despite everything', confessed a French official in 1921, 'after two years we have not succeeded in achieving peace. In fact the war goes on. In my opinion we risk increasingly frequent and violent crises.'[22] The Franco-German cold war revolved around reparations. The lesson of the First World War was that in a conflict France would be overwhelmed. At the Paris Peace Conference France had been persuaded to drop the demand for an autonomous Rhineland in exchange for an Anglo-American guarantee. The American Senate refused to ratify the guarantee and the British had then reneged on their part of the bargain. The French endeavoured to fill the gap in several ways: alliances with Germany's neighbours in eastern Europe; requests for a pact with Britain; efforts to strengthen the League of Nations; reparations. At first glance reparations offered major economic, political and diplomatic advantages. Siphoning off German wealth would retard economic and military recovery, German gold would fund French reconstruction and keep taxpayers happy, non-payment would activate sanctions and reinforce the peace settlement.

Closer inspection revealed serious flaws. The peace treaty had settled only the deadline for billing Germany – 1 May 1921 – not the total sum. The resulting uncertainty helped to polarize French and German attitudes. American policy was a further complication. The United States refused to cancel war debts and withdrew capital from Europe during the economic crisis of 1920–21. Consequently, France and Britain, in order to cover their American debts, tended to inflate the final reparations bill. Germany's ability to pay large sums depended on rapid economic recovery, yet rapid recovery menaced French economic ambitions. Demanding large amounts would put Germany's back up, antagonize ex-allies and cause long delays. But small payments would anger French voters and fall short of capital needs for funding reconstruction and war debts. Reparations presupposed a willingness to coerce Germany, yet coercion was fraught with risk. Hitting Germany hard – occupation of the Ruhr, for example – might kill the goose either by breaking the country apart or by driving it into the arms of Bolshevik Russia. And a reconstituted Germany might be even more revanchist than the existing one. Simply poking and prodding the tiger might turn out to be equally counter-productive. Force, to be most effective, required allied unity, yet London and Paris were at sixes and sevens on the treatment of the ex-enemy. Thus France was in a quandary.

For a while insistence on full execution of the treaty seemed successful. When the German army entered the demilitarized zone in March 1920 to suppress a protest strike, the Millerand government, without informing the Allies, immediately occupied Frankfurt and Darmstadt. At the Spa Conference of August 1920 France secured the lion's share of reparations – 52 per cent – Britain got 22 per cent; Italy 10 per cent; Belgium 8 per cent. At the same time a French military mission assisted Poland in repelling a Soviet offensive. In September a secret military agreement tied Belgium to France's alliance system. The Briand cabinet followed the same course for most of 1921. The London Conference of March 1921 fixed a high reparation bill of 220 million gold marks. Predictably, Germany refused to pay and delayed payments in kind. France and Britain riposted by occupying three Ruhr towns. Then, under British pressure, the bill was reduced to 132 million gold marks and a Franco-British ultimatum of 5 May forced German acceptance.

The apparent success of coercion concealed two serious snags. First, France's iron and steel programme was in trouble while German steel was on the mend. At the July 1920 Spa Conference, Germany secured a 43 per cent reduction in agreed coal deliveries and the British persuaded their ally to take smaller amounts of British coal. This was a blow to French steel which depended on the Ruhr for most of its coal. German heavy industry recovered much more quickly than anticipated, compensating for the loss of Lorraine iron ore by importing Swedish and Spanish ore and by utilizing scrap metal. The construction of modern steelworks, financed partly from government indemnities for the loss of Lorraine, partly from loans, gave Germany a competitive edge. High inflation, by reducing the real cost of loans, aided recovery. Second, significant differences of approach emerged among French leaders. Millerand and leading advisors, Seydoux and Maurice Paléologue, secretary general of the Quai d'Orsay, had worked for a Franco-German economic *entente* which would combine raw material deliveries and payments of paper marks, allowing French industry to buy a stake in German companies. French orders would go to German industry. Briand, however, preferred to engage the British by associating them in coercive measures. He also stressed the importance of economic aid for allies. The new secretary general, Philippe Berthelot, abandoned a plan to help Hungary, supporting instead France's Little Entente allies – Czechoslovakia, Romania and Yugoslavia. Germany took the initiative and revived schemes for economic cooperation. Two industrialists, Walter Rathenau, minister for reconstruction, and Louis Loucheur, minister for liberated regions, signed the Wiesbaden Agreements of 6 October 1921, providing for payments in raw materials and finished products for French reconstruction. British opposition, augmented by French industrialists who were reluctant to see their markets flooded by German imports, killed the agreements. By the end of 1921, Briand concluded that, since German recovery seemed unstoppable, diplomatic isolation could only be avoided by close cooperation with Britain.

The next initiative was British. Lloyd George proposed to reintegrate Germany and Russia into the international system by establishing an international consortium for Russian economic reconstruction. The Germans were baited with talk of reduced reparations, the French were offered a guarantee for their frontiers. At Cannes in January 1922 Briand and Lloyd George agreed to call an international economic conference at Genoa in the spring. But discussion of Germany's capacity to pay was like a red rag to the bullish Bloc National majority. President Millerand vetoed any concessions and Briand resigned. At Genoa (April–May 1922) Poincaré, Briand's successor, took a hard line on Russian debts. The German and Soviet foreign ministers, Rathenau and Chicherin, upstaged the conference by signing at nearby Rapallo a separate agreement, reestablishing diplomatic relations, renouncing financial claims and giving each other most favoured nation treatment.

Growing exasperation with Germany reflected awareness of slipping prestige – in the Middle East, Europe and North America. The outcome of the 1921–22 Washington Naval Conference was 'a very real diminution of prestige and authority in America'.[23] Capital ships ratio agreements gave France fourth place with Italy; Briand, who represented France at the opening session, was accused of having 'gambled and lost our money in London and our navy in Washington'.[24] In reality France had not done badly. Accepting parity with Italy on capital ships allowed her to retain superiority by concentrating on auxiliary vessels like destroyers and submarines. Why, then, was the conference perceived as such a defeat? Partly because of unrealistic expectations, partly faulty public relations, and partly because the French, having suffered setbacks in the Middle East and Europe, were hyper-sensitive. Paris aimed to profit from Anglo-American naval rivalry by playing the honest broker. Anglo-American gratitude, it was calculated, would then be expressed in a strengthening of French security in Europe. Several incidents made the French feel victimized. Briand, the only head of government leading a delegation, could not find a seat among great-power delegates and had to sit with the British dominions. And the 'Big Three', Britain, the United States and Japan – excluded France from discussions on capital ships ratios. Albert Sarraut, colonial minister and leader of the French delegation at the close of the conference, believed the Anglo-Saxons had ganged up against France. 'We must expect concealed and constant British opposition in Washington', concluded one observer, 'France is the great obstacle preventing England from recovering Anglo-Saxon hegemony over America and reconquering what she lost in the revolution of 1776.'[25]

At the close of 1922 France's position had deteriorated, European diplomacy was deadlocked. The German problem defied solution: how could Germany be prevented from tearing up the treaties in fifteen to twenty years time? The weak eastern allies offered no comfort; Franco-British pact talks proved abortive. Reparations and debts came to a head at the same time. Washington demanded full repayment of debts, denying linkage with reparations. The Balfour Note of August 1922 served notice that if London had to repay American debts it would also insist on repayment of French debts. No substantial sums had been extracted from Germany. Berlin continued with its delaying tactics, renewing a moratorium request of November 1921. The Bolsheviks refused to pay Tsarist debts to France. Banker T. W. Lamont of Morgan and Co., a leading American bank, warned the French government that only a conciliatory attitude on reparations and debts would win American friendship and capital.[26] One idea mooted was an international loan raised on the American market allowing Germany to pay reparations and so fund French debt payments. But the success of a loan depended on Germany's financial solvency and this was in doubt until reparations were reduced. Poincaré refused to consider a reduction. Another way out of the maze was an international enquiry. On 22 December 1922, secretary of state, Charles Hughes, suggested that a committee of experts, with American participation, should study reparations. However, Poincaré opted for military occupation of the Ruhr. A German failure to make deliveries in kind provided a pretext for a Franco-Belgian force to enter the Ruhr on 11 January 1923.

Ruhr occupation

What were Poincaré's aims? The operation which had been discussed since 1919 sprang from a deepening sense of insecurity and frustration. Endless international conferences had not fulfilled the victory. The French were convinced of Germany's bad faith and believed London was encouraging German footdragging. The German-Soviet *rapprochement* at Rapallo raised fears of a military alliance against France. Also the speed of Germany's economic recovery triggered alarm and anger. In 1922 the German steel industry completed reorganization well ahead of France. Lorraine was working at only 50 per cent capacity – its iron ore could not be fully exploited because of a lack of coke and foundries. German political developments confirmed the interventionist mood. Rathenau, a proponent of Franco–German *entente*, was assassinated on 24 June 1922 and the Cuno government abandoned its commitment to treaty fulfilment. To an embattled France the occupation seemed a sword that would cut the Gordian knot of postwar frustrations. Poincaré's political future depended on making Germany pay – taking over from Briand in January 1922, he had promised to make Germany pay. His declared objective was to seize the Ruhr as 'a productive guarantee' for a satisfactory international settlement of reparations and debts. Privately he hoped that, under cover of military occupation, the Ruhr and Rhineland could be detached from the Reich. Poincaré may also have accepted Foch's thesis that British power was crumbling, giving France the chance to settle the German problem on her own terms.[27]

The occupation had overwhelming parliamentary and popular approval. 'Public opinion has not changed', police reports confirmed in July 1923. 'It continues to believe the operation necessary and legitimate.'[28] An interallied control commission for mines and factories (MICUM) supervised the collection and delivery of reparations. Berlin riposted by declaring passive resistance and strikes paralysed industry. MICUM took draconian measures, imprisoning industrialist Fritz Thyssen and expelling 100,000 Germans. Acts of sabotage followed and troops fired on Krupp workers, killing thirteen. By September France had the upper hand; on the 26th the

Stresemann government called off passive resistance. Subsidizing strikes had stoked hyper-inflation, jeopardizing the currency. MICUM negotiated agreements with industrialists in October–November which restarted the Ruhr economy. A Franco-Belgian company ran the railways, a customs barrier was erected and efforts were made to establish a new Rhenish currency. With risings in Bavaria, the Rhineland, Saxony and Thuringia, the Reich's dissolution appeared imminent.

Poincaré made two crucial mistakes that wrecked the operation and determined the course of European diplomacy. In September he refused Stresemann's offer of direct talks; on 19 October he accepted an American proposal for a committee of experts, a suggestion he had rejected in December 1922. Direct Franco-German talks were refused on the grounds that interallied negotiations were the only way forward. In fact Poincaré was playing for the big prize – German decomposition and a separate Rhineland under French sway. Within days of accepting an international solution, Poincaré backed a separatist *putsch* in the Rhineland. These conflicting moves have puzzled historians. The international experts would require German currency stabilization and almost certainly scale down the total debt. This would spur German recovery. Did the decision to support the separatist rising mean that Poincaré wanted to backtrack on his 19 October acceptance of an international enquiry? Did the premier know what he wanted? Pressure on the franc did not become serious until December, so financial anxiety was not at issue. 'No coherent and consistent policy can be inferred from the sources', concludes Marc Trachtenberg.[29] Despite the mishmash of confusion and incoherence, some sense can be made of Poincaré's actions. From January to November he gambled on Germany's disintegration and therefore avoided direct talks that might give the Reich a breathing space. Amid the signs of impending disintegration, two factors induced him to accept the offer of a committee of experts. Essentially cautious by temperament, Poincaré hedged his bets. Should Berlin against all the odds recover, then France needed insurance. The premier reckoned that possession of the Ruhr would give him the strong bargaining position hitherto lacking in interallied talks. Second, domestic politics induced the premier to play safe and mend fences with London and Washington.[30] With elections set for April 1924, the conservative Bloc National majority and the Cartel des Gauches alliance of radicals and socialists manoeuvred for advantage. The Bloc was eager to exploit popular endorsement of the occupation. On 14 October 1923 President Millerand abandoned presidential neutrality and called for constitutional reforms to create a much stronger executive. As a liberal parliamentarian, Poincaré preferred the existing balance. Millerand's programme threatened to isolate him. In opting for an international initiative, the premier sought to build bridges with the radicals and socialists who advocated international cooperation based on a strong Franco-British *entente*. Thus Poincaré's posture in October was ambivalent. Like most Frenchmen he wanted to smash Bismarck's Germany but not at the price of an internal right-wing coup. Yet he hankered for the jackpot. If Germany splintered quickly before the experts got to work, then France would be able to dictate terms to London and Washington.

Germany's revival from late November spiked the main thrust of French policy. The Reichswehr restored order, suppressing Hitler's 9 November Munich *putsch*. Funded by London and Washington, Berlin stabilized the currency with a new Rentenmark which drove the franc out of the Ruhr. By December the tables were turned and the franc was on a downward spiral. The uncertainties of the occupation, combined with shaky public finances, undermined confidence. In January 1924 the French got less from the Ruhr than they had done before the occupation in 1922. The steady post-1918 depreciation snowballed into a headlong descent that destroyed France's bargaining power. 'It is absolutely necessary to re-establish our currency', officials desperately signalled. 'The more it depreciates the more the Germans increase their resistance.'[31] The franc, which in January 1922 stood at 15 to the dollar, slumped in December to 19.21, a 30 per cent loss. German and Anglo-Saxon speculators were accused of trying to topple Poincaré. In fact French speculators started the slide and played a leading role until January when foreigners took over. Some evidence suggests that the German government had a hand in the speculation. The British treasury reviewed financial pressure on the franc in November 1923, but the incoming Labour government of Ramsay MacDonald took no action.

The franc's fall delivered Poincaré to Anglo-Saxon creditors. The only effect of a 20 per cent tax hike in February 1924 was to make the government unpopular. Tax revenues took time to collect; only a large and immediate cash transfusion could have saved government and currency. The electoral campaign precluded drastic retrenchment. 'It was now generally recognised in political circles', cabled the British embassy, 'that the Ruhr was a failure.'[32] Poincaré frantically backtracked, assuring MacDonald of his desire for a close *entente*: 'Those of your fellow countrymen who believe that France dreams or has dreamt of the political or economic annihilation of Germany are mistaken ... no reasonable Frenchman has ever dreamt of annexing a parcel of German territory.'[33] On 13 March Poincaré secured a 100 million dollar American loan which lifted the franc from 123 to the pound sterling to 61 at the end of April. The price tag was an international settlement. The Dawes Committee, appointed in November, submitted its report on 9 April, proposing a five-year reparations settlement, funded by an international loan to Germany and supervised by a Berlin-based commission. The total debt would be reduced. Germany accepted at once; Poincaré hesitated until 25 April. On 11 May the Cartel des Gauches electoral victory swept him from power.

The Ruhr intervention need not have ended so dismally. Greater force – imposing a separate Rhineland, for example – might have worked; so too might greater moderation – direct talks with German leaders. Agreement with Berlin might have given Paris substantial leverage in interallied negotiations. The critical mistake was to accept the international initiative on 19 October without first exploring possibilities of bilateral agreement. By supporting outright separatists, while refusing to talk to moderates like Cologne mayor, Konrad Adenauer, Poincaré backed the wrong horse. 'The story might have had a very different ending', writes Marc Trachtenberg, 'if French policy had had a firmer conceptual foundation. Poincaré failed ... not because success was impossible but because he had no clear idea of what his aims were ... if France had succeeded in the Ruhr events after 1923 might have taken a completely different course.'[34]

Herriot and the London Reparations Conference

E douard Herriot, leader of the Cartel des Gauches alliance of radicals and socialists, was the exact opposite of the cold, withdrawn dossier-obsessed Poincaré – open, warmhearted and allergic to official files. The new premier's eloquence, culture and geniality made him one of the most popular and influential interwar politicians. Born in 1872, a historian by training, mayor of Lyons since 1905, he presided over the Radical Party until his death in 1957. He formed three interwar cabinets – 1924, 1926 and 1932 – and from 1936 to 1940 was president of the Chamber of Deputies. Opposition to Marshal Pétain's collaborationist Vichy regime brought house arrest and deportation to Germany. Physically huge, hair *en brosse* giving a slightly warlike appearance, puffing tobacco smoke out of an enormous curved pipe, he would discuss the latest left-bank literary fashions or give a virtuoso performance of Mozart on the piano. His passions were scholarship, women and food. Vain, touchy and over-sensitive he displayed his annoyance with someone by receiving them coldly, extending a single finger and then pushing his glasses to the back of his head, staring fixedly at the ceiling.

In 1919 he wrote a two-volume study calling for the modernization of France, proposing improved technical education, women's rights, scientific management and greater international cooperation. None of this vision was realised in his short-lived administrations – the 1924 Cartel barely lasted a year, the 1926 cabinet only a few days. Herriot's preference for compromise, conviviality and camaraderie were lubricants for the machine, not propellants. Friendship and agreement mattered more to him than controversial reforms. The verbal acrobatics in which he excelled defused strife while blocking change. Deeply liberal, the premier shrank from imposing an equitable income tax because it would curtail individual freedom. But domestic talents were defects abroad. The wiliness and killer instinct necessary for success in the international arena were wanting. Everyone agreed he was wet and weak. Thomas Lamont of the Morgan Bank cabled home: 'Herriot does not seem to be a strong man' and 'has no experience in national statecraft'. 'He is a child', remarked Belgian premier Georges Theunis.[35] The Cartel chief's craving for approval and desire for conciliation led him to concede too much. Thorny questions were fudged with a witticism and a generality. A highly strung temperament made him easy game for predators like British premier Ramsay MacDonald. At the London conference of July–August 1924, Herriot, suspicious that delegates had been meeting behind his back, had 'a most terrible outburst of rage and tears' and 'more than once cried' in MacDonald's presence.[36] He overloaded himself by trying to do three jobs: premier, foreign minister and mayor of Lyons – travelling to Lyons most weekends to catch up on business. A month after taking office, Herriot admitted that he had been mistaken in thinking that 'goodwill and sincerity alone' could solve Europe's problems.[37]

Traditional historiography contrasted the Bloc's bullying of Germany with Cartel conciliation. This is misleading. To be sure, right and left espoused opposing theses. The right considered Germany incurably militarist and aggressive. The left talked of two Germanies: the bad Germany of Kaiser, *Junkers* and industrialists versus the new democratic republican Germany. The Cartel advocated encouraging the new Germany while tightening security through the League of Nations and a Franco-British alliance. And the style of the Cartel was different. 'Our friends of the left meet in cafés and discuss confidential affairs in the most open manner', reported a shocked British diplomat.[38] But in practice the difference between the Bloc and Cartel was one of emphasis, not substance. The Cartel stressed conciliation and compromise. From 1919 the Bloc had mixed conciliation and coercion, attempting at times to realize *ententes* with London and Berlin. By 1922 growing frustration resulted in the Ruhr occupation and hopes of crushing Germany for good. However, Germany's revival from December 1923 forced Poincaré to return to his declared aim of securing the Ruhr as a pledge for a general settlement of reparations, debts and security. Acceptance of the Dawes Plan was the first step towards a wider settlement. This was the legacy Herriot inherited. The premier, even had he wished, could not change course quickly – most radicals supported the occupation and the Cartel would have collapsed without their support. Herriot admitted that he favoured evacuation of the Ruhr but only 'when France had obtained sufficient guarantee for reparations'.[39]

The ex-Allies had to decide how to implement the Dawes Plan. This process involved hard bargaining in the summer of 1924. Herriot's naivety, inexperience and slapdash style ensured that he got the worst of the bargain. The story of Cartel diplomacy is a lesson in how not to conduct negotiations. Having just taken office, Herriot barely had time to glance at official papers before rushing to England on 21 June for a meeting with Ramsay MacDonald at the premier's country residence, Chequers. The sole preparatory meeting on 20 June revealed strong disagreements between Gaston Bergery, head of Herriot's office, Peretti de la Rocca, political director at the foreign ministry, and war minister General Nollet. Herriot disabled himself by boycotting London envoy Saint Aulaire. The ambassador was in the Cartel's black books because he had defended President Millerand against critics calling for his resignation. The left viewed the president as the chief architect of the Ruhr occupation. From June until his replacement in November Saint Aulaire was ignored. Herriot, despite 'very sketchy' English, had a naive optimism that man-to-man talks with a brother democrat would work wonders. One comic incident speaks volumes for Cartel wimpishness. Whitehall made it clear that it would welcome Seydoux or Bergery but not Peretti. Instead of telling the British to mind their own business, Herriot's entourage promised cooperation. Then at the Gare du Nord Herriot suddenly asked Peretti to join him on the Paris–Calais train and the official arrived in London minus overcoat, toothbrush or dinner-jacket. Smuggling Peretti into Chequers did not save Herriot from being checkmated by a canny MacDonald, fully apprised of 'desperate attempts' at the last minute to coach his counterpart.[40] If Herriot had done some homework, he would have known that the British were no longer interested in a defensive pact. 'We must reckon on a growing tendency . . . to treat France and Germany on the same footing as regards security', Saint Aulaire cabled on 24 March.[41] The military attaché in London sent a plain warning on 16 June: 'the religion of the British cabinet is clear and firm: only the Dawes Plan will be discussed and nothing but the Report . . . it is essential not to follow Ramsay MacDonald . . . we must discuss at the same time the three questions: reparations, security and interallied debts.'[42] At Chequers Herriot meekly accepted MacDonald's agenda: 'let us therefore settle first . . . the Dawes Report; then we will go to . . . interallied debts, then . . . security'. An emotional plea for an alliance was fobbed off with the offer of 'constant collaboration', which Herriot interpreted as 'a sort of moral pact of continuous cooperation'.[43]

Both leaders agreed to summon an interallied reparations conference in London on 16 July. The outcome of the conversations was a serious defeat for Herriot: 'on every essential issue – economic evacuation, maintenance of a military presence, restrictions on future sanctions, limitations on the Reparations Commission's powers – Herriot had made substantial concessions . . . without receiving any compensation'.[44]

MacDonald's 'continuous cooperation' took the form of sending notes to interested powers worded as if substantial agreement had been reached on the London conference agenda. Herriot, already censured for the Chequers concessions, was accused of betraying national interests. The French were particularly infuriated by a British proposal that, under the Dawes Plan, the Reparations Commission should lose the power to declare Germany in default. This seemed like deliberate downgrading of the Versailles Treaty. MacDonald went to Paris on 8–9 July to save Herriot's face. Again, the French premier pleaded for an alliance against a resurgent Germany. MacDonald, who as a Scot disliked incurring unnecessary expense, replied that he wanted 'to conclude the closest of alliances that which is not written on a sheet of paper'.[45] Herriot got a palliative: an ambiguously worded memorandum as a basis for the London conference. So a pact of sorts had been forged. Both countries needed each other: Herriot's fall would have endangered Britain's reparations strategy; equally, Herriot required proof that the *entente* was alive and well in order to satisfy Cartel supporters.

The London Reparations Conference was the most important international gathering since the Paris Peace Conference. When the Germans, who had been barred from the first half of the conference, entered the plenary session on 2 August, Herriot 'looked as though he were having a tooth drawn'.[46] The United States for the first time since 1919 participated officially in a European conference. In the wings hovered the international bankers whose agreement was necessary for funding the Dawes Plan. As at most conferences, crucial compromises were reached off-stage in private huddles between bankers, officials and politicians. For France the proceedings were one long humiliation. Indeed, before the conference met, Herriot appeared reconciled to defeat. In discussions the premier 'incessantly made big speeches in which he talked of peace among mankind and a new era, while he designated all pertinent matters as technical questions which he had not yet studied'.[47] He seemed lost amid the crowd of hangers-on, deputies and journalists who swarmed around the French delegation. The premier alienated the Belgians, France's Ruhr partners, by failing to consult and cooperate with them – at one point agreeing 'to the immediate evacuation of Ruhrort, apparently without realising that this ... city served as the focal point of transport and logistics in the Belgian occupation zone'.[48] Attempts to raise interallied debts were blocked by MacDonald.

Herriot's forte was histrionics, not statecraft, and some sessions were more opera than conference. When MacDonald proposed evacuation in stages beginning as soon as possible, the prickly premier 'flared up, shouted, gesticulated, threatened to resign, lifted up his papers and went to the door'.[49] Sharp personality conflicts kept blood pressures high. MacDonald's Francophobe chancellor of the exchequer Philip Snowden hunted Herriot like a terrier. Wounded by the chancellor's spite and sarcasm the premier exploded: 'If Snowden speaks tomorrow against me and my country I shall with my delegation leave the Conference. Snowden is my enemy and the enemy of my country.'[50] Herriot had trouble enough controlling his war minister General Nollet, a staunch opponent of evacuation. Nollet gatecrashed a Downing Street meeting and had a violent altercation with Herriot. At midnight MacDonald went to bed leaving the French still fighting in the cabinet room.

Decisions on all substantive points went against the French – evacuation of the Ruhr within a year; abandonment of French economic exploitation; curtailment of the powers of the Reparations Commission – leaving France with virtually no right of independent action in the event of German defaults. Britain frustrated attempts to make the execution of Dawes dependent on effective German disarmament. Nor did the French win any relief on payment of American war debts. The only face-saver was payment of part of the Dawes annuities in coal and coke – sorely needed by French steel.

The League and collective security

After London, Herriot attempted to salvage something from the wreckage of Cartel hopes. MacDonald had promised that after reparations he would discuss disarmament and security. Since the British had set their faces against a bilateral pact, the only way forward seemed to be via a multilateral League scheme. In July Britain turned down the draft treaty of mutual assistance which obligated all members to come to the rescue of a victim of aggression. In the first week of September Herriot and MacDonald both addressed the League Assembly. This was the first visit to Geneva of British and French heads of government. The strong French delegation included Aristide Briand and Léon Bourgeois.

MacDonald called for arbitration machinery for international disputes. Next day Herriot stressed that arbitration, security and disarmament were inseparable. An Anglo-French resolution proposed a disarmament conference as soon as possible. The outcome of negotiations was the Geneva Protocol, the most important interwar initiative towards strengthening the League. It provided for compulsory arbitration. States which refused would be deemed aggressors and subject to sanctions. However, the protocol would only come into force when the disarmament conference scheduled for June 1925 had reached agreement. The protocol would have beefed up the League by imposing compulsory military sanctions and by making council action conditional upon a two-thirds majority instead of unanimity. The protocol represented 'a brilliant compromise between Herriot and MacDonald ... France was to be lured into disarmament by the promise of British participation in a system of collective security; Britain was to be lured into a system of collective security by the promise of French disarmament.'[51] Despite council endorsement and the adhesion of ten states, the protocol was torpedoed by the conservative government which succeeded the labour cabinet in November 1924. The new foreign secretary Austen Chamberlain and prime minister Stanley Baldwin disliked the protocol, alleging that the whole effort of imposing sanctions would fall on the royal navy and this might lead to conflict with the United States. The fallout from the battles over reparations and collective security strengthened France's Anglo-Saxon complex. Anglo-American plans for European reconstruction, Herriot was warned, were intended to depoliticize European affairs by handing over responsibility for reparations and disarmament to committees of experts: 'their goal is to break up the political system of which France is the centre and her army the guarantee; they want to reinforce the political system of which England and America are the centre and their fleet the guarantee.'[52]

End of predominance?

What was the balance sheet? The Ruhr occupation backfired and constituted the most serious reverse since 1919. The French now appeared more than ever the bullying top dogs of Europe, the Germans the underdogs. The British people, MacDonald wrote to Poincaré, were beginning to believe that France was out to 'ruin Germany and dominate the Continent'.[53] The Weimar Republic survived but the memory of 1923 – hyper-inflation, middle-class impoverishment, the humiliation of French colonial troops on German soil – contributed to the Republic's collapse after 1929. Poincaré's defenders claimed that without the occupation there would have been no Dawes Plan. This argument is hardly convincing. Dawes or a similar package would almost certainly have resulted if Poincaré had accepted the American initiative of December 1922. Poincaré's original purpose had been to force Anglo-American participation in an international settlement of reparations, debts and security. All he got for his pains was a highly unsatisfactory reparations scheme – unsatisfactory because Dawes downsized German repayments below the agreed 1921 level and made no reference to interallied debts. Moreover, Dawes, by recommending re-establishment of German economic unity, implicitly called for the evacuation of Franco-Belgian forces. Yet an imaginative and constructive negotiator might have extracted much more from the Ruhr occupation than coal and coke.

The Ruhr was no isolated setback. Little remained of the ambitions of 1919; plans for a powerful steel industry collapsed, economic penetration of Danubian and east central Europe registered only modest gains. Anglo-Saxon capital had the whiphand – in Czechoslovakia British interests held first place. Ironically, the Compagnie Française des Pétroles set up in 1924 to counter Anglo-American oil interests, tended in practice to strengthen Anglo-American hegemony. French imperialism, in contrast to the business-led Anglo-Saxon variety, has been called 'a poor man's imperialism' because the state had to take the lead in coaxing reluctant businessmen to invest.[54] Not that businessmen were by nature overcautious – they were ready to invest when opportunity offered. The difference between France and the Anglo-Saxon world was that the French state pursued political ambitions by economic means, and capital was reluctant to see its interests subordinated to political ends. There was a design of sorts for predominance but not a comprehensive one. Diplomatic alliances did not mesh with military strategy. Military planners provided for an offensive against Germany using the Rhineland as a springboard but no fundamental rethinking of army organization and strategy took place. As a result, France never had the army of its diplomacy – a rapid-response force ready to assist allies. Finally, imperial ambitions were unsatisfied. Sarraut's 1921 colonial investment project was overambitious. It assumed that colonial development could produce almost instant improvement in metropolitan France's economic situation. With the franc and reparations at risk, governments were unwilling to finance the Sarraut Plan and the Trans-Saharan railway. Initial technical surveys for the railway were delayed until 1928 and it was never built.

By the end of 1924 France was weaker than in 1919 or 1923: no Ruhr pledge; no debt settlement; no British or international guarantee; no autonomous Rhineland and no safeguards therefore against a German invasion fifteen or twenty years later. Why did coercion come to grief? Why did the Cartel's conciliation achieve so little? Most writers take the view that France was simply not strong enough to enforce her will.[55] An overstretched, under-resourced second-rank power bit off more than it could chew. Coercion, therefore, never stood a chance. Cartel conciliation did not show significant gains because Poincaré's blunders left no room for manoeuvre. This reading of French policy, although plausible, is open, however, to criticism on a number of points. It is much too neat and deterministic – failure appears unavoidable. Stressing the limitations on French action minimises both statecraft and institutional incoherence. Restraints were real enough yet the interplay of policy, personality and circumstance was more open-ended than supposed. Arguably coercion failed not for want of muscle but because it was not consistently applied.

Statecraft was the San Andreas fault of French policy. Poincaré lacked temperament and judgement for the Franco-German duel. In 1923 he blundered badly, accepting an international enquiry in October without first exploring informal German overtures; backing the outright separatists while refusing to talk to moderates like Adenauer. Opportunities for agreement on French terms were squandered for the big prize of German disintegration: 'by pursuing an unobtainable optimum solution the chance of an acceptable compromise was lost'.[56] Herriot's defenders advance two arguments in his favour. First, his predecessor left him no leeway. By March–April 1924 Poincaré had admitted defeat – accepting the Dawes Plan, arranging an Anglo-American loan to save the franc, trying to sweeten the British. Herriot had to live with the consequences of currency and foreign policy in pawn. Second, Herriot, it is said, was a realist who wanted to give France a fresh start by repudiating force and renewing Franco-British friendship. His inept performance reflected not so much lack of political skill as lack of belief in the premises of the negotiating position Poincaré bequeathed to him. So why, then, did Herriot have nothing to show for his own ideas? Surely a more skilful negotiator would have combined the liquidation of Poincaré's legacy with a distinctive achievement of his own. Herriot, alas, possessed neither the necessary conviction to maximize Poincaré's negotiating position nor the ability to sell his own beliefs. The margin for manoeuvre was tight, but wiser leadership might have delivered a combined reparations, debts and security package. France had three aces: military power, the Ruhr occupation and Britain's need for France. In July Britain's Paris embassy advised MacDonald:

> To let M. Herriot fall is indeed only too easy ... but it would ... be a great mistake not to make a supreme effort to save him ... 'the last stage of this strange, eventful history' might well be reached in a renewed and possibly prolonged re-appearance of M. Poincaré ... France, if she be squeezed too tight will finally throw prudence to the winds, remembering only that she is at present the one great military power with overwhelming military strength.[57]

Here was Herriot's game plan – if he had possessed the necessary gall to apply it. Ruhr evacuation might have been made conditional upon effective German disarmament and a debt settlement. Herriot, by exploiting Cartel fragility and his own moderation, had the chance to extract substantial concessions.

At issue between 1919 and 1924 was less a dearth of resources than finding the will and means to tap and focus existing energy, wealth and skills. The pyrrhic victory of 1918 might have been transformed into a French peace. But the prerequisite was a coherent strategy to restore national self-confidence and to persuade Bloc National voters to pay higher taxes. No cabinet attempted this task. In the last analysis, political judgement and choice made the final and decisive contribution to the frustrations of these years. Yet the Ruhr fiasco and the Dawes Plan were not the end of an independent foreign policy. Militarily France remained the most powerful continental state; from 1925 the leadership launched a second and final bid for predominance.

7

Locarno, 1925

A country like ours cannot always be asked to stretch its will to the point where at certain hours it can break ... At this time, and to prepare for the future, permit this country to rest a bit ... We must think of all the problems facing us. We must reconstruct a solid financial framework ... We must avoid being obliged to keep daily watch over our exchange rate.

 Edouard Herriot, Chamber of Deputies, 23 August 1924, in Stephen A. Schuker, *The End of French Predominance in Europe* (Chapel Hill, 1976), pp. 392–3

I rub my eyes and wonder whether I am dreaming when the French foreign minister invites the German foreign minister and me to celebrate my wife's birthday, and incidentally talk business, by a cruise on the Lake in a launch called Orange Blossom, *habitually used for wedding parties.*

 Austen Chamberlain, Locarno Conference, October 1925, in David Dutton, *Austen Chamberlain: Gentleman in Politics* (London, 1985), p. 230

I won't hide from you that in making foreign policy I ask myself what French resources are, from the financial and military standpoints. You must not be a megalomaniac. You must have the foreign policy that your country's finances and ability to use force allow. The day you go beyond leads them to Sedan.

 Aristide Briand, Chamber foreign affairs committee, 23 August 1926, in Edward David Keeton, *Briand's Locarno Policy: French Economics, Politics and Diplomacy, 1925–1929* (Yale, 1975), p. 117

A bas-relief at the entrance of the French foreign ministry commemorates Aristide Briand 'Pilgrim of Peace'. Of interwar French statesmen, Briand was the best known and respected. His seven years as foreign minister were France's Indian summer as a great power. Contrary to what is often asserted, predominance did not end in 1924. It would be quite misleading to depict the second half of the 1920s as a retreat from power. Financially and economically the country was stronger in 1930 than in 1924. Conciliation from strength superseded coercion as the formula for hegemony. Undeniably, a change of mood occurred in 1924. Poincaré diagnosed a 'tired' France, Herriot prescribed a period of 'rest'.[1] But fatigue was the consequence of the financial crisis and Ruhr failure, not a symptom of chronic debility.

Briand's goal was European pacification and reconciliation anchored in a Franco-German *entente*. This was to be accomplished through a mix of regional security pacts and bilateral understandings with Germany, Britain and the United States. The system would be animated by the League of Nations Covenant. How genuine was the call for universal reconciliation? Was it old-fashioned imperialism in new dress? The French sincerely dreaded war and wanted reconciliation with Germany – but on their own terms. Briand's rhetoric served both practical and idealistic ends. It aimed at seizing the high moral ground from the Anglo-Saxons and restoring the image of a peace-loving Marianne, guardian of enlightened values. The League commitment, it was hoped, would make Geneva rather than Paris the chief defender of the status quo. Thus, internationalist opinion would be mobilized in France's cause. Above all, Germany would be corralled within a European concert carrying an Anglo-Saxon seal of approval. Carefully measured concessions, it was believed, would tempt the new republican Germany into partnership. Was the idealist duped by his wily German counterpart, Gustav Stresemann, into sacrificing essential security interests? Briand was nobody's fool. 'I am perhaps a little naive but not to that extent', was his comment on the rumour that he had sold the towers of Notre Dame to the Germans. He did not trust Germany. Should conciliation fail, then a well-constructed treaty net would give early warning of German expansion while rallying world opinion to France. Essentially, the pilgrim of peace was a tough and shrewd negotiator bargaining from strength, insisting, for instance, that troops would only be withdrawn from the Rhineland in return for a final reparations settlement. Fundamentally, Briand's goal did not differ from that of Clemenceau, Poincaré and Herriot – security through European predominance. In 1919 Clemenceau attempted to ensure great-power survival via a postwar allied coalition against Germany. Disillusioned by allied quarrels and German recalcitrance, Poincaré tried to put a stranglehold on the ex-enemy. But coercion risked driving Germany into the arms of the Soviet Union. From May 1924 Herriot abandoned coercion and reverted to Clemenceau's goal of allied cooperation – but with a crucial difference. Cooperation now meant accepting Germany as an international partner in interallied negotiations.

Briand, Berthelot, Léger

A Breton born in Nantes in 1862, son of an innkeeper, Briand studied law before going into politics. Five pre-1914 premierships made him one of the Republic's inner circle. He was the archetypal figure of the regime: middleman and conciliator, ceaselessly forming and reforming coalitions. From 1914 he held office as an independent socialist almost continuously until 1932. After Delcassé, his seven-year tenure of the foreign ministry (1925–32) was the longest in the Third Republic. From head and shoulders he looked like a friendly lion with a mane of dark hair, heavy-lidded eyes and drooping moustache, alternately chain-smoking and dozing through international conferences. Eloquence, charm, and adroitness replaced the abrasive intransigence of Poincaré. Briand's sparkling, hypnotic extempore style was sheer delight after the usual bombastic droning. He was equally at ease with large audiences and individuals – after a spellbinding speech at the League Assembly in Geneva he lobbied persuasively in the corridors. Instead of reading long dossiers he preferred to sit in his armchair and talk through the issues with advisors. Visitors would find him behind a desk cleared of everything except a packet of cigarettes. Meetings with envoys filled up mornings; afternoons were spent in the Chamber of Deputies; at 5 p.m. he returned to the ministry to sign papers. Since he hated paperwork and did not dine because of a strict diet, he had plenty of time for the salons. Like British premier Ramsay MacDonald he got on better with women than men, especially duchesses. Weekends were spent fishing from his house at Cocherell in the Eure.

   Briand had the defects of his qualities. His chameleon-like character thrived on the ambiguities of Third-Republic politics. Political acrobatics were second nature: an up-and-coming socialist in the 1890s, he preached a general strike and revolution; premier in 1909–10 he took draconian measures against striking railway workers; in 1916 he denounced German peace offers yet within months advocated a negotiated peace; in 1921 he occupied German towns; by 1925 he was the apostle of conciliation. The charm was largely professional. 'It is only in his fine speeches that emotion plays a role', observed a German diplomat. Close associates considered him a cold fish: 'One is no further with him years later than the first day.' Secretiveness made him difficult to work with: 'he has avoided me all day', complained Berthelot, 'finding a thousand excuses not to have to tell me what the cabinet decided.' British academic Harold Laski compared him to a benevolent snake: 'his mind never comes directly upon anything ... it was most amusing to watch his endeavour to discover what my own views of the prime minister [Ramsay MacDonald] were before committing himself to the disingenuous epigrams he was anxious to make.' With colleagues and advisors he kept his own counsel, explaining policy to the cabinet as if giving a lesson in primary school – usually repeating what was in all the newspapers. His working methods were casual in the extreme. He read out papers without having looked at them beforehand, scanning faces to gauge the effect while carefully adjusting the argument. His 'only concern', opined ambassador Paul Cambon, was 'to create defences against his colleagues and parliament. He does not read the despatches he receives nor those that Berthelot sends in his name.'[2] If he was known to be out of Paris the British discounted his signature.

Briand needed a minder, otherwise his casualness and paperwork allergy would have been serious liabilities. Philippe Berthelot played the part to perfection. If just one functionary of the time could be resurrected for an interview, Berthelot would have first claim. Permanent head (secretary general) of the foreign ministry for most of the decade (1920–21, 1925–33) he was born in 1866 the son of Marcellin Berthelot, one of the founders of modern chemistry and foreign minister in the 1890s. A stellar personality, he belonged to a cultural as well as political elite, enjoying the friendship of Stéphane Mallarmé, Alfred de Musset, José-Maria Héredia and Jean Cocteau. Taller than average, thickset, with a high forehead, his distinctive feature was a sharp staccato voice which dispensed irony, sarcasm and wit. While indulgent towards his nursery of writer-diplomats like Jean Giraudoux, Paul Morand, Paul Claudel and Alexis Léger, he could be merciless towards colleagues and politicians.

Berthelot had two priceless gifts: an incomparable memory, winning Curzon's admiration by conducting an entire meeting without notes and assistants; and tremendous stamina. Managing on only three or four hours sleep, he transacted everything by hand – drafts, memoranda, correspondence. Modern paintings and *objets d'art* filled his office and he relieved the tedium of telegrams by reciting aloud Musset or Mallarmé. There were important political friendships with Herriot, Maurice Barrès and socialist leader Léon Blum, who shared the same apartment building in the boulevard Montparnasse. A great cat lover, the secretary general cabled news of his three Persians to French missions. In youth he gambled heavily on horses and cards – poker winnings paid for a tennis court at the ministry. Always unflappable, his safety valve was a blend of cynicism, paradox and aphorism: 'We must rest on our principles until they give way'; 'The only way to have the Italians usefully for one is to have them against one'; 'People prefer civil wars to foreign wars because they know the people they are killing'; 'There is nothing Briand hates more than thinking save action.' Cynicism was softened by humour. Apropos a London telegram advising 'Sir Edward Grey, [British foreign secretary] will think about the matter,' he replied, 'Grey is going to think – we are lost.' When straitlaced Huguenot diplomat Gabriel Puaux who had recommended a woman for a post protested on being asked whether he was sleeping with her: Berthelot replied 'I don't blame you – I only ask.'

Was Berthelot the power behind Briand? In one sense obviously so, since he did most of the paperwork. However, did he make policy? Assessing his influence is difficult because he shunned publicity, burning his papers and leaving no memoirs. His career had ups and downs. Director of Briand's office in 1915–17 he wielded more power than top officials like political director Pierre de Margerie and secretary general Jules Cambon. With Briand's departure, Berthelot was out in the cold and Clemenceau passed him over for the headship of the French delegation to the peace conference. Then in December 1919 with foreign minister Pichon semi-paralysed and Clemenceau caught up in the presidential election, Berthelot was briefly 'the real minister of foreign affairs'. At the London Conference of December 1919 'the main lines of the Turkish treaty were remitted to him and Lord Curzon'. But Clemenceau's successor, Alexander Millerand, kept him on a tight leash. Obstructing the British at the San Remo Conference in December 1920, Berthelot confessed 'he was acting under instructions' and 'hated it'.[3] In January 1922 Poincaré suspended him, alleging that he had misused his position in order to avert the collapse of his brother's Banque Industrielle de Chine. Privately, he opposed the Ruhr occupation, considering it too dangerous. Restored by Briand in April 1925, he felt confident enough to advance his own ideas, even criticizing Briand. Sceptical of the League and Geneva tea parties he was less than enthusiastic about the prospects for Franco-German understanding. Talking to the German ambassador, he would damp down hopes raised by Briand in discussions with Stresemann. Yet blowing hot and cold in this way may have been a deliberate double act, designed to give Briand maximum freedom of manoeuvre. There were limits to Berthelot's power; he never discovered precisely what Briand said to Stresemann at Thoiry in September 1926. Clearly Berthelot, although influential, was never master of French policy. Briand was front rider on the tandem.

From 1928 Alexis Léger, assistant political director and from 1931 political director, was increasingly influential. His literary reputation as Nobel prize winning poet Saint John Perse has obscured his diplomatic career. He is better known in the novels of the period than in the histories, appearing as 'Léger' in Marcel Proust's A la Recherche du temps perdu, Jules Romains' Les Hommes de bonne volonté, and Jean-Paul Sartre's Les Chemins de la liberté. Like Berthelot he kept his head down, leaving few traces in the record. His name was a byword for taciturnity verging on mutism. When a colleague warned of rising nationalism in Germany, Léger enigmatically replied: 'We are moving towards a revision of the Treaty of Versailles.'[4] Exiled in the United States after 1940, he kept tight-lipped, writing poetry but no memoirs. Coming from a French settler family in Guadaloupe, he wrote his first poems while studying law. The poet Francis

Jammes introduced him to Paul Claudel through whom he met Berthelot. Briand's patronage propelled him from assistant consul in Peking in 1916 to assistant political director (third most senior post) by April 1927. From 1928 rumours circulated that he intended to supplant Berthelot as secretary general. His influence was considerable since he was closer to Briand than Berthelot. Briand's 1929 European Union proposal owed much to Léger's ideas. However, essentially he was an executor, not an animator, largely content to follow Briand's lead.

Briand never achieved total command of policy. His influence peaked between 1925 and 1927; thereafter he was hemmed in by premier and colleagues. The elections of April 1928 strengthened the right and centre, making Briand more dependent on premier Poincaré's protection. From late 1929 his star waned rapidly as two dynamic right-wing premiers, André Tardieu (1929–30) and Pierre Laval (1931–32), in turn asserted themselves. Age and failing health took their toll. Yet Briand knew how to make the most of the free-wheeling enjoyed by Third Republic foreign ministers. Poincaré shared his aims and shielded him from a trio of right-wing cabinet critics – André Tardieu, Louis Marin and Louis Barthou. Also, Briand profited from popular backing and did not have to battle with powerful domestic lobbies. That said, not all was sweetness and light. There was a clash of temperaments and style between premier and foreign minister. Poincaré, it was said, 'knows everything and understands nothing', Briand 'understands everything and knows nothing'. The premier suspected Briand of withholding information from the cabinet, complaining that 'after a council of ministers Briand appears to accept the majority of his colleagues, and then goes off to the Quai to take a line in some respects different'. 'Important questions of foreign policy', noted British ambassador Lord Crewe, were 'hardly ever examined' at the informal cabinet meetings chaired by Poincaré at the Quai d'Orsay. Only President Doumergue's 'very remarkable tact and skill' in chairing formal cabinets at the Elysée kept the machine 'in working order'.[5] Conflict came to a head in January 1927 when Briand had to promise to consult cabinet and parliament before further negotiations on the Rhineland. On the whole, differences with Poincaré concerned style rather than substance. Briand, in Berthelot's words, was a man who said 'Yes, but' while Poincaré said, 'No, however'.[6] Moreover, Poincaré had mellowed since the Ruhr occupation and by 1928 was willing to consider early evacuation of the Rhineland, subject to a satisfactory final reparations pay-off.

Why conciliation?

Why did France swap the big stick for an olive branch? The strongest motive was a sense of inferiority – too few French, too many Germans. It was Hobson's choice. Abandonment of coercion in 1924 left no option. The time element concentrated French minds. Versailles stipulated that the three Rhineland occupation zones, France's most important treaty advantage, had to be evacuated in stages, starting in January 1925, ending in 1935. The 1924 London Reparations Conference imposed withdrawal from the Ruhr within a year. French leaders, all too conscious of eroding bargaining power, had to move fast in order to secure some accommodation with Germany.

Another compelling argument for conciliation was an empty treasury. The franc's fall from December 1923 blighted French policy for almost three years, torpedoing the Ruhr occupation and making Paris dependent on London and Washington. The pound sterling rate of 93 in May 1924 tumbled to 164 by April 1925, then plunged to 243 in July 1926. Empty coffers forced ministers to borrow large amounts from the Bank of France to fund immediate debts. By the end of 1925 total bank advances reached 36 million francs. The government's inability to meet short-term debts, except by borrowing from the central bank, signalled imminent bankruptcy and the risk of defaulting on bonds. Rapid depreciation produced a political crisis in July 1926. Hostile crowds surrounded the Chamber of Deputies and police guarded the Elysée. The Poincaré government of 'National Union' formed on 6 July was said to be the last hope of avoiding a military coup.

The financial crisis revived pet hates – tourists, foreign speculators, priests. Police watched those suspected of exporting capital. One suspect arrested had no gold but the police believed he had 'reactionary connections. Sontag himself had in his possession a rosary . . . his family includes three priests and a Trappist brother.'[7] The foreign ministry reinforced Bank of France admonitions to Herriot's Cartel:

> France is at present the only large European state which has not yet put its finances on a sound footing . . . this situation draws all the speculators to the Paris bourse . . . the world's admiration earned by our wartime conduct has completely disappeared; people are surprised that France has not shown in peacetime the energy that she showed in the war.[8]

Since the Cartel's fragility excluded steep tax rises, an American stabilization loan seemed the sole remedy. But Washington's price tag was a Franco-American debt accord and a conciliatory European settlement. Pressures from industry contributed to the new course in foreign policy. Industrialists enjoyed two advantages in German markets – booming sales, thanks to the weak franc, and preferential commercial terms under Versailles. But commercial advantages expired in 1925 and business leaders were anxious to consolidate newly won markets by arranging cartel agreements with German counterparts.

Military considerations buttressed Briandism. From 1919 to 1926 military planning provided for an offensive against Germany, using the occupied Rhineland as a springboard. After 1926 a defensive strategy, embodied in the

Maginot Line from 1929, prevailed. The reshaping of defence and foreign policies reflected the obvious and inescapable fact of Germany's demographic and industrial superiority. Resurgence, it was assumed, was only a matter of time and military leadership could not be retained indefinitely. France's two biggest assets, a large standing army and the Rhineland occupation, had only a short life span. Evacuation of the three Rhineland zones would begin from January 1925. Time, therefore, was of the essence. Since coercion had failed, conciliation had to be tried while France could still bargain. The army had diminishing value because the wartime slump in the birthrate would reduce the number of conscripts. In any future conflict France would not be able to mobilize the same number of men as in 1914. The unpopularity of conscription brought a reduction from three years to eighteen months in 1925 and to one year in 1928. The financial crisis made it imperative to reduce defence spending. Nationalist risings in Syria and North Africa diluted the army's strength on the Rhine. After prolonged debate, Marshal Pétain's ideas triumphed. He advocated a continuous line of fortifications as a mobilization shield after Rhineland withdrawal. Fortifications would compensate for a smaller army. In December 1925, war minister Paul Painlevé initiated detailed planning; in 1928 his successor André Maginot authorized the building of the Maginot Line. Continuing fears of a sudden German descent strengthened the case for defensive fortifications. Needless to say, the German army was far too weak to launch an attack. The new defensive posture and conciliatory foreign policy were mutually reinforcing. *Détente* offered the prospect of budget and tax reductions; fortifications proclaimed France's pacific intentions. This linkage was underlined by the president of the republic, Gaston Doumergue. 'People say that the reason why we have not organised our North East frontier defence is because we want to stay indefinitely on the Rhine, by starting our defensive work we will destroy the argument against us.'[9]

Diplomatic isolation since 1919 strengthened the case for *détente*. Repeated bids to muster Anglo-American military and political support had drawn a blank. The east central European alliances did not compensate for the lack of a great power ally. At the time, Anglo-Saxon critics condemned the alliances as proof of French militarism. This was a serious misreading of the pacts. They did not form a coherent military system. France had only two military agreements, with Belgium (1920) and Poland (1921). Originally, Paris had envisioned Poland, Czechoslovakia, Romania and Yugoslavia forming an anti-German and anti-Soviet barrier, pegging down the settlement in the east and imposing a two-front war on Germany. The disarray, however, of the east central European allies sharpened the argument for a west European regional security pact. More lame ducks than guard dogs, the client states were nearly as suspicious of each other as of Germany and the Soviet Union. The principal acolytes, Czechoslovakia and Poland, had little in common. Poland contested Czechoslovakia's possession of the Polish-speaking Silesian territory, Teschen. The centrepiece of the system was the Little Entente, a regional alliance of 1920–21 linking Czechoslovakia, Romania and Yugoslavia in three bilateral treaties. But it was targeted against revisionist Hungary, not Germany.

Support for Briand

B riand's pursuit of Franco-German understanding attracted diverse groups, ranging from left-wing pacifists and internationalists to right-wing tycoons. The pacifist and internationalist schools in French thinking which writers Henri Barbusse and Romain Rolland had kept alive during the war challenged the prevailing Germanophobia. Internationalists believed in two Germanys – the old nasty nationalist Germany bent on revenge v. the new democratic Germany committed to peace, prosperity and reconciliation. Novelist André Gide declared Franco-German reconciliation 'indispensable in the present situation of Europe'.[10] Barbusse's 'League of international solidarity for the triumph of the international cause' recruited stars like Georges Duhamel, H. G. Wells and Stefan Zweig. The philosopher Alain (Emile Chartier), who was influential among radical socialists proclaimed in *Mars ou la guerre jugée* (1921) that war could be contemplated only as a last resort to save France. Citizens were morally obliged to prevent its glorification.

The pan-European Union, launched by Austrian Count Richard Couden-hove-Kalergi in 1923, had Briand's blessing and set up headquarters in Paris. Louise Weiss, daughter of a wealthy Alsatian textile manufacturer, affirmed in the Parisian weekly, *L'Europe Nouvelle*, that European union was the best defence against the Americans and Russians. American, Japanese and Soviet competition worried industrialists. Centre right intellectual Lucien Romier, editor of the business paper *Journée industrielle*, summoned European business elites to close ranks against the extra-European threat. The steel manufacturers association (*comité des forges*) expressed interest in German industrialist Arnold Rechberg's schemes for a Franco-German military and economic alliance against the Soviet Union.

Backing came also from advocates of Franco-German understanding. In 1926 Luxembourg steel magnate Emil Mayrisch founded the Franco-German Information and Documentation Committee. Divided into French and German sections, its mission was to sell an *entente* to elite opinion in both countries. The list of founding members read like a Franco-German *Who's Who*: publicist Count Wladimir D'Ormesson, René Duchemin, president of the leading chemical concern Etablissements Kulhmann, Henri Peyrimhoff representing the coal owners (*comité des houillères*), Lucien Romier, sociologist André Siegfried, novelist E. R. Curtius, future chancellor Franz von Papen, von Stauff, president of the Deutsche Bank. Socialist deputy Pierre Viénot was first secretary general and the committee's patron was Marshal Lyautey, former resident general of Morocco, whose family home in Lorraine had been burnt by the Germans in 1914.

The Franco-German committee's activity was too rarefied and academic to appeal to the general public. In 1931 the German film director G. W. Pabst made the film *Kameradschaft*. With dialogue in French and German the film was an impassioned plea for a better understanding between nations. It dealt with a disaster in a French coalmine just across the Franco-German border. German miners go to the rescue of entombed French workers and to do so they smash their way through frontier posts. Pabst's portrayal of solidarity between French and German workers was good cinema but not real life. More indicative of the mental gulf separating the two peoples was the experience of German students who went to Paris by motorbike. They stopped for lunch in a French village and the innkeeper's wife who served them said: 'There is not a single French boy of your age who would have a motorbike like you. We French are economical and careful people. You Germans come over in the most flashy cars and motorbikes, and then you claim you cannot pay us any reparations.'[11]

France's renewed bid for international leadership rested in part on a strong League of Nations presence. The high-powered Geneva delegation impressed British delegate Robert Cecil with its 'extreme vigour and capacity ... Not only do its leaders consist of some of the most outstanding political figures in Paris but . . . a number of their very best officials.'[12] Every morning the delegation met for a brainstorming session, liaising with Belgian and east central European allies. Cecil complained of the French practice of mobilizing 'countries like Czechoslovakia, Poland and Yugoslavia to out-vote on naval questions England, America and Japan. The small countries voting with the French not only had no navies but were not even represented by a naval officer at the Conference'.[13] The powerhouse of France's League policy was the foreign ministry's League of Nations service. Empire-building made it virtually a ministry within a ministry. It had a decisive voice in general disarmament and bilateral negotiations, often short-circuiting senior ambassadors. As a result, 'the French had studied disarmament far more carefully than had any other nation'.[14]

Locarno honeymoon

The years 1925–29 are often called the Briand era; more accurately, they were the Briand-Stresemann era. Until 1924 French leaders held the initiative; now they had to share it with German counterparts. Stresemann's nationalist critics accused him of being a soft touch. A 1927 film showing in Berlin depicted Stresemann working on scaffolding around the Brandenburg

Gate, the symbol of old Germany. An onlooker asks: 'What is he doing?' Another says, 'Don't you know? He is taking the gates down to send to France.' In reality, Stresemann and German nationalists had the same aim – the destruction of Versailles. Stresemann, however, believed that Germany's military weakness made treaty fulfilment the only practical policy. Compliance, or at least a show of compliance, would foster international goodwill and strengthen Germany's case for treaty revision. Stresemann, like the nationalists, had a long shopping list: evacuation of the Rhineland and Saar; revision of the German-Polish frontier; union of Germany and Austria (*Anschluss*); return of all German peoples in central Europe.

In January 1925 Stresemann proposed a new western security pact. The proposal was prompted by a Franco-British refusal to evacuate on time the first Rhineland zone. Paris and London alleged German delays in disarming. The German minister's initiative was a canny move. Offering France pledges for the western frontier would make it difficult to refuse Rhineland and Saar evacuation, The offer was accepted. Beggars cannot be choosers. There were no alternatives. Coercion had come to grief, as had efforts to secure a Franco-British alliance and tighten collective security through the Geneva Protocol. President Doumergue had appealed directly to British chancellor of the exchequer Winston Churchill, stressing their common mission: both countries 'were responsible for great Mahometan populations, both were affected by the rapidly developing propaganda of Bolshevism among the coloured people'.[15] Unmoved, Churchill recommended a three-way Franco-Anglo-German agreement. More candidly, he told colleagues that France should be left 'to stew in her own juice'.[16] Even foreign secretary Austen Chamberlain avowedly 'the most pro-French member of the government',[17] opposed a Franco-British military alliance, describing Britain's role as that of an honest broker, seeking to reconcile France and Germany. Other pressures determined French decision-making. Washington informed Paris and Berlin that further loans depended on negotiating a security pact. But trust was lacking. 'All of them distrust Germany to the point of regarding it almost as an insult to suggest that they should make a pact with her', remarked Chamberlain after meeting French leaders in March 1925.[18]

Between 5 and 16 October 1925 Briand, Chamberlain, Stresemann, Italian fascist leader Benito Mussolini, and Belgian foreign minister Emile Vandervelde conferred at Locarno, a small Swiss resort on Lake Maggiore. The outcome was the Rhine Pact. Germany, France and Belgium recognized their existing borders as permanent, including the demilitarized Rhineland zone; Britain and Italy guaranteed the accord. All disputes would be referred to the League of Nations for arbitration. Germany concluded arbitration treaties with France, Britain, Poland and Czechoslovakia. Chamberlain and Briand wept, Briand embraced German chancellor Hans Luther. The public greeted Locarno as the start of real peace, the Promised Land in sight. In truth, the treaty was a mixed blessing for France. To be sure, Germany recognized the Versailles order in the west and promised to arbitrate disputes in the east, but this implied no renunciation of territory in the east. Locarno confirmed the deadlock of French policy. France at last had a guarantee of sorts but not her eastern allies, Czechoslovakia and Poland. Indeed, Locarno made their position more vulnerable because it discouraged French assistance. If Germany attacked Poland and Czechoslovakia, France could only respond by counter-attacking in the west across the Rhine; yet this might be construed as aggression against Germany, endangering the guarantee. The deadlock could only have been ended in one of three ways: by a British decision to underwrite the settlement in the east; by a French decision to act offensively on the assumption that Britain would follow; or by French disengagement from eastern Europe. It was this third path that France followed after Locarno. Even for western Europe Locarno had serious drawbacks. The guarantee was only half a guarantee. The guarantors, Britain and Italy, were sole judges of what constituted unprovoked aggression. There was no military machinery for implementing the guarantee nor inspection procedures for monitoring demilitarization.

Locarno, by excluding eastern Europe from the guarantee, destabilized France's position. Poland and Czechoslovakia were alarmed and anxious for the future. Austen Chamberlain's 'constant repetition of his indifference to all happenings east of the Rhine', noted one observer, 'is most demoralizing for central and eastern Europe'.[19] League membership in September 1926 gave Germany a platform for a more aggressive minorities policy aimed at undermining Poland and the successor states. Briand retuned France's eastern pacts, plugging them into the League and de-emphasizing their offensive potential. Additional treaties were signed with Poland and Czechoslovakia, pledging assistance in the event of unprovoked aggression. But the pacts were linked to the League so their implementation depended on the interpretation of the Covenant. Significantly, no military agreements were concluded. Although a 1924 Paris-Prague exchange of letters mentioned military cooperation, only one staff meeting took place. A June 1926 Franco-Romanian accord included a secret military protocol affirming collaboration but there was no follow-up. When France's envoy in Bucharest suggested that a watch be kept on Romanian defences, the foreign ministry denied that the military protocol implied staff talks. In 1928 Paris rejected Yugoslavia's request for military talks. Of course, the Franco-Polish military alliance of 1921 still stood; however, in 1927 Paris proposed that the pact should be harmonized with the League Covenant. Warsaw refused dilution, declaring that if Germany attacked France Poland would at once fulfil the terms of the alliance. What would France do in the event of a German attack on Poland? The response, Warsaw was told, would depend on Britain's attitude. In short, Poland could no longer count on the alliance.

Not that media hype bamboozled French politicians. Parliamentary debates disclosed great scepticism. 'For the Rhine the door has now been closed', one deputy remarked, 'England and Italy held it closed with us . . . these two powers have abandoned us . . . As regards east central Europe, before Locarno there was no doubt among our allies; we were at their side unreservedly. Today ... all is changed.'[20] Another speaker accepted the treaty but 'without conviction ... there was not one German in a million who was inspired by the spirit of Locarno. It would be folly not to vote for the Treaty but ... greater folly to believe in it.' Deputies admitted powerful constraints: 'France negotiated at Locarno under the pressure of English policy which is dominated by ignorance and lack of foresight ... We are oppressed by political and financial pressures. It's a dramatic, terrible situation [strong signs of approval] ... France was as threatened today as in 1914.' Only a handful hailed 'the start of a postwar policy. Attitudes will change ... One of the benefits of Locarno is to do away with the formulas which kept alive a war mentality. The world must be educated as children are educated.'

Notwithstanding strong French reservations, Locarno generated its own dynamic. The selling of the settlement, mid-decade economic prosperity and Stresemann's revisionist agenda all supplied a momentum for continuing negotiations. Expectations of universal peace and disarmament gained a new lease of life. Germany's entry to the League in September 1926, the Briand-Stresemann meeting at Thoiry in the same month, together with the 1926 international steel agreement and the Franco-German commercial treaty of 1927, nourished political optimism. 'No French politician, not even Poincaré,' declared Blum, 'could now go back upon the Locarno policy.'[21] Locarno 'tea parties' – informal get-togethers three or four times a year of Locarno power representatives meeting in one another's hotel rooms at Geneva – fuelled continuing talks. This personal diplomacy, while publicly preserving the Locarno spirit, had snags. It tended to devalue the League Council, leaving it little of substance. The casualness of the tea parties encouraged each one to interpret discussions in their own best interest and subsequent misunderstandings damaged goodwill. However, secrecy benefited France because the status quo was not openly challenged.

The franc's plight in the summer of 1926 offered Stresemann an opportunity to advance his agenda. Stresemann proposed a comprehensive Franco-German settlement. The two foreign ministers talked over lunch on 17 September 1926 in a small village inn at Thoiry in the French Jura across from Geneva. The package called for evacuation of the Rhineland, return of the Saar and the ending of the Inter-Allied Military Control Commission (IMCC), created by Versailles for the supervision of German disarmament. In return, Stresemann offered ready cash to be realized by the public sale of German reparation bonds under the Dawes Plan. France stood to gain 780 million gold marks. Nothing came of the scheme, partly because the franc recovered, partly because the scheme's 'grandeur and impracticality' meant that it was doomed.[22] Heavy flak from the cabinet and general staff forced Briand to retreat. Earlier in the year Marshal Foch had made the views of the high command crystal clear:

By abandoning the Rhine we will give Germany the ability to dominate and subjugate central Europe – beginning with Austria . . . There can be no question of France withdrawing from the Rhineland before the expiration of 15 years . . . evacuation will mean a national disaster coming on the heels of the financial crisis. Security, foreign policy, reparations will all collapse with it [Rhineland withdrawal].[23]

Who picked up the bill for the Thoiry lunch is not recorded. If Stresemann did, then he certainly got his money's worth. Although the comprehensive settlement was not realized, Germany secured in December 1926 without quid pro quo the ending of allied military control.

8

Indian summer, 1926–1931

Faced with French strength, England is not seeking to cooperate with us but to reduce our power. The idea that it is high time to curb French power is a national idea ... common to Labourites, Liberals and even Conservatives. For monetary, financial and economic reasons we are envied, we are becoming a nuisance, more than that, dangerous, if we are allowed to have the army and fleet corresponding to our resources ... If we claim a directing role in the unification of Europe let us not give ... the great maritime powers the instrument of an hegemony which they will use to neutralise ... the forces of Continental Europe.
    Memorandum on London Naval Conference of 1930 for French prime minister, 13 January 1930, MAE. Tardieu Papers, vol. 41

Since France and the United States by force of circumstances had become the two strongest nations in the world the rest of the world looked at this visit of the French Premier with keen anticipation and hoped for great results.
    Message from British secretary of state Lord Reading, US Department of State, *Foreign Relations of the United States, 1931,* II (Washington, USGPO, 1946), p 251

The rub came in the definition of the word 'security'. If the French meant the perpetual freezing of the postwar status quo, including the maintenance of unjust and bitterly resented treaty solutions, and a preponderant military force to guarantee it, then we could not agree with them. Our idea of security was a tranquillised Europe, which meant the solution, one by one, and by peaceful means of the problems preventing it from settling down.
    Memorandum by state department official Jay Pierrepont Moffat, 2 October 1931, in Melvyn P. Leffler, *The Elusive Quest, America's Pursuit of European Stability and French Security, 1919–1933* (Chapel Hill, 1979), p. 262

Decline of the Locarno spirit

O utwardly the Locarno spirit seemed to go from strength to strength: the Kellogg-Briand pact (1928), the Young Plan (1929), European Union (1929). In fact the achievement was much less than met the eye. Far from a blissful marriage stricken by world depression and an eruption of German nationalism, Locarno was a union of convenience severely stressed before the onset of economic crisis in late 1929. France clashed not only with Germany but Britain and the United States.

Locarno did not dispel underlying distrust of Germany. Within weeks ambassador Lord Crewe detected 'an increasingly strong undercurrent of distrust of Germany in official circles here'. The knowledge that the German military was evading Versailles disarmament clauses through secret cooperation with the Soviet Union confirmed traditional mistrust. 'While Stresemann was talking reason to Briand', complained war minister Painlevé in January 1927, 'his colleague at the ministry of war was doing his best to evade the Treaty in every possible way.' 'Germany', Foch fulminated, 'would only bow to force ... it is essential that Great Britain and France should remain united.' Over lunch, reported a British diplomat, the Marshal 'even muttered something uncomplimentary about Locarno but so quickly and so low that I preferred to think that he was talking to himself'. Politicians kept more open minds. Poincaré asked Berthelot if he thought the Germans sincerely wanted a *rapprochement*. The Germans, replied the secretary general, were 'probably sincere, and also insincere like all other nations whose vital interests were at stake'. Increasingly after 1926 Briand 'placed less confidence in "atmosphere", "goodwill", and verbal promises from Stresemann'.[1]

Franco-German relations were more duel than duet. It was a conflict neither side could win without Anglo-Saxon intervention. Accordingly, Briand and Stresemann competed for Anglo-American financial and political support. Three intractable issues – debts, disarmament and reparations – obstructed a Paris-London-Washington axis. However, the biggest roadblock was mutual jealousy and suspicion. French fears that Anglo-Saxon dominance would lead to an Anglo-German-American combination were matched by British apprehensions that 'the Europeans are constantly trying to drive a wedge between this country and the United States'.[2] The Americans for their part disliked being seen walking down the street with Europeans, believing that London and Paris were trying to dupe them into European commitments. Washington took a dim view of French leadership. 'Only a roulette table croupier', was the verdict on finance minister Joseph Caillaux.[3]

On debts the French wanted Uncle Shylock, as Uncle Sam had been

renamed, to do one of two things: either to cancel debts because they had
been incurred in a common cause or link repayment to German reparations.
The Americans seemed like loan sharks, telling them to settle big debts now
so that they could borrow more for currency stabilization. After Anglo-
American debt wranglings, Churchill warned Paris: 'They are going to bleed
you white like us.' Caillaux, on the eve of Washington debt talks in
September 1925, reiterated French doctrine: 'It would be quite impossible
for France to pay to America and Britain more than she received from
Germany. If I consented to such a thing I would be stoned in the streets.'
Right-winger Louis Marin urged Caillaux to stand up for France since the
'surrender all' policy of the past seven years had 'stripped us of the few fruits
of victory'. War loans were such an emotive and contentious issue that
officials 'considered offering colonial territory or a naval base instead of
cash'.[4] Yet without a settlement the dollars and goodwill needed for currency
stabilization and modernization would be denied. Caillaux's 1925 mission
failed and Briand had to settle for repayment without reparations linkage in
the Mellon-Bérenger accord of April 1926. Anti-American feeling prevented
ratification. On 11 July 1926, 25,000 veterans protested against the accord.
The sight of Americans on spending sprees, buying on the cheap as the franc
fell, whipped up public fury. Tourists were pulled off sightseeing buses and
police had to be deployed in force on main tourist boulevards. Washington
assumed that France's financial crisis would provide leverage for hustling the
French into a comprehensive political and economic settlement with
Germany. Yet, almost miraculously, the franc recovered, enabling Poincaré
to begin stabilization in December 1926 without American credit. Although
the Mellon-Bérenger accord remained unratified, Poincaré quietly started
repayments. Charles Lindbergh's landing at Le Bourget in May 1927, at the
end of the first solo transatlantic flight, temporarily restored some amity.

Franco-American goodwill, like the Locarno spirit, evaporated on
exposure to the complexities of disarmament. Incompatible approaches to
disarmament divided the powers. The wartime Allies were pledged several
times over to disarm by the League Covenant, by the preamble to the
Versailles Treaty, by declarations at Locarno. Powerful domestic and
international pressures forced governments to take active steps towards
general disarmament. Disarmament appealed to two of the strongest
instincts – the wallet and the heart. Smaller defence budgets bringing lower
taxes were vote-catchers. The pre-1914 armaments race was widely believed
to have caused World War I. Disarmament would bring nearer the abolition
of war. Moreover, on a practical note, without general disarmament it would
be increasingly difficult to justify Germany's disarmament. From December
1925 the League of Nations Preparatory Commission on Disarmament
deliberated in Geneva. Anglo-Saxon attitudes vexed the French:

> The Anglo-Saxons have ... this notion, false and dangerous ... that
> land armaments are perverse because they prepare for war whilst naval

power has a moral value because it prevents war. So they don't hesitate to say that the use of the British fleet (or American) against League decisions is inconceivable ... by opposing this viewpoint categorically we will avoid allowing the Anglo-Saxon powers, already masters of primary products, credits and the seas . . . from dominating the world.[5]

France demanded new security guarantees covering eastern Europe as a *sine qua non* for significant arms reduction. French representatives called for interdependence of land, sea and air armaments, conscript armies and limitations on industrial capacity.

In contrast, London and Washington considered French armaments, not German revisionism, to be the bugbear. Anglo-Saxon analysts believed that French disarmament on land, including abolition of conscription, would promote a Franco-German settlement and a prosperous Europe. This scenario offered the best guarantee for peace, and for American capital. Britain and America had no objection to greater security for France, provided it did not hinder German recovery and did not involve additional political and military obligations. For France stability meant enforcing the status quo, for Britain and the United States it meant a contented Germany. London and Washington acted as mediators, reconciling unruly French and German clients, arbitrating without taking sides. Disagreements extended across the board. Britain wanted to limit fleets by specific categories while France favoured limitation by overall tonnage – enabling her to compensate for inferiority in large warships by building up submarines and auxiliaries. On land armaments London and Washington were at one, on naval matters they were bitterly at odds. Parity was accepted in principle but without agreement on a practical formula, especially for cruisers. Winston Churchill was one of the few defenders of French arms, reminding colleagues that the French army was Britain's first line of defence and a guarantee of peace. But it was catch-22. Germany would use French armaments to justify rearmament and so increase the likelihood of conflict. Yet if France disarmed, Germany might still rearm and establish hegemony.

Understandably, Briand before disarming wanted to tighten collective security. Progress was stymied by disagreement over neutrality rights. Leading neutrals, principally the United States, insisted on their right to trade in non-contraband goods with belligerent states. France scouted British willingness to enforce League sanctions by naval power. The British, who were embroiled with the Americans over fleet strengths, refused to contemplate measures that might bring Anglo-American conflict over neutral trade. Tit for tat the French refused to discuss British plans for land armaments. In 1927 President Coolidge, in a bid to break the logjam, called a naval conference at Geneva. It was a fiasco; France and Italy refused to attend because they wanted an agreement to include land and air armaments. Britain, the United States and Japan failed to agree.

Briand, hoping that a Franco-American bilateral understanding might reduce the risk of a clash over neutral rights, proposed a Franco-American pact outlawing war. But he was outmanoeuvred. The Americans did not want to be corralled into an agreement that might be perceived as endorsing French alliances. Accordingly, they neatly side-stepped the French lasso by suggesting a general pact open to all. Their revised proposal made one concession – signatories promised not to protect the trade of those who violated the pact. But this small concession was withdrawn and the final American version accepted by Briand made no mention of trade or neutrality rights. On 27 August 1928 fifteen nations signed the Kellogg-Briand pact (Pact of Paris) outlawing war. It was a high-sounding declaration against sin, without enforcement clauses – an 'international kiss' as one American politician called it.[6] Like Locarno and Thoiry, the Kellogg-Briand pact fuelled expectations of universal disarmament without providing the means to realize the ideal.

No amount of cosmetic surgery like the Kellogg-Briand pact could mask the widening fissures in international politics. The summer of 1928 marked a change in German policy, a determination to take the offensive and secure maximum concessions or allow cooperation to die. Even a very limited naval compromise was stillborn. An Anglo-French compromise of July 1928 conceding parity in submarines and cruisers was denounced by the United States, Germany and Italy as an underhand effort to protect Britain's naval supremacy. Without agreement on essentials there was no hope of significant progress on disarmament. Calling a conference, warned socialist Henry de Jouvenel, would be dangerous because it would be merely an arms stabilization conference: 'consequently it would be a catastrophe for French democracy for it would make Germany the leader of reducing military budgets, a catastrophe for socialism by reinforcing Communist arguments, and a catastrophe for the cause itself because it would bring no progress, no means of control'.[7]

The longer disarmament talks lasted, the greater the price of failure. No power wanted to be saddled with responsibility for deadlock and breakdown. Nor could a League enterprise be abandoned without discrediting the League and demoralizing international opinion. In 1928 the search for scapegoats had already started. 'We can try to shift some of the blame on to the French', suggested the British foreign office. De Jouvenel blamed the Poincaré government for tying itself to British conservatives: 'We are working to strengthen the shaky position of the conservatives instead of profiting from their weakness to persuade them of our viewpoint.' Fellow socialist and member of France's League delegation, Joseph Paul-Boncour, denied slavishly following Britain, arguing that the conservatives were a safer bet than the opposition: 'I confess my anguish when I consider the francophobia of the liberals and labourites, their extraordinary conception of disarmament matters'.[8] Disarmament was a divisive issue at home as well as abroad. In addition to civilian-military and left-right differences, the left had its own disagreements. In October 1928 Paul-Boncour claimed that France had already made substantial reductions in defence spending. Compared with 1913, military expenditure had fallen by 13 per cent. Radical socialist leader Edouard Daladier challenged Paul-Boncour's figures, pointing out that the one-year law of 1928 had not reduced effectives since the general staff compensated by increasing the number of regulars.[9]

Franco-British financial rivalry

The Kellogg–Briand pact allowed Stresemann to recover the initiative. Since war was now outlawed, he asked, why occupy the Rhineland? Briand and Poincaré, knowing that the second Coblenz zone had to be evacuated in January 1930, endeavoured to make the best deal. They offered full evacuation for a satisfactory final reparations settlement. A committee of experts chaired by American banker Owen D. Young produced the Young Plan in June 1929. Adopted at the First Hague Conference in August 1929 the plan downsized German debts, fixing the final reparations repayment at about one-third of the 1921 total. Payments would extend over fifty-nine years until 1988. After haggling over dates the French agreed to withdraw fully by June 1930 without securing the international verification of demilitarization that Briand had wanted. The Young Plan left one permanent legacy, the Bank of International Settlements, established at Basle in May 1930 for reparation transfers and promotion of European central bank cooperation.

The First Hague Conference turned into a Franco-British squabble over reparation spoils. The French suspected the British of playing 'their old game of setting the Continental powers against each other in order to make a good deal for themselves'. British chancellor of the exchequer Philip Snowden belittled French claims, demanding a larger slice of the German cake. When the French press called him one of Joan of Arc's executioners his wife remarked, 'He is a Yorkshireman, and they do not understand the Yorkshire character.' The dispute became personal; Snowden described a speech by his French counterpart, Henri Chéron, as 'grotesque and ridiculous' and threatened to leave the conference. Chéron a 'fat, excitable man anxiously concerned about his position' took the comments as a personal affront and sent his seconds to demand an apology.[10] Foreign secretary Arthur Henderson announced that whatever the French decided Britain would withdraw her troops from the Rhineland by Christmas 1929.

Of course, rowing over reparations was nothing new. One cause of renewed bickering was a change of government. Labour defeated Baldwin's conservative administration in the elections of May 1929. Premier Ramsay MacDonald and colleagues did not share Austen Chamberlain's pro-French

Table 2 Gold and foreign exchange holdings (millions of francs) of the Bank of France

End of	Gold reserve	Foreign exchange		
		Sight deposits	Bills	League of Nations figures (US$m)
1925	18,142	316	a	13
1926	18,146	418	a	116[b]
1927	18,126	252	a	850[b]
1928	31,977	13,510	19,215	1,287
1929	41,668	7,249	18,693	1,021
1930	53,578	6,792	19,387	1,027
1931	68,863	12,354	8,757	842
1932	83,017	2,938	1,545	176
1933	77,098	16	1,143	—

[a]Not distinguished as separate items in the accounts of the Bank
[b]Estimate
  Source: David Landes, *The Unbound Prometheus* (1966), p. 386

feelings. Early in 1928 former Oxford don Alfred Zimmern, deputy director of the Institute for Intellectual Cooperation in Paris, urged a reluctant MacDonald to come to France in order to remove misunderstandings about labour: 'the general feeling is that a labour government would exhibit all the existing disagreeable features of British policy . . . there is very little realisation of the practical possibilities of cooperation . . . between the British and French left. Yet those possibilities are immense and could make a new League of Nations and a new Europe.' After much persuasion MacDonald finally spoke on French radio and met Daladier and Herriot. Zimmern counselled: 'If you can kill these two bogeys – (1) that the Conservatives are pro-French and Labour anti-French – (2) that the Labour Party is not in earnest about pooled security and cannot be trusted to make the League machinery effective in an emergency – your visit will have been a thousand times worthwhile.' Once in power, however, Labour's anti-French flavour soon surfaced. 'If France were to show a willingness to consent . . . to substantial cuts in her own fighting forces, it would . . . give a great impetus to events', wrote junior foreign office minister Hugh Dalton. 'Quite frankly I am . . . both astonished and impatient at the way in which some of our critics in France appear to forget all about this little Swiss Health Resort [Locarno] and what happened there. Is it not worth anything and has it no bearing on French security . . . that by the Locarno Treaty the whole force of the British Empire has been pledged to France in the event of an attack upon her by postwar Germany?'[11]

   Financial rivalry added extra tensions to cross-Channel relations. After years of financial weakness France was now ready to challenge Lombard

Street. By 1929 the franc had been successfully stabilized and the Bank of France had amassed the largest foreign exchange reserves of any central bank in the world, as well as acquiring large sterling reserves on deposit in London (see Table 2). French banks had considerable short-term holdings in Berlin. France's new-found power – attaching political conditions to loans and selling short-term holdings at opportune moments – impacted powerfully on the markets. The British and Americans, who in 1924–26 monopolized financial diplomacy, resented French competition in European financial reconstruction. Bank of England governor Montagu Norman claimed that the French 'for political purposes' were bypassing the League of Nations in providing loans for Poland and Romania. Emile Moreau, governor of the Bank of France, riposted: 'England . . . the first European country to re-establish a stable and secure currency had used that advantage to establish a basis for putting Europe under a veritable financial hegemony. The Financial Committee at Geneva has been the instrument of that policy.' At a Paris financial summit in April 1928 the central bankers had a battle royal. Moreau denied political considerations in France's loan to Romania, threatening: 'if the Bank of England were to refuse participation' he would regard it 'as an unfriendly act . . . He would then have no further regard to the interests of the Bank of England'. Later Moreau lost patience: 'these so-called questions of principle were simply childish . . . they were a mere pretext and the fact of their being dragged in again . . . revived in his mind all the unpleasant suspicions about the sincerity of the Bank of England . . . He then proceeded to bring a series of charges, supported by detailed accounts of what at various times had been said and done in London and New York.'[12]

Breakdown, 1929–1931

From late 1929 the fragile Locarno *détente* disintegrated. Firstly, world depression signalled by the Wall Street crash of October 1929 dragged down national economies and destabilized international relations. Economic breakdown led to political upheaval which in turn toppled the international order. Mass unemployment in Germany stoked up resentment against Versailles and Weimar democracy. Overnight Hitler's National Socialist Party became a serious political force and its representation in the Reichstag jumped from twelve seats in 1928 to 107 in September 1930. Weimar's deflationary economic policy kept both unemployment and political extremism high. Chancellor Heinrich Brüning saw in deflation a device to free Germany from reparations. Second, new national leaderships, Tardieu and Laval in France, MacDonald in Britain, Brüning in Germany, were much more willing to accept deadlock. Stresemann, in bad health for several months, died in October 1929. Briand stayed at the foreign ministry until January 1932, but his influence ebbed rapidly, especially after defeat in the presidential elections in May 1931. Brüning and foreign minister Julius Curtius played for popular support by adopting an uncompromising stance on reparations, disarmament and the project for an Austro-German customs union.

Billed as the 'conference on the final liquidation of the war', the outcome of the First Hague Conference spurred Briand to make one final attempt to prevent the liquidation of the peace. From Geneva in early September 1929 Briand called for a European union, a political and economic federation. In May 1930 he submitted a detailed proposal for League scrutiny. It was then quietly shelved for want of great-power support. What were Briand's motives? Primarily the desire to protect France's primacy by ensnaring Germany in a new web of international agreements. Withdrawal from the Rhineland and the deadlock over disarmament made a bold and imaginative initiative urgent. Briand aimed at retaining moral and political leadership in Europe. Economic and political conditions favoured a new initiative. While the world economy slowed down, the French economy was riding high, registering better growth rates than the United States. Chemical, electrical and motor car manufacturers benefited most. Expansion created confidence: 'France for the first time perhaps for ten years', enthused one official, had abandoned 'the inferiority complex created by the war, devastated regions, fear of Germany, the franc's fall.' Confidence was, however, tempered by apprehensions of the American economic colossus. Poincaré spoke with 'real despair of the Americanization of France'. In June 1929 Stresemann asserted that the issue was no longer one of Germany's isolation in Europe but 'one of Europe as a whole in fee to the power of the United States'. French officials glimpsed an opportunity to build bridges with Berlin. One purpose of European union was to help organize Europe against American economic expansion. The bait for Germany was a Franco-German economic *entente* which would exclude Britain and keep American multinationals at bay. 'People who have business interests with Germany', MacDonald was warned in late 1928, 'maintain that it is the natural thing for France and Germany to stand together apart from or against England.' 'Loucheur [Labour minister] and Léger and under their influence Briand', London heard, 'were definitely out for the federalization of Europe on the economic basis of the organisation of production, rationalisation etc . . . they were ready with Germany to organise Europe without us.'[13]

Britain played a leading role in killing Briand's European union proposal, first emasculating it then discouraging others from supporting it. Stresemann was strongly encouraged to reject a European federation. Britain opposed regional trading blocs and wanted to keep imperial economic links. The German foreign ministry did not want a political union because it would impede territorial revision of the eastern frontier. Moreover, a French authored political union would have been very difficult to sell to a stridently nationalist public which denounced the Young Plan as 'Young slavery', and demanded the return of the Saar.

The 1930 London Naval Conference confirmed the estrangement between France and the Anglo-Saxon powers. MacDonald, preparing for the five-power conference, met first with President Hoover in October 1929. The emphasis on Anglo-American relations stoked French fears of Anglo-Saxon hegemony. The French still smarted from the 1922 Washington Naval Treaty and wanted to overturn it. Pressure on French land armaments, advised a disarmament expert, had to be resisted 'by making it clear to the British that we will create difficulties for them in naval discussions unless they finally abandon their perpetual attacks against our land forces'. Passions ran high before the conference assembled in January 1930. Premier Tardieu summoned the American ambassador on Christmas morning 1929, charging him: 'You Anglo-Saxons are trying to disarm France to the advantage of Germany and Italy.' Tardieu's advisor explained France's conference strategy:

> Technical and as secret as possible is how the Americans and British would like this Conference. Political and as public as possible is how we want it ... for the French government it will be something of a success in domestic and foreign policies – because of the anxieties of our Geneva friends – if this Conference fails in the narrow and personal form which the Anglo-Saxons intend it to have.

Yet there was no wish to alienate the United States:

> But we must do our utmost not to discourage America. If its imposing delegation – the first to be sent to Europe since the end of the war – returns empty-handed, we may have to wait another ten years ...
>
> It is by trying to find a way for America to collaborate with Europe that we will bring her back to Europe and towards the League of Nations, which England would like to be free of.[14]

The French geared the conference to their security needs, asking for a Mediterranean guarantee pact. Negotiations resembled a dialogue of the deaf. MacDonald insisted with moral earnestness that French anxieties were illusory and that more pacts would afford only a false security. But his real concern was that guarantees would give France 'a free hand in determining European policy with Great Britain a bound follower ... that will mean alliances and war'. Tardieu was told that MacDonald was manoeuvring 'to reduce Conference difficulties to a Franco-Italian conflict so as to hide the Franco-British clash and throw on us the responsibility for a rupture'. The French resisted Italian demands for full parity. The Washington treaty had accorded France and Italy parity in battleships, but France objected to Italy's demand for parity in auxiliaries arguing that, unlike Italy, she had fronts to protect on the Atlantic and North Sea as well as the Mediterranean. Conceding full parity would in effect give Italy superiority in the

Mediterranean and endanger France's lifeline with her North African empire. Months of fruitless negotiations embittered MacDonald: France's 'mentality is purely militarist . . . war is the central fact of its mind'. Fortunately, French propaganda was better ordered than at the 1922 Washington conference. Paris enlisted the support of American peace groups and Hoover urged secretary of state Henry Stimson to take the offensive 'before the American public shall have become completely prejudiced against us through the French'.[15] Hoover vetoed Stimson's proposal for a consultative pact, fearing it would create a moral obligation to defend France. The conference ended with a three-power accord between the United States, Britain and Japan, establishing a 10:10:7 ratio across the board.

Germany's announcement in March 1931 of an Austro-German customs union demonstrated Berlin's new uncompromising stance. The long-range objective was a union (*Anschluss*) between the two countries as a foundation for an economic *Mitteleuropa*. France's clients, Poland and Czechoslovakia, would be pulled into Germany's orbit. Economic domination would speed revision of the German-Polish frontier. Paris immediately condemned the customs union because it jeopardized Austria's independence under the peace treaties. At this point Briand discredited himself by declaring on the day Germany announced the union that an *Anschluss* was no longer the danger it had been. He was now a political embarrassment and Laval tried to kick him upstairs by promoting his candidacy for the presidency of the republic. The collapse of Austria's largest bank, the Credit-Anstalt, on 31 May enabled France to crack the financial whip, insisting that Austria refer the proposed union to the International Court of Justice at the Hague.

The world-wide slump returned reparations to centre stage. The run on the German mark in the summer of 1931 offered Brüning a heaven-sent opportunity to ditch reparations. However, before he had time to announce a postponement of payments, Hoover, on 20 June, unilaterally proposed a one-year moratorium for all intergovernmental debts. The Hoover moratorium enraged the French because of its implied threat to future reparations. 'If we do renounce our right to reparations payments', asked Laval, 'what guarantee will be given to us by the United States and Great Britain that these payments will be resumed at the end of one year?' French ministers, by delaying acceptance of the moratorium, gained a breathing space during which they sought to reach agreement with Germany on future payments. The Germans, despite desperate financial straits, rejected Laval's offer of a ten-year loan of $500 million for a moratorium on political demands – 'even a temporary sacrifice of their legal right was out of the question'.[16]

German rejection of French demands reflected two considerations. Brüning knew that Laval would have to accept the Hoover moratorium. Washington threatened to negotiate separately with leading powers, leaving France high and dry. Brüning also knew that even without political strings the French loan was unacceptable to London and Washington. The British upstaged the French by calling a London conference on the financial crisis. The conference accepted the American moratorium and appointed a committee to examine Germany's plight. It was standstill all round. The financial storm deepened. Britain's departure from the gold standard on 21 September 1931 marked the final collapse of the old nineteenth-century international economy based on the gold standard, free trade and the City. Sterling's collapse pointed up the strength of the French franc, but a Franco-German summit in Berlin on 27 September achieved virtually nothing. The nationalist upsurge tied Brüning's hands and Laval, in his own words, 'had no authority from his cabinet to discuss any of the important unsolved questions between France and Germany'.[17] The sole result was the creation of a Franco-German economic committee to promote cooperation and cartelization.

After Berlin, Washington. This time Laval travelled without Briand. The encounter generated only ticker-tape. Pre-visit signals from Paris were unpropitious: 'Everybody ... was afraid of Laval's going wrong ... so far from home on new untried land ... they [the French] are willing to have matters opened, not finished . . . we shouldn't expect to get far with disarmament.' Hoover regarded the summit as 'just a nuisance', lambasting the French for speculating against the dollar. Both sides restated their positions. Laval blamed German revisionism for Europe's instability, suggesting a ten-year political moratorium; Hoover castigated the French: 'France always goes through this cycle. After she is done and begins to recuperate ... she gets rich, militaristic and cocky; and nobody can get on with her until she has to be thrashed again.' Privately, Laval agreed that the Polish Corridor was 'a monstrosity'.[18] The United States refused to make political commitments or sign consultative pacts.

New alliances? Italy and the Soviet Union

Did *détente* have to end in deadlock? France lacked the clout to impose a solution. Only the active participation of one or more great powers might have helped to resolve the Franco-German impasse. From 1919 Paris repeatedly canvassed Anglo-American support, but London and Washington wanted to be arbitrators, not allies. Yet there were two potential allies in the wings – Italy and the Soviet Union. Together or singly they might have given France greater political leverage. Ideology and the Soviet repudiation of Tsarist debts were formidable obstacles, but not perhaps insuperable. After all, ideological differences did not prevent German-Soviet cooperation. However, Comintern activities in France angered French leaders.

Communists spread anti-colonialist and anti-militarist propaganda, protesting against the Ruhr occupation and the Riff war of 1925–26. Diplomatic recognition of the Soviet Union in 1924 did not lead to *rapprochement*. The perceived ideological threat overrode foreign policy interests. 'Russia instead of serving as a counterpoise to Germany had only one desire and that was to stir up trouble everywhere', opined senior Quai d'Orsay official Jacques Seydoux. When Britain broke off relations with Moscow, after the raid on the Soviet trade mission in London in May 1927, French ministers wanted to follow suit. 'Communism is the enemy', proclaimed interior minister Albert Sarraut. While the Chamber was on holiday communist deputies were proscribed and arrested. Poincaré considered Soviet interference in French internal affairs 'absolutely intolerable', telling the Russians that he knew for a fact that French military documents had been stolen and examined in the Soviet embassy.[19] France responded to initiatives instead of making them. In September 1927 Moscow proposed a Franco-Soviet non-aggression pact. Negotiations limped along because Briand and Poincaré insisted on prerequisites: repayment of 1.2 million French bondholders, compensation for confiscation of French concessions and settlement of the Russian state debt to France. In 1930 Soviet foreign minister Maxim Litvinov reaffirmed Soviet willingness to sign pacts with France and Poland. In the summer of 1931 a right-wing hue and cry, started by a press leak, halted discussion of a non-aggression pact.

Italy, like the Soviet Union, might have made a makeweight against Germany. However, in the 1920s and early 1930s Paris and Rome battled over colonial expansion, naval parity and French support for Yugoslavia's Adriatic ambitions. The Italians felt doubly cheated because France refused to honour promises of colonial compensation along the Libya-Tunisia border and the Peace Conference had denied them League of Nations mandates. Since the 1922 Washington conference, Italy had claimed naval parity with France. In short, both countries wanted to be top dog in the Mediterranean. The French as first comers with a large North African empire had no intention of abdicating. The French foreign ministry had 'a rooted distrust' of Italy and Berthelot was credited with a 'well-known dislike and mistrust of everything Italian'. Briand accused Mussolini of 'making every sort of difficulty for France', alleging that during the Ruhr occupation the Italian leader had offered Germany arms to fight France.[20] In 1928–29 Franco-Italian exploratory talks stalled on the mandate issue. Mussolini wanted assurances that in the event of a redistribution of mandates Italy would receive a share. Poincaré closed the door firmly, saying that mandates would be retained until the mandatory power decided to give independence to a territory. Foreign secretary Austen Chamberlain rejected Berthelot's suggestion that in order to accommodate Italy new mandates might be carved out of independent Abyssinia or Portuguese colonies.

Political talks restarted in 1931, with Mussolini expressing interest in meeting Laval. Again, discussions dragged on for months before fading out. Laval's chief advisor blamed Berthelot and the foreign ministry for sabotaging the talks. In fact, both sides were at fault. Naval rivalries intensified after Italy failed to win parity at the 1930 London Naval Conference. In 1931 Franco-Italian political and naval conversations took place. The French navy's Italophobia helped to torpedo an agreement. Berthelot, far from blocking political talks, wanted to divert Italy from North Africa by offering her 'a free hand in Abyssinia'. The suggestion was not pursued, but four years later it resurfaced as part of the Rome Agreements, the Franco-Italian reconciliation of January 1935. Mussolini was also responsible for lack of progress. His 'main aim' was 'grand policy in Europe and expansion at Yugoslavia's expense'. He wanted 'an impressive diplomatic victory, such as the cession of a real French colony'. The obstacles to Franco-Italian and Franco-Soviet agreement, although considerable, were not necessarily insuperable. Arguably, stronger initiatives would have given France at least one much-needed ally.

Missed opportunity?

A nnus terribilis was historian Arnold Toynbee's description of 1931. There was economic misery and international deadlock on all substantive questions: the Saar, disarmament, reparations, economic cooperation. The Japanese invasion of Manchuria in September 1931 provided the first serious challenge for the League and collective security. In October came rumours of a German-Polish war. Of the European great powers, France alone seemed secure: 'the dominant military power in Europe in the air as well as on land ... the Bank of England was shocked to find itself dependent on the Bank of France, and the Federal Reserve Bank [of the United States] to find itself not altogether independent of French goodwill.'[21] In 1930–31 the economy reached a peak which it was not to equal again until the early 1950s. Prosperity was greater than at any time since the Second Empire. Coal, iron and steel topped record levels for the 1920s. Yet despite her ascendancy, France remained isolated internationally, at odds with friends and foes and in the worst possible position for the World Disarmament Conference which opened in Geneva in February 1932.

Could 1931 have been France's *annus mirabilis*? Briefly in 1919–23 France had the power to impose a European settlement; from 1929–31 she had an opportunity to propose a settlement. Ironically Germany gained more from skilful exploitation of her own weakness than France gained from financial and political strength. Why, excepting the Kellogg-Briand pact and European Union, did France risk no major initiatives? 'It has to be admitted,' wrote assistant League secretary general Joseph Avenol, 'that for some time we have lost all the initiative and we have been outmanoeuvred and thrown on the defensive.' The French knew their strength. 'We have never been in a stronger position', judged Berthelot. 'We can lean on England while the pound is at our mercy', another senior official advised: 'We can make her understand ... that if she wants our help as a lender, other questions must first be settled ... the same with America'. Curiously, nothing happened. One obvious curb was the timidity of military and political leaders. There was no dearth of ideas but politicians preferred to shore up the status quo. Second, parliament and public shied away from imaginative solutions. Parliament buried finance minister Paul Reynaud's plan for reducing taxes on overseas investments as an incentive for further investment, especially in central Europe. At Franco-German summits in 1931 premier Laval was handcuffed by cabinet hardliners. It was assumed that France was strong enough to bide her time. There was a third restraint. Exercising financial diplomacy carried high risks because France as both creditor and debtor was in an ambiguous position. Insistence on securing reparations from a near-bankrupt Germany seemed avaricious; footdragging on interallied debts looked like a means of funding armaments. Simultaneous attempts to keep the pole position in disarmament discussions made it seem as if the French were trying to have their cake and eat it. Hoover answered French reservations about his moratorium proposal with a brutal 'Let them disarm.'[22]

Why did Briand's policy fail? Three explanations have been advanced. According to one view, the Locarno era was one of solid achievement swept away by the whirlwind of depression and German nationalism. Alternatively, détente, it is said, had fundamental flaws which surfaced under the stress of economic crisis. Third, the Locarno period, it is argued, was one of missed opportunities. In sum, détente failed because it did not go far enough. None of these explanations is adequate. Conciliation collapsed partly because of the incompatibility of Franco-German interests, partly because the depression and nationalist frenzy in Germany poisoned the international climate.

The notion of 'missed opportunities' was the product of Locarno rhetoric. Leaders promised more than they could deliver. There was no willingness to radically reassess national interests. Briand and Stresemann were not trammelled by military advisors and public opinion. The fact is that both leaders held different and opposing conceptions of European security; Briand wanted a French Europe, Stresemann a German one. However that still left some middle ground for cooperation without sacrificing treaty rights and revisionist claims. But the Locarno years were not ones of solid achievement. To be sure, there were gains; dismissing the Locarno era as one of illusion is too negative. The Young Plan of 1929 was 'adequate, definitive and relatively secure'. By 1929 Stresemann had realized all his 1925 agenda save the Saar. Yet long-term objectives were not realized: 'Briand did not make Europe safe for France; Stresemann did not win French acceptance for German revisionism; Chamberlain's entente did not give the French the assurance and security they craved.'[23]

What went wrong? The most important factors were structural: the conflict between France's treaty predominance and German revisionism, the impact of the depression. Locarno limited but did not liquidate the Franco-German conflict. The spirit of Locarno meant different things to different leaders. As one French official quipped: 'There are three things, the Locarno spirit, *l'esprit de Locarno* and the *Locarnogeist*.' For Stresemann, Locarno was the first step towards treaty revision; for Briand the first step on the road to compliance; for Chamberlain it was an assertion of British detachment. By guaranteeing the Franco-German frontier Britain explicitly repudiated responsibility for any other European frontier. By the summer of 1928, *before* the slump, Germany showed a new determination to assert its demands.

Was *détente* doomed without the depression? A key theme of this book is the importance of political leadership in influencing the outcome of conflict. Briand, Stresemann and Chamberlain achieved a personal rapport that concealed the cracks. Their successors were much less committed to cooperation. Nevertheless, it is arguable that, but for the depression, some formula would have been found to manage Franco-German rivalry. Locarno would then have stood as the first step towards stabilization of international politics. But the conjuncture of slump, new leaders and nationalist upsurge ended prospects of comprehensive settlement. However, Laval, Tardieu, Brüning and Curtius did not necessarily assume that irreconcilable differences would lead to war. Rather they risked deadlock and breakdown because they assumed they could handle the consequences of failure. Depression killed Locarno-style *détente*, it did not exclude limited opportunities for agreement. Franco-German differences did not have to be settled by war; national goals could be reassessed. The judgement of Weimar leaders, as Jonathan Wright argues, might have been different 'if . . . they had been negotiating on matters which involved the risk of war and peace such as the *Anschluss* and the Polish Corridor'.[24]

9

Economics, armaments, decision-making

[T]he old formula, 'We must have an army which corresponds to the needs of our policy', has lost none of its value . . . an army can be organised according to just principles only if the policy which it must see carried out is clearly defined . . . If we leave questions of this magnitude without examining or solving them we shall be led inexorably day by day, under the pressure of budgetary necessities, political influence or international blackmail, to take measures which will gradually drain our forces of their substance.

General Maxime Weygand, inspector general of the army, 16 January 1933, *DDF, 1932–1939*, First Series 1932–5, II, (Paris, 1966), no. 203

His opinion was that the British and French are by their rearmament . . . incurring a serious danger of financial and economic collapse . . . France . . . will find it difficult to continue for more than a year at the present pace.

Report of talk with Charles Spinasse, minister for national economy, 13 April 1937, *FDR and Foreign Affairs*, Second Series, January 1937 to August 1939, vol. 5, ed. Donald B. Schewe (New York, 1975), pp. 53–6

Who, in France, would have imagined in 1930 that in less than 10 years this great democratic nation would become a second-rate power shorn of its influence in central Europe and dependent on a stubborn and demanding ally for its own security?

United States secretary of the treasury Henry Morgenthau, September 1938, in J. M. Blum (ed.), *From the Morgenthau Diaries*, I (Boston, 1959), p. 525

Slump

F rom late 1929 an economic blizzard struck the world economy, causing stock markets to collapse, driving currencies off the gold standard, creating mass unemployment and pushing down agricultural prices. Capitalism seemed on its last legs; hunger marchers converged on Washington; bankrupt businessmen committed suicide; millions of Germans lived on potatoes. Economic nationalism manifested itself in protectionism and beggar-my-neighbour policies derailed the international economy, scuppering hopes of international cooperation. Until the last months of 1931 France escaped the storm. In 1931 sociologist André Siegfried published *England's Crisis* – Britain, not France, was on the rocks. By the end of the year, however, industrial production in France fell by 17 per cent; unemployment jumped from negligible levels to 260,000 in 1932 and 426,000 in 1935. Good harvests in 1932 and 1933 flattened agricultural prices, reducing peasant purchasing power for industrial goods.

The depression enfeebled France and contributed to the collapse of 1940. This was because it hit France later than other countries and lasted longer (see Table 3). The delayed onset deluded both rulers and ruled into thinking

Table 3 Recovery from the Great Depression

	Real national income 1937–8 as % of:		Real income per head 1937–8 as % of:		Manufacturing output 1937–8 as % of:	
	1928–9	1913	1928–9	1913	1928–9	1913
United Kingdom	119	135	114	120	131	139
Germany	119	129	113	114	122	144
France	88	110	88	110	86	119
Sweden	135	188	131	169	161	231
United States	98	163[a]	92	123[a]	96	164[a]

[a]The denominator is 1909–18, rather than 1913
Source: David Landes, *The Unbound Prometheus* (1966), p. 394

the economy was fundamentally sound and would weather the storm without major surgery. The country seemed to be passing through temporary turbulence created by the unsound fiscal policies of competitors and needed only to stay on course. Staying on course meant preserving gold reserves and the value of the franc as stabilized by Poincaré in 1928. A modest upturn in industrial production in mid-1932, coinciding with the creation of a gold bloc, reassured ministers that all was basically sound. As the economy wound down in 1933 governments applied the orthodox medicine of deflation, retrenchment and balanced budgets. A successful foreign policy depends on a healthy economy. The depression, by persisting almost to the end of the decade, flawed foreign and defence policies. While the British, German and American economies convalesced in the mid-1930s, France stayed in the doldrums. Between 1929 and 1938 industrial production increased by 20 per cent in Britain and 16 per cent in Germany while in France it fell by 24 per cent. Not until the winter of 1938–39 did the economy show signs of recovery. The slump's timing and duration had three consequences: it widened the gap between French and German industrial strength, accentuating France's sense of inferiority and pessimism; second, it intensified domestic strife; third, the burden of rearmament on an ailing economy undermined social and political cohesion. The speed of German recovery unnerved the French. In 1933 France produced one kilo of steel for one German kilo, by 1938 Germany produced three kilos for one French kilo.

Rearmament fuelled internal conflict. Accelerated defence spending from 1935 consumed the state's social and economic budget, weakening social cohesion. The Republic's lethargic response to social reform in the 1920s left large holes in the social security net. The Popular Front introduced paid holidays and a forty-hour week but not old-age pensions and unemployment insurance. Family allowances were paid by employers and varied from department to department. They were not extended and improved until Daladier's Family Code of July 1939. In June 1939 parliament was told that there was no money for the provision of old-age pensions which deputies had voted for three months earlier.

Society was riven by the depression. The propertied lived in dread of a general social collapse. The conjuncture of internal crisis and external peril sharply polarized politics. The ideological battle between left and right spilled on to the streets. The upheaval prevented national unity when it was most needed. Foreign policy, an integrating force before 1914, became a source of division. The inability of governments to cure economic ills bred anger and disillusionment which exploded in the anti-parliamentary riots of 6 February 1934. For conservatives the electoral victory of the left-wing Popular Front in May 1936 heralded revolution. 'Evening with the Countess Murat', recorded one diarist, 'where all the guests talked of the imminence of revolution.'[1]

Why did the depression last so long and bite so deep? Unlike German chancellor Adolf Hitler and American president Franklin Roosevelt who were prepared to break with economic orthodoxy, French policy-makers clung to the gold standard and a balanced budget. There were few heretics. It was well into 1934 before conservative politician Paul Reynaud began to advocate devaluation. Finance minister Pierre-Etienne Flandin 'laughed out of court the idea of any currency being based on anything but gold'.[2] Britain's devaluation of September 1931 was followed by a host of countries, with devastating effect. It left the franc overvalued and French exports uncompetitive. Devaluation of the US dollar in 1933 disadvantaged the franc still more. Nevertheless, from 1931 to September 1936 politicians of all persuasions fought to stay on gold. Premier Pierre Laval's deflationary decrees of July 1935 enforced 10 per cent salary and expenditure cuts. Even before the slump the fixation with fiscal policy had obscured the problems of the economy as a whole. In 1929, for instance, parliament rejected André Tardieu's 'national retooling' proposal for investing budgetary surpluses in better transport and infrastructure. Surpluses had to go into reducing the national debt. The weak franc and long inflation of the 1920s had created a mindset resistant to further devaluation. Depression and deflation appeared lesser evils than devaluation and inflation.

Other considerations determined responses to the slump: the doctrine of a balanced economy, neglect of economic data, the casualness of decision-makers. Writers sang the praises of the balanced economy in which resources were almost evenly divided between town and country. The state tried to perpetuate the world of the small independent peasant farmer. The peasant represented the true stock and heritage of France. 'The land', in Marshal Pétain's words, did not 'lie'.[3] Protectionism and under-industrialization, while warding off mass unemployment on the scale of Britain and Germany, also lengthened the crisis by preserving inefficiency and stagnation. Modernization of urban industry was patchy and uneven. Charles Spinasse, Popular Front minister of national production, spoke of 'industries organised and equipped as they were in the middle ages'.[4] The average life of machine tools at the end of World War II was said to be six to seven years in the United States, seven to nine in Britain and twenty-five in France.

The neglect of economics reflected the political elite's classical and literary formation. In the universities the law faculties controlled the teaching of economics which was of a low standard. Ignorance of economic indicators critically affected Blum's 1936 Popular Front. The 25 per cent devaluation of the franc in September 1936 boosted the economy but the premier did not know of the upswing because production and unemployment indices were not consulted. In November 1938, when revisions to the Popular Front's forty-hour-week law were proposed, the labour minister said no changes were needed because no one was working the full forty hours. In fact 81 per cent were working forty hours – the figures were available in the ministry's own factory inspectorate reports.

Politicians tended to be dismissive of economics and economists. In 1932 premier Edouard Daladier, asked if he would devalue, replied: 'My advisors are firm. Some tell me: 'Above all no inflation or you are lost', the others: 'Above all no deflation or you are finished'. There you have it. If you know two economists who are in agreement send them to me.'[5] Much more harmful was the mix of inertia and improvisation that characterized decision-making. On 5 October 1938 parliament empowered government to tackle financial and economic problems. Nothing happened. On 17 October a leading treasury official warned the finance minister that if no action was taken the state of public finances would lead to disaster. He got a kick in the pants for exceeding his duties. On 3 November the new finance minister Paul

Reynaud instructed an astonished advisor: 'I need for 10 November at the latest decree laws which will transform the economy of the country.'[6]

Deflation as well as delaying rearmament inflicted severe cuts on existing modernization programmes – a 22 per cent cutback in spending in 1932–34.[7] Even when rearmament started in 1934, it was a far cry from the total modernization that might have transformed France's performance. It took the form of selective doses of limited spending – air force (1934–35), army (1936–37), air force (1938–40). When Hitler attacked in the west in May 1940 France was well equipped both quantitatively and qualitatively but the effort came too late and at too great a cost politically. Robert Frankenstein argues persuasively that the financial strain of armaments sapped the nation's cohesion and resistance in the phoney war of 1939–40.[8]

Two notions – the doctrine of the balanced budget and the assumption that another war would be a long one – made it axiomatic that financial and economic strength should be conserved, not squandered on massive armaments. Large spending on arms was seen as the short road to ruin because it would prevent economic recovery. Popular Front finance minister Vincent Auriol feared that even the modest level of rearmament begun in 1936 would prove 'unbearable'.[9] The perceived lessons of 1914–18 were added reason for caution. It was believed that the pre-World War I armaments race had been a prime cause of war. No one wanted to recreate the alliance blocs and international anarchy of 1914.

According to orthodox opinion, a stable franc and gold reserves constituted a second Maginot Line sheltering the economy until prosperity returned. Falling tax receipts and the emphasis on balancing the books meant that rearmament could only be financed by modest borrowing. Consequently, rearmament had to be phased since a general all-out effort was deemed unaffordable. This selective approach left critical gaps in defences, creating dependence on British sea power and on the United States for aircraft production in 1939–40. Weakness in air power during the Munich crisis of 1938 supplied a powerful argument for appeasement.

Financing rearmament

Borrowing to pay for rearmament shackled governments to the money markets and Anglo-Saxon allies. The connection had decisive effects. France, at a critical moment in the struggle to stay a great power, was in hock to Britain and the United States. Paris got an American loan of $33 million in May 1935 and short-term loans from Britain in 1936–37. London and Washington facilitated the devaluation of September 1936 in the Tripartite

Table 4 Military expenditure in France, Germany and Great Britain, 1930–1939, as a percentage of GNP and national income (in thousand millions of local currency)

Year	France Nat. Inc.	Mil. Exp.	Francs %	Germany GNP	Mil. Exp.	RM %	Gt. Britain Nat. Inc.	Mil. Exp.	£ %
1930–1	332	15.1	4.3	–	–	–	–	–	–
1931–2	312	12.9	4.1	58	0.8	1	–	0.1	–
1933	259	11.7	4.5	59	1.9	3	3.7	0.1	3
1934	237	10.2	4.3	67	4.1	6	3.9	0.1	3
1935	221	10.4	4.7	74	6.0	8	4.1	0.1	2
1936	239	14.4	6	83	10.8	13	4.4	0.2	5
1937	304	20.8	6.8	93	11.7	13	4.6	0.3	7
1938	347	28.4	8.2	105	17.2	17	4.8	0.4	8
1939	407	92.7	22.8	130	30	23	5	1.1	22

Source: A. Adamthwaite, *France and the coming of the Second World War* (1977), p. 164

Stabilization Agreement aligning the franc with the US dollar and sterling. The franc received Anglo-American support in the money markets. Unfortunately, the 1936 devaluation was too little, too late. A stagnant economy and continuing gold exodus forced two further devaluations in 1938. The sliding franc discredited the country. Lending money to France was 'just like throwing money into the Atlantic', declared US treasury secretary Henry Morgenthau, 'someone had ... to tell the French they were a bankrupt fourth-class power.'[10] By May 1938 the franc was fettered to the pound sterling.

Dependence on the markets made the Popular Front cabinets of 1936–38 prisoners of capital-holders. Blum, by proclaiming confidence in capital and playing according to the rules, allowed the wealthy to call the tune. The casualty was the Front's social programme. The 'pause' of February 1937 cut social expenditure and left armaments intact. Blum, who was fearful of antagonizing the wealthy and Anglo-Saxon allies, rejected exchange controls to stop the export of gold. Appeasing lenders undercut the socialist premier's popular base. Supporters were disillusioned by a left-wing government that spent more on guns than butter (see Table 4) and whose much-vaunted public works programme was a sham. In May 1937 the Senate safely unseated Blum without provoking a popular protest. Paradoxically, rearmament weakened rather than strengthened the country. It fashioned a double dependence – on allies and on capital-holders. Reliance on Britain was economic, financial and military. Vital raw materials like coal (30 per cent), copper, oil and rubber came from Britain and her empire, carried in British bottoms.

The defeat of 1940 provoked a search for scapegoats. The right blamed the Popular Front, calling it an alliance of Jews, freemasons and pacifists. The left indicted the 'wall of money' and a fascist fifth column. The surrealist poet and communist Paul Elouard pictured the proletariat banging its head against 'the wall of money'. A financial and industrial oligarchy, composed of the 200 principal shareholders of the Bank of France, allegedly plotted the downfall of the Popular Front and subverted the Republic.

Was there a moneyed mafia bent on savaging the left? Conspiracy theories are inherently suspect because they lump together and grossly oversimplify complex and often disparate phenomena. Evidence too is a problem. Not enough is known about the interaction of political, industrial and financial elites. However, it is clear that the so-called 'bastille of 200 families' did not exist as a continuous organized force. connections between big business, banks, the press and politicians certainly existed but they were not close enough to constitute a coherent and homogeneous pressure group against the left. There was no conspiracy of the rich, no treason of the propertied. A plurality of decision-making centres functioned separately, frequently at sixes and sevens – treasury, Bank of France, government, influential politicians, industrialists. In 1925–26 industrialist Francis de Wendel, regent of the Bank of France and president of the iron and steel association (*comité des forges*) undermined Herriot's Cartel, but his action was only one of several causes of the Cartel's collapse. And Wendel's success, as he recognized, was counter-productive because it excited powerful suspicions and jealousies. Wendel's greatest triumph lay in facilitating Poincaré's return to power in July 1926. However, in the currency debates of 1926–28 between stabilizers and revaluers, it was Poincaré who decided on stabilization against Wendel who favoured revaluation. In 1936 the Popular Front reformed the Bank of France, curtailing its influence. Nevertheless, Robert Frankenstein argues that the wall of money operated through 'strikes' by capital holders. By selling francs and exporting gold they attacked the currency and created a financial crisis which toppled the left. But the record is inconclusive. How does one distinguish between a legitimate desire for profit and a political campaign to bring down the Popular Front? On balance, the 'wall of money', like the Bastille of 1789, was more symbol than reality.

Empire

France's colonial empire of sixty million was the second largest in the world. Could it have compensated for the demographic and economic inferiority of metropolitan France? After World War I ambitious colonial development plans were floated; on the eve of World War II politicians projected the empire as a great arsenal of men and resources. Post-1918 enthusiasm was short-lived but the empire attracted investment – between 1914 and 1940 its share of the total overseas portfolio jumped from 9 per cent to 45 per cent. Colonial imports increased by 30 per cent in the years 1929–38. After 1925 colonial history became compulsory in the school curriculum with textbooks depicting France as 'heir to Rome'. André Gide, Paul Morand, Roland Dorgelès and Georges Simenon reported on Africa and Asia. The popular press published colonial features. The 1931 Colonial Exhibition in Paris drew seven million visitors. The 1921 Sarraut Plan was revived in a bid to integrate the colonies in the French economy. However, traditional indifference quickly reasserted itself. Plans to keep the exhibition open into 1932 were shelved. Le parti colonial, the parliamentary colonial pressure group, ceased to exist after the 1932 elections.

The razzle-dazzle of the Colonial Exhibition concealed, as one leading colonial specialist put it, 'the crisis of colonisation'.[11] This was less a moral crisis – although self-questionings about colonialism existed – than a realization that colonialism probably had no future. The European civil war of 1914–18 had compromised Europe's prestige – 'the renaissance of Asia confronts the decline of the West'. Mingled with pride in national grandeur was a recessional mood. 'The time of colonial Africa is running out', prophesied Georges Simenon in a 1932 reportage: 'Tomorrow the black who has today bought a fuschia-coloured suit at a French department store will be dressed in impeccable black and take his seat at international meetings, dignified and unbending.'[12] Simenon cited an old-time colonialist who had gone native: 'Believe me, the Africans' answer to us whites is merde and right they are.' Rebellions in Syria (1925, 1936), in Morocco (1925–26), and in Indo-China (1930) challenged French rule. In Morocco control was not fully regained until 1934. Celebrations of the first centenary of Algerian colonization in 1930 drew the comment from Algerians: 'They [the French] will not celebrate a second.'[13] By the mid-1930s popular unrest showed itself in most of French North Africa. 'Generally French prestige has weakened', concluded an official report, 'No need to stress the dangers of this situation in the event of a European conflagration.'[14] Photographs of Hitler, together with flyers praising his anti-Semitism, circulated in Morocco.

Disaffection was partly of France's own making. The Republic's civilizing mission displayed little civility towards the ruled. Promises of political reform were not honoured and a repressive colonial regime forfeited the loyalty which Africans and Asians had demonstrated during the war. In Indo-China 700 summary executions took place in the suppression of the 1930 Tonkin rising; by 1932, 10,000 Vietnamese nationalists were under arrest. Thousands of France's black African subjects fled into British territory to escape taxes and forced labour. Gide in Le Voyage au Congo (1927) condemned conditions: 'the companies are ruining the colony. The natives die or desert in great numbers.'[15]

As Germany revived, the empire became first a bargaining counter then a rallying point for wounded pride. In the early 1930s leading politicians condemned the confiscation of German colonies. Euroafrica, a plan for mobilizing European energies in Africa, was mooted. Colonial condominium schemes in Africa were the staple of Franco-German discussions in 1936–37. By the autumn of 1938, however, the surrenders in central Europe had refocused attention on the empire. At the Radical Party congress in October 1938 premier Daladier spoke of 'a vast zone of strength outside Europe', which France would defend 'as she will defend her home territory'.[16] Opinion hardened rapidly against colonial appeasement. In October 1938 59 per cent of those polled favoured appeasing Hitler with colonies; by December, 70 per cent said no. On the outbreak of World War II government propaganda exploited the imperial myth: '110 million strong, France can stand up to Germany.' 'If necessary our empire will be able to raise 2 million soldiers and half a million workers', boasted colonial minister Georges Mandel.[17] In the event, France's small merchant marine, mostly concentrated in Europe, could ferry only a small number of the 70,000 Vietnamese work troops promised by Mandel. By January 1940 Japan had sucked Indo-China into its economic orbit, taking a third of its ore.

Could the empire have recharged France? Maybe. It is too easy to write off France's interwar imperial myth as a mirage. The 1921 Sarraut Plan and the trans-Saharan railway, while vastly overambitious, were not in principle flawed. A long-range development plan was needed, but it had to be part of an integrated strategy linking foreign and defence policies. This was never attempted. No one listened to strategist Admiral Raoul Castex who in 1931 advocated abandoning an 'indefensible' Indo-China and focusing on the axis Europe–Africa. The fault lay with the perception of empire as an economic quick fix for metropolitan France. The grand design of the early 1920s collapsed because the will and machinery were lacking. Three ministries – foreign affairs, colonies, interior – shared responsibility for the empire without an overall czar. The French would not dig into their pockets to pay for colonial improvement and capital exports were not allowed until 1928. The colonial ministry lacked the expertise and resources for long-range planning. In 1922 the request of the higher national defence council (*conseil supérieur de la défense nationale*) for a study of economic mobilization in war elicited the reply that ministry staff were incapable of conducting such an investigation. Faced with competing development strategies, governments were indecisive. In June 1936 Popular Front colonial minister Marious Moutet declared that all colonial peoples were 'on the same level of equality, social justice and brotherhood with the workers and farmers of France'.[18] Some concessions were made in Indo-China but French settlers blocked a bill to enfranchise 20,000 Algerian Muslims. A commission of enquiry into the 'political, economic, and moral situation' of the colonies was so slow in getting started that the Popular Front fell before it reached the Far East.

Table 5   Armies and navies of the great powers in 1913 and 1932

		Germany	United States	France	Great Britain	Italy	Japan	USSR
Peacetime effectives in hundreds of thousands	1913	800	97[b]	786	247	275	274	1,200
	1932	100[a]	126	565	193[c]	275	241[d]	900
Naval strength in thousands of tons	1913	1,000	833	645	2,221	320	530	317
	1932	157	1,078	669	1,139	432	890	184

[a]Limit imposed by Versailles Treaty
[b]Regular army strength: no conscription
[c]Regular army strength (no conscription): plus 170,000 Indian Army
[d]1926 figures. In 1932 because of the war in Manchuria the figure was higher
Source: Girault and Frank, *Terbulente Europe et nouveaux mondes, 1914–1941* (1988)

Defence

The armed forces, like the empire, generated anxiety. Ironically, while Anglo-Saxon critics fulminated against French militarism, strength dwindled. The army that was intended to provide security was itself a source of insecurity. In the 1930s military unpreparedness made leaders overcautious and pessimistic. In the mid-1920s the army phased out offensive planning for a thoroughly defensive strategy dedicated to the defence of national frontiers and empire. The army of 1931 was a *trompe l'oeil* force, 'dislocated, without a coherent strategy, badly equipped'.[19] In effect, it was little more than a training machine for conscripts, requiring a ten- to twelve-day general mobilization to bring it up to war combat strength. The slump, political instability and the growth of pacifism all contributed to this weakness. Between 1931 and 1935 the defence budget fell by 32 per cent. Cutbacks were across the board – equipment, training, personnel, modernization. For hard-pressed ministers struggling to make ends meet national defence meant defence of the franc. 'I am convinced,' wrote socialist deputy and disarmament supporter Pierre Viénot, 'that the state of our finances will make us wise. Even moderate circles think that a reduction of military expenses is indispensable.'[20]

What was France's military profile in the early 1930s? The active army of twenty-five divisions, about 565,000 strong (see Table 5), was heavily dependent on the horse and wedded to a defensive strategy. It lacked a rapid reaction force. Real strength was nearer sixteen divisions since the Maginot

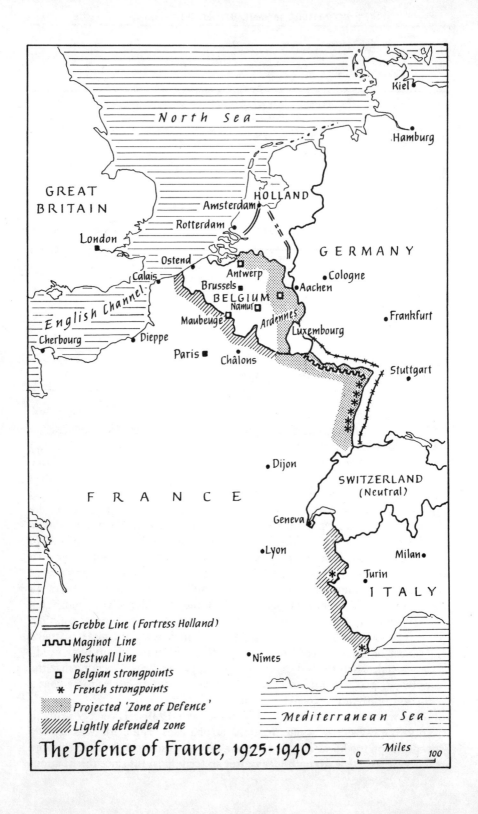

Kiel

Hamburg

North Sea

GREAT
BRITAIN

HOLLAND

Amsterdam

Rotterdam

GERMANY

London

Ostend

Cologne

Calais

Antwerp

Aachen

Brussels

BELGIUM

English Channel

Namur

Ardennes

Frankfurt

Cherbourg

Dieppe

Maubeuge

Luxembourg

Paris

Châlons

Stuttgart

Dijon

SWITZERLAND
(Neutral)

F R A N C E

Geneva

Lyon

Milan

Turin

I T A L Y

Nîmes

Grebbe Line (Fortress Holland)

Maginot Line

Westwall Line

Belgian strongpoints

French strongpoints

Projected 'Zone of Defence'

Lightly defended zone

Mediterranean Sea

The Defence of France, 1925-1940

Miles

0   100

Line absorbed nine or ten divisions. The active army served as a backbone for a citizen army of reservists in the event of war. Modernization was slow and uneven. There were no armoured units. Even in the late 1930s manoeuvres were hindered by lack of modern weapons and equipment. Financial cutbacks and disarmament talks halted naval building in 1933. The navy which had counted on holding its own against Germany and Italy was handicapped by the Anglo-German Naval Agreement of June 1935 allowing Germany to build up to 35 per cent of British tonnage. By 1936 the navy, while still in fourth place after the United States, Britain and Japan, barely kept ahead of Italy. In 1930 ministers were told that the state of the air force, especially fighter defences, was 'incontestably very serious'.[21] There were no reserves and if war came there would be 'a delay of four months' before aircraft losses could be replaced. The first phase of air rearmament started in 1934 but various constraints limited its effectiveness: financial stringency, differences over the role of air power, disarmament talks and insufficient industrial capacity. While the generals relegated the air force to a tactical supporting role, air chiefs argued for an independent strategic mission overriding army cooperation. Responding to disarmament preoccupations, the French adopted a multipurpose aircraft designed for bombing, combat and reconnaissance. This was the worst of compromises since specialist aircraft outclassed it in different roles.

France's deteriorating international position after 1933 evoked not reassessment but a deepening of the defensive mentality. Extension of conscription to two years in March 1935 in response to Hitler's reintroduction of military service gave little relief since 1935–40 were the lean years when the number of conscripts would fall because of the low World War I birthrate. Not that new ideas were in short supply. Captain Charles de Gaulle in *Vers l'armée de métier* (1934) advocated a professional force of 100,000 organized in seven armoured divisions. It would be a spearhead for the main army, strong enough to act as an independent striking force in limited operations. Another strategist, Admiral Castex, proposed a strategy of total defence. The Maginot Line would be extended to the sea, creating a Franco-British fortress. Castex adopted de Gaulle's armoured divisions but in a defensive mode. Both men were blackballed by the political and military establishment.

Institutional inertia, received ideas and personality influences stifled innovation. 'No one could change anything in our army', admitted the deputy chief of the general staff, 'but it is because of this very fact that we have survived at all.'[22] Years of exhausting struggle against internal foes – parliament, the treasury, the government – bred a fortress-like outlook. Pacifist sentiment and the expectations focused on the Geneva Disarmament Conference of 1932–34 made the military virtues seem outdated. As a result, military chiefs felt vulnerable and disinclined to take risks. The fault lay not in the adoption of a defensive strategy – no other course was practicable in the Locarno era – but in the failure to review and redefine strategy and tactics in the light of changing technology and international perils. The lessons of the First World War were codified in an official manual, the *Instruction on the Tactical Use of Major Units*, which as late as 1936 insisted that despite post-1918 technical advances the guiding concepts of 1918 remained valid. There was a lack of curiosity about new military thinking. The shapers of military doctrine ignored the prophets of modern warfare – General Jean-Baptiste Estienne in France, Captain Basil Liddell Hart in Britain. Translations of General Guderian's *Achtung Panzer* sent to garrison libraries remained unread. Construction of the Maginot Line discouraged fresh ideas by making them appear foolhardy and unnecessary. 'How can anyone believe', asked war minister General Maurin, 'that we can still think of the offensive when we have spent millions to establish a fortified barrier? Would we be foolish enough to go in front of this barrier chasing all kinds of adventure?'[23]

De Gaulle's professional army project endangered the orthodoxy of the nation-in-arms. True republicanism, it was held, rested on a citizen army in the *levée-en-masse* tradition of the French Revolution. Elite long-service professionals, it was feared, might become shock troops for a far-right *putsch*. In Blum's words, 'In order to save national independence, you expose the nation to the loss of its natural liberty.'[24] De Gaulle's presentation of his case supplied ammunition for critics. He argued that the 'economic, political and moral crisis' made a 'specialist corps' necessary for the preservation of 'internal order'.[25] The high command rejected Admiral Castex's total defence strategy because extending fortifications to the sea, as well as being expensive, would drive Belgium into full neutrality and demoralize eastern allies. French war plans provided for an advance into Belgium. After Belgium's return to full neutrality in October 1936 the high command continued to hope that the coming of war would frighten the Belgians into cooperating with France.

Three leaders moulded interwar defence policy: Marshal Philippe Pétain, General Maxime Weygand and General Maurice Gamelin. In 1929 George Orwell watched Foch's funeral procession. Pétain's appearance left a lasting impression. 'As he stalked past – a tall, lean, very erect figure, though he must have been seventy years old, with great sweeping white moustaches like the wings of a gull – a whisper of "Voilà Pétain" went rippling through the vast crowd.'[26] Pétain was the most illustrious Frenchman from the retirement of Clemenceau in 1920 to the advent of de Gaulle in 1944. Born in 1856 of a peasant family in the Pas de Calais, by 1914 he was a fifty-eight-year-old colonel nudging retirement. At the Ecole de Guerre his heterodox emphasis on the defensive was unfashionable. The war gave him his chance. Already in 1915 he saw clearly that it was 'a war of attrition. There is no longer a decisive battle as in the past.'[27] The defence of Verdun in 1916 made him a national hero; from 1917 he was commander in chief.

Pessimism, mistrust of the British, contempt for politicians and confidence in his own judgement distinguished his outlook. From 1918 to 1944 he was in turn vice-president of the supreme war council and inspector general of the army (1920–30), war minister (1934), ambassador to Spain (1939–40) and head of the Vichy state (1940–44). Tried for treason in 1945 he was sentenced to life imprisonment on the Ile d'Yeu off the Vendée coast and died there in 1951. His icicle-like exterior was deceptive. Among friends he unbuttoned and relished a good joke. Military life was not his only passion. He had a string of affairs, claiming to have made love at eighty-six.

Weygand was Foch's chief disciple. Reputedly the natural son of the Habsburg Emperor Maximilian of Mexico, he became Foch's chief of staff in 1914. Unlike Foch, however, who lived only for his job, Weygand's contributions to the arts and literature won him election to the French Academy. In 1920 during the Russian-Polish war the government sent him to advise the Poles. The right wrongly credited him with vanquishing the Bolsheviks. In fact this was the achievement of Polish leader General Pilsudski. Ever since the neo-Bonapartism of General Boulanger in 1889 and the Dreyfus affair of 1894 politicians and generals had been deeply suspicious of each other. Many on the left regarded the army as a nest of anti-republicans and clericalists. Weygand's record as high commissioner for Syria and commander in chief in the Levant alarmed the centre and left who believed him 'up to his neck in priests'.[28] When Marshal Lyautey suggested him as his successor in Morocco, premier Painlevé objected: 'If he does down there what he did in Syria we will no longer be able to control him.'[29] Before appointment as chief of the general staff in 1930 he had to reassure parliament of his loyalty to the Republic. The following year he succeeded Pétain as vice-president of the supreme war council. Recalled from retirement by premier Paul Reynaud in May 1940, the septuagenarian quickly concluded that an armistice was unavoidable. After service as Pétain's war minister he was imprisoned by the Germans at Schloss Iter in Austria with politicians like Daladier and ex-president Lebrun whom he detested. Following the Liberation in 1944 the High Court exonerated him from treason charges. He refused to fade away – opposing the European Defence Community in 1952, censuring the Fourth Republic, campaigning to keep Algeria French, demanding the reburial of Pétain's remains at Verdun. In 1930–35 Weygand crossed swords with ministers over disarmament and effectives. His conservative sympathies and abrasive manner embittered civil–military relations, arousing fears of Boulangism. Short on tact, Weygand talked back at the politicians, quarrelling with war minister Daladier and openly ridiculing his successor Paul-Boncour.

Historians have not been kind to Gamelin, chief of the army general staff (1931–40), allied commander in chief (1940). 'A nice old man, not remotely equal to his enormous job', commented a British officer in 1939.[30] Weygand succeeded him as allied commander in chief after the German breakthrough in the west in mid-May 1940. Why, then, did Gamelin preside over the army's fortunes for nearly a decade? Firstly, he had talent, ending World War I in command of a division. In 1925 he was promoted to general over many more senior rivals. Political patronage helped him on the ladder. Socialist Albert Thomas recommended him to war minister Painlevé as 'an open character, a sympathetic man ... he should definitely be kept in the army.'[31] Gamelin's self-effacing personality and modesty of ambition made him an ideal peacemaker at a time when army morale was low. The unease felt by army leaders at the Republic's convulsions sapped civil–military confidence. Weygand's impulsive, intransigent conservatism stretched relations almost to breaking point. 'Weygand is a wall, Gamelin an eiderdown', opined Daladier.[32] The phlegmatic, loyal republican could be relied upon to keep the army out of politics. As a mark of confidence he was allowed to combine the two highest posts – vice-president of the supreme war council and chief of army staff, an honour denied Weygand. Gamelin, as Martin Alexander persuasively argues, was essentially a manager, not a warrior.[33] As such he deserves credit both for mending fences with the republican political elite and for France's well-stocked armaments in 1940. But Gamelin's adroit management was too successful. It stifled innovative and original insights. The general trapped himself 'in a system in which submission no longer allowed for saving initiatives. The philosopher took precedence over the man of action.'[34]

How accurate was the evaluation of the German menace? French military intelligence reported on the evolution of Germany's strategic and tactical doctrine, especially the revolutionary role of tanks and aircraft, but it shared the defensive assumptions of the general staff. For example, a 1938 study on the use of tanks and air power in the Spanish Civil War concluded: 'In general terms we are finding nothing which would cause us to renounce the basic ideas which we have held up to now.'[35] In early 1939 a report suggested that in the light of Spain German officers were wondering whether tanks were really worth their cost.

Fear impelled French leaders to exaggerate German army strength. In April 1935 Gamelin spoke of a German army of thirty-two divisions, perhaps doubling by the end of the year, reinforced by fifty divisions of frontier troops. The objective was a force of 120 divisions, against which France's metropolitan army mustered only thirty-one divisions. Gamelin took it for granted that in a long war – the only kind he envisaged – Germany had the advantage. But military intelligence (*Deuxième Bureau*) estimates were different. In March 1936, on the eve of the Rhineland reoccupation, intelligence put German strength at twenty-nine divisions (a figure confirmed by German studies). This force, it was stressed, had a crippling weakness in the severe shortage of trained officers. Accordingly, the *Deuxième Bureau* discounted the huge paramilitary formations in Germany because they could not be effectively mobilized without officers.

Diplomacy

Navigating a safe passage through international storms required an efficient foreign ministry. The close of the 1920s brought renewed calls for modernization; a 1933 parliamentary enquiry indicted the ministry on several counts: inadequate publicity and propaganda, insufficient consultation between the central administration and overseas representatives, absence of established procedures – many conversations went unrecorded. Some improvements came in 1934 but the final tally was negative. The diplomats failed to avert a war which the nation did not want and for which it was unprepared.

Criticisms of the ministry had force. 'Our ministry is an old machine, slow and cumbersome', admitted junior minister Pierre Cot in 1933.[36] The untidiness of the news department shocked one visitor: 'The room was at the back of the building. To reach it I had to pass through a dark passage and wade through stacks of old newspapers as well as dust and dirt.'[37] A small, overworked cipher section enciphered and deciphered by hand. This had serious consequences for diplomacy. The London embassy, France's most important mission, had only one cipher clerk who was frequently overwhelmed by a rush of cables. The embassy had no direct radio contact with Paris. British post office telegraphists brought and took away printed forms to which the embassy attached cipher messages. 'This procedure', recalled one official, 'caused numerous mistakes and despite all the keys we had certain messages were indecipherable.'[38] Negotiations for a Franco-Turkish alliance in 1939–40 were impeded by the delay with which instructions reached the ambassador in Ankara. There were free riders. Staff in the small American section whiled away the day gossiping, intriguing for promotion, going to book sales. Ministers did not systematically keep and circulate records of talks with foreign envoys and statesmen. While Louis Barthou (1933–34) and Yvon Delbos (1936–38) regularly circulated papers, Pierre Laval (1934–36) wrote little and sometimes mislaid files at home. Georges Bonnet (1938–39) would withhold notes of talks for several days and these sometimes conflicted with the versions given by his interlocutors. Nor were incoming papers consistently minuted – occasionally an official might annotate a telegram or a despatch, but it was not standard practice. Although senior advisors did not screen ministers from agents in the field, they showed scant regard for the morale of overseas colleagues. In the thick of the Italo-Abyssinian war of 1935–36 France's man in Addis Ababa complained: 'I've been working flat out for ten months and I've not yet received from the department either a word of appreciation or the slightest gesture of encouragement.'[39] Teamwork was the exception – only rarely did ministers, envoys and advisors meet to debate general or regional issues.

Most officials appear to have worked hard. Membership of an elite does not seem to have unduly coloured judgements; reporting was not noticeably reactionary or partisan. The tradition of state service overrode class and ideological prejudice. The diplomats, unlike the military, were free from far-right infiltration. In 1939 they strove conscientiously for a Soviet alliance. More's the pity, then, that organizational deficiencies prevented better use of talents and energies. Shortcomings had two main causes: the decline of the professional diplomat and the reluctance of the politicians to impose root and branch reform. Post-1918 trends – international conferences, personal diplomacy of heads of government and foreign ministers, the rise of economic, financial and military experts – undermined career professionals. The experts had the edge over career officials with a generalist training. Increasing use of the telephone kept envoys on a tight leash, with instructions liable to be revised or rescinded up to the last minute. Military and financial attachés communicating directly with their own ministries made coordination both within embassies and with Paris more difficult. Diplomats played only a peripheral role in negotiations for the Tripartite Monetary Agreement of 1936. Aware of declining influence and apprehensive for their jobs, the mandarins were too cautious to press for restructuring and the necessary credits to pay for it. Ministers who could expect no more than a few months in office had neither the time nor the incentive to take bold measures. It was easier to short-circuit the system than initiate reforms which risked political infighting. The rapid succession of international crises in the 1930s kept a run-down system in a permanent state of shock. Only survival mattered.

Morale suffered accordingly. The Quai's inability to defend the status quo in the early 1930s depressed officials. 'The almost tragic battle which our diplomacy wages today', acknowledged a disarmament expert in December 1933, 'is on the verge of being lost'. Accelerated appeasement of Germany, initiated by the Daladier government of 1938, sowed distrust and unease. A leading member of the London embassy was quite sickened by the terms of the Franco-British plan for the cession of the Sudetenland to Germany. After Munich political director René Massigli and news department chief Pierre Comert were purged – Massigli despatched to Turkey, Comert shunted to the American department. But no one resigned, bureaucratic loyalty to the state came first. A cluster of top functionaries talked of opposing foreign minister Bonnet. Unfortunately, secretary-general Léger (1933–40) was the very model of a self-effacing mandarin – hardly the person to restore morale and attempt reform. He had a lot in common with the Leader of his poem, *Anabase*, who in the midst of all the parleyings with ambassadors and princes, is continually distracted by the contemplation of his own soul. At the time critics targeted him as a grey eminence, manipulating ministers for the sake of an outmoded Briandism. Léger was certainly a faithful Briandiste but no grey eminence. He lacked Berthelot's appetite for work. More to the point, he was not a fighter and shunned confrontation. His watchword was 'never react violently against a person so as not to be dependent on him'. British foreign secretary Anthony Eden believed he lacked 'the strength of character ... to impose his judgements on men like Laval and Flandin'. In the Czech crisis he adopted an ambivalent stance, leaning on the Czechs to accept the Franco-British cession plan but speaking so firmly at the Munich Conference that Daladier had to ask him to be more conciliatory. The Rhineland *coup* overturned what he called 'the great rules of French diplomacy' and he had nothing to put in their place. By 1938–39 he succumbed to a fatalistic pessimism.[40]

Coordination

E ffective responses to German and Italian expansionism demanded a fast and flexible policy-making machine capable of maximizing resources and articulating choices. The critical weakness of French policy in the approach to World War II was that defence and diplomacy were out of sync. The defensive doctrine embodied in the Maginot Line ran counter to the rationale of alliances. To be sure, the Polish pact of 1921 was the only full military alliance but all the pacts assumed France was a great power determined to protect its interests. But what were those interests? In January 1933 Weygand called for a fundamental policy review in order to give France an army tailored to national goals. No review took place and nothing was done to integrate foreign and defence policies.

The cabinet was too unwieldy and slow-moving to have a significant say in foreign policy-making. In 1933–34 foreign minister Paul-Boncour spent weeks trying to secure an urgent decision on French Morocco. Informal consultation was the norm; senior ministers went into a huddle. In 1936 Blum held special meetings of senior colleagues on foreign and defence issues. No records have survived. Similarly, in 1938 Daladier formed an inner cabinet to meet daily. Again, no records. In the Munich crisis of 1938, the most important international threat since 1918, the cabinet was not at the centre of decision-making. The decision to tell the Czechs that they must accept the cession of territory to Germany was taken by premier Daladier and foreign minister Bonnet. The president of the republic was not a coordinator. Albert Lebrun, last president of the Third Republic, was mediocrity itself. He had trained as an engineer. Shortly before his election in 1932 Madame Lebrun, daughter of a director of the Ecole des Mines, is said to have exclaimed nostalgically: 'When I think that if Albert had not gone into politics he could have been an inspector general of mines.'[41]

Some centralized machinery existed but it was not used systematically. Until 1936 the high military committee (*haut comité militaire*) and the supreme war council (*conseil supérieur de la guerre*) handled defence policy.

The council had a membership of Uncle Tom Cobbleigh and all: war minister, chief of army staff, marshals of France, certain generals, plus a maximum of twelve divisional generals. It spoke only for the army; navy and air force had their own supreme councils. The high military committee set up in 1932 to streamline decision-making included premier, service ministers, chiefs of staff, vice-presidents of the supreme councils of the armed forces, and Pétain. In June 1936 Blum replaced it with the permanent national defence committee (*comité permanent de la défense nationale*). The activity of both the high military committee and the permanent national defence committee was curiously spasmodic. Between March 1932 and December 1934 the high committee had eight meetings; from January to September 1935 it met monthly, then fortnightly on an informal basis. Its successor had only thirteen meetings in three years (1936–39). In 1938 it met only twice. No adequate machinery existed for integrating foreign and defence policies. The need for a defence ministry was recognized in the 1920s but its creation in 1932 had more to do with window dressing and costcutting than restructuring. In June 1936 Blum subordinated it to the war ministry. War minister and national defence minister Daladier fought off moves to give the new ministry overlordship for the armed forces. Army chief of staff Gamelin doubled as chief of national defence staff but had no separate defence staff and his authority was confined to the army.

Defective machinery meant that important decisions were reached informally at unprepared and unminuted meetings. Policy was often made not in cabinet and committees but in the Parisian salons, the lobby and at the dinner table. This informality compounded confusion in two ways. First, the desire of senior colleagues in the coalitions that ruled France to be cooperative and conciliatory tended to vitiate the articulation of real choices. In sum, conciliation and compromise fostered ambiguity and indecision. Second, informal discussions, unsupported by prepared papers, promoted a casual, careless style of leadership. On New Year's Day 1935 foreign minister Laval called a conference to finalize arrangements for his Rome meeting with Mussolini. Instead of businesslike discussion, anecdotes and jokes were exchanged. This was no festive exception. A month later Laval and premier Flandin got ready for a London visit. The two discussed travel arrangements. Such was the casualness of permanent committee of national defence deliberations that the secretariat was hard put to compose minutes. Lack of seriousness discredited ministers and destroyed confidence. After a session of the high military committee chaired by Laval in November 1935 Gamelin 'wept' for his country 'which until now ... has found the men it needed'.[42]

Interdepartmental strife and organizational defects help to explain the poor record of French military intelligence. Timely and accurate warning of Germany's intentions would have redressed the strategic balance. The failures make depressing reading: the full implications of German innovations in armour and air power were missed; the opportunity to break

Germany's secret machine code Enigma was not grasped; many French diplomatic codes were compromised; intelligence drew a blank on German-Soviet negotiations in 1939. Organizational restraints were huge. Six independent agencies flourished – army, navy, and air force ran separate services and from 1937 the ministry of colonies had its own intelligence service. In addition, the *sûreté nationale* and Paris prefecture of police supervised home intelligence and counter-intelligence in metropolitan France. No machinery existed for the coordination and centralization of information.

Without proper reflection and organization France drifted helplessly on the tide. Bureaucratic shortcomings retarded military preparedness. In 1938 aircraft were ordered from the United States to make up the shortfall in domestic production. President Roosevelt blamed the French for the slowness of deliveries: 'The delays which have ensued have been due to their ways of doing business.'[43] In September 1939 deficiencies were as serious as ever. Almost no preparations had been made for economic warfare; 'administrative chaos' reigned in the newly created blockade ministry.

Why did the hugger-mugger prevail? Civil–military distrust blocked the appointment of a supreme commander in peacetime. Daladier, who from 1938 combined premiership, war and national defence portfolios, perhaps believed that informal partnership with Gamelin would ensure defence coordination. Unhappily, this did not happen. Weeks went by without contact. Gamelin claimed that the premier was too immersed in administration. After several requests he would eventually be received but no sooner had a conversation started than a secretary announced another visitor. Such was the extent of civil–military distrust that in 1938 a socialist deputy warned British labour leaders to be sceptical of estimates of French military strength because 'if the truth were told, many high officers of the general staff should be immediately court-martialled and shot'. The military reciprocated. At Franco-British staff talks in 1939 'the French made no bones about distrusting their politicians' and 'told them as little as possible'. The lack of trust confirmed the preference for informality, bypassing the machine.

Interservice rivalry was another obstacle. Each service jealously guarded its independence. 'Our leaders', wrote a senior air force officer, 'seem powerless to take new initiatives ... it is discouraging to struggle without result, each time that we try to get a few concessions from the army and navy ... we have the feeling of being kept at a distance.' Interservice liaison was minimal even in a major crisis. In 1938 the army was said to be 'entirely unaware of what they could count on from the air force'. Mutual distrust between high command, war ministry and foreign ministry stymied decision-making. The communication gap can be gauged from the fact that in February 1936 the foreign ministry initiated a formal correspondence to ask what the army intended to do if Germany reoccupied the Rhineland. In 1935 military intelligence complained that although they delivered diplomatic decrypts to the Quai d'Orsay they got nothing back. After the *Anschluss* in March 1938 Léger, secretary general of the Quai, told Gamelin that the ministry had not been kept sufficiently informed of German moves. Thereafter weekly liaison meetings started but were confined to routine exchanges of information.

Distrust of a powerful executive inhibited far-reaching change. The calls of Léon Blum, André Tardieu and others for a fundamental overhaul of government fell on deaf ears. An elite civil service training school, the Ecole nationale d'administration, first mooted after 1848, was not realized until 1945. The executive was too dependent on parliament which tended to favour local rather than national interest. The resulting stalemate promoted confusion, timidity and casualness. Ministerial instability evoked a *Tour de France* syndrome – nose to the ground, seeing only the immediate road ahead. Clinging to office for a few months at a time, leaders were torn by the competing demands of a precarious parliamentary base, day-to-day administration and forward thinking. In October 1936 Charles de Gaulle endeavoured to explain to Blum his project for a professional armoured force. While they talked the telephone rang ten times. 'You see', sighed Blum, 'how hard it is for the head of government to concentrate on the plan you have outlined when he cannot remain five minutes with the same idea.' Understandably, in a fractured society politicians shrank from contentious measures. Streamlining the machine, it was feared, would destroy democracy. In 1938–39 Daladier strengthened the executive by stealth. The consolidation was crisis-driven. By skilfully exploiting international threats the premier secured decree powers. A prime minister's office was developed. The reinforcement, however, was ill-managed and too late to revitalize French policy. And it was too much for some left-wingers. Writer Simone Weil claimed that by September 1939 Daladier's decrees had turned France into a 'mild dictatorship'.

Horrendous as the problems were they were not thereby insoluble. What made them so was the corrosive interplay of the system and the leadership. The inadequacies of the decision-making machine had a self-reinforcing effect which impaired France's ability to define a role. Why did leaders remain mired? First, the whole complex of issues and maladies induced a mood of fatalistic resignation. 'The decadence of public order, parliament and institutions', Barthou believed, was 'so great that ... one cannot act ... the day of reckoning will be fatal ... war inevitable'. Second, the alternatives were unattractive. André Siegfried in *La Crise de l'Europe* (1935) emphasized the danger posed by expectations of higher living standards. The authoritarian model of economic autarchy, five-year plans and military mobilization of the masses would destroy democracy. Model II, Americanization *à la* Babbitt, would enable the authorities to satisfy expectations but at the cost of national and European identities. How to stay an independent power? The options looked bleak. Acquiescence in German and Italian demands portended national humiliation, demoralization, perhaps revolution. Yet resistance meant reorganization and this threatened democracy. As Aldous Huxley warned: 'A democracy which ... effectively prepares for modern scientific war must necessarily cease to be democratic.' War promised at best another pyrrhic victory, at worst annihilation and enslavement. Whatever France did, a loss of power seemed inevitable. This apparent dilemma paralysed political will, creating a gulf between thought and action. Thus in April 1937 foreign minister Delbos criticized advocates of firmness and conciliation as equally mistaken but offered no way forward.

10
Ideology, opinion and foreign policy

Many foreigners have left Paris in a hurry. They believe in an immediate revolution. In spite of the enforced prudence of the press and radio, the news which reaches us from abroad is heartbreaking, for many consider that France is lost ... there is talk of the collapse of the franc and even the taking over of private houses, of the hoarding of money and flight to the provinces and abroad. (A friend), who is very worried, asks me if I think he ought to allow the family to remain in Paris?

    Abbé Desgranges, 11 June 1936 in Geoffrey Warner, *Pierre Laval and the Eclipse of France* (London, 1968), p. 133

Every time I hear a political speech or I read those of our leaders I am horrified at having, for years, heard nothing which sounded human. It is always the same words telling the same lies ... the fact that men accept this, that the people's anger has not destroyed these hollow clowns, strikes one as proof that men attribute no importance to the way they are governed.

    Albert Camus, August 1937, *Carnets, 1935–1947*, trans. and introduced by Philip Thody (London, 1963), pp. 26–7

To understand the attitude of Georges Bonnet [foreign minister] during the crisis [Czech] it must ... be borne in mind that he was resolved not to allow war because war would have meant the disappearance of the privileged class ... a desperate struggle, resorting to all methods ... was organised in certain Parisian circles ... The French press, largely nourished by GB (the secret funds are exhausted) orchestrated each day its different themes.

    Pierre Comert, head of the French foreign ministry news department, letter of 2 October 1938 in Anthony Adamthwaite, *The Making of the Second World War* (London, 1977), p. 195

B y the mid-1930s France's international persona had changed – for the worse. The vindictive, militaristic Marianne of the 1920s had become the sick woman of Europe, crisis-ridden, beset by scandals and flirting with Bolshevism. A great power seemed set to self-destruct. After the debacle of 1940, French exiles presented a picture of betrayal and subversion by a fascist fifth column. The classic statement was André Géraud's (Pertinax) *The Gravediggers of France* (1944). Meanwhile, Vichy and the right pursued their own vendetta against the Third Republic and the Popular Front. A special political court at Riom arraigned Blum, Daladier, Gamelin and others. Did the contemporary image of a diseased regime going downhill fast reflect reality? How influential were fascism and pacifism? Was France already defeated psychologically before the military collapse of 1940? To provide some answers to these questions this chapter looks in turn at the political parties, fascist and pacifist movements, and the media and public opinion.

Political parties

' A h if only there were political parties in France and if these parties had an organisation and a doctrine', lamented Blum.[1] The notion of organized parties was disliked and politics was a byzantine affair, pivoted on personalities and volatile coalitions. The economic and ideological hurricanes brought polarization and further fragmentation. The radical socialists, the traditional governing party, resembled a radish, red on the outside, white inside – essentially a centre right party. It had 'friendships, not definitions', and barely any organization. Radicalism, in Herriot's words, was a 'state of mind'.[2] Such woolliness offered refuge to all moderates who found that recommending 'moderation with extreme vehemence' satisfied their zeal.[3] To a party based on peasant proprietors, small businessmen and shopkeepers, moderation meant skirting social reform and other controversial issues. Radicalism was the chief victim of the polarization of the 1930s. Unable, despite efforts by 'young radicals', to fulfil its centrist role of accommodating right and left, the party was hijacked after 1938 by the right.

The left was in disarray throughout the interwar years, holding power briefly only twice – the Cartel of 1924 and Popular Front of 1936. The left majority parliaments elected in 1924, 1932 and 1936 were captured within two years by the centre and right. Although the socialists, the main left-wing party, had a strong organization and membership, they were deeply divided on doctrine. The party's parliamentary section followed Jean Jaurès in working for unity and reform rather than revolution. The left never fully recovered from the Congress of Tours in December 1920 when a communist majority led by Marcel Cachin and L.-G. Frossard seceded from the socialists and set up a Communist Party adhering to the Comintern. Despite a large initial membership, the communists did not transform the left's electoral fortunes. Internal quarrels and secessions drained away strength – only Moscow's roubles kept the party afloat. From 1934 under the leadership of Marcel Thorez the communists began to reconquer lost ground.

The Tours schism reduced the socialists to a rump of 40–50,000 members, with few resources and no newspaper – L'Humanité having passed to the communists. Shepherded by Léon Blum who helped found Le Populaire, the party recovered. With 132 seats in the 1932 parliament, the socialists were potentially powerful but fratricidal battles dissipated energies. Splinter groups on the extreme left led by Marceau Pivert and Jean Zyromski, including semi-fascist neo-socialists grouped around Marcel Déat and Pierre Renaudel, reflected the deep ideological eddies. The party had a strong pacifist wing – secretary general Paul Faure parted company with Blum in the Munich crisis of 1938. Blum would have fought Germany in order to save France's ally Czechoslovakia. For Faure, however, conciliation had no limits. 'We desire', he announced, 'a pact with the devil if necessary.'[4]

The traditional right lacked a strong conservative party which might have stabilized society by offering a social reform and national recovery menu. The right was a hotchpotch of factions ranging from the rabid royalism of Action Française to more moderate parliamentary combinations. Until mid-decade the right was united on a staunchly nationalist foreign policy and resistance to social reform and communism.

While Germany rearmed, France was absorbed by domestic broils. The right exploited the Stavisky affair to discredit government and parliament. Daladier's radical socialist cabinet was accused of protecting the financial swindler Serge Stavisky. Right-wing indignation exploded in the riots of 6 February 1934 which left seventeen dead and over 2,000 injured. Feelings ran so high that radical leader Herriot, on leaving the Chamber of Deputies, narrowly escaped being thrown into the Seine. The left denounced the right for plotting the Republic's overthrow. Counter-demonstrations were mounted. During 1934–35 a Popular Front coalition of radicals, socialists and communists took shape.

Did the right pose a real threat to the regime? Hardly. The 6 February riots were not a premeditated coup against the Republic. Extreme right and fascist groups, although noisy, lacked the strength to stage a successful coup. And the traditional right did not need to use extreme methods to return to power – from 1937 it had a partnership with the radical socialists. However, the fact that left and right believed each other to be conspiring against the state was in itself destabilizing. Accusations and counter-accusations bred an introverted atmosphere of rumour, conspiracy and anger. In October 1937 conservative senator Jacques Bardoux accused communists of planning the subversion of western Europe at a secret meeting on 16 May 1936.[5] On 10 November 1937 the general staff warned the government of an imminent communist *putsch* for 15–16 November.[6] Future Vichy leaders, Marshal Pétain and Pierre Laval, had contacts. In March 1938 Laval proposed a committee of public safety under Pétain, governing by decree. But there is no evidence of actual plotting. Ultra-right terrorist groups existed. The *Cagoulards* (hooded men), an underground anti-communist organization with military connections, attempted a coup on 15 November 1937. The leaders were tried and imprisoned. While *Cagoulards* were too few to present a serious danger, their activities contributed to the general mood of violence and vilification. In February 1936 royalist thugs (*Camelots du roi*) dragged Blum from his car, beating him savagely. Police and left-wing demonstrators fought in the Clichy riots of March 1937 leaving seven dead and several hundred injured.

Fifth columnists

The fall of France spawned accusations of betrayal by a fascist fifth column. Some historians have in part endorsed this interpretation. Nazi propaganda is said to have taken advantage of the pacifist climate in order to infiltrate numerous sectors of society, anaesthetizing opinion and weakening the will to resist.[7] Subversion of morale on such a scale would provide a major explanation of the collapse of French power. But did it in fact occur? Italy poured lire into the French press, but German propaganda was more comprehensive and sustained. Berlin followed two approaches: indoctrinating opinion by buying press support and converting political and cultural elites through the France–Germany Committee.

The Germans concentrated on buying individual journalists rather than newspapers. This was the most economical and efficient method because journals, once bought, would be quickly identified as German mouthpieces. But with skill and care individual journalists could exercise a wider and longer influence. In 1934 the proprietors of two newspapers made unsuccessful bids for German subsidies. Nevertheless, Berlin did buy a clutch of small-circulation papers and minor news agencies. After Munich a new agency, Interpress, opened in Paris. It placed articles in the French press and commissioned French journalists. The material offered was of good quality and high prices were asked. In November 1938 Interpress negotiated with the mass circulation *Paris Soir* for the publication of a feature by a German general on Germany's Western Wall. The conclusion of the piece was that the fortifications were impregnable. French journalists working for the agency were well paid but not excessively lest suspicions might be aroused.

The main propaganda thrust, however, was directed at the political and cultural establishment. Berlin's instrument was the subsidized France–Germany Committee formed by journalist Count Fernand de Brinon in

1935. It replaced the Comité France–Allemagne of the 1920s. As well as publishing a review, *Cahiers Franco-Allemands*, it fostered youth, veteran and cultural exchanges. Brinon liaised with German foreign minister Joachim von Ribbentrop's personal representative in Paris, Otto Abetz. Two leaders of veteran associations, Jean Goy and Henri Pichot, were committee members. German propaganda plugged the Franco-German community of arms – if the veterans of Verdun could come together then all would be well.

Brinon, the impresario of German propaganda, was close to radical socialist leader and premier Edouard Daladier. He accompanied French ministers to a London conference in April 1938 and may have undertaken secret missions to Berlin. During the Munich crisis of 1938 Brinon's conduct was little short of treasonable. He passed to Berlin summaries of secret cabinet discussions obtained from two ministers. But one Brinon does not a fifth column make. The France–Germany Committee's activities should not be exaggerated. To be sure, in 1938 foreign minister Georges Bonnet tried to endow it with greater influence. Herriot was nominated chair of the French section and contributed an article for the review. But in August 1938 he declined an invitation to the Nazi Party's annual Nuremberg rally, despite hints that Hitler would meet him. Bonnet failed to persuade Daladier to write for the review. In March 1939, following Hitler's occupation of Prague, public fury forced the closure of the Committee's Paris office. Novelist Jules Romains, active in the Committee since 1935, resigned. Brinon, denounced as a German agent, retired to his country estate. In sum the Committee certainly influenced some opinion-makers, but to say that Nazi propaganda effected a psychological neutralization of opinion is far-fetched. In the summer of 1939 the hue and cry over spies and fifth columnists netted only two journalists.

Fascism and anti-Semitism

S ome might claim that France was already more than half fascist, therefore there was no need for a fifth column. For many years French historians either denied the existence of French fascism or treated it as an insignificant fringe movement. However, Israeli historian Zeev Sternhell argues that France was 'the real birthplace of fascism' and political life was heavily impregnated by fascism in the 1930s.[8] The resulting polemic became front-page drama in 1984 when French writer Bertrand de Jouvenel who had been quoted by Sternhell sued the historian for defamation. Controversy centres on two issues: the role and beliefs of the extra-parliamentary leagues and second, the cultural and political penetration of fascist ideas in society at large.

As regards organizations, fascist or fascist-type parties existed but mostly without a mass following. Before 1936 the only mass-membership extreme-right force was Colonel de la Rocque's *Croix de Feu* (451,000). He denied the label fascist but his movement had fascist traits. After 1936 the most formidable movement was Jacques Doriot's *Parti populaire français* with 100,000 adherents, many of whom were working class. Ceremonial, personality cult and anti-liberalism gave it a fascist flavour, yet glitz should not be confused with substance. Doriot's party 'never had the aggressive dimension of Italian fascism and nazism which exalted war'.[9] In fact, French fascism as an organized force was 'fragmented, incoherent and badly coordinated'.[10]

Did fascist ideas penetrate society? 'Our society is rotten, dying ... We are ... flying towards Fascism', wrote Louis-Ferdinand Céline after the Stavisky riots.[11] Since opinion polls did not begin until 1938 and newspapers did not regularly publish readers' correspondence there is no way of knowing whether Céline's view was widely shared. In any case, one is dealing with imponderables because there is no consensus on the components of a fascist mindset. Historians and political scientists do not agree on definitions and paradigmatic cases. Concepts like 'fascist impregnation' and 'fascist spirit' are too woolly to offer adequate descriptions and explanations of the empirical evidence. Perhaps the term 'fascism' lacks explanatory force.

Racism, however, was a major component of fascism. According to Bernard Henri Lévy, it was endemic in twentieth-century France. 'What the devil are all these foreigners doing in France?', asks magistrate Cornéliau in George Simenon's *Pietr-le-Letton* (1931).[12] The Dreyfus affair demonstrated the strength of anti-Semitism and it is a fact that during the German occupation the French outdid the Germans in racialist zeal. The French authorities were responsible for deporting more than 70,000 Jews from France to the death camps. Understandably, the influx of foreign workers (*les métèques*) and Jewish refugees seemed to threaten jobs and culture. 'Down with the wogs [*les métèques*] ... France for the French', shouted right-wing student demonstrators who included in 1935 future socialist and Fifth Republic president François Mitterrand. By 1939 the Republic, in addition to nearly 2.5 million foreign workers, sheltered about half a million refugees, including 40–50,000 Jews and over 300,000 Spanish Republicans. The Spanish were herded into internment camps. The great mass of Jewish refugees lived a ghetto existence, cut off from French contacts. Yet it would be wrong to conclude that Vichy's anti-Semitism was the logical and natural culmination of interwar racism and xenophobia. There was 'nothing in the widespread but partly submerged anti-Semitism of the 1930s that would make inevitable the anti-Jewish policy of Vichy ... the Vichy racial laws of 1940–41 are inconceivable without the seismic shock of June 1940.'[13] In fact France deserves credit for accepting more refugees than any other European country in the 1930s. Leon Feuchtwanger wrote of his internment in 1939–40: 'I do not believe that behind the whole procedure there was any

particular malice or cruel intention, and if the internment made many of us for ever wretched, if it cost some of us our lives ... it is highly probable that this was the outcome not of malice, but of sheer thoughtlessness.'[14] To be sure, Feuchtwanger was writing during World War II and perhaps errs on the side of charity. Nevertheless, generalizations on the lines of 'France was fascist and racist' are far too wide and sweeping. Instead of facile assertion the changing face of anti-Semitism over different periods has to be carefully scrutinized.

Pacifism

One of the few apparently safe generalizations about French opinion in the interwar years is that it was profoundly pacifist. International critics condemned French 'militarism' while the French described themselves as pacifist. In the May 1932 elections most candidates called for disarmament. France, in Winston Churchill's phrase, was 'armed to the teeth and pacifist to the core'.[15] How pervasive was pacifism? Did it inhibit France from defending its interests?

Labelling France pacifist or fascist does not in fact tell us much about opinion. Pacifism meant different things to different people. Integral or absolute pacifists, opposed in principle to all wars and violence, were a tiny minority. Curiously, some integralists, inspired by anarchist tradition, preached the use of force to purify society – violence to end violence. Simone Weil on the pacifist left preferred German hegemony to war even though it would mean 'certain laws of exclusion against Communists and Jews'.[16] But for the vast majority pacifism meant no more than a vague internationalism – condemnation of war, support for the League and disarmament. It did not signify readiness to accept foreign occupation rather than fight. Most were prepared to fight for national frontiers and interests.

Pacifism permeated society but it was a balkanized, splintered movement, lacking a single large organization like the British Peace Pledge Union. Scores of different groups campaigned independently, often unknown to each other. Nor was pacifism a constant; its influence fluctuated considerably, waning after 1936. Notwithstanding the slaughter of the trenches, it was a minority movement in the early 1920s. Poincaré's occupation of the Ruhr had popular approval. As the war receded, pacifism grew stronger. In the late 1920s a pacifist majority emerged, inspired by Locarno and the 1928 Kellogg-Briand pact outlawing war. With the darkening of the international horizon after 1930 the pacifist majority broke into two groups: those who wanted disarmament yet insisted that security came first; second, the campaigners for general disarmament. In August 1932 writers Jean Giono and Romain Rolland organized in Amsterdam a world congress against imperialist war.

This sparked a counter-campaign calling for the strengthening of national defence. The fracture cut across party lines. Two senior radicals held opposing views. Herriot announced: 'I do not believe in disarmament as a means of security', to which Daladier replied, 'Either disarm together or die together, you must choose.'[17]

How strong was pacifism? Public support cannot be quantified. There was no French counterpart of the 1935 British Peace Ballot. Estimates of support vary wildly. In 1930 the League for the Rights of Man collected signatures for peace and disarmament. Instead of an expected one million, by autumn 1931 the numbers were: 109,000 for disarmament, 111,000 for peace. Yet in 1937 the International Association for Peace (*Rassemblement universel pour la paix*), led by Robert Cecil and Pierre Cot, claimed sixteen million French members. Surprisingly, pacifism grew stronger after the failure of the Geneva Disarmament Conference (1932–34). Between 1934 and 1938 pacifist sentiments were most influential, peaking in 1936. In 1935 Jean Giraudoux's play *Tiger at the Gates* used the classical legend of Troy as a vehicle for a protest against the stupidity of war. The pacifist climate made the pursuit of disarmament and conciliation the only widely acceptable policy. For many, however, it was the consequences of war that mattered, not war *per se*. Right-wing Wladimir d'Ormesson, editor of *Le Figaro*, considered a war to stop Hitler too appalling to contemplate because it would be 'the end of civilisation, the end of the Christian era'.[18] After Germany's invasion of the Rhineland in March 1936 virtually everyone from left to right cried 'no war'.

Veterans, school teachers and left-wingers formed a pacifist core. The adage 'if you want peace prepare for war' cut no ice with veterans who argued that it implied acquiescence in the likelihood of war. They believed that Hitler as an ex-combatant wanted peace with France. Peasant organizations, traumatized by the war, feared that peasants would again have to pay a large blood tax. They did not reject national defence but had no stomach for the defence of distant allies. The 100,000-strong school teachers' union demanded general disarmament and arbitration. Socialists claimed to be the party of peace. War was hated *per se* and for the damage it might inflict on the working-class movement. Demonstrably, the war of 1914 had fractured the European left and promoted fascism in Italy. The exception was the Communist Party which from 1935, on Stalin's order, rediscovered the virtues of national defence.

But it would be simplistic to conclude that pacifism predetermined French policy in the run-up to war. Pacifism waned after 1936. Blum initiated a major rearmament programme in September 1936 without provoking a pacifist backlash. To be sure, pacifist voices, especially school teachers and peasants, were some of the loudest during the Munich crisis. 'A victorious war would be almost as disastrous as a war lost', proclaimed a peasant paper. However, pacifism in 1938 was not a unified lobby. A variety of motives were at work: anxiety about military unpreparedness, fear of

The left calls for the nationalization of French armament firms: 'The voice of the merchants of death: "Kill one another – we serve victors and vanquished alike!" '
CGT poster

revolution, anti-communism stimulated by communist bellicosity against fascism, continuing hopes for Franco-German understanding. Mathematician André Weil assumed that France would fight for Czechoslovakia and went to Switzerland to escape conscription – not protesting against war but 'to devote myself to mathematics as much as I was able'.[19] Significantly, a million reservists were mobilized without serious incident. Police reports reveal that even in September 1938 opinion accepted the idea of war as inevitable – without enthusiasm but with determination to see it through. The winter of 1938–39 brought an upsurge of confidence and patriotism. Two leading veteran groups now opposed Hitler and peasant associations rallied to Daladier. At the CGT (*Confédération générale du travail*) Congress in November a motion against war received only 28 per cent of votes.

Realignment and the Popular Front

The mid-1930s witnessed a fundamental realignment of viewpoints on international affairs. Until the end of 1934 the right preached the necessity of resisting Germany while the left advocated disarmament and collective security. Over the next two years many on the left modified their faith in the League and disarmament. Blum's Popular Front accelerated rearmament, spending more on guns than social reforms. In September 1938 the left, although divided, displayed more enthusiasm for defending Czechoslovakia against Germany than did the right. Conservatives, encouraged by Hitler's noisy beating of the anti-communist drum, shed traditional Germanophobia. By the autumn of 1936 opposition to communism and the Popular Front eclipsed hatred for Germany. Hence the slogan: 'Better Hitler than Blum'. The ratification of the Franco-Soviet pact exemplified this reorientation. In May 1935, in the shadow of German rearmament, most of the right endorsed the pact; nine months later, frightened by the Popular Front, 164 conservatives voted against ratification.

The internal bear-garden distracted attention from international menaces. Socialists and communists insisted that fighting fascism at home came first and that even to envisage the possibility of war would be playing into the hands of the right. In May 1935, for instance, socialists and radicals, fearing the thin end of a militarist wedge, vehemently denounced the Flandin government proposal to extend military service from one to two years as a riposte to Hitler's reintroduction of conscription. The mix of domestic and international alarms raised political temperatures to fever pitch. When Mussolini invaded Abyssinia in September 1935 left and right fought over the imposition of League sanctions on Italy. For many conservatives Mussolini could do no wrong.

The electoral victory of the Popular Front in May 1936 and the outbreak of the Spanish Civil War in July intensified the ideological paroxysm, generating an atmosphere close to civil war. The Popular Front was a largely socialist ministry with radical socialist participation and communist parliamentary support. 'The crisis of May–June 1936', wrote General Gamelin, chief of the general staff, 'terrorised a great section of the French bourgeoisie. It made many of us lose sight of the dangers of Hitlerism and fascism . . . because behind the Popular Front one saw the spectre of Bolshevism.'[20] Blum's long overdue social and economic package of paid holidays, wage increases and a forty-hour week attempted to heal one of the chief fissures in French society – the alienation of the working class. But the socialist slogan 'everything is possible' sounded more threat than promise to the propertied. Horrified by the sit-in strikes and revolutionary ferment, the wealthy considered Blum's government an unmitigated disaster. Bitterness infected social life. 'In the past I used to lunch and dine with all sorts of people', recorded a left-wing journalist. 'Now I can be on friendly terms only with people who more or less share the same political convictions as I have.'[21] The coming of the Spanish war transformed the war of words into a real battleground. Volunteers crossed the Pyrenees to fight for Republicans or Nationalists. Right-wing press persecution drove socialist interior minister Roger Salengro to suicide.

The eve of World War II found the left in full retreat. After Blum's fall in June 1937 subsequent administrations edged to the right. The bourgeoisie's dread of social revolution shaped foreign policy until the outbreak of war. Daladier's radical socialist cabinet (1938–40) did more to erode parliamentary democracy than any fascist fifth column. Daladier buried the Popular Front, dismantling the forty-hour week. Reliance on decree powers which did not need immediate parliamentary approval enhanced the executive at the expense of parliament. Until early 1938 the interaction of domestic and international crisis had fostered weak and indecisive cabinets. Daladier restored governmental authority by demanding special powers to deal with the financial and international crisis. The price paid was a tacit alliance with the right. 'We are voting for you – you will govern for us', conservatives instructed the premier after Munich.[22] Threatened with a general strike on 30 November 1938 the government reacted ruthlessly, tear-gassing striking Renault workers and requisitioning mines and railways. Union leaders were warned that attempts to disrupt the railways would bring criminal proceedings. Finance minister Paul Reynaud's deflationary decrees restored investors' confidence and capital flowed back. Industrial unrest yielded to an uneasy capital–labour truce. In September 1939 Daladier, taking advantage of the Nazi–Soviet pact, closed down the communist press and locked up communist deputies.

Vive la France

Projecting an upbeat image was a necessity in a decade of depression and ideological strife. Dynamic and skilful propaganda might have offset the perception of Marianne as the sick woman of Europe. In 1936 France had a potentially strong world-wide network of institutes, *lycées* and schools. Several hundred teachers were seconded overseas and the *Alliance Française* offered language courses in many major cities. Sadly, the pioneers of cultural diplomacy were outclassed by the Germans and Italians. In the early 1920s Paris established institutes and teaching posts but did not make the most of the intense postwar interest in French culture. Financial cutbacks restricted programmes. France spent much less on propaganda than Germany. When in 1936–37 the French began to get their act together it was too late.

The great interwar event was the Paris International Exhibition of 1937. It did little to restore prestige. The opening, announced for the 1 May 1937, was postponed for over three weeks. Many pavilions were still unfinished. The exhibition site was the scene of numerous meetings, strikes and demonstrations. 'Workmen spit at you and shout "parasite"', complained a Swiss visitor.[23] The exhibition incurred heavy financial losses – costs were 380 million francs, receipts 160 million. Fifty million visitors were expected, thirty million came. The huge German and Soviet pavilions faced each other, sharply symbolizing the ideological conflict.

After 1931 France's cultural influence wilted. In the early 1920s French teachers and students gained scholarships to the United States while thousands of Americans studied in Paris. From 1926 American enthusiasm faded and France competed against the marketing of German language and science. In 1931 France had thirty-two scholars in the United States, Germany eighty-five. France's continuing prosperity in the early stages of the depression strengthened long-standing anti-French sentiments. 'The best way to assure the peace and happiness of the world would be to wipe France off the map and share out her territory among neighbours', announced one newspaper.[24] American students in France grumbled about bad accommodation, lack of academic guidance, difficult access to libraries and the unsociability of French students. A frequent visitor to the United States pointed out that German propaganda was better organized than French. The German ambassador travelled extensively, placed material in the press and had a stream of VIPs from Germany giving talks. By contrast, the French ambassador left visitors with the impression that they bored him.[25] A 1936 parliamentary report called the situation critical: 'It is undeniable that we are losing ground rapidly in Belgium, Romania, Yugoslavia, Turkey and even Czechoslovakia ... the same danger threatens in the Far East.'[26]

France lost the radio war. Broadcasts were badly timed and reached a much smaller audience than German, Italian and British transmissions. Complaints spoke of poor-quality broadcasts which were rarely announced in advance. Transmitters were low-powered. In 1932 France did not have a powerful enough transmitter to send and receive broadcasts from the United States.[27] The Popular Front rushed to make up for lost time. A coordinating committee for overseas propaganda was set up, and fleetingly in March–April 1938 a propaganda ministry. Overseas propaganda targeted Europe which by 1938 accounted for 41 per cent of the budget. But increased spending could not compensate at this late stage for contracting political and economic power. The Munich Agreement of 1938 dealt a body blow to the Descartes line in central Europe. Czechoslovak sections of the *Alliance Française* dissolved themselves, protesting France's betrayal of a loyal ally. Holders of French decorations returned them. The Franco-German contest was an unequal one; in Bulgaria Germany awarded thirty-six scholarships against France's six. By 1938 Germany had recovered its pre-1914 position in China. The numbers of Chinese studying French fell because of the decline of Franco-Chinese trade and a lack of career openings. Japan preferred Britain, Germany and the United States for specialist services and expertise in most fields. English was compulsory in Japanese schools, French a minority language. The days when French was the universal language of diplomacy and culture were long gone and Paris fought a losing battle to protect the language. The Havas newsagency reprimanded its London bureau for Anglicisms in reporting. In March 1937 the French Institute in Berlin was informed that English would replace French in German schools.

Why did France miss the boat? Propaganda services were criticized for being under-manned, under-resourced and lacking professionalism. Embassies did not have specialist cultural attachés. Elderly clapped-out lecturers, it was said, gave their country a tired, exhausted image. The bits and pieces of a propaganda service were scattered among different ministries and the various agencies were poorly coordinated. Poor coordination betrayed a reluctance to call a spade a spade. Propaganda was identified with dictatorships, not democracies. Budgets already modest in the 1920s were slashed in the early 1930s. The foreign ministry publicity section (*service des oeuvres*) had a small staff and a low budget. Part of the problem was the message itself. Playwright and diplomat Paul Claudel analysed the differences between French and American propaganda: 'The realistic and practical teaching given by the United States has now a very marked attraction for a lot of Brazilians who are acquiring . . . a taste for action and achievement. This is a point that France, always convinced of the animating role of general ideas . . . should reflect on more.'[28] There were calls for action but nothing was done until 1936 when Blum established the coordinating committee for overseas propaganda. Years of neglect could not be repaired overnight. In 1938 France did not have foreign-language broadcasts and

Daladier's radio talks were relayed in French only. Later in the year an effort was made to provide transmitters to deal with German and Italian propaganda in Africa but the project was not fully realized. The ineffectiveness of French propaganda reflected the hesitations and uncertainties with which France responded to Italian fascism and German nazism. In the end no propaganda, however skilful, could make good the retreats of 1936–39. Ironically, at the eleventh hour the government finally created a central coordinating agency, the Commissariat General for Information. During the phoney war of 1939–40 officials complimented themselves on keeping open French schools and institutes. Cultural prestige had become a substitute for power.

The media

Press

Newspapers were by far the most important source of information on international affairs. In the 1930s France had 253 daily newspapers, 200 of which were small-circulation journals. The Paris press, which published forty papers with a circulation of nearly seven million, was the most influential. It was also, because of its ownership, cautious and conservative. The big five morning papers were *Paris Soir* (1.8 million), *Le Petit Parisien* (1.5 million), *Le Journal* (0.9 million), *Le Jour Écho de Paris* and *Le Matin*. *Le Matin* belonged to right-wing political and business interests. *Paris Soir*, owned by textile magnate Jean Prouvost, professed itself non-political but usually came down in favour of the government of the day. The semi-official *Petit Parisien* belonged to the Italophile Pierre Dupuy; editor Jules Elie Bois was on the foreign ministry's payroll. *Le Journal* was avowedly right-wing. *Le Matin*'s proprietor, Maurice Bunau Varilla, a shady financier who had profited from the pre-1914 Panama scandal, was an admirer of Hitler. *Le Jour Écho* of Léon Bailby spoke for the far right, opposing the Popular Front. In the Munich crisis Bailby condemned 'the really criminal and Bolshevik attempts to render a general conflagration inevitable'.[29] The leading evening paper *Le Temps* represented big business and toed the official line on foreign policy. Editor Jacques Chastenet, representing the coal owners' association, visited Hitler in 1933 and remained under the dictator's spell, writing in September 1938: 'Hitler has often both publicly and privately posed as a champion of peace, there is no reason to doubt his sincerity.'[30]

Corruption was endemic. In 1934 Daladier admitted that four-fifths of all the press lived on subsidies of one sort or another. The large number of papers, the decline of advertising revenue during the depression and the low pay of journalists all encouraged venality. Foreign and domestic buyers vied for influence. Before 1914 Russian roubles were distributed in order to lubricate the raising of loans on the Paris bourse. In World War I Germany paid considerable sums; in the 1920s Americans were said to have spent 'enormous sums on the French press'.[31] After 1918 the Soviet Union subsidized both the communist *Humanité* and the semi-fascist *La Liberté* of Jacques Doriot. From 1934 Italian lire poured into the coffers of several papers; British intelligence and the Trades Union Congress were accused of funding some papers.

But the main influence on the press was the government of the day. The levers were many: the Havas news agency; secret funds; advertising contracts; informal contacts with editors, proprietors and journalists. Following the end of wartime censorship in 1919 official influence was consolidated and extended. The foreign ministry created a news department in 1920; from 1925 the principal ministries established press offices, with journalists on their payrolls. The Bank of France and business concerns followed suit. The pivot of official control was the semi-official Havas news agency, counterpart of Reuters in the United Kingdom. Havas, by combining news and advertising services, acquired a virtual monopoly of press advertising. It was also a majority shareholder in Radio Luxemburg and other stations. The agency was backed by big financial interests such as the Banque de Paris et des Pays Bas. From the Second Empire the agency functioned as a semi-official body, its overseas representatives doubling as unofficial diplomatic agents, liaising with French missions. In 1933 premier Daladier asked Havas 'not to publish anything on internal and external policy of the government without having first informed me'.[32] In 1938 the government tightened the reins by assuming responsibility for ten years for the deficit on news services in the Havas budget.

Advertising contracts were another means of informal control. Blum set up a special department to allocate state advertising. Unsurprisingly, most of it went to friendly newspapers. The secret funds were slush monies enabling ministers to buy journalists and papers. The monthly *Notre Temps* did so well out of Briand that it became a weekly. In 1938–39 Bonnet paid the same journal 20,000 francs a month for supporting appeasement. Informal day-to-day contacts with the press allowed ministers to keep a close eye on news and editorial opinion. The foreign minister briefed the diplomatic correspondents of the principal papers twice a day. The authorities had no qualms about suppressing unwelcome news. Overall, the press tranquillized rather than informed opinion. When Germany reoccupied the Rhineland in 1936 the prestigious radical daily *Dépêche de Toulouse* reassured readers that Germany had in fact suffered a setback in failing to breach Franco-British solidarity. The *Dépêche* was one of the few provincial papers to run a weekly defence feature, but its 'blind and complacent conformism' helped to maintain the illusion of an all-powerful army and high command.[33]

Radio

Until well into the 1930s radio was regarded as a source of music and entertainment rather than of news. Politicians distrusted radio, viewing it as a threat to their self-appointed role as mediators between government and citizens. For the political nation the print media and political meetings mattered most. André Tardieu was criticized for using radio in the 1932 elections. By 1937 France had about 5 million radio receivers compared with Britain's 8.3, Germany's 8.4 and America's 26 million.

State controls on programming came in 1934 with the reorganization of the broadcasting network. Two days before the 1934 Stavisky riots the government installed a news censor on the two main state news channels. Journalists protested against the suppression of news in the Stavisky riots. The first widespread use of radio in elections came in 1936. The Popular Front accused the state radio network of bias and purged twenty journalists. The right in turn condemned biased news presentations. The *Gazette de Lausanne* claimed the Swiss were so shocked by tendentious reporting that they gave up listening to French stations.

The crisis over Czechoslovakia in 1938 brought centralization of controls over state radio. During the crisis, news and information services were actually reduced. From 1 July 1938 press reviews were banned on state and commercial networks and news reduced to three brief daily bulletins, each lasting only seven minutes. This was in part a victory for the press which had long campaigned to restrict competition from radio. From the summer, radio underwent a transformation, becoming an instrument of government foreign policy. A decree of 19 September imposed news censorship on private radio stations. Munich was the first international crisis in which broadcasting played a significant role. Daladier broadcast before and after Munich, emphasizing his dedication to peace, complimenting the public on its unity, industry and strength and presenting the Munich Agreement as a victory for peace. Ministerial broadcasts contributed to the failure of the general strike called for 30 November 1938. Again, news reports were censored. Radio reflected the government's movement to the right. In December 1938 the state radio programme *Journal de France*, which had become more and more critical of the left, sacked the well-known socialist commentator Pierre Brosolette. From February 1939 official controls were tightened further; all news and information broadcasts were supervised by an agency attached to the premier's office. In the summer, state radio services were merged under a director general responsible to Daladier. In the approach to war radio played almost no part in informing opinion. Quite the contrary. The torrent of songs, games and serials had a tranquillizing, euphoric effect on popular attitudes. Arguably, without government censorship, news services might have given the public greater awareness and understanding of international issues.

Cinema

After World War I the authorities recognized the cinema's propaganda potential, but there was no unified control. Central government, prefects and mayors all exercised separate censorships. Taboo or highly sensitive issues included war, the armed forces, poverty, criminality, national traditions and institutions. In *All Quiet on the Western Front* (1930) scenes showing French women welcoming German soldiers were suppressed. A Soviet film, *The Mother* (1930), was banned as Soviet propaganda. Censorship applied to newsreels. Not surprisingly, newsreels showing the unemployed marching on Paris singing the *Internationale* were confiscated. Film of the 6 February Stavisky riots deleted scenes of police repression. Censorship was often arbitrary, contradictory and bumbling to an extent verging on the farcical. In 1931 a prefect banned newsreels on Hitler, banks and Corsican bandits. A film banned in Paris might be seen in the provinces. Abel Gance's *Napoleon* (1927) had a shot of a guillotine removed but the version projected at a gala performance for the president of the republic kept the guillotine shot intact. Generally, the cinema reinforced stereotypes; the French were always lovers of liberty and justice contending against cruel and barbarous Germans flouting international conventions.

From 1936 official policy became more systematized and centralized. Newsreel producers had to submit in advance details of filmed material, including a list of cinemas. In addition, an interministerial committee monitored the newsreels. The premier's office circulated a weekly list of recommended and forbidden topics. Safe, staple subjects were theatre and film first nights, sport, fashion, new cars, official ceremonies. In short, nothing controversial. As a result, by 1938–39 ministerial intervention was much more pervasive than hitherto. Foreign minister Bonnet stopped two whole issues of the English edition of *March of Time*, one on Munich, the other on refugees. For the first time the government made a determined effort to project national values. Films worshipping the military virtues, the empire and *entente cordiale* received funding and patronage. France – ran the message – with its spiritual superiority, empire, allies and citizens would triumph. The documentary 'Are we defended?' (*Sommes nous défendus?*, 1938) opened on a map of France; next came the aerial plan of a village followed by close-ups of work in the fields. A peasant closes his door with a padlock. Then several close-ups of doors, of blinds being drawn, of keys and locks. Storm clouds mass and a hen gathers its chicks. Strangely, war itself was hardly present in these films. War was rehabilitated by being emptied of its real content of blood and suffering. Subjects were drawn from the start of

World War I – *Le Héros de la Marne* (Hero of the Marne, 1938) – in a context of partial or total victory with a minimum of battle scenes.

Government, opinion and foreign policy

Morale as much as armaments and economic muscle is one of the sinews of power. In their apologias French statesmen asserted that pacifism and divided opinion excluded action against Germany until the spring of 1939. In March 1936 the public did not want to fight to stop Hitler remilitarizing the Rhineland; in September 1938 pacifist feeling again ruled out war to save France's ally Czechoslovakia. It was Hitler's Prague coup of March 1939 that galvanized opinion against German aggression. This defence soon found its way into textbook accounts and has gone unchallenged.

Yet there is an alternative view. Historian Marc Bloch's analysis of the fall of France (*Strange Defeat*, 1946) highlights the failure of successive governments to inform opinion. Indeed, the evidence reveals extensive government management of opinion through the media. In effect, official policy tended to shape opinion. The public showed little sustained interest in international issues because it was not encouraged to do so. After Hitler's Rhineland coup a senior American diplomat observed: 'The facts with respect to Germany are known but they have not been faced. In some countries there has been an effort through press control . . . to keep the facts from the people.'[34] Two years later a top state department official commented: 'Through all this crisis [Munich] what has surprised me is that the governments of the democracies have not taken their peoples or their parliaments into their confidence.'[35] Attitudes towards Germany and Italy hardened in the spring of 1939. In June 1939, 76 per cent of those polled said that a German attempt to seize Danzig should be stopped by force.[36] Arguably, this U-turn might have come much sooner but for official efforts to sell appeasement by suppressing and minimizing dissent. A government determined on opposing Germany might have successfully mobilized support for its cause. In April 1938, in the midst of anti-Czech press campaigns, the German ambassador in Paris shrewdly observed: 'If the government knew how to inculcate in the people the conviction that sooner or later hostilities between France and Germany were inevitable, Czechoslovakia would assume an entirely different significance in the minds of the people.'[37]

The May 1936 Popular Front election, noted *Manchester Guardian* correspondent Alexander Werth, revealed an 'almost unbelievable indifference to international affairs'.[38] To be sure, the public did not protest against unpopular foreign policies. There was nothing to match British

outrage against the Hoare–Laval pact of December 1935 dismembering
Abyssinia. The reading public seriously interested in other countries was
small. The Soviet Union provoked more interest than any other country in
the 1930s yet most titles sold only 5,000 copies. Lack of curiosity about
other countries partly reflected the urgency of domestic problems, partly the
assumption of cultural hegemony. The French perceived themselves as the
cynosure of world attention and considered that they had nothing to learn
from others. 'Our comrades who have travelled to the United States, or
across Latin America, have been telling us how closely those peoples are
following events in France', enthused writer Jean Guéhenno. 'On the success
or failure of the Popular Front may depend they assure us the political
orientation of the world for the next fifty years.'[39] But lack of interest in
international affairs was also the product of news management shaping and
controlling the public agenda.

What were the landmarks in the management of opinion? The *Anschluss*
of March 1938 was followed by a violent press campaign against France's
alliance with Czechoslovakia. In the early summer the campaigns died down
and government influence seems to have been directed towards restricting
and discouraging discussion of the international crisis. Far from mobilizing
support in defence of Czechoslovakia, Daladier tranquillized it. On 8 July
1938 the cabinet received warning of German mobilization and the
probability of a war within six weeks. Justice minister Paul Reynaud called
on Daladier to accelerate rearmament and talk to the unions: 'It will be said
that it is dangerous to alert opinion. The greater danger, however, is its
present passivity. It is this passivity which encourages the dictators . . . Let us
beware of weakening opinion by giving it the impression that something is
being withheld.'[40]

In September 1938 stiffening resistance to concessions to Germany obliged
ministers to pull out all the stops. Public meetings on international affairs
were banned and government influence increased. By the end of the month
the secret funds were exhausted. The best documented instance of official
intervention was the treatment of the British foreign office communiqué of
26 September. Foreign secretary Lord Halifax authorized a statement that if
Germany attacked Czechoslovakia France would assist her ally and would
be supported by Britain and the Soviet Union. This was bad news for foreign
minister Bonnet and associates who were working frantically to keep France
out of war. Their reaction took two forms: circulation of the statement
within France was restricted as much as possible, and second, it was
rumoured that the statement had not been officially authorized and could
therefore be discounted. The French morning press of 27 September barely
mentioned it. Ambassador Charles Corbin in London wired Paris,
underscoring the communiqué's official character. Pierre Comert, head of
the foreign ministry's news department, claimed that this telegram never
reached him.

Almost total press approval of the Munich Agreement on Czechoslovakia did not necessarily reflect opinion. The press had been fine-tuned in advance. 'German and Italian money has poured over the past few days into the whole French press ... to persuade our poor people that it was necessary to give way and to terrorize it by the threat of war', wrote Charles de Gaulle.[41] Two polls conducted shortly afterwards illustrate the fluidity of opinion and the existence of a large minority opposed to Munich.[42] Replying to the question 'Do you approve of the Munich agreements?', 57 per cent said yes; 37 per cent said no. The second poll asked 'Do you think that France and Britain should in future resist further demands by Hitler?' and replies were: yes 70 per cent, no 17 per cent.

Lack of interest in foreign policy was the result of inanition, not apathy. The executive deprived public and parliament of information and opportunities for debate. In 1938–39 key foreign-policy decisions were taken when parliament was in recess. In June 1938 Daladier, armed with decree powers, sent the Chambers on holiday. Only two foreign-affairs debates were held in 1938 – a major review in February and a cursory discussion of the Munich Agreement on 4 October. Before 1914 and into the 1920s governments regularly published documentation on foreign policy. But in the 1930s there was nothing on the pre-World War II crises.

The phasing out of appeasement after March 1939 did not produce a relaxation of official pressures. On the contrary, Daladier tried to tackle the dictators with their own weapons. The strengthening of the executive through decree powers produced much tighter control of the media. On 21 March 1939 the government assumed wide powers of censorship and confiscation of newspapers, letters and telegrams. On 30 July a commissariat general for information, a propaganda ministry in all but name, was created. These measures have to be seen in perspective. Compared to the Nazi propaganda juggernaut the Daladier government initiatives were lilliputian.

Why was the selling of France neglected until 1938–39? Depression was one reason. While France lay becalmed on an economic Sargasso Sea, the dictatorships appeared dynamic and purposeful. By comparison, liberal democracy looked faded and uncertain. Appeasement was another factor. The traditional mantras of revolution, army and empire did not fit a policy of compromise and retreat. And ministers preferred to let sleeping dogs lie. Rallying the public and renewing morale risked refuelling appeasement's critics as well as encouraging France's central European allies to resist Hitler instead of yielding. There was a deeper reason for the propaganda failure. Creating national cohesion presupposed a confident leadership and a readiness to heal internal wounds by accepting Popular Front legislation. Both requirements were wanting in 1938–39. The right held Daladier in thrall so there was no question of accepting Popular Front reforms. And Daladier was no charismatic leader. After Munich he invited foreign-policy specialists to a discussion: 'Sympathetic but sententious and weary, the premier seemed elsewhere.' Shocked by the premier's lassitude, one participant concluded: 'We are finished.'[43] Daladier's indecision was symptomatic of a double crisis of confidence – about Europe's future and France's role. The stocktaking that followed 1918 was tempered by hopes that in time pre-war Europe would be restored. By the mid-1930s it was realized that not only had Europe lost its political and economic primacy for good but its cultural identity was endangered. Awareness of a broken world was heightened by self-doubt about France's role in a German- and Anglo-Saxon-dominated universe. The ending of an innovative creative period in French culture, as H. Stuart Hughes argues, may have contributed to this crisis of confidence.[44] Whatever the precise causes, serious doubts existed. As Pétain put it in April 1936: 'Neither Germany nor Italy have doubts. Our crisis is not a material crisis. We have lost faith in our destiny ... We are like mariners without a pilot.'[45]

11
Challenges, 1932–1936

One cannot live in Germany as a French person without feeling the threat, without noticing the unavoidable and impending day of reckoning. The interminable disarmament negotiations only serve here to pass the time while rearmament is pushed ahead as fast as possible.

Jean Dobler, French consul general in Cologne, letter of 26 January 1934 to Edouard Herriot, MAE, Herriot Papers, 34

We have just witnessed in France an imbecile and almost criminal right-wing action [in the Abyssinian crisis]. I am ashamed of it for my country ... the artificial frenzy is only momentary. It is noisy because those who are making most noise have plenty of money ... But the mass of the French people rejects the provocation with horror. More than ever we must remain united. We are at a great turning point in history.

Edouard Herriot, radical socialist leader, letter of 19 October 1935 to former British foreign secretary Sir Austen Chamberlain, BUL, AC41/1/63

Last night I experienced one of the most painful moments in my life. After leaving ... the High Military Committee, chaired by Laval ... I wept ... for the destiny of my country, which until now has found the men it needed, not only a Joffre, a Foch, but a Poincaré and a Clemenceau ... [Laval] explained to us his general policy: 'Hitler has shown his desire on several occasions for an entente with France.' Is this policy without grandeur, of continual bargaining, worthy of France?

General Maurice Gamelin, chief of the general staff, notes on a meeting of the High Military Committee, 21 November 1935 in Servir, II: *Le Prologue du drame (1930–1939)* (Paris, Plon, 1946), pp. 177–81

F rance's headaches came thick and fast: depression and political turmoil, a deepening Manchurian crisis, Germany's demand for equality of arms, disarmament deadlock, Hitler's advent, Mussolini's invasion of Abyssinia. Fortunately, the expansionist powers, Germany, Italy and Japan, did not launch a concerted challenge to the status quo. A full Axis alliance of Berlin, Rome and Tokyo was delayed until 1940; Mussolini and Hitler went separate ways until 1936, concluding a military alliance only in 1939. This lack of unity gave French statecraft an opportunity to rethink strategies. Writer Wladimir d'Ormesson called for 'a skilful, informed, coherent ... self-confident diplomacy'.[1] Alas, French diplomacy proved anaemic, lethargic, temporizing. The initiative passed to Britain and Germany. Briand had pursued conciliation from strength – a strong franc, massive gold reserves, the largest army in western Europe. After 1932 conciliation was largely driven by internal weakness and fear.

Manchuria

'T here has scarcely been a period in the world's history when war seemed less likely than it does at the present', the League Assembly was told on 10 September 1931.[2] Within a week Japanese forces seized key points in Manchuria from Chinese garrisons. In May 1933 the Japanese swept southwards menacing Peking and the North China plain. At this point they stopped and concluded a truce with the Chinese. The truce lasted until July 1937 when the eight-year Sino-Japanese war began. Chinese appeals to the League were answered by the dispatch of a commission of enquiry, the Lytton Commission. Meanwhile, the Japanese conquest proceeded unhindered. The League voted against recognition of the Japanese puppet state of Manchukuo, imposing derisory sanctions – refusal to recognize Manchukuo passports, currency and postage. Japan walked out of the League in March 1933.

Manchuria demonstrated that the League was toothless. Was France, mainstay of the League, responsible for the collective security failure? To be sure, single-handed she was barely strong enough to police Europe, never mind Asia. Collective security depended on the agreement of the great powers to defend the status quo. France, like Britain and the United States, had a large stake in the Far East but Manchuria was not perceived as a direct threat to western commercial and colonial interests. The United States, not France, was the crucial factor. 'I have always believed that Japan could be stopped by strong action without any risk of war', wrote League advocate Robert Cecil, 'but that should only be done with the full cooperation of the United States.'[3] Yet a more far-sighted French leadership might have attempted to coordinate western action – if only to show solidarity for

League principles. Sadly, French policy was reactive, confused and indecisive.

Reparations, war debts and disarmament monopolized the agenda. For the first year of the Far Eastern crisis 'little was attempted in the Quai d'Orsay in the nature of long-term analysis of the Far Eastern scene'.[4] Second, Briand, foreign minister since 1925, was shipwrecked by age, ill-health and disappointment at losing the elections for the presidency of the republic in May 1931. Because of his illness the League Council met in Paris in October 1931: 'He cut a pathetic figure. He could hardly speak. He was overcome by a continuous fit of coughing and could continue only by sipping Evian after every few words, and gasping for air.'[5] Over the twelve months following his resignation in January 1932 four different foreign ministers came and went. Third, high officials and much political opinion favoured Japan. 'Japan, civilized nation, our loyal wartime ally', preached the semi-official daily *Le Temps*, 'represents and defends in the Orient the social order . . . against . . . the bloody surge of Bolshevism.' Japan was one of 'the invisible ramparts of our Indo-China'.[6] Both Berthelot, secretary general until 1933, and his successor Alexis Léger were said to be sympathetic towards Japan. René Massigli, head of the Quai's League of Nations section, assured Tokyo that France would take 'the greatest care to maintain friendly relations . . . and lose no opportunity to show its friendship'.[7] One socialist deputy believed 'the armament firms are working for the Japanese in order to discredit the League before the Disarmament Conference starts, and that the Japanese are buying up the Paris press'.[8] Plagued by political and economic uncertainty, France got the worst of all worlds – alienating League supporters, annoying the Japanese, vexing the Americans and British. The policy of impartiality to China and Japan, combined with support for the League, was an impossible one. It was widely believed that Paris and Tokyo had reached a secret understanding – support for Manchurian expansion in return for Japanese backing at the Geneva disarmament conference. No such agreement existed although the Japanese were ready to scratch France's back. Would a Paris–Tokyo axis have eased France's isolation? There was no mileage in a bilateral understanding. A Paris–Tokyo arrangement, by antagonizing Anglo-American opinion and disabling the League, would only have worsened France's plight. French Indo-China was expendable, Europe was France's very lifeblood. Anglo-American distrust of France sprang from the conviction that French militarism, not German or Japanese, constituted the main threat to peace. There were fears that Paris might annex the Chinese province of Yunan on the border of French Indo-China. Japan's attack in January 1932 on Chapei, close to the Shanghai international settlement and French concession, did not jolt the French into a tougher attitude. They tamely followed Anglo-American initiatives. Should France have taken a firmer line? Arguably, there was a potential role for Paris in shoring up League defences by coordinating and animating the responses of the major powers. Certainly a frustrating task but one which would have salvaged some moral kudos for France and the League. In the event, French wishy-washiness only served to reinforce Anglo-American dissatisfaction with French policy. 'Undoubtedly, a bolder policy in Paris would not have altered the course or the outcome of the Shanghai crisis', argues John E. Dreifort, 'but it might have led to a more serious analysis of the general situation in the Far East and a fuller appreciation of the future dilemma of simultaneously defending France's interests in that area and in Europe.'[9]

France's dilemma

Although Manchuria, by discrediting the League, contributed to the breakdown of the peace settlement, the fate of the settlement hinged on relations between the European powers. The first big challenge for French security in Europe came during the Geneva Disarmament Conference of 1932–34. Germany's demand for equality of armaments challenged France's military superiority. Berlin served notice that France had to surrender her lead or compete in an arms race. The Conference laboured for two years to no result. Germany increased its military spending; France announced in a note of April 1934 its withdrawal from disarmament discussions. By the end of 1934 the initiative in Europe had passed to London and Berlin. Britain became the senior partner in the *entente cordiale*. Saving a brief assertion of independence in the spring of 1939, France followed her British governess.

Why did France become so dependent on Britain? Internal unrest was part of the answer. The Molotov cocktail of economic crisis and political disorder enfeebled foreign policy-making. Economic recovery engrossed decision-makers, leaving scant time or energy for external affairs. The 6 February 1934 Stavisky riots, triggered by the exposure of the financial swindler Serge Stavisky, convinced many that France was teetering on the brink of civil war. Ministerial crises impeded decision-making. In the four months from Germany's departure from the League in October 1933 to the 6 February riots the country had four changes of premier. In mid-February 1934 foreign minister Louis Barthou told the British that the government was so preoccupied with internal problems that it had not been able to decide its attitude on disarmament. Statesmanship was lacking when most needed. Briand's close disciple, socialist Joseph Paul-Boncour, foreign minister from December 1932 to January 1934, treated the Quai like a part-time job, arriving at 10.30 a.m. and insisting on three-line summaries of telegrams. His windy oratory did nothing for France. 'Spoke for an hour and a half and said absolutely nothing', commented one bored listener. 'It's amazing how he rolls on, like Old Man River.'[10] At a time when France desperately needed to mend fences Paul-Boncour, over a period of thirteen months, made no foreign trips, except to Geneva.

But the chief cause of France's loss of the initiative was the fact that Germany's rearmament brought the French face to face with the dilemma inherent in the nation's international position since 1919. Accepting German rearmament seemed suicidal, resisting it equally so. The problem appeared insoluble. French leaders did not bury their heads in the sand. They knew what they were up against. It was precisely because they could recognize the true nature of the threat that they could not make up their minds how to meet it. 'I have no illusions', premier Herriot told advisors in October 1932. 'I am convinced that Germany wishes to rearm ... We are at a turning point in history. Until now Germany has practised a policy of submission . . . Tomorrow it will be a policy of territorial demands.'[11]

The response was to mark time and stay close to Britain. The French had no insurance – no major European alliance – but they knew their value as Britain's first line of defence. 'Thank God for the French army', Winston Churchill had told the British parliament.[12] If the worst happened and Germany attacked, then Britain, to preserve its independence, would have to fight for France, alliance or no alliance. This calculation made sense, yet interdependence need not have become passive dependence. There was an opportunity for a real partnership if French leaders had played their cards skilfully. In 1932 political scientist Raymond Aron returned from Germany full of anxiety about Hitlerism. He secured an interview with a junior Quai minister. 'What would you do if you were in Herriot's place?' asked the minister. Aron was lost for words.[13] The political will to devise a solution was frozen by fear. There was a feeling, reported the British embassy, 'approaching resignation that in every issue arising from Germany's urge to emancipate herself from the bonds of 1919 France can only fight at best a rearguard action.'[14] The dice seemed loaded against France: Britain and the United States behaved more like foes than friends; military superiority could not be kept indefinitely.

Hitler's accession to power on 30 January 1933 did not reenergize the French. The significance of Nazism was not understood. An hospitalized emigré writer was asked by a nurse why he had not stayed in Germany. His explanation of the nature of the regime and the reasons for flight met with total incomprehension. 'When one has done nothing wrong', replied the nurse, 'one has nothing to fear.'[15] The new German chancellor seemed no different from other Weimar Republic leaders like Brüning, Schleicher, and Hindenburg. Nazism was perceived as a temporary infection of extreme nationalism. Daladier even declared to parliament that Hitler's advent improved France's diplomatic prospects because his mistakes would isolate Germany and enlist sympathy for France. Nazism, instead of galvanizing the French, 'transformed even the most far-sighted ... into spectators', passively waiting for the regime's downfall.[16] Dramatist and diplomat Paul Claudel, ambassador in Brussels, exemplified the blend of breast-beating, scapegoating and wishful thinking that characterized French reactions to Hitler. The League and international conferences, wrote Claudel, were unsuited to the resolution of international problems. France's 'narrow and unintelligent nationalism' was also at fault. 'All Briand's generous and enlightened initiatives' had been hobbled by domestic opponents; 'all the concessions made to Germany were made too late'. France, however, 'was not directly threatened. Hitler proclaims it . . . and I believe him to be sincere'. 'Germany', concluded Claudel, 'swept along by the new dynamism, led by mediocrities and fanatics, intoxicated by its success, will commit new follies which will do more than the League ever could to unite Europe in fear and common interest.'[17]

French policy was not wholly passive. Efforts were made to consolidate influence in Danubian Europe. Following the defeat of Germany's Austro-German customs-union project in September 1931 France sought to retain leadership in central Europe with a scheme for a Danubian economic *entente* embracing Austria, Hungary, Czechoslovakia, Yugoslavia and Romania. A tariff agreement based on a reciprocal preferential system among the Danubian countries was recommended but the scheme ran into flak. The Stresa Conference of September 1932 concentrated on the economic problems of the Danubian area but failed to find permanent solutions. Great-power rivalries were too closely involved.

French appeasement featured a new emphasis on peace-treaty revision and Franco-German reconciliation. Revisionists grew more visible. The radical socialist newspaper *La République*, said to be Daladier's mouthpiece, called for treaty revision. In December 1932 Jacques Kayser, vice-president of the radical socialist party and advisor to Daladier, condemned the 1919 settlement. Franco-German discussions took place. In 1932–33 industrialists and civil servants from France, Germany, Belgium and Luxemburg discussed outstanding political issues – the Polish Corridor, disarmament, reparations, colonies. But German foreign minister von Neurath rejected the conclusions, while the French government does not appear to have formed any opinion.

Did the French read *Mein Kampf*? Forewarned is not always forearmed. Although an abridged translation was not available in France until 1938, keynote passages on Franco-German relations were publicized in the press and parliament. In 1934 one deputy 'made a great impression merely by reading out, word for word', the sections in which Hitler expressed his determination to settle scores with France.[18] *Mein Kampf* did not shock the French into action. There were several reasons for this passivity. Since few believed Hitler would last long, it did not seem necessary to take the message too seriously. Hitler's self-projection as a peace-loving Führer who wanted only amity with France went some way towards counteracting *Mein Kampf*. Experienced observers like Berlin ambassador André François-Poncet played down Hitler's writings, arguing that he had changed his views since the mid-1920s. Those who did not trust Germany whatever the regime in power learnt nothing from *Mein Kampf* that they did not already know. The difficulty was not knowing the enemy but knowing what to do and discovering the necessary will.

Were alternatives to appeasement canvassed? Some voices called for firmness but all shrank from the only certain way of stopping German rearmament – force. A preventive war was not practical politics. The only prominent proponent of force, General Weygand, advocated reoccupation of the Rhine bridgeheads, provided Britain gave moral, and later naval, support. Since British assistance was unlikely in the extreme Weygand was not proposing a realistic alternative. France was backed into a corner. A repetition of the Ruhr adventure of 1923 would endanger the Locarno guarantee. Public opinion was another constraint. The May 1932 elections returned a solidly left-wing Chamber which would not have tolerated coercion. Finally, France did not have an effective military instrument for intervention.

Hawkish ministers like Tardieu and Doumergue were not as tough as they sounded. They were not prepared to fight and they assumed the early fall of Hitler. When in April 1934 François-Poncet pleaded the case for a disarmament agreement he was told by Tardieu: 'You are wasting your time, the agreement which you proposed will not be concluded ... Hitler will not last long ... An agreement ... would only strengthen him. If war comes, within a week he will be deposed ... by the Crown Prince.'[19] Only two individuals, François-Poncet and Charles de Gaulle, advocated coherent and realistic options. François-Poncet, like the British, advocated recognizing German rearmament while there was yet time to limit its pace. France lacked two things: the political will to act and the military means to do so. Between full war mobilization and acquiescence no intermediate military response capability existed. It was all or nothing. Political passivity was partly a function of the lack of an intervention capability. Charles de Gaulle's originality was to argue, not for preventive war, but for the creation of an intervention instrument, a professional armoured striking force.

Disarmament

Disarmament offered no solution. In disarming Germany the Allies pledged themselves to work for general disarmament. The Geneva Disarmament Conference of 1932–34 was the most important interwar initiative. The debates were replays of the arguments of the 1920s. France was at loggerheads with both Germany and the Anglo-Saxons. The Americans saw high arms spending as the main cause of Europe's troubles. 'The stupendous increase in military expenditures since before the war', President Hoover told Congress, 'is a large factor in world-wide unbalanced national budgets ... unstable credit and currencies and ... loss of world confidence in political stability.'[20] Many in Britain and the United States saw France, not Germany, as the chief threat to peace and harmony in Europe.

France was the strongest military power on the continent; Germany was disarmed and her economy in ruins; the French had suffered less from the depression than the British had. British premier Ramsay MacDonald considered 'the diplomacy of France ... an ever active influence for evil in Europe'.[21] Before the conference assembled the British cabinet decided two fundamental points: it was opposed to the idea of an international peace-keeping force, and no new guarantees would be given to France. For France, however, there could be no disarmament without security – in short, fresh guarantees. French opinion believed London and Washington were intent on disarming France. 'The government', wrote one expert, 'finesses and manoeuvres to make the world believe we have the Anglo-Saxons with us ... they are effectively with us on condition that we disarm on land, at sea and in the air.'[22] Between France and Germany there was an abyss of suspicion. 'At bottom', as the British recognized, 'the trouble' was 'that the French and Germans utterly mistrust each other and nothing that we can do or say makes the least difference'.[23]

Since Germany was determined to rearm it was plain that a disarmament pact would have to legalize some level of German armaments. This might have offered a basis for negotiation. But the demand for equality of rights placed France in a quandary. Lacking Germany's demographic and economic muscle, France either had to make herculean efforts to keep up or abdicate her lead. An armaments race carried too many risks for the economy and society; surrendering a military lead spelt insecurity and German dominance. The first French scheme, the Tardieu Plan, presented in February 1932, suggested an international peace-keeping force composed of national contingents from League-sponsored regional pacts. The force would have had heavy weapons denied to national armies. The scheme called for the revival of the Geneva Protocol of 1924. This was followed by President Hoover's Plan of 22 June, calling for the reduction by one-third or a quarter of all existing armaments. The Americans warned the French that their 'European allies' would 'become too bankrupt to maintain their present scale of armaments'.[24] In effect, disarm or risk losing allies. Germany tried to short-circuit Geneva discussions by proposing a Franco-German under-standing – cancellation of reparations in return for a customs union and economic cooperation in eastern Europe, plus a military pact and staff talks in return for equality of rights. German chancellor von Papen offered a four-power cooperation pact. In September 1932 France rejected the Franco-German overture. It offered nothing for the eastern allies and assumed German good faith. Germany withdrew from the conference pending acceptance of her claim.

France responded with the 'Constructive Plan', insisting that disarmament and security should be in tandem. Heavily armed units from League members would be placed at the League's disposition to enforce collective security. All other heavy arms would be stockpiled under international control. International experts would verify compliance at least once a year.

The government adopted the plan against Weygand's advice. Finalizing the plan provoked acrid civil–military debates. Premier Herriot and Weygand both dreaded German resurgence but differed on remedies. The Germans, insisted Weygand, could not be trusted. France had already reduced its strength by adopting one-year military service: 'I ask the Committee to understand my state of mind. I have the responsibility of defending the frontiers with forces, not words.' Herriot reminded military chiefs that abandoning disarmament talks might mean complete isolation. 'The government's great fear', he said, 'was that one day France would find herself alone facing Germany.'[25]

Why did the Disarmament Conference fail? The fundamental difficulty was that disarmament meant different things to different powers. In June 1932 Herriot reminded the conference of the grammatical irregularity of the verb 'to disarm'. 'It is conjugated', he said, 'only in the future sense and it has only the forms of the second person. The task of the Conference is to give it a present tense and a first person: to transform "you shall disarm" into "we are disarming".'[26] But learning a language takes time and effort. A meeting between premier Tardieu and British minister J. H. Thomas illustrated the communication problem. After Tardieu had explained at length France's need for security and a British official had translated, Thomas commented only, 'Oh 'ell.' 'What does M. Thomas say?' asked Tardieu. 'The minister', replied the interpreter, 'had listened with great attention and interest and would report most faithfully to his colleagues.' Tardieu eyed the interpreter with thinly veiled mistrust.[27] The conference met in the worst possible conditions. Economic and financial collapse had intensified international tensions. The twelve months of preparatory talks had been largely wasted. The conference resembled the Dover Mail in Charles Dickens's *A Tale of Two Cities* – everyone suspecting one another. Entrusting technical preparations to the military courted failure because 'the very purpose of their existence was to guarantee the security of their country'.[28] The left blamed the arms manufacturers, 'the merchants of death', for failure. However, the accusation can be supported in one instance only. In 1932 proposals for controlling arms manufacture were defeated by the armaments lobby and the general staff.

Three factors moulded France's negotiating position: the influence of the general staff, civil–military discord and French diplomacy. Until June 1932 and after February 1934 the general staff determined disarmament policy, insisting on the status quo and preventing effective disarmament. From June 1932 to February 1934 politicians and generals quarrelled and their disputes hindered both modernization and disarmament initiatives. More discreet than the army but equally effective was the navy's opposition. The admirals torpedoed a proposal for Franco-German *rapprochement*. French diplomacy, in bondage to Britain, contributed to the disarmament fiasco. By sticking to the strict letter of the treaties France sacrificed flexibility. The League of Nations section of the foreign ministry had a virtual monopoly on disarmament policy-making. Its head, René Massigli, was much too subservient to Britain. Disarmament was perceived exclusively in multilateral terms at the expense of promising bilateral initiatives. The bias towards personal diplomacy and Geneva negotiations marginalized France's senior ambassadors. Poor liaison between the ministry and the Berlin embassy meant that François-Poncet was still talking to the Germans about collective security after the government had changed its mind. Politicians, like the diplomats, had their faults. They were oversensitive to military pressures and popular feelings. Hitler's pretended pacifism could have been unmasked sooner if premier Daladier had had the courage to pursue his instinct for dialogue. Yet France cannot be saddled with the principal responsibility for the collapse of the conference. Britain and the United States determined the conference's fate. Both powers wanted influence without responsibility; both knew the scale of German rearmament, yet insisted on substantial French disarmament. Disarmament discussions did not delay French rearmament. The 22 per cent cut in defence spending between 1932 and 1934 was the result of deflation, not disarmament.

By 1932 the key issues of debts, depression and disarmament had grown into one dark maze. During the Disarmament Conference two attempts were made to find a way out of the labyrinth – the Lausanne Conference of June 1932 and the World Economic Conference of June 1933. The Hoover moratorium of 1931 gave only a year's respite on debts. Chancellor Brüning declared that it was impossible for Germany to continue reparations payments. Lausanne was to have opened in January 1932 but was delayed until June because of Tardieu's illness and French elections in May. Ramsay MacDonald, chairing the conference, favoured outright cancellation of reparations and 'had a long stand-up contest lasting several days with the French' who wanted continuing payments.[29] Once again ministerial instability stymied French diplomacy. 'The new French Cabinet', reported MacDonald, 'has not settled down and will take a little time to get the experience which is necessary to decision ... one feels when meeting them a lack of coherence that strengthens Herriot's own fault of hesitancy.'[30] MacDonald bullied and blarneyed the French into dropping a demand for annual payments and accepting a smaller lump sum compensation. The carrot was an offer of a consultative pact. It offered no new commitments – as in 1924 Herriot was outmanoeuvred with kind words. Arguing that without reparations the war debt to the United States could not be paid, France requested postponement of the instalment due in December 1932. The United States would not recognize a connection between debts and reparations and refused postponement. Herriot then asked parliament for authority to pay the instalment. This was refused and the government fell.

The World Economic Conference of June 1933 was inauspiciously housed among the fossils in the Geological Museum in South Kensington. Britain and France were anxious to secure agreement on currency stabilization. With the depreciation of the dollar they feared cheap American imports. Great hopes were pinned on President Roosevelt's leadership in sponsoring the conference. On 2 July Roosevelt wrecked the conference by rejecting even temporary stabilization of the dollar against sterling for the duration of the conference. By the end of 1933 the only way forward seemed to be to legalize German rearmament. 'If Hitler is sincere in proclaiming his desire for peace', counselled France's military attaché in Berlin, 'we will be able to congratulate ourselves on having reached agreement; if he has other designs or if he has to give way one day to some fanatic we will at least have postponed the outbreak of a war and that is indeed a gain.'[31]

Barthou

A ll too briefly Louis Barthou, foreign minister in the Doumergue government of February 1934, offered a solution – a renewed search for security through League-sponsored regional and bilateral pacts. Barthou's dynamism gave French diplomacy a new vigour and firmness. The seventy-two-year-old minister was an author, bibliophile, and keep-fit enthusiast. 'I get up at 5 a.m. to take a cold bath, do my exercises and go to my desk at 6.30. My breakfast is at 7.30 and my barber comes at 8. That would be a good time to talk to me', he told secretary general Léger.[32] He was tireless, reading and annotating papers so fully that they served as drafts for replies.

Reassertion of French influence took several forms: withdrawal from disarmament talks, an eastern Locarno, a Franco-Soviet alliance and Franco-Italian *rapprochement*. In March 1934 Hitler increased Germany's military budget and demanded an army of 300,000. Britain pressured France to come to an agreement with Germany. By refusing an agreement, France appeared to be blocking progress on disarmament. Yet legalizing rearmament without guarantees seemed madness. France's note of 17 April 1934 rejecting further disarmament talks brought temporary relief from international pressures. It was a victory for Doumergue rather than Barthou who would have preferred some agreement. The logic of the April note was rearmament. 'We are initiating a policy of force', affirmed one minister.[33] Apart from a modest air force modernization programme nothing happened. Rearmament did not start in earnest until September 1936. Not that Barthou was to blame – balancing the books excluded large spending. Barthou concentrated on repairing friendships. In late April he renewed contact with Mussolini and set off on a European tour. Could the eastern pacts be given some credibility? Barthou's answer was an eastern Locarno, a mutual assistance pact under the aegis of the League, linking the Soviet Union, Germany, Poland, Czechoslovakia, the Baltic States, and Finland. Reactions were mostly negative or lukewarm. Poland, having just signed a non-aggression pact with

Germany in January 1934, showed no interest in links with the Soviet Union. Poland's ruler Marshal Pilsudski defended the flirtation, alleging the 'uncertainties' of French policy and 'its continual concessions under the pressure of England'.[34]

Barthou's two main initiatives were Franco-Italian *rapprochement* and negotiations for a Franco-Soviet pact. Previous talks with Italy had led nowhere. In March 1933 Mussolini proposed a Four-Power Pact of France, Britain, Germany and Italy inviting the powers to adopt a policy of peace. Innocuous enough. But the pact also mentioned treaty revision and France's eastern allies jibbed at a clause threatening their existence. The pact was signed in July 1933 but never ratified. The wooing of Italy had the blessing of the French general staff. Italy would fill the need for a major continental ally. Of the two candidates, Italy and the Soviet Union, Italy was favourite. French conservatives mistrusted Moscow. Moreover, Germany and the Soviet Union did not have a common land frontier and France could not therefore expect direct Soviet help in a conflict. Italy seemed the best bargain: protecting France's exposed Mediterranean flank, bridging alliances in western and eastern Europe, allowing France to concentrate troops on the Rhine. Besides, Austria's independence depended on Italy. When Austrian Nazis murdered Chancellor Dollfuss in July 1934 Mussolini had sent troops to the Brenner frontier. Suddenly, Barthou's career ended. On 9 October 1934 a Croatian terrorist assassinated King Alexander of Yugoslavia at Marseilles during a state visit. Barthou at his side was hit. In the general panic he wandered off on foot bleeding to death. 'His death marked the end of a great policy, the only one which could still have saved France from war and aggression.'[35]

Laval

Pierre Laval, Barthou's successor, was probably the most hated of French leaders in the quarter of a century 1919–45. The biggest black mark on his reputation was his premiership of Vichy France from 1942–45. He was widely believed to have sold out to the Germans and betrayed his country. In 1935 historian Richard Cobb, rushing to get the last Metro, ran straight into Laval as he was coming up the steps at the Rond Point des Champs Elysées. 'I apologised most profusely to M. le Président. He accepted my apologies: "It's nothing" [*de rien*] he said.'[36] However, Laval's informality in political life was more vice than virtue. He had all the faults of France's interwar political leadership – casualness, insularity, opportunism, preoccupation with the political machine. A self-made man of a peasant family in the Auvergne he began his career as a socialist; by 1934 he was of the right and had amassed a large fortune, including two newspapers, a radio station, a stud farm and the chateau in his native village. Bottles of the local mineral water were in every railway dining car. With his swarthy, squat figure, rather Asiatic in appearance, and white silk tie – looking more waiter than politician – he personified for many observers all that seemed tricky and suspect in French politics. He was 'like a French peasant' said British foreign secretary Sir Samuel Hoare, 'who was always thinking of getting the better of someone over the price of a chicken'.[37] He had the tight-fistedness and canniness of the Auvergnat peasantry, allegedly signing official documents as close as possible to the last line of text to prevent the insertion of additional material. Success sprang from a combination of intelligence, immense personal charm and unrivalled knowledge of the machine. In 1930 as Labour minister he had a deputation of angry strikers eating out of his hand within minutes. Like Briand, once orally briefed he quickly sized up complex issues. He was contemptuous of diplomatic procedure, preferring face-to-face meetings without witnesses or papers. Secretary general Léger was in awe of him. In October 1935 at Geneva Léger, who had been helpful to the British in Laval's absence, 'begged' British minister Anthony Eden 'to make it clear to Laval that he had been as stubborn as possible'.[38] Laval knew how to maximize his influence, handing people their letters of recommendation so that they could post them themselves without delay. Instead of the customary twice-yearly lists for the coveted Legion of Honour he put out small batches of a few names throughout the year – so applicants could always be told that they would be on the next list.

Was Laval a fascist mole undermining the Republic in preparation for Vichy? British premier Stanley Baldwin suspected him of being paid by Mussolini. The left accused him of conspiracy to establish a dictatorship. The charge was renewed at Laval's trial in 1945 and revived in 1970 following the publication of Italian documents. On trial, Laval vehemently denied pre-war plotting with foreign powers and the charge was dropped. Italian lire certainly bought French journalists and newspapers in the 1930s, but Laval was not paid by Mussolini or Hitler. Italian records confirm his commitment to an understanding with Italy and Germany as well as hopes of a Laval–Pétain government, but there is no evidence of active conspiracy against the Republic. Nor did Laval utilize French fascist groups or the terrorist *Cagoule*. Like Pétain, he was critical of the regime and wanted a more authoritarian style, but the two were not hand in glove. Laval's ideas throughout the decade were of a piece with his policies in power in 1931–32 and 1935–36 – *rapprochement* with Rome and Berlin, mistrust of Britain, anti-communism. Laval's principal fault was not duplicity or opportunism but a misperception of the nature of international politics. 'He had a vision of a united Europe resting on a Franco-German *entente* in which Russia would be thrust back to Asia and the Anglo-Saxon countries would lead an autonomous existence with the United States and France serving as the points of contact with the European and Anglo-Saxon world.'[39] Hitler, however, wanted domination, not dialogue; Britain would not allow French leadership in Europe; Russia would not be excluded. Naively, Laval believed that wheeler-dealing and charm would work wonders in the international arena. 'He himself would certainly convince the Führer if only he could speak to him personally', he told the German ambassador: 'Admittedly he spoke no German but the Führer would nonetheless receive the impression that his intentions were honest.'[40]

Laval's handling of the Saar plebiscite demonstrated his desire for an understanding with Hitler. Versailles provided for a plebiscite after fifteen years of international administration. 'The Saar is not worth a war', Laval told the Germans.[41] The plebiscite on 13 January 1935 offered Saarlanders three choices: union with France, maintenance of the status quo or reunion with Germany. Of course, German-speaking Saarlanders would not vote for France but some might have opted for the status quo. Barthou tried to encourage supporters of the status quo in the hope of forcing concessions from Hitler. Laval did not try to bargain, telling the Germans that the Saar was 100 per cent German and should be returned as soon as possible. He ignored evidence that the Germans were preparing to rig the plebiscite. The 90 per cent pro-German vote gave Hitler his first big foreign policy success. Laval was rewarded with a few crumbs – compensation for the Saar mines and Hitler's declaration that he had no more territorial claims against France.

Abyssinia

The European security system, already severely shaken by Germany's departure from the League of Nations and denunciation of the Versailles disarmament clauses, underwent a decisive test in the Abyssinian crisis of 1935–36. The consequences of Mussolini's invasion of Abyssinia were far-reaching: the Stresa front of France, Britain and Italy crumpled, as did the Franco-Italian alliance of 1935; the battered League received its *coup de grâce*; Britain and France were estranged. Under cover of the Italo-Abyssinian war Hitler proceeded with the remilitarization of Germany's western Rhineland frontier a year earlier than he had thought possible. Italy's isolation led directly to the emergence of the Rome–Berlin Axis in October 1936, which in turn brought the abandonment of Italy's interest in preserving Austrian independence. The way was cleared for Germany's annexation of Austria in March 1938.

Italy's invasion was not a bolt from the blue. It marked the culmination of colonial ambitions entertained for over half a century. After the occupation of Corfu in 1923 Mussolini followed a peaceful path for the rest of the decade. Plans for an attack on Abyssinia were not discussed until 1932 because it was only in that year that Italian forces finally completed the subjugation of the Senussi in Libya. Gradually, the diplomatic disappointments of 1933–34, beginning with the miscarriage of the Four-Power Pact of July 1933, confirmed the resolve to act in Africa. Mussolini believed that an invasion of Abyssinia would succeed provided Italy had no problems in Europe. The assassinations of Austrian Chancellor Dollfuss in July 1934 and King Alexander of Yugoslavia in October brought quarrels with Germany and Yugoslavia. A decision on Abyssinia was postponed.

What decided the issue was the conclusion of the alliance with France. On 7 January 1935 Laval and Mussolini signed the Rome Agreements promising to consult together if Germany violated Versailles disarmament obligations. The most controversial of the agreements was a secret one on Abyssinia by which France signed over to Italy her economic interests in the country. In a private conversation with the Duce, Laval used the phrase a 'free hand'. The Italian leader understood this to mean that France would turn a blind eye to the military conquest, whereas Laval probably assumed that Italy would stop short of war. No record of the talk was kept and the ambiguity was no doubt intentional.

By the spring of 1935 Italy's intentions were common knowledge, but there was no common front to restrain Mussolini. Hitler's reintroduction of conscription and plans for a thirty-six-division army enhanced Mussolini's value as a makeweight against Germany. Accordingly, France and Britain pursued accommodation. Meeting at Stresa on 11–14 April, France, Britain and Italy reaffirmed Locarno obligations in Europe without alluding to Abyssinia.

Laval's preference for Mussolini rather than Stalin was never in doubt. He journeyed to Moscow on 13 May 1935, having in his own words 'purged' the Franco-Soviet pact of 2 May 'of the most dangerous elements'.[42] Barthou had wanted a real alliance; Laval emasculated the pact by subordinating it to League procedures. Stalin's proposal for staff talks was sidestepped and parliamentary ratification delayed until February 1936. The pact's significance was more internal than external. It helped Laval's reelection in his Paris working-class constituency of Aubervilliers. The foreign minister secured a declaration from Stalin approving France's rearmament. This silenced French Communist Party criticism of the army. Laval's colleagues had no enthusiasm for the pact. 'Far too much importance was attached to the Russians', wrote navy minister François Piétri. 'We are going to deceive ourselves about the new Russia just as we did about the old.'[43] Quai d'Orsay press chief Pierre Comert stressed its 'purely negative' importance in preventing a new German-Soviet collaboration.[44]

No time was lost in consummating the Franco-Italian union. On 27 June 1935 French and Italian military chiefs signed a military convention providing for concerted action in the event of a German threat to Austria. There was talk of sending an Italian contingent to the Rhine and of French troops crossing Italy en route to central Europe. Franco-British discord spurred Mussolini to finalize plans for conquest. Independently, Britain had negotiated the Anglo-German Naval Agreement of 18 June 1935, allowing Germany to build up to 35 per cent of British fleet tonnage. French ministers who had been kept in the dark about Anglo-German naval talks felt betrayed by this unilateral violation of Versailles.

The Italian invasion of Abyssinia on 3 October 1935 brought League anathemas, followed by the imposition of 'soft' economic sanctions on 18 November. French and British ministers were unremitting in their efforts to buy off Mussolini. These efforts peaked in the Hoare–Laval plan of 8 December, ceding two-thirds of Abyssinia to Italy. Abyssinia would have retained a corridor to the sea, a 'corridor for camels' as the London *Times* contemptuously dismissed it. Why did France allow Italy to overrun Abyssinia and discredit the League and collective security? The Italian attack on a League member was an open and shut case of aggression. Internal politics and strategic fears determined France's response. Some sections of opinion did not see any intrinsic evil in Italian expansion in Abyssinia. Germany, not Italy, was the troublemaker. As a Locarno guarantor and guardian of Austrian independence, Italy had to be appeased, not warned. Italy was France's sole continental ally. The general staff calculated that in war with Germany Italian neutrality would release seventeen divisions from the Alps and North Africa for service on the Rhine. And a hostile Italy would play havoc with France's communications with her North African empire.

The Italo-Abyssinian conflict coincided with mounting domestic turmoil. Ultra-nationalist leagues battled with the Popular Front electoral alliance of communists, socialists and radical socialists. Since the Stavisky riots of February 1934 ring-wing ministries had held office. Laval's cabinet of June 1935 clung to a precarious parliamentary existence, dependent on radical-socialist and conservative support. Laval was trapped by financial and ideological storms. His deflationary decrees were unpopular and Popular Front demonstrators hanged his effigy on 14 July. The flight of gold continued. Political survival presented Laval with an agonizing dilemma. France, like Britain, was in a pre-election period, with elections due in April–May 1936. The right sang Mussolini's praises while the left and centre defended the League and collective security. Staunch support for sanctions would have maddened the right and destroyed the government's parliamentary base. Equally, abandonment of the League would have enraged the radicals. The fact that some radicals had reservations about the Popular Front made it all the more desirable to retain their votes. Since there were no French opinion polls until 1938 we do not know how much support sanctions enjoyed in France. The pro-Laval press consulted readers in October 1935 in the first nationwide poll on foreign policy. Of 850,000 respondents, 553,000 wanted absolute neutrality on Abyssinia; 310,000 supported economic sanctions; only 10,000 demanded military measures. Doubtless, a left-wing-organized poll would have produced a different breakdown.

British policy added to Laval's tribulations. London demanded a clear-cut commitment from Paris. Unequivocal French backing for the League, it was thought, might persuade Italy to withdraw. If Italy stayed put, French military help was considered indispensable for police action. In November fears of a 'mad-dog act' by Mussolini – perhaps a sudden swoop on the British fleet at Malta – strengthened the argument for French cooperation. Alternatively, it was reasoned, a French negative or evidence of shilly-shallying would be a useful alibi for British inaction. Faced with British requests for naval assistance, Laval trod water, striving to keep Rome and London happy. His tightrope act came near to success. If the Hoare-Laval Plan had not been leaked to the press it might have tempted Mussolini.

There is no question that joint Franco-British naval action to enforce an oil embargo would have cut Mussolini's lifeline, forcing a withdrawal. But France would have lost a new ally and deepened her isolation. Only one thing could have tempted Laval off the fence – a new British commitment to compensate for the loss of Italy. Laval might have ridden out a domestic storm, provided he could have shown a significant reinforcement of French security. On 10 September 1935 Laval asked if Britain would enforce collective security in Europe. In short, Britain was being asked once again to extend Locarno commitments to central and eastern Europe. The answer, as Laval must have anticipated, was negative.

The failure to restrain Mussolini did not make a European war inevitable but it did make it highly probable. 'Us today, you tomorrow', were the Emperor of Abyssinia's parting words at Geneva. Instead of uniting France and Britain in defence of the League the crisis drove them apart. Both felt cheated. The French appeared evasive and unreliable because they were half-hearted about sanctions. The French right believed Britain wanted to destroy the Italian alliance. 'England must be reduced to slavery', thundered the far-right journal *Gringoire*. The police guard on the British embassy had to be strengthened. Herriot apologized for 'an imbecile and almost criminal right-wing action'.[45] Abyssinia toppled France's main security pillar, the League of Nations. Japan and Germany had withdrawn in 1933, Italy exited in 1937. Laval too was discredited and his government fell at the end of January 1936. As he left office the premier was heard to say: 'Mussolini – what a bastard!'[46]

Laval's fellow citizens would have used ruder epithets to describe the shambles of French diplomacy in January 1936. All France's initiatives had fizzled out: the Italian alliance battered, the Franco-Soviet pact still awaiting ratification, disarmament dead, the League crippled, Britain estranged, Germany rearming fast. To be sure, the whole national and international climate was adverse: the sagging economy and the exodus of gold captured headlines and drained energies. The conjuncture of debts, depression and economic nationalism was inimical to cooperation. The fragile world community represented by the League and international conferences was overwhelmed by Brobdingnagian problems. 'Proceedings at Geneva', confessed League stalwart Robert Cecil, 'become more and more like a nightmare – vast exertions without any result.'[47] That said, French statecraft was unequal to the challenges. 'The brigands have more energy than the honest men', observed Berthelot in one of his last letters.[48] The political elite was a soft target for predatory dictators. Instead of a connected narrative of his 1932 government, Herriot's memoirs present a series of episodes, like a card index. The refusal to analyse and draw conclusions was symptomatic of an inconclusive, hesitant and lethargic leadership. Barthou was the exception. There was little or no attempt to think through options and devise solutions. The impasse of 1932–35 induced a profound pessimism. In his multi-volume novel *Les Hommes de bonne volonté* Jules Romains, who was close to the elite, depicts the despair which oppressed them. 'For men like us', the fictitious Jerphanion tells Grenier, 'I mean like Daladier, like Paul-Boncour, like myself, there is no longer anything to be done.'[49]

12
War again, 1936–1939

When Blum [the French premier] went this morning to see the President of the Republic, ... he [the President] said, 'What is being planned, this delivery of armaments to Spain may mean war or revolution in France' ... The position of the President of the Republic is shared by several ministers ... 'My soul is torn' said Blum, who is as convinced as we ourselves of the European significance of the struggle that is being fought in Spain.

Fernando de los Rios, to Spanish prime minister, 25 July 1936, in William Foss and Cecil Gerahty, *The Spanish Arena* (London, Robert Hale, 1938), p. 374

As usual, we surrender without a fight to the insolent demands of the Germans and deliver our allies, the Czechs, to the common enemy ... This surrender will give us a brief respite, like old Madame du Barry with her head on the block begging: 'Just a few more seconds, Mr Executioner.'

Charles de Gaulle to his wife, September 1938, in *Lettres, notes et carnets 1919–Juin 1940* (Paris, Plon 1980, pp. 473, 474

To say 'yes' – it's an immediate demoralisation for France ...
– it's the loss of the best trumps of our game; namely our military and moral force ...
To say 'no' – it's a serious risk of war
– it's perhaps the resignation of ministers
– it's perhaps the unleashing of a strong pacifist campaign in France.
Solution proposed: don't close all doors ... !

Premier Edouard Daladier's manuscript notes on Mussolini's conference proposal, 31 August 1939, in FNSP, 2DA 7/Dr.5

The pre-war period that began in 1936 had two distinctive features: extreme rapidity of change, and an atmosphere of undeclared war. The accelerando of events made western policy-making difficult. The initiative lay with the dictators. As in the approach to World War I, the cumulative effect of the crises – Rhineland, Spain, Austria, Czechoslovakia, Poland – was to speed up the collapse of the international system. An effect became a cause, reinforcing the original cause. The multiplying of tensions and pressures set up intolerable stresses. Moreover, there was no sharp transition from peace to war. The outbreak of the Spanish Civil War in July 1936 was the beginning of three years of 'a reign of terror and international lawlessness'. 'We are already in a state of mobilisation and at war, the only difference is that there is no shooting yet', Field Marshal Hermann Göring announced in 1936.[1] The Sino-Japanese war began in July 1937 without a Japanese declaration of war. The sense of impending doom created by the rush of events made French and British statesmen lean over backwards to stave off disaster. By March 1939 when they at last accepted that Germany might have to be stopped by war within a matter of months, it was too late to convince Hitler that they meant business.

Rhineland

On 7 March 1936 Hitler, alleging a contradiction between the Franco-Soviet pact and the Locarno treaty, sent a force of 22,000 into the demilitarized Rhineland, violating Versailles and Locarno. His gamble that Britain and Italy, guarantors of Locarno, would acquiesce and that France would not dare to act alone, proved correct. Paris expected Hitler to open negotiations for remilitarization. However, instead of negotiating, he used force. The pretext for action was provided on 11 February 1936 when, after months of procrastination, the Franco-Soviet pact was submitted to the French parliament for ratification.

Traditionally Hitler's Rhineland coup has been seen as *the* crossroads on the road to war, a last chance to reverse German expansion and save French power. 'If the French government had mobilised', wrote Winston Churchill, 'there is no doubt that Hitler would have been compelled by his own General Staff to withdraw, and a check would have been given to his pretensions which might well have proved fatal to his rule.'[2] Why then, did France not expel German troops from the demilitarized zone? She was not entirely caught off guard: a German coup had been predicted since the summer of 1935. Stephen Schuker argues compellingly that the French never seriously considered opposing Germany by force.[3] Several factors induced passivity: public lack of interest in chastising Hitler, Franco-British estrangement over the continuing Abyssinian war, military and financial weakness, impending elections, a Locarno commitment to conciliation, the pursuit of appeasement.

Diplomatically, France's hands were tied. The cardinal principle of French policy since 1924 was to keep in step with the British because France had no major continental ally. Since the Abyssinian war had weakened the *entente* the French did not want to make matters worse by quarrelling over the Rhineland. Second, Locarno required France to maintain consultation with partners and avoid unilateral action. Thus, the French were committed to consultation with partners who did not want to resist Germany. 'I suppose Jerry can do what he likes in his own back garden', encapsulated the British response. France's predicament evoked little sympathy. 'The damned French are at their old game of dragging this country behind them in their policy of encircling Germany', wrote former labour chancellor Philip Snowden.[4] In February 1936 the government decided that no forcible action could be undertaken without British agreement. On 7 March, following German occupation, foreign secretary Anthony Eden counselled the French not to take any action without prior consultation.

The Paris press, with few exceptions, rejected a riposte. Though Hitler's claim that the Franco-Soviet pact and Locarno treaty were incompatible did not command wide assent, French and British conservatives strongly deplored the ratification of the pact on 27 February. The French right-wing press argued that ratification had needlessly provoked Hitler. An outraged and bellicose French public would doubtless have catapulted the government into action against Germany. On 10 March the French Chamber gave a very chilly reception to a suggestion of unilateral action. Given the apathy of opinion, and with a general election only six weeks off, the broken-backed caretaker administration led by Albert Sarraut had no choice but to acquiesce in a *fait accompli*.

Financial and military weaknesses dictated acquiescence. The treasury warned the government on 8 January 1936 that it could no longer borrow on the home market and was teetering on the edge of bankruptcy. France lacked a rapid reaction force to deal with the Rhineland crisis. Expelling Germany would have been like taking a sledgehammer to crack a nut. The government was told that it was not possible to expel German forces without general mobilization, involving the risk of war. War with Germany could not be contemplated without the certainty of allied support. 'The idea of sending quickly into the Rhineland a French expeditionary force, even if only a token force, was a chimera' because the army was a 'static' force and 'no offensive action could be undertaken until the twelfth day of mobilisation'.[5] The generals feared that France no longer had a clear lead over Germany. The high military committee was told on 18 January 1936 that 'as regards equipment, Germany was on the point of overtaking us outright'.[6] To have mobilized against Germany would probably have brought financial crisis and devaluation. The Abyssinian crisis had weakened France on the Rhine. Fourteen divisions, about a fifth of France's total war strength, had been transferred to the Alps and Tunisia. Yet in trained manpower France still had numerical superiority over Germany. The number of German troops in the Rhineland was grossly overestimated. The fact of the matter was that no one really wanted to march for the Rhineland. Fighting to keep demilitarization would have gone against the grain of French policy since 1924. Demilitarization, it was believed, could not be indefinitely enforced and was not worth a war. Accordingly, attention was focused, not on ways and means of preventing reoccupation, but on using the Rhineland as a bargaining chip to secure concessions from Germany and to collect insurance from Britain. On 18 February the general staff advised the government to seek a defensive alliance with Britain as 'compensation' for remilitarization.[7]

This strategy brought only meagre returns. In London on 19 March four of the five Locarno powers – France, Britain, Belgium and Italy – renewed their obligations and agreed to open staff talks. Anglo-Franco-Belgian talks followed on 15–16 April. It was agreed that in the event of an unprovoked German attack on France, and subject to the decision of the government of the day, two infantry divisions would be sent to France. This was minimal, not comprehensive cover, but the French accepted on the principle that half a loaf is better than none. Like Locarno, the new undertaking was more constraining than supportive. If France wanted to rescue her Polish and Czech allies by attacking Germany she risked losing the British pledge. Yet if France did not fight for Poland and Czechoslovakia, Germany would become unstoppable. The effect of the new commitment was to bind France more closely to Britain.

Focusing on the many curbs on French policy in the approach to March 1936 can give a misleading impression of impotence. In fact, the Rhineland had been written off as early as 1932–33. Constraints certainly bulked large, but acquiescence in the coup was part of a deliberate strategy. Gamelin, as Nicole Jordan convincingly argues, advocated a strategy of 'cut-price war on the peripheries'. His assumption was that Hitler, after remilitarizing the Rhineland, would expand in the east. It made no sense therefore to risk a Franco-German contest in the west. 'The interest for us', explained Gamelin, 'is in a conflict beginning in central Europe, so that we could act as a secondary force against a Germany already engaged'. Military diplomacy from 1933 concentrated on the construction of a central European front. The Franco-Italian alliance played a pivotal role in this scheme since it enabled France to envisage sending an expeditionary force to spearhead a war of coalition in the east. Although the timing and manner of remilitarization took the generals by surprise, the coup itself was considered to have validated Gamelin's game plan. The chief of the general staff blundered very badly, neglecting the coup's demoralizing impact on domestic opinion and on eastern allies. 'By attempting to fight the war elsewhere', as Nicole Jordan shrewdly observes, he 'made it impossible to fight at all'.

The Rhineland marked a turning point in international politics. It was the beginning of the end for the eastern allies. The strategic balance was never again as favourable to France. By bolting and barring German's western door Hitler could block or delay a French offensive in aid of Poland and Czechoslovakia. German rearmament received new impetus in the Four Year Plan of August 1936 setting a deadline of 1940 for war readiness. Moreover, the coup demoralized French opinion. No one had wanted to fight, no one wanted to face the consequences of passivity. Over two weeks later a British visitor found 'everywhere a sort of resigned despair' and recognition that 'in about two years' Germany would swallow Austria and Czechoslovakia 'without let or hindrance'.[8] In government a psychological denial of the implications of reoccupation prevailed. 'The essential point is that France cannot allow Germany to build fortifications ... We could find it impossible to intervene effectively in order to assist our eastern allies', premier Sarraut told military chiefs on 4 April.[9]

France's acquiescence in the coup dismayed her eastern allies. 'If on 7 March you could not defend yourself, how will you defend us against the aggressor?' asked the Romanians. Austria felt more exposed than ever to the German dragon; 'if Germany is allowed to fortify the Rhineland, we are lost',[10] declared Vienna. On Italian advice, Austria concluded a new agreement with Germany, the *modus vivendi* of 11 July 1936. In return for a German promise to respect Austrian sovereignty, Austria acknowledged herself 'a German State'.

Paradoxically, the eastern pacts were more important to France after 7 March than before the coup. Until 7 March the military were fairly confident of holding their own against Germany in a defensive war, though it was recognized that the decisive superiority enjoyed in the early 1930s had gone. But the rapidity with which Germany exploited her victory and the disarray of the eastern allies made the general staff anxious to strengthen France's defences. By May 1936 Krupp was turning out prefabricated concrete sections round the clock and armies of workmen were constructing defences in the Rhineland.

Consequently, the general staff re-emphasised the Czech and Polish alliances. In an appreciation of 25 June Gamelin stressed the fragility of France's position. Taking into account British, Belgian and Czechoslovak forces, there was a balance between France and Germany. Yet if Germany accelerated rearmament and Italy adopted a neutral or hostile attitude the situation would be precarious. Reserves of manpower were exhausted and reliance on colonial troops might prove dangerous if political unrest occurred in the colonies. On 9 July the military chiefs talked of a 'central European front' provided Italy remained friendly. French troops might be sent to central Europe, 'certain and effective help' would be given to the eastern allies by means of 'pressure' or 'an offensive' in the west.[11] Italy confirmed that the military accord of 1935 remained in force, provided sanctions were lifted. Sanctions were lifted on 15 July but events in Spain quickly shattered the alliance.

Spain

France's sorrows came in battalions. On 18 July 1936 the Spanish Civil War began. It was to last almost three years. On 20 July the Spanish Republic asked France for arms and at the same time General Franco, leader of the military insurrection, requested help from Germany and Italy. Within weeks Germany, Italy and the Soviet Union were supplying men and arms. For the rest of 1936 and into 1937 it seemed likely that Spain would spark off a general conflagration. Spain was the beginning of a war of creeds and a continuity of resistance to fascism. In 1944, after the liberation of France, General de Gaulle inspected partisan forces of Toulouse. Stopping before one raggedly dressed man, he asked: 'And when did you join the Resistance, my friend'. The partisan replied: 'Well before you, general' – he had fought in the Spanish war.

Only speedy and substantial French aid could have saved the sister Popular Front. 'Arms for Spain' was the cry in Paris and London. Blum's Popular Front ministry promised assistance and then reneged. On 2 August France, seconded by Britain, proposed a non-intervention agreement. Although Germany, Italy and the Soviet Union signed the agreement, it proved a complete farce. Britain alone respected it while France allowed a trickle of supplies to reach the Republic. The European left claimed that Britain bullied France into non-intervention. Certainly pressure was applied in Paris but the decisive considerations which weighed with Blum were the danger of general war and the threat of civil war in France. With German and Italian forces engaged in Spain it seemed likely that French intervention would ignite a European war. The president of the republic, the presidents of the Chambers and the foreign minister all impressed on Blum the menace of a general conflict. One minister, a married man who had lost three brothers in the war of 1914–1918, told foreign minister Yvon Delbos, a lifelong bachelor: 'They should never appoint bachelors to key positions. They should appoint fathers of families like myself, I tell you that I will not go to war under any circumstances.' A tortured Blum could neither eat nor sleep. The paroxysms of left and right convinced him that sending arms might topple his government and destroy its reforms. Charity began at home.

It would be hard to exaggerate the impact of the war on French policy. The subsequent political and strategic anxieties explain in part the retreat from east central Europe in 1938. The military implications were terrifying. It was assumed that if Franco won the civil war France would be encircled by a triple alliance of Germany, Italy and nationalist Spain. As well as the threat to the Pyrenees land frontier, air and sea links with French North Africa were endangered. A third of the French army was in North Africa and survival in war depended on the speed and safety with which troops could be ferried across the western Mediterranean. The nightmare of encirclement made France cleave closer to Britain. Presented with almost simultaneous threats to her Mediterranean flank and to geographically remote allies in central Europe, France put her frontiers first. Spain was a warning of what might happen in France. 'I met peaceable Frenchmen, for whom I had never before felt contempt and who would never have dreamed of any killing themselves', wrote Simone Weil, 'but who savoured that blood-polluted atmosphere with visible pleasure.'[12] The domestic bitterness of the summer of 1936 extinguished any hope of an effective Franco-Soviet alliance. The Soviet Union needed good French patriots, declared Soviet commissar for foreign affairs Maxim Litvinov. But the traditional Germanophobia of the right was dissolved by Blum's Popular Front and the Spanish war. Stalin, not Hitler, was the enemy.

Spain strengthened expectations of war. In 1934–35 analysts wrote about 'the next war'; by 1936 international war had become highly probable. Negotiations with Germany for a European settlement were punctuated by cries of alarm: 'Europe is on the verge of general war', announced foreign minister Yvon Delbos in November 1936. From Berlin François-Poncet signalled: 'The present state of affairs in reality was no longer peace but undeclared war.'[13]

Popular Front

In Paris the proposition remained peace. The Rhineland and Spain added urgency to the search for *détente* with Germany, but it was not a gadarene rush. Blum took the most important decision of the decade in defence policy – the launching in September 1936 of a major four-year rearmament programme. The quest for conciliation would ultimately be based on renewed military strength. In the meantime, until the tanks and aircraft were delivered in quantity, solutions had to be found. The Popular Front pursued conciliatory overtures to Germany in tandem with efforts to revive and strengthen the eastern pacts. By the summer of 1937 ministers were at the end of their tethers. On 5 May Delbos admitted being 'at his wit's end' to devise an effective foreign policy. A fortnight later Blum 'agreed that Hitler had the political initiative ... he did not see any way to take the initiative out of the hands of Germany ... the situation was beginning to resemble more and more the situation before 1914.'[14] Not only was agreement with Germany no nearer but negotiations to reanimate the Little Entente failed. Worse still, Belgium in the autumn of 1936 abandoned her 1920 military agreement with France and returned to the pre-1914 policy of full neutrality. This pulled the plug on French plans to advance into Belgium to meet a German attack. Extending the Maginot Line in 1937, apart from being ruinously expensive, would only have consolidated Belgium's new stance. French leaders could only hope that the coming of war would frighten the Belgians into asking for help.

Only a military alliance with Britain or the Soviet Union could have repaired the breaches in French defences. Secret talks in 1936–37 for a Paris–Moscow military understanding were probably the last chance of an alliance. But French generals had no stomach for supping with the devil and repeatedly advised against them. And Britain sternly warned France against military links with Moscow. The role of ideology in shaping military assessments of the Soviet Union is exemplified by the Loizeau and Schweisguth missions of 1935 and 1936. Within a year two separate French general-staff missions visited the Soviet Union and reached contradictory conclusions. Impressed by Soviet strength Loizeau urged contacts. General Colson, deputy chief of the general staff, blocked Loizeau's report, ensuring that neither Gamelin nor the war minister saw it. The Rhineland coup did not soften military attitudes. *Rapprochements* with Italy, Poland and Czechoslovakia were recommended but Moscow was anathema – 'its help can only be limited, late and uncertain'. In September 1936 General Schweisguth attended Red Army manoeuvres and advised against a military agreement. Moscow was castigated because it seemed 'to be seeking even greater co-operation ... in order to force France into a confrontation with Germany'. Thus the USSR would 'become the arbiter in an exhausted Europe'.[15]

Appeasement

F rom late 1937 the immediate origins of the Second World War can be discerned. Hitler set Germany on a course of territorial expansion in central Europe which threatened France's allies Czechoslovakia and Poland. France's response was to speed up the search for *détente*. Only after Hitler's annexation of rump Czechoslovakia in March 1939 did France and Britain begin to consider stopping him by force. By allowing Hitler to believe that his territorial ambitions would not be opposed, French appeasement contributed to the making of the war.

Why did the French appease Germany for so long? The standard view was that France had no choice – fear, social strife and military unpreparedness dictated conciliation. French policy-makers blamed Britain for adding to internal pressures. 'The Munich Agreement', François-Poncet subsequently recorded, 'was the logical consequence of the policy practiced by Britain and France, but principally inspired by Britain.' French historians have endorsed the stereotype of a British 'governess', bullying and cajoling unwilling French charges along the road to war.[16]

This traditional interpretation requires substantial modification. Hitler's advent from 1933 presented France with three options – preventive war, submission or appeasement. Preventive war, as noted in Chapter 11, was not feasible. Submission would have meant accepting a settlement on Hitler's terms, abandoning allies. In short, vassal status in a German Europe. This was as unthinkable as preventive war. That left diplomacy – in other words, appeasement. The objective was a European settlement negotiated from strength. In the interim, diplomacy had to use all its tricks in order to gain time for rearmament. But the hope was that, with perseverance and German goodwill, a satisfactory compromise could be negotiated quickly – avoiding war and a ruinous arms race.

French appeasement was not solely fear-driven. Like its British counterpart, it was an amalgam of many influences. French leaders, far from being reluctant recruits in a British-inspired enterprise, were convinced appeasers. They sincerely wanted a Franco-German *rapprochement* and believed they could achieve one. Fear of Germany did not exclude genuine idealism – revisionism, passionate detestation of war, desire for disarmament and European harmony. France had to stay close to Britain because she had no other ally. However, the French made a virtue of necessity. By encouraging and exploiting British leadership French ministers provided themselves with an alibi for disengagement from east central Europe. While Paris seemingly bowed to British initiatives, in practice it pursued an active and independent line.

The strongest motive impelling French ministers was undoubtedly fear. 'The ambitions of Napoleon', declared premier Daladier in April 1938, 'were far inferior to the present aims of the German Reich ... if and when Germany had secured the petrol and wheat resources of Romania she would then turn against the western powers.'[17] Loss of influence since 1931 aroused apprehensions of decline. 'France', said Daladier in November 1938, had to choose 'between a slow decline and a renaissance through effort'.[18] But apprehensions of Germany and of decline were not the only motives at work. French leaders were filled with a hatred of war, as a result of the fighting in the trenches in 1914–18. Both Daladier and foreign minister George Bonnet had seen front-line service. France, Daladier insisted, must 'not sacrifice another million or two million peasants'.[19] Revisionism was another influence. There was sympathy for German grievances against Versailles. Both Daladier and Bonnet, cabled the American ambassador in September 1938, 'are convinced that the treaty [Versailles] must be revised and at bottom regard an alteration in the Czechoslovak state as a necessary revision'.[20]

Appeasement was also a response to social conflict and an ailing economy. The economy showed no upturn until the winter of 1938–39. From 1936 to 1938 governments battled to save the franc. Investors scared by the Popular Front sold their francs and exported gold. In May 1938 the franc was devalued for the third time in less than two years. In August 1938 a serious financial crisis erupted. Rearmament provoked deep despondency. 'If France should continue to arm at the present rate', declared one minister, 'it would be necessary to regiment the entire country, placing the civilian population on soldiers' wages and soldiers' rations.'[21]

The Popular Front fractured French society. Blum's conciliatory approaches to Germany in 1936–37 were partly motivated by the desire to protect social reform. International *détente* was needed for domestic *détente*. His radical socialist successors, Camille Chautemps and Edouard Daladier worked for *détente* but for different reasons. Agreements with Germany and Italy, it was hoped, would assuage the anxieties of the propertied. War, it was feared, might bring social revolution and the return of the Popular Front. Given peace abroad, Popular Front legislation could be quietly dismantled. 'Germany would be defeated in the war', affirmed Daladier, 'but the only gainers would be the Bolsheviks as there would be social revolution in every country of Europe.'[22] In September 1938 when war over Czechoslovakia seemed imminent, former premier Joseph Caillaux believed that 'heavy air bombardments of factories around Paris may well cause another Commune'.[23]

Was there an alternative to the Franco-German duel? Although the primary motivating instinct of French policy was fear, French leaders, like their British counterparts, nursed illusions about Germany. They believed that, with goodwill, agreement might be achieved. In 1936–37 Blum and Delbos made strenuous efforts to reach an understanding. On taking office Blum at once declared his readiness for an *entente*, provided Hitler accepted a new western security pact in place of Locarno. Indeed, Popular Front ministers departed from protocol and called on the newly appointed German ambassador. One illusion shaping appeasement was the notion that ideological differences were really secondary and should not hinder agreement. 'I am a Marxist and a Jew', Blum told German economic minister Dr Schacht, but 'we cannot achieve anything if we treat ideological barriers as insurmountable'.[24] Bonnet shared this illusion. 'It was necessary', he said in 1938, 'to get rid of ideological prejudices and, in the world as it exists today, employ the type of diplomacy which seeks to have as useful relations as possible with every country.'[25]

The main thrust of French appeasement in 1936–37 was the search for an economic and colonial arrangement with Germany.[26] Economic and colonial concessions, it was hoped, might win over German moderates, represented by Dr Schacht. Satisfaction of German claims would give the moderates leverage over party fanatics and discourage aggression. In August 1936 Schacht stressed Germany's need for colonies and markets. Blum and Delbos pursued this red herring assiduously. A settlement of the Spanish Civil War, Delbos informed Berlin, would provide the basis for a Franco-German pact. Germany 'should have raw materials, colonies and loans in return for which the only compensation was peace'. In February 1937 the French envisaged 'the creation of consortiums to develop sections of Africa ... all the African colonies except French North Africa and British South Africa would ... be put in a common pot'. Germany, it was admitted, would not be able to put up much money but a large proportion of the development would be done by German equipment. The plan was so secret that Blum and Delbos had not discussed it with the cabinet.

In 1938–39 Daladier and Bonnet cherished hopes of a Franco-German agreement. A sharp contrast is often drawn between the two men – Bonnet the out-and-out appeaser, Daladier the realist, bowing to British pressure but deeply suspicious of Germany. Physically, the two were a contrast. The stockily built, bull-necked, shortish premier looked much like a bundled-up Teddy Bear, projecting stolid, purposeful strength; the foreign minister, of taller build, had a prominent nose and a mobile, foxy countenance, exuding restlessness and subtle manoeuvrability. In truth, Daladier had more faith in conciliation than supposed. Despite or perhaps because of his recognition of the German danger he could not resist the lure of Franco-German reconciliation. The desire for a European settlement was not a panic response to the Czech crisis. As premier in 1933 he had agreed to join Mussolini's Four-Power Pact. Plans for a secret Hitler–Daladier meeting and a Franco-German declaration were mooted in 1933. On his return from the Munich Conference he defended the agreement: 'It's my policy, it's the Four-Power Pact.' He told the cabinet that contacts with Hitler might be fruitful. Although he recognized Munich as a major diplomatic defeat, his faith in negotiations was unshaken. At Marseilles he told the Radical Party Congress: 'When at Munich I heard the heart of the German people beating, I could not prevent myself thinking as I had done at Verdun, that between the French and German peoples ... there are strong ties of mutual respect which should lead to loyal collaboration.'

Anschluss and Munich

From the summer of 1937 to March 1939 France pursued appeasement with consistency and determination. Publicly the Chautemps cabinet of June 1937 declared its determination to fulfil all obligations; in practice it was willing to make substantial concessions in central and eastern Europe. At the Radical Party Congress in Lille in October 1937 Delbos's reaffirmation of alliance pledges did not mention Czechoslovakia by name. French ministers were said to be willing to do their 'utmost to effect a general settlement with Germany' and would raise no objection 'to an evolutionary extension of German influence in Austria ... or in Czechoslovakia'.

Chautemps was inhibited from explicit disengagement by the fear of breaking up the Popular Front majority. 'Chautemps', cabled the American ambassador, 'will wish personally to enter into direct negotiations with Germany and perhaps make the necessary concessions: in other words, to abandon Austria and the Germans of Czechoslovakia to Hitler. But he will know that his government will fall if he tries to put this policy into practice.' However, where Britain led, France could safely follow. In May 1937 British foreign policy came under new management. Conservative premier Neville Chamberlain in his eagerness to negotiate a European settlement was willing to take France in tow. Acceptance of British leadership provided France with both a scapegoat and an insurance cover. The closer France stayed to Britain the more the British would feel committed to her. In London on 29–30 November 1937 British ministers refused to guarantee Czechoslovakia. Chautemps and Delbos offered only token resistance to British designs. It was agreed that London should take the initiative in approaches to Berlin and Rome.

By mid-February 1938 the leadership seemed resigned to the erosion of influence in the east. Fatalism prevailed. Chautemps thought it 'probable' that 'central and eastern Europe would slip into the hands of Germany without war'.[27] On 12 March German troops marched into Vienna and Hitler proclaimed the union (*Anschluss*) of Germany and Austria. Hitler, by two bloodless victories in two years, had almost reversed the verdict of 1918. French requests for British support for Austria were diplomatic flourishes, designed to reassure parliament and the Czechs. French prestige in central Europe, signalled the military attache in Vienna, had been 'almost completely annihilated, even among those who claim to be the most loyal'.[28]

After the *Anschluss* Czechoslovakia's days were numbered. With a strong army of thirty-five divisions and alliances with France and the Soviet Union, Czechoslovakia was a barrier to German control of central Europe. Blum's fleeting return to power did nothing to change policy. Buffeted by storms on all sides – the loss of his wife, political intrigues to unseat him, industrial unrest, Senate opposition to his financial reforms, ill-concealed British antipathy – the premier and his foreign minister Paul-Boncour had no real chance to reappraise options. France and Britain in the week after the *Anschluss*, without consulting each other, decided their policies on Czechoslovakia. On 15 March the permanent committee of national defence concluded that France could not help Prague directly. The major part of the meeting was an examination of the possibilities of French intervention in Spain. Blum's desire to save the Spanish Republic elicited a biting comment from war minister Daladier: 'One would have to be blind not to see that intervention in Spain would unleash a general war.' The meeting confirmed France's impotence. As Léger put it: 'France can only react to events, she could not take the initiative.'[29]

VOILA CE QUI NOUS ATTEND, SI LE GOUVERNEMENT N'EST PAS CAPABLE DE SORTIR L'AVIATION FRANÇAISE DE LA SITUATION DRAMATIQUE OÙ L'A PLACÉE LE FRONT POPULAIRE!

'Here's what's in store for us if the government cannot rescue the air force from the terrible state in which the Popular Front left it.'
Poster.

Throughout the summer France and Britain pressurized the Czechs into conceding more and more to the Sudeten German minority. By September 1938 German storm troops were massed on the frontiers of Czechoslovakia. Appeals for a conference reached Hitler from Mussolini, Chamberlain and President Roosevelt of the United States. Since his public demands for the German-speaking Sudetenland were virtually assured, Hitler issued invitations to a conference in Munich on 29 September. The Munich

Agreement dismembered Czechoslovakia by ceding the Sudetenland to Germany. Militarily there was a case for resisting Germany in September 1938. France had a last chance of fighting on better or at least even terms. Gamelin saw clearly what was at stake, warning Daladier on 27 September that if Germany was not resisted then within a decade France would become a 'second class power'.[30] With Germany nearing the peak of rearmament and amassing more trained reserves, France's position could only deteriorate. At sea France and Britain were more than a match for Germany. Their weakness lay in air power. But Germany's shortcomings were serious – shortage of trained reserves and of oil, for which she was heavily dependent on purchases from the west. Moreover, the bulk of the German army had to be deployed against Czechoslovakia, leaving only ten divisions in the west facing the French army. Since the concrete in the Siegfried Line was not dry there was little to stop a determined French offensive. Needless to say, although France mobilized, there were no plans for an offensive. Apologists of Munich stressed the divisions of opinion and public support for the Munich Agreement. In fact, the government, through influence on the media, manufactured support for appeasement. Arguably, it could have mobilized support for resisting Germany (see Chapter 10).

 French military intelligence made two serious overestimates – the strength of the Siegfried Line and the number of German divisions available for immediate mobilization.[31] The general staff was told that the Siegfried Line in September 1938, although unfinished, could be utilized and constituted a formidable barrier. On 27 September, two days before Munich, military intelligence advised that Germany could mobilize 120 divisions and was ready for 'general war'. In official discussions with ministers Gamelin exploited this overestimate of German fortifications. Officially, he cited it as a reason for not fighting for Czechoslovakia; privately, he admitted that 'another year or even more would be necessary to make the Siegfried Line really formidable'.

French policy in the Munich crisis was much more assertive and independent than supposed. Following the British governess had two purposes: first, to ensure that Britain had the lion's share of responsibility for the abandonment of Czechoslovakia; second, to secure additional British commitments. Major modifications were secured, namely, the promise on 18 September of British participation in a guarantee for Czechoslovakia and on 26 September a British pledge of support for France in the event of war with Germany. When war appeared imminent on 27 September France not only seconded a British timetable for the transfer of the Sudetenland to Germany but tempted Hitler with a larger slice of the cake. During the summer Bonnet skilfully played a double game – encouraging London to believe that he was exerting strong pressure on Prague while discreetly following a cautious and moderate line until early July. When on the night of 20–21 September a French ultimatum was sent to Prague to enforce acceptance of the Franco-British cession plan, Britain was made to shoulder chief responsibility.

'No thanks . . . I'd rather "Live for France"!'
A right-wing cartoon showing a French soldier who prefers to live for France than die for other countries or causes.
Je Suis Partout, 11 November 1938

A free hand in the east?

After Munich the search for agreement with the fascist dictators quickened. Despite the acrimony which had soured Franco-Italian relations since Abyssinia, Daladier strove for understanding. Only Italian cussedness prevented agreement in October 1938. An orchestrated anti-French demonstration in the Italian Chamber on 30 November culminated in shouts of 'Nice, Corsica and Tunis'. Overtures to Germany were more successful. In December German foreign minister von Ribbentrop came to Paris for the signing of a Franco-German Declaration. It had three clauses: a declaration of friendship and goodwill, confirmation of the existing Franco-German frontier as fixed and final and an undertaking to consult together on matters of common interest. The Bonnet-Ribbentrop discussions, like the Laval–Mussolini conversations of January 1935, generated more heat than light. At the time and later the French minister was accused of giving Germany a 'free hand' in eastern Europe. But, with the exception of a single ambiguous phrase in the German record of the Paris talks of 6–7 December, no evidence has been found of such an assurance. Arguably, no assurance was given because none was needed. Merely signing such an agreement in the wake of Munich was a tacit acquiescence in Germany's claim to hegemony in eastern Europe.

Yet the French did not want to give Germany a completely free hand. They did not rush to liquidate interests in central and eastern Europe. Despite Bonnet's wish to abandon the Polish and Soviet alliances, the alliances were maintained and even reaffirmed on 29 January 1939. The ambiguity of the Franco-German talks, which Ribbentrop interpreted as a free hand for Germany in the east, was partly deliberate, partly inevitable. There were conflicting voices: Bonnet wished to disengage quickly from the east, Daladier wanted to maintain a French presence. Some confusion was unavoidable since France needed time to take stock. Ambiguity was a response to the uncertainty surrounding German intentions. Germany, it was hoped, would expand in the east, perhaps in the Ukraine, but there was no certainty. Until Hitler showed his hand it was prudent to postpone major policy decisions. Ambiguity was also dictated by the need to retain a bargaining position *vis à vis* Germany and Italy. The Franco-German accord was viewed as a possible lever against Italy. In return for French acceptance of gradual and peaceful German expansion in the east Hitler might be persuaded to muzzle Mussolini. It was imperative, therefore, not to surrender too much too soon.

Barcelona's fall on 26 January 1939 brought the end of the Spanish Civil War in sight. The consequences threatened to close in on France like a garrote. France was menaced on three fronts – the Rhine, the Alps and the

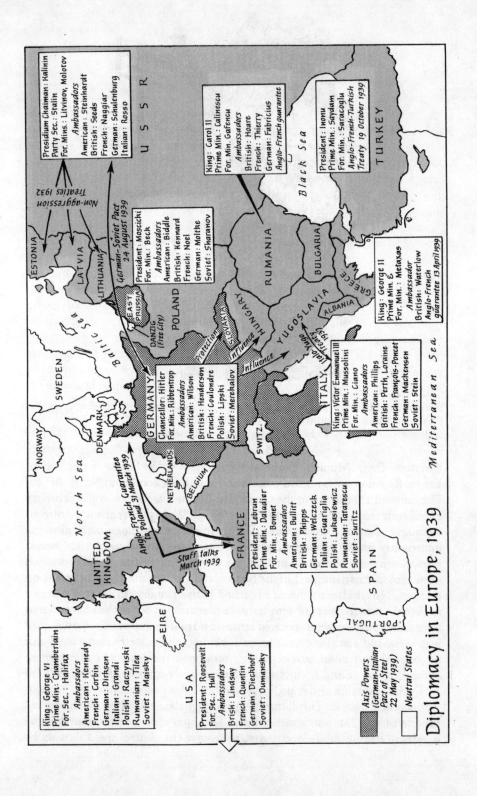

USSR

Presidium Chairman: Kalinin
Party Sec.: Stalin
For. Mins.: Litvinov, Molotov
Ambassadors
American: Steinhardt
British: Seeds
French: Naggiar
German: Schulenburg
Italian: Rosso

Non-aggression Treaties 1932

German–Soviet Pact
24 August 1939

King: Carol II
Prime Min.: Calinescu
For. Min.: Gafencu
Ambassadors
British: Hoare
French: Thierry
German: Fabricius
Anglo–French guarantee

TURKEY

President: Inonu
Prime Min.: Saydam
For. Min.: Saracoglu
Anglo–French–Turkish
Treaty 19 October 1939

Black Sea

RUMANIA

BULGARIA

GREECE

ALBANIA

King: George II
Prime Min. &
For. Min.: Metaxas
Ambassador
British: Waterlow
Anglo–French
guarantee 13 April 1939

President: Moscicki
For. Min.: Beck
Ambassadors
American: Biddle
British: Kennard
French: Noel
German: Moltke
Soviet: Sharanov

POLAND

DANZIG
(Free City)

EAST
PRUSSIA

ESTONIA

LATVIA

LITHUANIA

SWEDEN

Baltic Sea

NORWAY

DENMARK

North Sea

Anglo–French Guarantee
to Poland 31 March 1939

Staff talks
March 1939

GERMANY

Chancellor: Hitler
For. Min.: Ribbentrop
Ambassadors
American: Wilson
British: Henderson
French: Coulondre
Polish: Lipski
Soviet: Merekalov

Protectorate

SLOVAKIA

Influence

HUNGARY

Influence

YUGOSLAVIA

Italy 1937

ITALY

SWITZ.

NETHERLANDS

BELGIUM

King: Victor Emmanuel III
Prime Min.: Mussolini
For. Min.: Ciano
Ambassadors
American: Phillips
British: Perth, Loraine
French: François-Poncet
German: Mackensen
Soviet: Stein

UNITED
KINGDOM

King: George VI
Prime Min.: Chamberlain
For. Sec.: Halifax
Ambassadors
American: Kennedy
French: Corbin
German: Dirksen
Italian: Grandi
Polish: Raczynski
Rumanian: Tilea
Soviet: Maisky

EIRE

FRANCE

President: Lebrun
Prime Min.: Daladier
For. Min.: Bonnet
Ambassadors
American: Bullitt
British: Phipps
German: Welczeck
Italian: Guariglia
Polish: Lukasiewicz
Rumanian: Tatarescu
Soviet: Surits

SPAIN

PORTUGAL

Mediterranean Sea

USA

President: Roosevelt
For. Sec.: Hull
Ambassadors
Brish: Lindsay
French: Quentin
German: Dieckhoff
Soviet: Oumansky

Axis Powers
(German–Italian
Pact of Steel
22 May 1939)

Neutral States

Diplomacy in Europe, 1939

'And now, I'm coming – to work in France'
A right-wing cartoon demonizes defeated Spanish Republicans seeking refuge in
France as Bolshevik bandits.
Gringoire, 26 January 1939

Pyrenees. Since Munich, Franco-Italian relations had gone from bad to
worse. By February both countries were poised for conflict in North Africa.
The only light at the end of the tunnel was Britain's tardy offer on 3 February
of full staff talks. For the first time since World War I the French were offered
a military alliance. The revolution in British policy was the result of growing
uncertainty and suspicion of Hitler's intentions. In January 1939 secret
reports – mostly the work of German opposition groups – warned of an
imminent German invasion of the Netherlands, coupled with an air attack on
London. No similar intelligence reached Paris. The only crisis that worried
the French was the dispute with Italy. Leaders responded to the international
uncertainty in three ways. First, in central and eastern Europe the watchword
was wait and see. Despite intense lobbying, the eastern pacts were not
denounced or revised, and a French economic presence was maintained.
Second, Daladier and Bonnet strove energetically for a *modus vivendi* with
Berlin, encouraging and expediting economic discussions under the Franco-
German declaration. Third, ministers made it clear that they would defend
Mediterranean interests against Italy. The failure of a secret mission, the
Baudouin mission of 2–3 February, to resolve the quarrel was followed by

military confrontation in North Africa. Fears of an Axis-controlled Spain were partly allayed by the Bérard–Jordana agreement of 25 February giving General Franco *de jure* recognition. On the eve of Hitler's occupation of Prague, France was bracing itself for Mussolini's next move. The government, wired the American ambassador, 'believe unacceptable demands will be made by Mussolini between tenth and end of March ... France may expect Mussolini to make war at any time after the middle of March.'[32]

Prague

The shock of Hitler's Prague coup of 15 March 1939 revitalized French policy. Franco-British guarantees were showered on eastern Europe and the Balkans: on Poland on 31 March, on Greece and Romania on 13 April, on Turkey on 12 May. In mid-April France and Britain opened negotiations with the Soviet Union for a treaty of mutual assistance. On four key issues – the Romanian guarantee, British conscription, contacts with Italy and negotiations with Moscow – France had her own way. Léger urged Daladier to stand firm, writing: 'London has been accustomed for so long to see Paris follow the English watch-word that there was complete surprise to see us maintain our point of view in spite of English objections or scruples.'[33] Though London considered that the announcement of a guarantee to Romania was best left until after the conclusion of negotiations with Poland and Turkey, Daladier demanded and obtained an announcement on 13 April. French appeals for the introduction of conscription reached a crescendo after Mussolini's invasion of Albania on 7 April. President Roosevelt's help was enlisted. Paris insisted on an announcement of conscription before Hitler's Reichstag speech on 28 April and Chamberlain complied on the 26th. As for Italy, Chamberlain believed that Mussolini might be persuaded to exercise a moderating influence on Hitler. To this end, he asked the French to kiss and make up with Italy. Notwithstanding repeated requests, including a personal appeal from Chamberlain in July, Daladier refused an approach to Rome. In the Moscow talks the French made all the running, urging reluctant British partners to close quickly with the Russians. Impatient of British procrastination the French, instead of keeping in step, released their own much firmer proposals to the Russians.

Why were French attitudes transformed so quickly? Of course, Britain in the light of the German peril now needed France and became more cooperative. The revival of the French economy in the winter of 1938–39 reversed the gold flow, generating new confidence. Daladier's tough stance towards Italy brought a huge fan mail, making him the most popular premier since Poincaré. Decree powers reinforced the government's political stability.

Public and parliamentary opinion contributed significantly to the change of gear. The Chambers were in session in mid-March and demanded energetic measures. By annexing non-Germans Hitler at a stroke destroyed the moral justification which his policy had hitherto enjoyed. Daladier, advised by Léger, took greater control of policy-making, bypassing Bonnet, the leading proponent of appeasement. But the most important factor in galvanizing the French was the atmosphere of imminent European war. The alarums and excursions of March–April, starting with Hitler's occupation of Prague, concentrated minds as never before. On 23 March Hitler occupied Memel; on 7 April Mussolini invaded Albania. The intelligence dimension deepened the climate of gloom and doom. Intelligence appreciations, by emphasizing the imminence of war, helped inject a new decisiveness into French policy.[34] On 16 March Daladier was advised that the Prague coup could be 'the start of a very serious crisis in the near future menacing France directly'. Joint German–Italian action might develop 'in a very short time . . . April is the leit-motiv in most of the information received'. The most likely option was German action against Holland, together with Italian operations from Libya. More alarms and confusions followed Hitler's occupation of Memel. From MAD, a secret source which had predicted 15 March for the Prague coup, came the warning: 'The Danzig affair will be settled on 1 April or 2nd at the latest . . . Germany intends to reorganise the Romanian army and make it a vassal force.' On the morning of 9 April Colonel Gauché, head of military intelligence (*Deuxième Bureau*), forwarded new information. War was 'inevitable and very near; the delay will not last beyond 20 April'. The conflict would begin with a massive air attack on London and Paris, accompanied by seizure of the Romanian oil fields. Gauché believed that unity of views had now been established between the three dictators, Hitler, Mussolini and Franco.

Last weeks

On 14 July 1939, the 150th anniversary of the French Revolution, 30,000 troops paraded along the Champs Elysées. As a mark of Franco-British solidarity the chief of the imperial general staff, Lord Gort, took the salute jointly with his French counterpart, General Gamelin. While Royal Air Force bombers thundered overhead, large black tanks advanced, each marked on its turret with hearts, spades, clubs and diamonds. 'France had put all its cards on the table', joked one observer. In fact, France was on the mend; gold continued to flow back and the industrial climate seemed more settled than it had been for three years. Rearmament was showing significant returns, especially in the air. Annual production of warplanes reached 2,000 in 1939, double 1938. In land forces France ranked third after

Germany and the Soviet Union; in naval and air power it held fourth place after Germany, the Soviet Union and Britain. Across the Rhine the Germans put up an enormous hoarding on which was painted 'Ein Volk, Ein Reich, Ein Führer'. In reply the French had an equally large hoarding proclaiming 'Liberté, Egalité, Fraternité'. France still believed herself the champion of culture, liberty and democracy. The head of the French pavilion at the 1939 New York World Fair, when asked what tomorrow's world would be like, replied: 'Tomorrow's world like yesterday's and today's, will be pre-eminently of French inspiration.'[35]

The self-confident facade, however, concealed doubts and divisions. To be sure, cries of 'Why die for Danzig?' did not reflect majority views; in July, 76 per cent of respondents said France should fight if Germany seized Danzig. Yet appeasement was far from dead. It had always been a mixture of conciliation and firmness. Firmness was now to the fore, but hopes persisted that war could be postponed or avoided. Moreover, Franco-British unity left a lot to be desired. In the vital first weeks of the Moscow negotiations the two western democracies were seriously out of step. At the beginning of August, French and British ministers were still arguing over travel arrangements for the military missions requested by the Russians. Although French and British staffs met regularly, no permanent machinery existed for the coordination of war plans.

The lengthy and frustrating Franco-British-Russian haggling of April–August 1939 allowed Hitler and Stalin ample time to reach agreement. The Nazi–Soviet pact of 23 August rendered war inevitable. The Soviet Union's benevolent neutrality freed Hitler from the danger of a two-front war. Poland could be attacked in safety. Would the course of events have been different if French leaders had known of the German-Soviet talks? Conceivably, France might have persuaded Britain to conclude an alliance quickly and forestall Germany. On hearing of the Nazi-Soviet pact Daladier reminded the American ambassador William Bullitt that 'at least six times since last January' the envoy 'had warned him that most serious negotiations were under way'. The premier asked for an investigation 'but had been reassured that there were no negotiations other than the commercial negotiations in progress between Germany and the Soviet Union'.[36] Since serious German-Soviet political talks did not take place until mid-July it would be wrong to criticize French intelligence too severely. They had precious little time to discover what was afoot. More blameworthy was the United States. Thanks to the German diplomat in Moscow, Johnnie von Herwarth, the United States was well informed of the German-Soviet contacts. But Washington kept Paris in the dark and von Herwarth did not confide in his French or British colleagues.

On 19 August Gauché predicted that Germany would be ready to attack Poland by the end of the month: 'It was not humanly possible to get closer to the truth.'[37] But the truth was now too close. The approach of war revealed a divided leadership. Publicly ministers proclaimed firmness and determination, privately they flinched from the impending conflict. Daladier and a majority believed Hitler was bluffing and all that they had to do was stand firm and indicate a willingness to talk. Bonnet and a smaller group of associates worked for a second Munich. Until 23 August Paris assumed that an alliance with the Soviet Union would deter Hitler. The German-Soviet pact of 23 August demolished this calculation. At Bonnet's behest, Daladier summoned a special war council. Bonnet planned to corner Gamelin and extract from him a counsel of despair – an admission that the armed forces were not ready for war. Poland could then be jettisoned. Gamelin gave no ground, pointing out that if France did not fulfil the alliance her security in western Europe would be endangered since Germany stood to gain most from a respite. More circumspectly, Daladier was also looking for an exit. The Poles, he told the cabinet on 24 August, 'must sacrifice Danzig. They ought to have done so earlier.'[38] He wrote a conciliatory letter to Hitler, offering his services as a mediator. French representations on 29 August induced Warsaw to postpone mobilization for several hours. These few hours were crucial, since they meant that a quarter of the army never reached the units at the front.

Misleading intelligence and wishful thinking contributed to the firmness of French declarations. Desperately, ministers and advisors clutched at reports of flagging German morale and wobbling in high places. On 30 August ambassador Robert Coulondre informed Daladier: 'Hitler has been hesitating. Irresolution has gripped the heart of the Nazi Party. Reports indicate a growing discontent among the people.' 'Hold Fast', counselled Coulondre.[39] On 31 August Mussolini proposed a conference. Bonnet was delighted at the hope of a last-minute reprieve. Frantically, he strove to keep the Italian conference proposal in play, even after the German attack on Poland. At a confused and stormy meeting of the cabinet on 31 August, Bonnet pleaded for the conference idea. Daladier, bristling with anger and contempt, turned his back.

At dawn on 1 September German armies invaded Poland. Hitler's aggression activated the Franco-Polish alliance of 1921 and the British guarantee of 31 March 1939. While Poland fought for her life, the French and British governments pursued Mussolini's proposal. Finally, the French ultimatum demanding a German withdrawal from Poland was delivered in Berlin on 3 September – with an expiry deadline six hours later than the British document. The failure to synchronize the ultimatums encapsulated the *mésentente cordiale* which had prevailed since 1919. The delays surrounding the declarations of war have been blamed on the French. But there was no plot to betray Poland and surrender to Germany. Daladier knew that France would not survive the demoralization of a second Munich. The truth was that neither Paris nor London was in a hurry to go to war. The assumption was that the war would be a long one and that nothing could be done to save Poland. For military and political reasons Daladier and Gamelin were as keen as Bonnet to delay the delivery of an ultimatum. They wanted

Table 6   Opposing forces, September 1939

	Great Britain	France	Germany
Combat divisions	4	110 (90 in France: 2,776,000 men out of 5 million mobilised)	103 (2,600,000 men)
Armoured divisions	–	1 in formation	5
Tanks	–	2,946	2,977
Naval strength (Capital ships+subs)	36+57	15+78	7+56
Total air strength	1,377	1,254 of which 463 modern	3,228

Source: Girault and Frank, *Turbulente Europe et nouveaux mondes, 1914–1941* (1988), p. 242

to gain time for mobilization and the evacuation of civilians. Pressed by London to advance the French ultimatum, Gamelin remarked: 'They want us to declare war today, but they are only going to send their aircraft tomorrow.' France went to war reluctantly – the confidence and optimism of 1914 replaced by a fatalistic 'let's finish this once and for all' (*il faut en finir*). Apart from Poland, France could count on only four British divisions (see Table 6). 'Never in her history would France enter a war in such initially unfavourable conditions', declared the chief of French intelligence.[40]

Epilogue

And you all know security
Is mortals' chiefest enemy

Macbeth III.v.32

It is easy, it is very easy for us to lose the war.
   Paul Reynaud speaking in French parliament, 13 December 1939, *In the Thick of the Fight 1930–1945* (New York, 1955), p.240

Can it be that France has had her day like Athens, Rome, Spain or Portugal in the past? Is it Germany's turn now? No. Our virtues and our culture, which only twenty years ago proved strong and full of life, have not been killed by a mere handful of politicians.
   Major D. Barlone, *A French Officer's Diary*, in Alistair Horne, *To Lose a Battle* (1990 edn), p.640

On 10 May German armies invaded Holland and Belgium. As French and British forces advanced into Belgium to meet the onslaught, German armour punched a hole through the French line at Sedan and raced to the coast, cutting the allied forces in two. 'We have lost the battle', premier Paul Reynaud told Winston Churchill on 16 May. 'We have no reserves', added Gamelin.[1] As leaders deliberated at the Quai d'Orsay, bonfires of secret papers blazed in the courtyard. When the government fled Paris on 10 June for Tours, confusion and panic brought tragi-comedy. French army headquarters were at the Château de Muguet, near Briare, which had fifteen bedrooms and stables for twelve horses but only one telephone near the toilet in a passageway at the back of the building. Reynaud's mistress, Countess Hélène de Portes, was observed standing in the courtyard of the Château de

Chissay, wearing a dressing gown over her bright red pyjamas and directing traffic.

The battle of France was over in six weeks. An armistice was signed on 22 June in the same railway carriage at Compiègne in which Germany had surrendered in November 1918. At the time, and later, Germany was believed to have had overwhelming superiority in men and material. This was not so. In numbers and equipment the opposing sides were well matched. Germany's advantage lay in strategic doctrine. Armoured divisions, backed by tactical air support, explained the German triumph. The defeat was primarily a military one. Political and ideological weaknesses contributed to the collapse but did not determine it.

The phoney war of 1939–40 had a demoralizing effect. From the start the war had been a half-hearted affair. Round one of the Second World War was a German–Polish duel. Apart from mobilizing, no effective help was given to Poland. 'Too many' members of the government, the Polish ambassador was told, were 'hostile to the war'.[2] On 8 September – the day German forces reached the outskirts of Warsaw – the French high command ordered that on no account should German troops be fired on. France was not committed to launch a relief offensive until the sixteenth day of mobilization. Unsurprisingly, no relief action was attempted. On 17 September Soviet armies attacked from the east, claiming Moscow's share of the spoils under the secret partition protocol of the 23 August Nazi–Soviet pact. By the end of the month Poland lay crushed and divided.

This was a 'funny kind of war' (*drôle de guerre*) in more senses than one. Millions were mobilized yet, except at sea, no one was fighting. From the Maginot Line the French watched German troops playing football. VIPs returned from visits to the Line with souvenir medals, as though from a shrine. All the action was on the home front. Instead of a political closing of ranks, a sacred union as in 1914, divisions and dissent grew. French conservatives, like their British counterparts, feared that the west was 'committing suicide, whilst Stalin laughs and the Kremlin triumphs.'[3] On Moscow's orders, French communists did an about turn, switching from an anti-fascist to an anti-war stance. Daladier dissolved the party on 26 September, stripping communist deputies of their parliamentary mandates. The repression of communists aroused more enthusiasm than fighting Hitler. Parliamentary pressures forced Daladier's resignation on 19 March 1940. He was blamed for military inaction, especially for not rushing to the defence of Finland when it was attacked by the Soviet Union on 30 November.

The military formula was one of war on the cheap – getting allies to do the fighting in the hope of weakening Germany and gaining time. Gamelin's attitude was 'deeply cynical'.[4] At Franco-Polish military talks in May 1939 Gamelin blatantly misled the Poles, encouraging them to believe that they could count on a relief offensive. The Poles were sacrificed on the wildly overconfident assumption that they would hold out until the spring of 1940, giving France extra time. The strategy of winning the war without fighting –

waiting for the economic blockade to do its work, gaining time for full British mobilization and American aid on 'cash and carry' terms, hoping too, for a Hitler–Stalin quarrel – was seriously flawed and self-defeating.

Little was done to repair the ravages of twenty years of *mésentente cordiale*. There was no common Franco-British strategy, only a common determination to avoid fighting. In the battle of France Britain did not commit her full air power. No unified interallied command existed. The supreme war council had no permanent secretariat to keep records and preserve continuity. The war of make-believe was expressed in conflicting plans. French ministers concocted a peripheral strategy, proposing offensives in Scandinavia, the Caucasus, Salonika and Petsamo – almost anywhere, in fact, except on the Rhine. British ministers devised schemes for offensive action on the Rhine and in the Ruhr. The result was vacillation and paralysis. When in April 1940 the Allies finally took the plunge and sent an expeditionary force to Norway the operation was muffed.

Moreover, reliance on economic asphyxia was misplaced since Germany drew on raw materials from eastern Europe and the Soviet Union. Belgian neutrality was another weakness in allied strategy. Instead of staying in prepared defences on the Belgian frontier, Gamelin's war plan was to move forward into Belgium in the event of a German attack. Yet Brussels, although apprehensive of a German onslaught in early November, refused to authorize the advance of French forces as a preventive measure. The waiting game was flawed in two vital respects: it assumed that time would work for the allies – in fact Germany gained more from the breathing space – and second, waiting encouraged doubts and self-questioning in the armies and at home. Sartre, serving as an army weather forecaster in Alsace, wondered why war had been declared. 'To defend democracy?' He asked. 'It no longer exists. To preserve the pre-war state of affairs? It was the most complete disorder ... '. Some argued that with Poland's destruction the original cause of the conflict had disappeared and peace could be made. Hitler's peace offer of 6 October on a 'forgive and forget' basis produced some intense lobbying in Paris. The French seemed to be between the devil and the deep blue sea. Peace was tempting but the price was high. Daladier rejected the offer: 'We will only lay down our arms when we have a guarantee of security which will not be challenged every six months.' His advisors warned that making peace would be a 'veritable catastrophe ... breaking the nation's moral spring. It would be difficult to mobilize again in case of danger . . . It would be a humiliation ... and a definitive establishment of German hegemony'.[5]

But marking time for months was demoralizing. A partial antidote would have been vigorous propaganda aimed at convincing the nation that it was fighting for an independent existence. On 18 October Hitler approved Operation Yellow, an attack on France through Luxembourg, Belgium and The Netherlands. The date was set for 12 November and then postponed because of bad weather. Unfortunately, France's commissioner for information, Jean Giraudoux, was no more effective than he had been as foreign ministry press chief in the 1920s. Home-front propaganda was a damp squib. Restaurants and stations displayed large maps of the world with French and British possessions coloured red. Below ran the caption 'We will win because we are the strongest'. It sounded more like a Sumo wrestling match slogan than a call to arms. The 'Let's finish it once and for all' (*il faut en finir*) inscription on scarves and handkerchiefs had all the passion of an old gas bill. In practice, the motto was 'Let's forget about it'. Hitler and the Siegfried Line became part of the Folies Bergère repertoire. Paris had a 'business as usual' mood. British pacifist Vera Brittain found the blackout much less severe than London and the atmosphere 'totally different from the tense, tragic city' of 1914–1918.[6]

Were the retreats that led to war and collapse avoidable? Could the game have been played differently? The received version holds that the victory of 1918 was too dearly bought. France had no choice. Two points are worth making – one philosophical, the other methodological. Inevitability is a magic word to mesmerize the unwary. Past events were once in the future and then they were not inevitable. 'The irresistible', Mr Justice Brandeis remarked, 'is often only that which is not resisted.' Second, the student of foreign policy relies heavily on the official record. This has its perils. The abundant, well-arranged documentation validates the establishment's perception of its problems and policies. Thus historians can conclude that ministers could have done only what they did. All the more reason therefore to explore alternatives. From 1919 to 1931 France had both the potential and opportunity to shape a European settlement. Wanting was the wit and determination. To be sure, France paid a high price for the victory of 1918 but Germany and Japan, although devastated and occupied in 1945, became leading economic powers in the second half of the century. After 1958, de Gaulle's France recovered quickly from incipient civil war and a crippling colonial conflict in Algeria.

Why, then, did French leaders not make more of their chances? One major fault line was organizational. The increasingly complicated and rapid interaction of military, diplomatic, domestic political and international political considerations demanded skilful coordination and integration of foreign and defence policies. However, the malfunctioning of the government machine inhibited the rethinking of grand strategy. Delays and confusion abounded. In February 1940 Daladier discovered that preparations for sending an expeditionary force to Finland had not been carried out – units which should have been at sea were still in France. In March 1940 France's economic warfare mission in London had to be reorganized as 'its members were not capable of handling the difficult problems with which they were confronted'.[7] The handling of political and military negotiations with Poland in May 1939 revealed a horrifying, almost unbelievable, lack of liaison between foreign ministry, war ministry and Daladier's office. The biggest obstacle to the modernization of government was liberal democracy. The effective conduct of foreign policy, De

Tocqueville observed, demands the perfect use of almost all those qualities in which a democracy is deficient. For a variety of reasons – civil–military friction, dislike of a powerful executive, interdepartmental jealousies, ephemeral cabinets and plain inertia – ministers and advisors lacked the proper means to judge priorities and devise solutions. 'We lived from day to day', Gamelin conceded, 'without prospects or plans.'[8] The nation's shortcoming was not inability to adapt but failure to adapt quickly enough. Before 1914 the Republic had been first off the mark with foreign ministry reform. To be sure, the disarray of government machines was common to all the great powers before 1914 and before 1939. The Third Reich had its own version of administrative anarchy, but Hitler, unlike French leaders, had the will and ability to act.

Defective decision-making was in part a function of an ailing political system – short-lived coalition cabinets at the mercy of an over-mighty parliament. The system is said to have excluded 'any coherent, long-term policy'.[9] This is too sweeping. In fact a highly constraining system allowed for substantial achievements – restoration of ravaged regions after 1918, rearmament from 1936. Explanations of France's disappointing per-formance have tended to minimize the responsibility of the players. Yet contemporaries were shocked by the inadequacies of French leadership. In January 1936 the American ambassador signalled 'a lack of courageous, vital, disinterested, resourceful and imaginative leadership'. Two years on, another American diplomat talked to the newly appointed French envoy to Washington: 'When I asked him whether he saw any possibility of preserving peace, he said that he saw none. He did not feel that there was anything France and England could do or should do except wait. I said to him that this seemed to me not the policy of a statesman but the policy of an undertaker.'[10]

Faulty statecraft hobbled the bid for power. Clemenceau's strategy at the Paris Peace Conference did not make the most of France's strengths. Poincaré's bungling of the Ruhr operation wrecked the first bid for hegemony. Even so, sharp statecraft might have salvaged something from the wreckage. Alas, Herriot bargained away his country's negotiating position. 1931 was, in Maurice Vaïsse's words, 'the year of missed opportunities'.[11] French financial strength could have served as leverage for *rapprochement* with Berlin. Germany's price was revision of Versailles. The conservative, unimaginative, overcautious outlook of political and military chiefs blocked concessions.

French statesmen were no match for Hitler. Laval's casual opportunism drove Gamelin to tears. Blum was a self-doubting intellectual: 'I do not know if I have the qualities of a leader ... it's a test that you are going to make on me and I am going to make on myself.'[12] The eel-like, arch-manipulator Chautemps, a political lightweight, was so pleased to escape from duties that 'even before a cocktail he turned somersaults on the lawn'.[13] Daladier, fortified by decree powers and the international crisis, enjoyed a much stronger position than any premier since Poincaré. Yet 'the bull of Vaucluse' (his constituency), as he was popularly known, belied his name. Self-doubt fettered his powers of initiative and decision; after being talked into making up his mind he would go back upon it or he would make himself inaccessible to advisors like Gamelin who wanted a ruling from him. In 1940 Reynaud, like Daladier, disappointed those who had seen in him a saviour figure.

Policy-makers were conditioned by various attitudes and assumptions. The preference for abstract, intellectual discussion became an end in itself. A problem discussed was a problem solved. In Proustian fashion, issues and information were painstakingly analysed from all angles but action shunned. Some general staff papers were so abstract that they had to be read several times to discover the sense. The waiting strategy of 1939-40 was in part a refusal to decide. A profound pessimism about the future of France and of Europe induced caution and compromise. 'The Great War for Civilization' had endangered civilized values. To abandon the quest for peace and prepare for war seemed a denial of 1914–18 losses and sacrifices. Yet pactomania – the obsessive search for security through treaties – was a snare and delusion. Complete security was a chimera. France had to live with risk and uncertainty. Another inhibition was the liberal assumption that there can be no final incompatible aspirations where the wishes of one person or community are wholly irreconcilable with those of another. Consequently, politicians underestimated the ideological divide between dictatorships and democracies. 'Certain people seem incapable of seeing that the only way to constrain a strong country is by war', exclaimed one minister in April 1936.[14] But readiness to resort to force presupposed confidence in one's cause. By the mid-1930s many assumed that the 1919 treaty structure was bound to collapse. The belief that the treaties were doomed stemmed partly from the feeling that they were unfair and unenforceable, partly from the conviction that, as new nations, Germany and Italy had the initiative. The tide of expansion could be ridden, not reversed. French leaders mistakenly assumed that the dictators shared their own detestation of war. In reality, for Hitler and Mussolini, war and peace were one keyboard. Force, threats of force, subversion, conciliation – all formed one process.

Yet a willingness to review options might have preserved French power after 1933. Given the ethos of liberal internationalism which inspired western leaders, surrender and preventive war were equally unthinkable. But the diplomacy adopted did not necessarily have to take the form that it did. A policy might have been devised which upheld liberal values and the desire for a peaceful settlement, yet demonstrated determination to defend allies and interests. Of course, it would have required teeth – a rapid reaction force and major alliances. Much more might have been done to make the *entente* with Britain work for France. However, France had to avoid putting all her eggs in one basket by relying exclusively on a Franco-British partnership.

French historians have stressed the constraint of the 'English governess', warning Blum against intervention in Spain in 1936, admonishing Paris against a Soviet military connection in 1936-37, refusing until the last minute to guarantee support for France in the event of German aggression against Czechoslovakia. Yet the French were their own worst enemies. Instead of exploiting Britain's need for a strong France they deliberately fostered British tutelage in order to provide a fig leaf for disengagement from east central Europe. 'The French have not been clever at taking their opportunities with us', noted British diplomat Ralph Wigram.[15] Firm alliances with Moscow and Rome would have been counterweights to Britain and Germany. On the eve of the Ruhr occupation, for instance, Moscow offered France 'Russian support in the event of German aggression'.[16] The Franco-Soviet pact of 1935 had little value without a military agreement. Stalin was anxious for staff talks with Paris. In February 1939 he offered to supply France with aircraft. France achieved a short-lived alliance with Italy in 1935 but it should have come much sooner. The Italo-Abyssinian war demolished the alliance. Could it have been revived? Perhaps. William R. Shorrock argues that France missed opportunities for conciliation during and after the *Anschluss* in 1938. 'Fumbling and dilatory' Popular Front diplomacy cemented the Italo-German relationship.[17]

To sum up the argument of this book: the dramatic reversal of French fortunes from victor to vanquished in twenty-two years has usually been interpreted as the inexorable outcome of deep-seated weaknesses. Everything unfolded with the inevitability of a Greek tragedy. A near-great power overreached itself by trying to turn the artificial predominance of Versailles into a real hegemony. The bid ended in 1924 with acceptance of the Dawes Plan and evacuation of the Ruhr. Unable to police the settlement single-handed France appeased Germany until Hitler's aggression left no alternative but to fight.

The standard view requires substantial modification. The five years following the German armistice of November 1918 were decisive for the relations of the European great powers. For the first time since Napoleon I the French army dominated Europe. It was an opportunity to translate a temporary advantage into a lasting hegemony. The problem was one of mobilizing and focusing military, diplomatic and economic power. Two bids were made – Poincaré's Ruhr occupation of 1923–24 and Briand's pursuit of conciliation and collective security from 1925 to 1931. Briand's appeasement was conciliation from strength, aimed at keeping France the dominant player in European decision-making. Lacking, however, was a victory culture – an assumption of a right to rule and dominate Europe. *Vis à vis* Britain and the United States, the French always had a chip on their shoulder. In response to the crises of the 1930s they developed a Maigret syndrome – reflective but passive observers, analysing data and waiting expectantly for things to sort themselves out.

The years 1932–39 witnessed a succession of ambushes – Abyssinia, the Rhineland, Spain, Austria, Munich and Prague. By 15 March 1939 Germany, without firing a shot, had achieved European hegemony. Yet there were no tramlines to Vichy. Crisis, not decline or decadence, best defines France's predicament. Grandeur did not have to end in misery. Energetically led and supported by allies France could have warded off the German challenge and survived as an independent great power. Unhappily, the elements for success were wanting; decisive leadership, a revised grand strategy, self-confidence. This brings us to the heart of the matter. The crisis of French power was in essence a crisis of confidence. Victories do not keep – 1918 required a continuing act of will. 'The mentality and habits of a victorious people' demanded by Clemenceau in 1920 were not realized. In 1917 Clemenceau visited a regiment. The men were enthusiastic in their welcome and Clemenceau asked the commander if it was genuine. 'Yes,' came the reply, 'for you were the first French leader to say *merde* to the Boches'. 'That's true', answered the Tiger, 'I've always liked dropping people in the shit – I started with my wet nurse.' [18] If rulers and ruled had possessed the courage to say *merde* to Hitler before 1939 the story would have had a different ending.

Finally, France's eclipse mattered. The collapse of 1940 shaped the pattern of international politics after the Second World War. For most of the interwar years Anglo-Saxons inveighed against 'French militarism'. In retrospect, however, France's fall was Europe's loss. A French Europe after 1919 would have made most Europeans happier and more secure. Viewing the century as a whole, Germany's rise and hegemony caused horrendous suffering and savagery. France was the last large democratic country left in mid-1930s' continental Europe. 'France is not only peaceful and orderly, which is the least that any government can be expected to achieve', the British ambassador in Paris reminded London, 'but is really free. France is governed without recourse to concentration camps or islands for inconvenient critics. The press is not bridled . . . and any political refugee can find a home here.'[19] Of how many countries can the same be said today?

Notes

Abbreviations

AC	Austen Chamberlain Papers
AN	Archives Nationales, Paris
BDFA	British Documents on Foreign Affairs
BN	Bibliothèque Nationale, Paris
BL	British Library, London
BLO	Bodleian Library, Oxford
BUL	Birmingham University Library
CC	Churchill College, Cambridge
CUL	Cambridge University Library
DBFP	*Documents on British Foreign Policy*
DDF	*Documents Diplomatiques Français*
DGFP	*Documents on German Foreign Policy*
FNSP	Fondation Nationale des Sciences Politiques
FRUS	*Papers Relating to the Foreign Relations of the United States*
FPA	French Parliamentary Archives
MAE	Ministère des Affaires Etrangères, Paris
PRO FO	Foreign Office Papers in the Public Records Office, Kew

1 France and the world

1 Cited R. Binion, *Defeated Leaders: The Political Fates of Caillaux, Jouvenel and Tardieu* (New York, 1960) p. 240.
2 Cited Ruth Emily McMurray and Muna Lee, *The Cultural Approach: Another Way in International Relations* (Chapel Hill, 1947), p. 9.
3 See Robert Aldrich, 'Late Comer or Early Starter? New Views on French Economic History', *Journal of Economic History*, 16.1.1987, p. 97.
4 Maurice Levy-Leboyer, *La Position internationale de la France: Aspects économiques et financiers XIX–XX siècles* (Paris, Ecole des hautes études en sciences sociales, 1977), p. 31.
5 Cited Pascal Ory, 'Introduction to an Era of Doubt. Cultural Reflections of French Power Around the Year 1948', in Josef Becker and Franz Knipping (eds.), *Power in Europe: Great Britain, France, Italy and Germany in a Postwar World, 1945–1950* (Berlin/New York, 1986), p. 405.
6 Op. cit., p. 405.
7 Cited Christopher M. Andrew and A. S. Kanya-Forstner, *The Climax of French Imperial Expansion, 1914–1924* (Stanford, 1981), p. 26.
8 Jules Cambon, ambassador in Berlin, letter of 23 February 1914 quoted in Christopher Andrew, 'Déchiffrement et diplomatie', *Relations Internationales*, 5, 1976, p. 56.
9 Cited Andrew and Kanya-Forstner, *Climax*, p. 26.
10 Cited Martin Ceadel, *Thinking about Peace and War* (Oxford, 1987), p. 123.
11 Cited Andrew and Kanya-Forstner, *Climax*, p. 17.
12 Cited Alec G. Hargreaves, *The Colonial Experience in French Fiction* (London, 1981), p. 9.
13 Cited Andrew and Kanya-Forstner, *Climax*, p. 13.
14 Cited Paul Gordon Lauren, *Diplomats and Bureaucrats: The First Institutional Responses to Twentieth Century Diplomacy in France and Germany* (Stanford, 1976), pp. 42–3.
15 Cited Henri Grimal, *Decolonisation* (London, 1978), p. 30.
16 Cited Bernard Auffray, *Pierre de Margerie et la vie diplomatique de son temps* (Paris, 1976), pp. 129–30.
17 Op. cit, pp. 129–30.
18 This paragraph draws on: Binion, *Defeated Leaders*, pp. 82, 364, n. 19; p. 387, n. 37; Richard Griffiths, *Marshall Pétain* (London, 1970), p. 94; Harold Nicolson, *Peacemaking 1919* (London, 1933), pp. 249, 289; Robert de Saint Jean, *Journal d'un journaliste* (Paris, 1974), p. 29.
19 Cited Binion, *Defeated Leaders*, pp. 56–7.
20 Op. cit., p. 245.
21 Cited Catherine Slater, *Defeatists and their Enemies: Political Invective in France, 1914–1918* (Oxford, 1981), p. 1.
22 Cited James Joll, *The Origins of the First World War* (London, 1984), p. 101.
23 *Saint John Perse: Letters,* translated and edited by Arthur J. Knodel (Princeton, NJ, 1979), Saint John Perse to J. Rivière, 21 July 1922, p. 109.

24 Cited Robert J. Young, *Power and Pleasure: Louis Barthou and the Third French Republic* (Montreal, 1991), p. 234.
25 *War Memoirs of David Lloyd George*, III (London, 1934), p. ix.
26 Paul Cambon, *Correspondance 1870–1924*, III (ed. H. Cambon), (Paris, 1946), p. 147.
27 Cited Christopher Andrew, 'France and the German Menace', in Ernest R. May (ed.), *Knowing One's Enemies: Intelligence Assessments Before the Two World Wars* (Princeton, 1984), p. 33.
28 Cited Walter Rice Sharp, *The French Civil Service: Bureaucracy in Transition* (New York, 1931), p. 33.
29 Cited Philippe Bernard, *La Fin d'un monde 1914–1929, Nouvelle histoire de la France contemporaine*, 12 (Paris, 1975), p. 46.
30 Cited John F. V. Keiger, *France and the Origins of the First World War* (London, 1983), p. 119.
31 Cited Christopher Andrew, *Theophile Delcassé and the Making of the Entente Cordiale* (London, 1968), p. 64.
32 Comte de Saint Aulaire, *Confessions d'un vieux diplomate* (Paris, 1953), p. 19.
33 Cited Douglas Porch, 'The French Army and the Spirit of the Offensive 1900–1914', in B. Bond and I. Roy (eds.), *War and Society: A Year Book of Military History* (London, 1976), p. 126.
34 Cited Andrew and Kanya-Forstner, *Climax*, p. 21.
35 In the 1920s ex-minister Albert Thomas, head of the International Labour Office, could not be persuaded to write minutes on a file – 'he dictated notes which were typed on little square pieces of paper and which circulated independently of the files' (E. J. Phelan, *Yes and Albert Thomas*, London, 1936, p. 65).
36 Brigadier General E. L. Spears, *Liaison, 1914* (London, 1930), pp. 3, 6.

2 Armageddon

1 See Arno J. Mayer, *The Persistence of the Old Regime* (London, 1981), p. 136; Madeleine Rebérioux, *La République radicale 1898–1914* (Paris, 1975), pp. 134, 194.
2 Cited James Joll, *The Origins of the Second World War* (London, 1992), pp. 119–20.
3 Raymond Poincaré, *Au Service de la France: Neuf années de souvenirs*, IV (Paris, 1932), p. 328.
4 Christopher M. Andrew, 'France and the German Menace', in Ernest R. May (ed.), *Knowing One's Enemies: Intelligence Assessment Before the Two World Wars* (Princeton, NJ, 1984), p. 143.
5 Joll, *The Origins of the First World War*, pp. 120–1; Norman Rich, 'Great Power Diplomacy 1814–1914' (McGraw-Hill, New York, 1992), pp. 458–9.
6 Cited Jan Karl Tanenbaum, 'French Estimates of Germany's Operational War Plans', in Ernest M. May, *Knowing One's Enemies*, pp. 169–70.
7 *Les Carnets secrets d'Abel Ferry, 1914–1918* (Paris, 1957), p. 24.

8 Paul Morand, *Journal d'un attaché d'ambassade, 1916–1917* (Paris, 1963), p. 36.

9 Marie Irène Curie, *Correspondance: Choix de lettres 1905–1934* (Paris, 1974), pp. 98–9.

10 Tanenbaum, 'French Estimates of Germany's Operational War Plans', pp. 169–70.

11 Alain-Fournier, letter of 4 August 1914, in Robert Gibson, *The Land Without a Name: Alain-Fournier and His World* (London, 1975), p. 264.

12 Cited D. Stevenson, *French War Aims Against Germany, 1914–1919* (Oxford, 1982), p. 21.

13 Cited Georges Soutou, 'La France et les marches de l'est, 1914–1919,' *Revue Historique*, CCLX, 1978, p. 345.

14 Op. cit., p. 348.

15 Op. cit., p. 355.

16 Cited Stevenson, *French War Aims*, p. 45.

17 Op. cit., p. 47.

18 Op. cit., p. 56.

19 Cited Stephen Roskill, *Hankey: Man of Secrets*, I (London, 1970), p. 523.

20 BL, Northcliffe Papers, 62160, André Tardieu to Lord Northcliffe, 20 October 1915, Add. Mss 62153–62397.

21 Alexander S. Mitrakos, *France in Greece During World War I: A Study in the Politics of Power* (New York, 1982), p. viii.

22 David Lloyd George cited in David Dutton, 'The "Robertson Dictatorship" and the Balkan Campaign in 1916', *Journal of Strategic Studies*, 1986, 9, p. 70.

23 Roskill, *Hankey*, I, p. 349.

24 Cited David Dutton, 'The Balkan Campaign and French War Aims in the Great War', *English Historical Review*, January 1979, p. 111.

25 Mitrakos, *France in Greece*, p. 280.

26 Op. cit., p. 180. For Briand and the Greek royal princesses see Paul Morand, *Journal*, p. 106. A double censorship operated on Greece. In addition to regular vetting, Briand's secretary went every morning at 3.00 a.m. to scrutinize the morning press and carried out a second check, deleting all criticism of Princess George of Greece (pp. 68–9).

27 AN, Painlevé Papers, 313 AP, 129dr, Interallied conference, 7–8 August 1917.

28 John F. Godfrey, *Capitalism at War: Industrial Policy and Bureaucracy in France 1914–1918* (Leamington Spa, 1987), p. 27.

29 Op. cit., pp. 67–8.

30 Cited Jean-Baptiste Duroselle, 'Strategic and Economic Relations During the First World War', in Neville Waites (ed.), *Troubled Neighbours: Franco-British Relations in the Twentieth Century* (London, 1971), p. 55.

31 Op. cit., p. 55.

32 Paul Cambon, *Correspondance, 1870–1924*, III (Paris, 1946), p. 129.

33 The civil service grew from 800,000 in 1914 to 1.25 million in 1926 (Godfrey, *Capitalism at War*, p. 296).

34 Op. cit., p. 214.

35 Cited Rudolph Binion, *Defeated Leaders: The Political Fate of Caillaux, Jouvenel and Tardieu* (New York, Columbia, 1960), p. 262.

36 Cambon, *Correspondance*, III, p. 130.

37 Op. cit., III, p. 101.

38 Op. cit., III, p. 89.
39 M. Hankey, *The Supreme Command, 1914–1918*, 2 (London, 1961), p. 733.
40 Cited M. C. Sanders and Philip M. Taylor, 'The Maison de la Presse and the Organisation of French Propaganda During the First World War' (unpublished paper).
41 George G. Bruntz, *Allied Propaganda and the Collapse of the German Empire in 1918* (New York, 1972), pp. 41–2. French propaganda was enterprising in developing the sausage method: 'small vials, containing messages for German troops were prepared to look like sausages and dropped behind the lines' (Bruntz, p. 45). And the French were said to be 'particularly adept at producing faked photographs as proof of German atrocities' (Sanders and Taylor, unpublished paper).
42 Pierre Renouvin, 'Le Gouvernement français et les tentatives de paix en 1917', *Revue des Deux Mondes*, 15 October 1964, p. 506.
43 Op. cit., p. 506.
44 Raymond Poincaré, *Au Service de la France*, IX, *L'Année trouble 1917* (Paris, 1932), p. 299.
45 'Journal de Russie d'Albert Thomas', *Cahiers du Monde Russe et Sovitique*, 14, 1973, p. 200.
46 Cited Renouvin, 'Le Gouvernement français', p. 512.
47 AN, 313 AP, 129, 'Etude du Commandant Herscher sur les conditions d'une paix française', 12 July 1917, Painlevé Papers.
48 'Etude du Commandant Herscher'.
49 Count Harry Kessler, July 1917, in André Schérer and Jacques Grunewald (eds.), *L'Allemagne et les problèmes de la paix pendant la Première Guerre Mondiale*, 2 (Paris, 1962), no. 180.
50 Jean-Jacques Becker, *Les Français dans la Grande Guerre* (Paris, 1981), p. 305.
51 Paul Morand, *Journal d'un attaché d'ambassade*, p. 28.
52 Philippe Berthelot cited in Morand, p. 174.
53 Jules Blondel, Washington, 24 March 1917, cited in Morand, p. 197.
54 Amie Joseph de Fleuriau, minister in London, cited in Morand, p. 212.
55 Cited Georges Soutou, 'La France et les marches de l'est', pp. 380–1.

3 Peace-making, 1919

1 Cited in D. Stevenson, *French War Aims*, p. 122; cited in Alan Sharp, *The Versailles Settlement: Peacemaking in Paris, 1919* (London, 1991), p. 13.
2 Cited in David Robin Watson, *Georges Clemenceau. A Political Biography* (London, 1974), pp. 334–5.
3 Stevenson, *French War Aims*, p. 129.
4 Cited in Georges Wormser, *La Republique de Clemenceau* (Paris, 1961), p. 341.
5 For Pétain and de Gaulle see Guy Pedroncini, *Pétain Général en Chef 1917–18* (Paris, 1974), pp. 428, 432, n. 2.
6 Cited in Pierre Renouvin, *L'Armistice de Rethondes* (Paris, 1968), p. 267.

7 Op. cit., p. 264.

8 John Maynard Keynes, *The Economic Consequences of the Peace* (London, 1919), pp. 20–1.

9 Cited in Pierre Miquel, *La Paix de Versailles et l'opinion publique française* (Paris, 1972), p. 426.

10 Stevenson, *French War Aims*, p. 137.

11 Cambon to Pichon, 26 April 1919, Pichon Papers (Institut de France), II, 4396.

12 AN 149AP, 21, Mangin Papers, Fayolle to his commanders, 10 March 1919.

13 Stevenson, *French War Aims*, p. 141; Agnes Headlam-Morley (ed.), *Sir James Headlam-Morley: A Memoir of the Peace Conference, 1919* (London, 1973), 10 May 1919, p. 102.

14 Paul Mantoux, *Les Délibérations du Conseil des Quatres: Notes d'un officier interprète*, I (Paris, 1955), p. 30.

15 Renouvin, *L'Armistice*, p. 265.

16 Clemenceau to Lloyd George, 9 November 1919, Lloyd George Papers, (House of Lords) LG/F/50/3/46.

17 Cited in Stevenson, *French War Aims*, p. 158; M. L. Dockrill and J. D. Goold, *Peace without Promise: Britain and the Peace Conference 1919–23* (London, 1981), p. 35.

18 Georges Clemenceau, *Grandeurs et misères d'une victoire* (Paris, 1930), p. 113.

19 Cited in Headlam-Morley, *Sir James Headlam-Morley*, p. 14.

20 Cited in Stevenson, *French War Aims*, p. 157; Headlam-Morley, *Sir James Headlam-Morley*, p. 31.

21 Charles Seymour, *Letters from the Paris Peace Conference*, ed. Harold B. Whiteman (Yale University Press, New Haven, 1965), p. 89; Frank Costigliola, *Awkward Dominion: American Political, Economic and Cultural Relations with Europe 1919–33* (Cornell, Ithaca, 1984), p. 170.

22 Seymour, *Letters*, pp. 156, 159.

23 Headlam-Morley, *Sir James Headlam-Morley*, p. 74; Dockrill and Goold, *Peace without Promise*, p. 272.

24 Headlam-Morley, *Sir James Headlam-Morley*, p. 102.

25 Mantoux, *Les Délibérations*, I, 28 March 1919, p. 71.

26 Cited in Dan P. Silverman, *Reconstructing Europe after the Great War* (Cambridge, Mass, 1982), p. 39.

27 BL, Cecil, Add. Mss 51131, 'Diary, British Delegation Paris 1919', 28 February 1919.

28 Cited in Roskill, *Hankey*, I (London, 1970), p. 510.

29 Hankey (Maurice) Lord, *The Supreme Command*, 2 (London, 1961), p. 822; Martin Gilbert, *Winston S. Churchill*, IV, *1916–1922* (London, 1975), pp. 97–8.

30 P. Cambon, *Correspondance*, III, p. 295.

31 For Clemenceau in action see H. Nicolson, *Peacemaking 1919* (London, 1937) p. 258; Seymour, *Letters*, pp. 155, 225–6; Stephen Bonsal, *Unfinished Business* (London, 1944), p. 194.

32 Camille Barrère to Harold Nicolson, cited in James Lees-Milne, *Harold Nicolson. A Biography 1886–1929* (London, 1980), p. 113.

33 Cited in C. M. Andrew and A. S. Kanya-Forstner, *France Overseas: The Great War and the Climax of French Imperial Expansion* (London, 1981), p. 183.

34 BL, Cecil, Add. Mss 51131. 'Diary, British Delegation Paris', 8 January 1919.

35 Raymond Poincaré, *Au Service de la France: Neuf années de souvenirs*, XI, *à la recherche de la paix 1919* (Paris, 1974), p. 283.

36 BL, Cecil, 'Diary, British Delegation Paris', 25 January 1919.

37 BL, Cecil, 'Diary, British Delegation Paris', 11 February 1919; See G. W. Egerton, *Great Britain and the Creation of the League of Nations, Strategy, Politics and International Organisation, 1914–1919* (Chapel Hill, 1978), p. 136.

38 Cited in Andrew and Kanya-Forstner, *France Overseas*, p. 181.

39 BL, Cecil, 'Diary, British Delegation Paris', 28 February 1919.

40 For Clemenceau and the Rhineland see Watson, *Georges Clemenceau*, p. 353; Stevenson, *French War Aims*, p. 158; J. R. McCrum, 'French Rhineland Policy at the Paris Peace Conference 1919', *Historical Journal*, 21, 3 (78), pp. 623–48.

41 Poincaré, *Au Service de la France*, 14 March 1919, p. 245.

42 See Stevenson, *French War Aims*, p. 173.

43 Poincaré, *Au Service de la France*, p. 337.

44 Cited in David Stevenson, *The First World War and International Politics* (Oxford University Press, 1988), p. 255.

45 Stevenson, *The First World War*, p. 255.

46 Cited in Watson, *Georges Clemenceau*, p. 354.

47 Poincaré, *Au Service de la France*, p. 390.

48 Colonel T. Bentley Mott (translator), *The Memoirs of Marshal Foch* (London, 1931), pp. xv–xvi.

49 Letter to Clemenceau, 28 April 1919, in David Lloyd George, *Memoirs of the Peace Conference*, I, (New Haven, 1939), pp. 281–4.

50 Poincaré, *Au Service de la France*, p. 15.

51 Cited in Stephen A. Schuker, 'France and the Demilitarization of the Rhineland 1936', *French Historical Studies*, XIV, 3, Spring 1986, p. 302.

52 Poincaré, *Au Service de la France*, pp. 390–1.

53 Cited in McCrum, 'French Rhineland Policy', p. 645.

54 Mantoux, *Les Déliberations*, II, p. 271.

55 See Marc Trachtenberg, 'Versailles after Sixty Years', *Journal of Modern History*, 17 (1982), pp. 487–505.

56 Op. cit., p. 497.

57 A. Lentin, 'What Really Happened at Paris', *Diplomacy and Statecraft*, July 1990, I (2), p. 269.

58 Op. cit., p. 269.

59 Miquel, *La Paix de Versailles*, p. 548.

60 Cited in Nicolson, *Peacemaking*, p. 242.

61 Miquel, *La Paix de Versailles*, p. 546, n.i.

62 Stevenson, *French War Aims*, p. 163.

63 Cambon, *Correspondance*, III, p. 303.

64 Poincaré, *Au Service de la France*, 31 January 1919, p. 104.

65 Clemenceau's words, 15.3.1919 in Louis Loucheur, *Carnets secrets, 1908–1932*, presented and annotated by Jacques de Launay (Paris, 1962), p. 72.

66 Derby to Balfour, 16 December 1918, Derby Papers (City of Liverpool Library), 920 DER (17).

67 G. A. Riddell, *Lord Riddell's Intimate Diary of the Peace Conference and After, 1918–1923* (London, 1933), pp. 37, 51.

68 Dockrill and Goold, *Peace without Promise*, p. 36.

69 Lentin, 'What Really Happened', p. 266; Jean-Baptiste Duroselle, *Clemenceau* (Paris, 1988), p. 773.

4 The price of victory

1 Stephen A. Schuker, *The End of French Predominance in Europe: The Financial Crisis of 1924 and the Adoption of the Dawes Plan* (Chapel Hill, 1976).

2 F. Scott Fitzgerald, *Tender is the Night* (Collier, NY, 1982), p. 57; Francis Partridge, *Memories* (London, 1981), p. 220.

3 Cited in Judith M. Hughes, *To the Maginot Line: The Politics of French Military Preparation in the 1920s* (Cambridge, Mass., 1971), p. 21; Cited in Theodore Zeldin, *France 1848–1945: Anxiety and Hypocrisy* (Oxford, 1981), p. 134; Stephen Roskill, *Hankey: Man of Secrets*, II (London, 1972), p. 161.

4 CUL, Baldwin Papers 125, Eyre Crowe memorandum of talk with Montagu Norman, governor of Bank of England, 31 May 1923.

5 MAE, Papiers Fleuriau, vol. 2, note of 6 May 1919.

6 AN, Painlevé Papers, 313AP, 188, rapport mensuel (Sûreté générale), October 1925.

7 J. F. Godfrey, *Capitalism at War*, p. 213.

8 Dan P. Silverman, *Reconstructing Europe After The Great War*, p. 20.

9 Carole Fink, *Marc Bloch: A Life in History* (London, 1990), pp. 102–3.

10 Charles Seymour, *Letters from the Paris Peace Conference*, p. 220.

11 Hughes, op. cit., p. 169.

12 Op. cit., p. 120.

13 AN, F 60699, *Commission interministerielle des affaires musulmanes, Correspondance*, Lyautey to war minister, 19 April 1920.

14 Michael J. Hogan, *Informal Entente: The Private Structure of Cooperation in Anglo-American Economic Diplomacy 1918–1928*, (Columbia, Missouri, 1977), p. 39.

15 Dan P. Silverman, *Reconstructing Europe*, p. 298.

16 C. M. Andrew and A. S. Kanya-Forstner, *The Climax of French Imperial Expansion 1914–1924* (Stanford, CA, 1981), p. 198.

17 Paul Gordon Lauren, *Diplomats and Bureaucrats*, pp. 223, 225.

18 Roskill, *Hankey*, II, p. 150.

19 Harold Nicolson, *Curzon: The Last Phase, 1919–1925: A Study in Post-War Diplomacy* (London, 1934), p. 398.

20 John Cruickshank, *Variations on Catastrophe: Some French Responses to the Great War* (London, 1982), p. 167.

21 Edward Spears, British military mission, 23 January 1919 in Keith Jeffrey (ed.) *The Military Correspondence of Field Marshal Sir Henry Wilson, 1918–1922* (London, 1985), p. 80.

22 Cited in M. L. Dockrill and J. D. Goold, *Peace Without Promise*, p. 34.

23 Cited in Nicole Jordan, *The Popular Front and Central Europe: The Dilemmas of French Impotence, 1918–1940* (Cambridge, 1992), p. 5.

24 DBFP, First Series, XVI, no. 768; C. M. Andrew and A. S. Kanya-Forstner, *The*

Climax of French Imperial Expansion 1914–1918 (Stanford, CA, 1981), p. 224.

25 Everyman edition (London, 1966), p. 296.

26 *Goodbye to All That* (London, 1957), p. 257.

27 BN, Fonds Millerand, 70M, note on French telecommunications, 1921.

28 *Lyautey L'Africain: Textes et lettres du Marechal Lyautey*, IV, covering 1919–1925 (Paris, 1957), presented by Pierre Lyautey, p. 114.

29 *DBFP*, First Series, XII, no. 14; Stephen Roskill, *Naval Policy Between the Wars*, I, *The Period of Anglo-American Antagonism 1919–1929* (London, 1968), p. 357 and pp. 382–3.

30 BN, Fonds Millerand, M71, 'Note sur la Conférence de Washington', 6.2.1922, citing Wells from *New York World*, 22 November 1921.

31 Roskill, *Hankey*, II, pp. 149–50.

32 *DBFP*, First Series, XV, no. 70.

33 *DBFP*, First Series, XV, no. 110.

34 Charles Dickens, *Our Mutual Friend* (OUP illustrated edn, 1952) pp. 131–2.

35 BUL, Austen Chamberlain Papers, Chamberlain to Crewe (Paris), 4 June 1926, AC50/86.

36 *DBFP*, First Series, XVI, no. 768.

37 *Les Silences du Colonel Bramble* (Grasset, Livre de Poche, Paris, 1950), p. 33.

38 Cambon, *Correspondance*, III, p. 389.

39 Marc Trachtenberg, *Reparation in World Politics: France and European Economic Diplomacy 1916–1923*, (New York, 1980), pp. 165–6.

40 Cambon, *Correspondance*, III, p. 389.

41 C. M. Andrew and A. S. Kanya-Forstner, *The Climax of French Imperial Expansion 1914–1918* (Stanford, CA, 1981), p. 232; Robert Rhodes James, *Memoirs of a Conservative: J. C. C. Davidson's Memoirs and Papers, 1910–1937* (London, 1969), p. 146; H. Montgomery Hyde, *Baldwin: The Unexpected Prime Minister* (London, 1973), p. 171.

42 MAE, Papiers Millerand, 19, 29 November 1921.

43 MAE, Serie Europe, Grande Bretagne, 69, note by Henri Fromageot, 27.12.21.

44 MAE, Serie Europe, Grande Bretagne, 71, 19 March 1922.

5 A flawed response

1 BUL, *Austen Chamberlain Papers*, Chamberlain to Crewe (Paris), 27 January 1927, AC50/28.

2 Harold Nicolson, *Diplomacy* (London, 1939), p. 150; FNSP, Auriol to Caillaux, 1 September 1925, Caillaux Papers ERJC4; Marcel Proust, *Correspondance*, XVIII: 1919, ed. Philip Kolb (Paris, 1990).

3 Paul Gore Booth, *With Great Truth and Respect* (London, 1974), p. 48.

4 Simone de Beauvoir, *Memoirs of a Dutiful Daughter* (Penguin edn, London, 1980), pp. 300–1.

5 FPA, foreign affairs committee, Chambre des Députés, 12ème législature, 25

February 1921; joint session of foreign affairs and finance committees, 3 March 1921.

6 Charles de Gaulle, *Lettres, notes et carnets, 1919–1940*, (Paris, 1980), p. 30; *Holmes-Laski Letters*, Mark Dewolfe Howe (ed.), 2 (London, 1953), p. 1300.

7 MAE, Papiers Millerand, 19, note of 5 November 1921.

8 Pierre Renouvin, *The Immediate Origins of the War* (Yale, New Haven, 1928), p. 1.

9 Letter of 16 August 1921 cited in Pierre Ordioni, *Le Pouvoir militaire en France*, 2 (Paris, 1981), p. 335; Poincaré, *Au Service de la France*, XI, p. 301.

10 MAE, Papiers Millerand, 19, note: 'situation économique européenne', 3 December 1921.

11 BN, Fonds Millerand, 70M, note of April 1921.

12 MAE, Papiers Millerand, 19, Jusserand (Washington), 29 November 1921.

13 CC, Phipps Papers, Phipps to Tyrell, 14 January 1927, 2/14; AN, police reports, September 1926, F7 12968; CC, Phipps Papers, Phipps to Eyre Crowe, 28 November 1923, 2/3; Ronald Hayman, *Writing Against: A Biography of Sartre* (London, 1986), p. 73; Carole Fink, *Marc Bloch: A Life in History* (London, 1990), pp. 102–3.

14 Sir Arthur Salter, *Personality in Politics* (London, 1947), p. 198.

15 David Lloyd George, *Memoirs of the Peace Conference*, I (London, 1939), p. 162.

16 Trachtenberg, *Reparation in World Politics*, p. 325.

17 Salter, *Personality in Politics*, p. 198.

18 Sharp, *The French Civil Service: Bureaucracy in Transition* (New York, 1931), p. 36.

19 Charles de Gaulle, *Lettres, notes et carnets*, p. 15.

20 Spears Papers, 1/21/1 (King's College, London), 22 April 1919.

21 CC, Phipps Papers, 2/5, Phipps to Eyre Crowe, 16 February 1925.

22 Cited in Maurice Vaïsse, *Sécurité d'abord: la politique française en matière de désarmement 9 dec 1930–17 avril 1934* (Paris, 1981), p. 45; Anne Hogenhuis-Seliverstoff, 'French Plans for the Reconstruction of Russia', in Carole Fink, Axel Frohn and Jurgen Heideking (eds.), *Genoa, Rappallo and European Reconstruction in 1922* (New York, 1991), pp. 145–6; Roskill, *Hankey*, II, p. 160, p. 162.

23 Jacques Body, *Giraudoux et l'Allemagne* (Paris, 1975), p. 269; see also Jacques Body (ed.), *Jean Giraudoux: Lettres* (Paris, 1975), pp. 211–14.

24 McMurray and Lee, *The Cultural Approach*, p. 17.

25 René Girault and Robert Frank, *Turbulente Europe et nouveaux mondes, 1914–1941* (Paris, 1988), p. 91.

26 William H. Keylor, 'How They Advertised France', *Diplomatic History*, Summer 1993, p. 367.

27 Auffray, *Pierre de Margerie*, p. 433.

28 Jacques Bariéty, 'Les Reparations allemandes après la première guerre mondiale: objet ou prétexte à une politique Rhenane de la France (1919–24)' *Bulletin de Société d'Histoire Moderne* 72 (1973), p. 33.

29 Schuker, *The End of French Predominance*, p. 83.

30 Jon Jacobson, 'Strategies of French Foreign Policy After World War I', *Journal of Modern History*, 55 (1983), p. 88.

31 Raymond Recouly, *Mémorial de Foch* (Paris, 1929), pp. 269–70.

32 Trachtenberg, *Reparation in World Politics*, pp. 396–7.

6 Predominance, 1919–1924

1 See Pierre Renouvin, *Histoire des relations internationales*, tome 7, *Les Crises du XX siècle*, I, *De 1914 à 1929* (Paris, 1957); Jean-Baptiste Duroselle, *Histoire diplomatique de 1919 à nos jours* (Paris, 1970); Maurice Baumont, *La Faillite de la paix 1918–1939*, 2 vols. (Paris, 1951).

2 See Walter A. McDougall, 'Political Economy versus National Sovereignty: French Structures for German Economic Integration After Versailles', *Journal of Modern History* 51 (1979), 4–23; March Trachtenberg, 'Reparation at the Paris Peace Conference', *Journal of Modern History*, 51 (1979), 24–55; Charles S. Maier, 'The Truth About the Treaties?', *Journal of Modern History*, 51 (1979), 56–67; Walter A. McDougall, 'Comment', *Journal of Modern History* 51 (1979), 78–80; Jon Jacobson, 'Is There a New International History of the 1920s?', *The American Historical Review*, 88 (1983), 617–45; 'Strategies of French Foreign Policy After World War I', *Journal of Modern History*, 55 (1983), pp. 78–95.

3 Silverman, *Reconstructing Europe*, p. vi.

4 Stephen A. Schuker, *American 'Reparations' to Germany 1919–1933: Implications for the Third World Debt Crisis* (Princeton, NJ, 1988), p. 46.

5 McDougall, *France's Rhineland Diplomacy, 1914–1924: The Last Bid for a Balance of Power in Europe* (Princeton, 1978), p. 379.

6 Op. cit., p. 375.

7 This follows Bariéty's argument in *Les Relations Franco-Allemandes après la première guerre mondiale* (Paris, 1977), pp. 134–49. It is contested by Trachtenberg, *Reparation in World Politics*, pp. 166–8.

8 Barrès cited in Andrew and Kanya-Forstner, *France Overseas*, pp. 209, 227.

9 Trachtenberg, *Reparation*, p. 165.

10 Op. cit., pp. 165–6.

11 Letter to Briand, 29 January 1923 in Georges Suarez, *Briand: Sa Vie, Son Oeuvre*, V, *1918–1923* (Paris, 1941), p. 429.

12 Trachtenberg, *Reparation*, pp. 165–6.

13 BN, Fonds Millerand, 70M, note by Louis Steeg, 'Situation actuelle en Turquie', 6 January 1921.

14 Andrew and Kanya-Forstner, *France Overseas*, p. 223.

15 FPA, foreign affairs committee, Chamber of Deputies, 12ème legislature, 11 November 1921.

16 Andrew and Kanya-Forstner, *France Overseas*, p. 224.

17 Op. cit., p. 226.

18 Dockrill and Goold, *Peace Without Promise*, p. 242.

19 Andrew and Kanya-Forstner, *France Overseas*, p. 215.

20 Op. cit., p. 234.

21 Letter of 29 January 1923 to Briand, Suarez, *Briand*, p. 430.

22 AN, Tardieu Papers 324AP, Pierre Comert writing to Tardieu, 14 May 1921 (118).

23 BN, Fonds Millerand, 71M, 'Note sur la Conférence de Washington', 6 February
    1922.

24 Donald S. Birn, 'Open Diplomacy at the Washington Conference of 1921–2: The
    British and French Experience', *Comparative Studies in Society and History*, 12,
    1970, p. 300; see also Joel Blatt, 'The Parity That Meant Superiority: French
    Naval Policy Towards Italy at the Washington Conference 1921–2 and Interwar
    French Foreign Policy', *French Historical Studies*, 12, 2, 1981, pp. 223–48;
    'France and the Washington Conference', *Diplomacy and Statecraft*, 4, 3, Sept.
    1993, pp. 192–219.

25 BN, Fonds Millerand, 71M, 'Note sur la Conférence de Washington', 6 February
    1922.

26 Hogan, *Informal Entente*, p. 67; BN, Fonds Millerand, 71 M, Morgan Bank
    cable to French government, 23 February 1922.

27 See Louis Loucheur's diary entry, 15 April 1923 in Louis Loucheur, *Carnets
    secrets 1908–1932*, presented and annotated by Jacques de Launay (Paris, 1962),
    p. 124.

28 AN, F7 12967, Police générale, rapport mensuel, July 1923.

29 Trachtenberg, *Reparation*, p. 329.

30 The following discussion is based on Pierre Miquel, *Poincaré* (Paris, 1961), pp.
    476–80; Paul Guinn, 'On Throwing Ballast in Foreign Policy: Poincaré, the
    Entente and the Ruhr Occupation', *European History Quarterly*, 18 (88),
    427–37.

31 MAE, Délibérations internationales, 158, Ruhr: procès-verbaux du comité
    restreint, 12 January 1924.

32 PRO FO 800/220, Mendl to Tyrrell, 26 February 1924.

33 PRO FO 800/218, Poincaré to MacDonald, 25 February 1924.

34 Trachtenberg, *Reparation*, p. 334.

35 Jean-Noel Jeanneney, *Leçons d'histoire pour une gauche au pouvoir: la Faillite du
    Cartel 1924–1926* (Paris, 1981), p. 55; Schuker, *The End of French
    Predominance*, p. 245.

36 Roskill, *Hankey*, II, p. 369.

37 Schuker, p. 271.

38 CC, Phipps Papers 2/4, Phipps to Eyre Crowe, 2 June 1924.

39 Jeanneney, *Leçons d'histoire pour une gauche au pouvoir: la Faillite du Cartel
    1924–1926*, p. 45.

40 CC, Phipps Papers 2.4, Phipps to Eyre Crowe, 22 June 1924.

41 MAE, Série Europe, Grande Bretagne, 71, 24 March 1924.

42 AN, Painlevé 313AP, 177, letter of Colonel Fagalde, assistant military attaché
    (London) to Paul Painlevé, 16 June 1924. Fagalde asked Painlevé to inform
    Herriot.

43 David Marquand, *Ramsay MacDonald* (London, 1977), pp. 339–40.

44 Schuker, *The End of French Predominance*, p. 241.

45 *DBFP*, First Series, XXVI, no. 508.

46 MacDonald's diary, 5 August 1924 in Marquand, p. 345.

47 Schuker, *The End of French Predominance*, p. 382.

48 Op. cit., p. 382.

49 Marquand, *MacDonald*, p. 350.

50 Op. cit., p. 349.

51 Op. cit., p. 355.

52 MAE, Herriot Papers, vol. 9, unsigned, untitled note dated 'Geneva, 4 September 1924'.
53 Marquand, *MacDonald*, p. 334.
54 See Georges Soutou, 'L'impérialisme du pauvre: la politique du gouvernement français en Europe centrale et orientale de 1918 à 1929', *Relations Internationales*, 7, 1976, pp. 219–39.
55 See Jean-Jacques Becker and Serge Berstein, *Victoire et frustrations 1914–1929* (Paris, 1990), p. 219.
56 Bariéty, *Les Relations Franco-Allemandes*, p. 261.
57 *DBFP*, First Series, XXVI, no. 519.

7 Locarno, 1925

1 Schuker, *End of Predominance*, pp. 231, 392.
2 Stevenson, *French War Aims*, p. 30; Morand, *Journal*, p. 62; *Holmes–Laski Letters*, 2, p. 1300; Cambon, *Correspondance*, III, p. 98.
3 Cambon, *Correspondance*, III, p. 365; Roskill, *Hankey*, II, p. 137.
4 Léon Noel, 'Souvenirs de la Conference de la Haye', *Revue d'Histoire Diplomatique* 3/4, 1983, p. 246.
5 AC, Crewe to Chamberlain, 3 and 4 January 1927, AC54/56: general correspondence 1927.
6 Cited Jon Jacobson, *Locarno Diplomacy: Germany and the West, 1925–1929* (Princeton, NJ, 1972), p. 306.
7 MAE, Herriot Papers, 4, Documents financiers 1924–5.
8 MAE, Herriot, 7, Jacques Seydoux note, 8 April 1925: 'Situation financière'.
9 Cited Jean Doise and Maurice Vaïsse, *Diplomatie et outil militaire 1871–1969* (Paris, 1987), p. 279.
10 André Gide, *Journals 1889–1949*, trans., selected and edited by Justin O'Brien (Penguin Books, Harmondsworth, 1967), p. 318.
11 Fritz Stern, *The Pillar of Fire* (London, 1951), pp. 89–90.
12 BL, Cecil Papers, Cecil to Austen Chamberlain, 7 September 1925, special correspondence, Add. Mss 51078.
13 BL, Cecil Papers, Cecil to Austen Chamberlain, 18 July 1926, Add. Mss 51079.
14 British expert General Temperley cited in Maurice Vaïsse, *Sécurité d'abord: la politique française en matière de désarmement 9 dec 1930–17 avril 1934* (Paris, 1981), p. 46, n. 95.
15 Martin Gilbert, *Winston S. Churchill 1874–1965*, V, *1922–1939* (London, 1976), p. 122.
16 Op. cit., p. 125.
17 AC, Chamberlain to Crewe, 20 February 1925, general correspondence 1925.
18 AC, Chamberlain to Eyre Crowe, 8 March 1925, AC52/50.
19 Cited David Dutton, *Austen Chamberlain, Gentleman in Politics* (London, 1985), p. 260.
20 FPA, Chamber Foreign Affairs Committee, 12 February 1926, 13ème législature, 50ème séance.

21 CC, Phipps Papers, Phipps to Orme Sargent, 2 August 1926, 2/7.
22 Jacobson, *Locarno Diplomacy*, p. 85.
23 AN, Painlevé 313 AP, 13 dr.2, Foch to the government, 8 March 1926.

8 Indian summer, 1926–1931

1 Cited Jacobson, *Locarno Diplomacy*, p. 79; CC, Phipps to Tyrell, 2/14; Phipps to Tyrell, 11 January 1927; Phipps to Tyrell, 6 February 1927; 2/15 Phipps to Tyrell, 3 August 1927; Jacobson, *Locarno Diplomacy*, p. 387.
2 *DBFP*, Series Ia, V, no. 490, memorandum by Mr Craigie, 12 November 1928.
3 Cited Melvyn P. Leffler, *The Elusive Quest, America's Pursuit of European Stability and French Security 1919–1933* (Chapel Hill, 1979), p. 135.
4 FNSP, Caillaux Papers, Fleuriau (London) to Seydoux, 17 July 1925; CC, 2/2 Phipps to Crewe, 17 September 1925; Marin to Caillaux, 22 July 1925; Frank Costigliola, *Awkward Dominion: American Political, Economic and Cultural Relations with Europe 1919–1933* (Ithaca, 1984), p. 133.
5 MAE, Herriot Papers, 9, note of 3 December 1924.
6 Cited Sally Marks, *The Illusion of Peace: International Relations in Europe 1918–1933* (London, 1976), p. 100.
7 AN, Joseph Paul-Boncour Papers, 11 October 1928.
8 *DBFP*, Series Ia, IV, no. 267; AN, Paul-Boncour, 11 October 1928; 17 October 1928.
9 AN, Paul-Boncour, correspondence with Daladier, 5 and 12 October 1928.
10 Cited Jacobson, p. 312; Philip Viscount Snowden, *An Autobiography*, II, *1919–1934* (London, 1934), p. 827; Jacobson, p. 330, n. 63.
11 BLO, Zimmern Papers, Zimmern to MacDonald, 1 February 1928, Zimmern to MacDonald, 30 November 1928, Dalton to Mrs Zimmern, 22 June 1929.
12 BUL, AC, AC55/300, Montagu Norman to Chamberlain, 'Financial Reconstruction and the League and France', 4 February 1928; Emile Moreau, *Souvenirs d'un gouverneur de la banque de France: Histoire de la stabilisation du franc (1926–1928)* (Paris, 1954), pp. 488–9; R. S. Sayers, *The Bank of England 1891–1944*, 3 (London, 1976), pp. 101–6; for commercial rivalry see Robert D. Boyce, *British Capitalism at the Crossroads 1919–1932: A Study in Politics, Economics and International Relations* (Cambridge, 1987), pp. 127–8.
13 BLO, Zimmern Papers, 22, Pierre Comert (director of information, League of Nations) to Mrs Zimmern, 16 November 1929; Georges Duhamel, *Le Livre de l'amertume* (Paris, 1983), pp. 162–3; Robert D. Boyce, 'Britain's First "No" to Europe: Britain and the Briand Plan, 1929–30', *European Studies Review*, 10 (1980), p. 21; Zimmern to MacDonald, 30 November 1928 PRO FO 371/14365/K5786, Tyrell to Vansittart, 11 February 1930.
14 AN, Painlevé, 313 Ap, 195, 'Mémento remis par le Général Requin à Monsieur Berthelot', 8 October 1929; Leffler, *Elusive Quest*, p. 222; MAE, Tardieu, 41, 'Les problèmes politiques de la Conférence de Londres', 13 January 1930.
15 MacDonald diary cited in Marquand, *Ramsay MacDonald*, p. 514; MAE,

Tardieu, 41b, Aubert to Tardieu, 23 March 1930; Costigliola, *Awkward Dominion*, p. 229.

16 Cited Geoffrey Warner, *Pierre Laval and the Eclipse of France* (London, 1968), pp. 33, 38.

17 Op. cit., p. 42.

18 Op. cit., pp. 44, 47.

19 CC, Phipps Papers, 2/12, Phipps to Tyrell, 29 April 1925; cited Anthony Adamthwaite, *France and the Coming of the Second World War* (London, 1977), p. 26; Phipps to Tyrell, 3 June 1927, 2/15.

20 This discussion draws on A. J. Crozier's, 'Philippe Berthelot and the Rome Agreements of January 1935', *The Historical Journal*, 26, 2 (1983), pp. 413–22, all quotations are from this source.

21 Cited Warner, *Laval*, p. xv.

22 Avenol to André François-Poncet, 21 June 1931, Vaïsse, *Sécurité d'abord*, p. 107; Berthelot, 18 August 1931, Auguste Bréal, *Philippe Berthelot* (Paris, 1937), p. 233; General Requin to Weygand, 2 February 1931, Vaïsse, pp. 99–100; cited Costigliola, *Awkward Dominion*, p. 263; Vaïsse, p. 101.

23 Jacobson, *Locarno Diplomacy*, p. 360.

24 Review by J. Wright of Franz Knipping, *Deutschland, Frankreich und das Ende der Locarno-Ära 1928–1931* (Munich, 1987), German Historical Institute London *Bulletin*, November 1989, p. 28.

9   Economics, armaments, decision-making

1   Robert de St Jean, *Journal d'un journaliste* (Paris, 1974), p. 198.

2   CC, Spears Papers, 1798, note of conversation with Flandin, 25 May 1932.

3   Cited Henry Bordeaux, *Histoire d'une vie*, XI (Paris, 1966), p. 54.

4   Cited Joel Colton, *Léon Blum: Humanist in Politics* (New York, 1966), p. 281.

5   Cited André Maurois, *Choses nues: Chroniques* (Paris, 1963), p. 65.

6   Cited Alfred Sauvy, *De Paul Reynaud à Charles de Gaulle* (Paris, 1972), p. 70.

7   Maurice Vaïsse, *Sécurité d'abord*, pp. 609–10.

8   Robert Frankenstein, *Le Prix du réarmement français*, 1935–1939 (Paris, 1982), pp. 296–7.

9   *FRUS*, 1936, I (Washington, 1955), p. 564.

10 J. M. Blum (ed.), *From the Morgenthau Diaries*, I (Boston, 1959), p. 460.

11 Cited Dominique Borne, Henri Dubief, *La Crise des années 30, 1929–38* (Paris, 1989), p. 61.

12 Georges Simenon, *African Trio* (London, 1979), pp. vii–viii.

13 Cited Jacques Thobie et al., *Histoire de la France coloniale 1914–1990* (Paris, 1990), p. 209.

14 BN, Flandin Papers, F65, 'Note sur la situation au Maroc', n.d.

15 Cited A. G. Hargreaves, *The Colonial Experience in French Fiction* (London, 1980), p. 85.

16 Cited Adamthwaite, *Coming of the Second World War*, p. 296.

17 Cited C. M. Andrew and A. S. Kanya-Forstner, *The Climax of French Imperial Expansion 1914–1918*, p. 250.
18 Cited Roger Levy, *French Interests and Politics in the Far East* (New York, 1941), p. 130.
19 Jean Doise, Maurice Vaïsse, *Diplomatie et outil militaire*, p. 279.
20 BL, Cecil Papers, Add. Mss 51143, Cot to Robert Cecil, 9 April 1932.
21 MAE, Tardieu Papers, 96: Aviation militaire, réunion du 19 november 1930.
22 General André Beauffre, *Mémoirs 1920–40–45* (Paris, 1965), p. 63.
23 Richard Griffiths, *Marshal Pétain* (London, 1970), p. 39.
24 Op. cit., p. 140.
25 Charles de Gaulle, *Lettres, notes et carnets 1919–1940* (Paris, 1980), p. 393.
26 The Collected Essays, *Journalism and Letters of George Orwell*, IV, *In Front of Your Nose 1945–50*, ed. Sonia Orwell and Ian Angus (Penguin, 1980), p. 317.
27 Herbert R. Lottman, *Pétain: Hero or Traitor, the Untold Story* (London, 1985), p. 50.
28 Philip C. F. Bankwitz, *Maxime Weygand and Civil–Military Relations in Modern France* (Cambridge, Mass., 1967), p. 29.
29 Op. cit., p. 26.
30 Cited Adamthwaite, *Coming of War*, p. 167.
31 AN, Painlevé, 313 AP, 188, Thomas to Painlevé 22 June 1925.
32 Adamthwaite, *Coming of War*, p. 168.
33 Martin S. Alexander, *The Republic in Danger: General Maurice Gamelin and the Politics of French Defence 1933–40* (Cambridge, 1992).
34 P. Le Goyet, *Le Mystère Gamelin* (Paris, 1975), p. 64.
35 Cited Adamthwaite, 'French Military Intelligence and the Coming of War 1935–1939', in Christopher Andrew and Jeremy Noakes (eds.), *Intelligence and International Relations 1900–1945* (Exeter, 1987), p. 192.
36 Cited Adamthwaite, 'France's Government Machine in the Approach to the Second World War', in Haim Shamir (ed.), *France and Germany in an Age of Crisis 1900–1960: Essays in Honour of Charles Bloch* (Leyden, 1990), p. 205.
37 Op. cit., p. 205.
38 Girard de Charbonnières, *La plus évitable de toutes les guerres* (Paris, 1985), pp. 33–4.
39 Adamthwaite, 'France's Government Machine', p. 206.
40 *DDF*, 1, V, no. 76; *St. John Perse: Letters*. Translated and edited by Arthur J. Knodel (Princeton, NJ, 1979), letter of 9 April 1918, p. 325 (as an historical record the letters from China in this collection are unreliable since many appear to have been concocted by Léger in the 1960s, Catherine Mayaux, *Les "Lettres d'Asie" de Saint John Perse. Les récits d'un poète, Cahiers Saint John Perse*, no. 12, Paris 1994); Anthony Eden, *Facing the Dictators* (London 1962), 232, 276–7; interview with Etienne de Crouy-Chanel (Léger's private secretary), 27 September 1985; Elisabeth R. Cameron, 'Alexis Saint-Léger Léger', in Gordon A. Craig and Felix Gilbert (eds) *The Diplomats 1919–39* (Princeton, NJ, 1953), p. 390.
41 Adamthwaite, *Coming of War*, p. 112.
42 General Maurice-Gustave Gamelin, *Servir*, II (Paris, 1946), p. 177.
43 Adamthwaite, 'France's Government Machine', p. 210. All quotations in the remaining sections of this chapter are from this source.

10   Ideology, opinion and foreign policy

1 Cited Daniel Halévy, *La République des comités* (Paris 1934), p. 52.
2 Op. cit., p. 52.
3 Anatole France, *Penguin Island* (Penguin edn, 1948), p. 240.
4 Cited Nathanael Greene, *Crisis and Decline: the French Socialist Party in the Popular Front Era* (New York, 1969), p. 225.
5 See Felix Bonafé, *Jacques Bardoux: Une vocation politique* (Paris, 1977), pp. 219–20.
6 FNSP, Daladier, 3DA 11.3, 'Renseignements sur l'activité communiste en 1937'.
7 See Maurice Vaïsse, 'Le pacifisme français dans les années trente', *Relations Internationales*, 53, 1988, I, p. 46; Fred Kupferman, 'Diplomatie parallèle et guerre psychologique', *Relations Internationales*, (1975), 3, p. 95.
8 Zeev Sternhell, *Ni droite ni gauche: L'Idéologie fasciste en France* (Paris, 1983).
9 Dominique Borne, Henri Dubief, *La Crise des années 30: 1929–1938* (Paris Seuil, 1989), p. 179.
10 James F. McMillan, *Twentieth Century France: Politics and Society 1898–1991* (London, 1992), p. 107.
11 Cited Patrick McCarthy, *Céline* (London, 1975), p. 125.
12 Penguin edition (1972), p. 113.
13 Cited Michael R. Marrus and Robert O. Paxton, *Vichy France and the Jews* (London, 1981), p. 14.
14 Leon Feuchtwanger, *The Devil in France* (London n.d.) pp. 26–7.
15 Winston S. Churchill, *The Second World War*; I, *The Gathering Storm* (London, Cassell, 1964), p. 40.
16 Cited Marrus and Paxton, *Vichy France*, p. 14.
17 Cited Vaïsse, 'Le pacifisme français', p. 41.
18 BUL, AC, 41/1/12. D'Ormesson to Austen Chamberlain, 30 March 1935.
19 André Weil, *The Apprenticeship of a Mathematician* (Basel, 1992), p. 126.
20 *Servir*, II (Paris, 1946), p. 219.
21 Cited Arthur Marwick, *Class, Image and Reality in Britain, France and the USA Since 1930* (London, 1980), p. 168.
22 Cited Léon Blum, *L'Oeuvre de Léon Blum*, IV, *1937–40* (Paris, 1965), p. 203.
23 Cited Thomas Jones, *A Diary With Letters 1931–50* (London, 1954), p. 367.
24 Cited MAE, Herriot Papers, 29, report by A. Desclos, assistant director, Office National des Universités et Ecoles françaises, 1931.
25 FPA, 15ème législature, Chamber foreign affairs committee, 8 March 1933, report on United States by General Taufflieb.
26 Cited A. Marès, 'Puissance et présence culturelle de la France', *Relations Internationales*, 33 (1983), 69.
27 See Annie Guénard, 'Cinéma et radio au service d'une politique culturelle à la veille de la deuxième guerre mondiale', *Travaux et Recherches*, 2 (Institut Pierre Renouvin), August 1988, 2–26.

28 Claudel to French foreign ministry, 30.4.1918, cited Gerald Antoine, *Paul Claudel ou l'enfer du génie* (Paris, 1988), p. 198.
29 *DBFP*, Third Series, II, no. 1197.
30 Cited Geneviève Vallette and Jacques Bouillon, *Munich 1938* (Paris, 1964), p. 109.
31 Emile Moreau, *Souvenirs d'un gouverneur de la Banque de France* (Paris, 1954), p. 104.
32 AN, Havas archives, 5AR 436, 8.4.1933.
33 H. Lerner, *La Dépêche: Journal de la démocratie* (Toulouse, 1978), II, p. 958.
34 *FRUS*, 1936, I, p. 219.
35 Nancy Harvison Hooker (ed.), *The Moffat Papers: Selections from the Diplomatic Journals of Jay Pierrepont Moffat 1919–1943* (Cambridge, Mass., 1956), p. 214.
36 *Gallup International Public Opinion Polls*, I, *France 1939–1975* (London, 1977), pp. 1–3.
37 *DGFP*, Series D, II, no. 120.
38 Alexander Werth, *De Gaulle: A Political Biography* (London, 1965), p. 84.
39 Cited Herbert R. Lottman, *The Left Bank: Writers, Artists and Politics from the Popular Front to the Cold War* (London, 1983), p. 55.
40 Paul Reynaud, *La France a sauvé l'Europe*, I, (Paris, 1947), pp. 557–8.
41 *Lettres, notes et carnets, 1919–1940*, pp. 473–4.
42 Christel Peyrefitte, 'Les premiers sondages d'opinion', in *Edouard Daladier, chef de gouvernement* (Paris, 1977), pp. 265–74.
43 Cited Louis Joxe, *Victoires sur la nuit: mémoires 1940–1946* (Paris, 1981), p. 16.
44 H. Stuart Hughes, *The Obstructed Path: French Social Thought in the Years of Desperation 1930–1960* (New York, 1968).
45 Cited Richard Griffiths, *Marshal Pétain* (London, 1970), p. 185.

11 Challenges, 1932–1936

1 *Le Temps*, 29 January 1933, cited in Vaïsse, *Securité d'abord*, p. 351.
2 Cited Christopher Thorne, *The Limits of Foreign Policy: The West, The League and the Far Eastern Crisis of 1931–1933* (London, Macmillan, 1973), p. 4.
3 BL, Chelwood, Add. Mss 51082, Cecil to Simon, 26 February 1932.
4 Christopher Thorne cited in John E. Dreifort, *Myopic Grandeur: The Ambivalence of French Foreign Policy toward the Far East, 1919–1945* (Kent State, Kent, Ohio, 1991), p. 49.
5 Dreifort, *Myopic Grandeur*, p. 49.
6 Op. cit., p. 51.
7 Cited R. A. C. Parker, *Europe 1919–1945* (London, 1969), p. 254.
8 British Labour Party Archives, International Department, box 8, Philip Noel Baker to Willie Gillies, 18 November 1931.
9 Dreifort, *Myopic Grandeur*, p. 69.
10 CC, Cadogan Papers, AVCAD 3/6, Cadogan to his wife, 8 February 1933.

11 DDF, Série I, no. 286.
12 House of Commons, 23 March 1933 in Winston S. Churchill, *The Second World War: The Gathering Storm* (London, Cassell, 1964), p. 64.
13 Raymond Aron, *Mémoires* (Paris, Julliard, 1983), p. 59.
14 DBFP, 2nd Series, IV, no. 90.
15 Cited Gilbert Badia, 'La France découverte par les émigrés', *Revue d'Allemagne*, avril–juin 1986, p. 181.
16 Vaïsse, *Sécurité d'abord*, p. 357.
17 MAE, Berthelot Papers, 23, Claudel to Berthelot, 16 November 1933.
18 DGFP, Series C, III, no. 399.
19 Cited Maurice Vaïsse, 'Against Appeasement: French Advocates of Firmness, 1933–8', in Wolfgang J. Mommsen and Lothar Kettenacker (eds.), *The Fascist Challenge and the Policy of Appeasement* (London, Allen and Unwin, 1983), p. 231.
20 *FRUS*, 1932, I, 19 December 1932, p. 22.
21 Cited Marquand, *Ramsay MacDonald*, p. 717.
22 *DDF*, Série I, V, no. 34.
23 CC, Hankey 3/39.
24 *FRUS*, 1932, I, Davis to Jouvenel, June 1932, pp. 235–6.
25 *DDF*, Série I, I, no. 286.
26 Cited Philip Noel Baker, 'Disarmament', *International Affairs* (London, 1934), 13, 1 p. 3.
27 Cited David Dilks (ed.), *The Diaries of Sir Alexander Cadogan 1938–45* (London, Cassell, 1971), p. 7.
28 Maurice Vaïsse, 'Security and Disarmament: Problems in the Development of the Disarmament Debates 1919–1934' in R. Ahmann et al., (eds.), *The Quest for Stability: Problems of West European Security 1918–1957* (London, OUP, 1993), p. 183.
29 CUL, Baldwin 119, MacDonald to Baldwin, 24 June 1932.
30 CUL, Baldwin 118, MacDonald to Baldwin, 15 June 1932.
31 *DDF*, Série I, V, no. 125.
32 Cited Laurent Greilsamer, *Hubert Beuve-Méry* (Paris, Fayard, 1990), p. 78.
33 François Pietri, 'Observations présentées par M. Piétri à la séance du conseil des ministres du 17 avril 1934' (document in author's possession).
34 Cited J.-B. Duroselle, *La Décadence 1932–1939* (Paris, Imprimerie nationale, 1979), p. 101.
35 Op. cit., p. 112.
36 Richard Cobb in the *Spectator* (London), 11 June 1988, p. 7.
37 Cited W. P. Crozier, *Off the Record: Political Interviews 1933–1943*, ed. with Intro. by A. J. P. Taylor (London, 1973), p. 58.
38 PRO FO 800/295 (Hoare), Eden to Hoare, 7 October 1935.
39 Geoffrey Warner, *Pierre Laval and The Eclipse of France* (London, Eyre and Spottiswoode, 1968), pp. 23–4.
40 DGFP, Series C, IV, no. 430.
41 Cited F. Kupferman, *Pierre Laval* (Paris, Masson, 1976), p. 38.
42 Gamelin's record of a meeting of the high military committee, 21 November 1935, cited in M. G. Gamelin, *Servir*, II, *Le Prologue du drame (1930–1939)* (Paris, Plon, 1946), p. 179.
43 CC, Spears 1846, Pietri to Spears, 4 April 1935.

44 CC, Spears 1969, Comert to Spears, 30 January 1935.

45 BUL, AC 41/1/63, Herriot to Austen Chamberlain, 19 October 1935.

46 Cited Martin Kitchen, *Europe Between the Wars* (London, 1988), p. 223.

47 BL, Chelwood, Add. Mss 51143, Cecil to Pierre Cot, 2 January 1933.

48 Cited Richard D. Challener, 'The French Foreign Office: The Era of Philippe Berthelot', in Gordon A. Craig and Felix Gilbert (eds.), *The Diplomats 1919–39* (Princeton, NJ, 1953), p. 85.

49 'Le 7 octobre' *Les Hommes de Bonne Volonté*, 27, (Paris, 1946), p. 221.

12 War again, 1936–1939

1 Cited Anthony P. Adamthwaite, *The Making of the Second World War* (London, 1977) p. 47.

2 Op. cit., p. 53.

3 Stephen A. Schuker, 'France and the Remilitarization of the Rhineland 1936', *French Historical Studies*, 14, 3 (1986), pp. 299–338.

4 CC, Grigg Papers, Snowden to Grigg, 14 March 1936.

5 Cited Adamthwaite, *The Making of the Second World War*, p. 54.

6 Op. cit., p. 54.

7 Op. cit., p. 54.

8 BL, Paul Emrys Evans correspondence, 58248, John McEwen to Emrys Evans, 24 March 1936; Nicole Jordan, 'The Cut-price War on the Peripheries: The French General Staff, the Rhineland and Czechoslovakia', in Robert Boyce and Esmonde Robertson (eds.), *Paths to War* (London, 1989), pp. 139, 157–8; Nicole Jordan, *The Popular Front and Central Europe* (Cambridge, 1992), pp. 72–3.

9 Cited Adamthwaite, *France and the Coming of the Second World War*, p. 41.

10 Op. cit., p. 41.

11 Op. cit., p. 42.

12 Op. cit., pp. 42–3; Simone Weil to Georges Bernanos 1938 cited Iganzio Silone, *Emergency Exit* (London, Gollancz, 1969), p. 124.

13 Cited *Making of the Second World War*, p. 58.

14 Cited *France and the Coming of the Second World War*, p. 56.

15 For the Loizeau and Schweisguth missions see Adamthwaite, 'French Military Intelligence and the Coming of War, 1935–1939', in Christopher Andrew and Jeremy Noakes (eds.), *Intelligence and International Relations 1900–1945* (Exeter University Press, Exeter, 1987), pp. 197–8.

16 Cited Anthony Adamthwaite, 'France and the Coming of War', in Mommsen and Kettenacker (eds.), *The Fascist Challenge and the Policy of Appeasement*, p. 246.

17 Op. cit., p. 247.

18 Op. cit., p. 247.

19 Op. cit., p. 247.

20 Op. cit., p. 247.

21 *Making of the Second World War*, p. 65.

22 *France and the Coming of the Second World War*, p. 248.

23 *Making of the Second World War*, p. 66.
24 'France and the Coming of War', p. 248.
25 *Making of the Second World War*, p. 44.
26 For this and the following three paragraphs see 'France and the Coming of War', pp. 248–9.
27 Cited *France and the Coming of the Second World War*, p. 75.
28 Op. cit., p. 77.
29 Op. cit., p. 88.
30 Op. cit., p. 226.
31 For this paragraph see 'French Military Intelligence', p. 192.
32 Cited *France and the Coming of the Second World War*, p. 263.
33 FNSP, 2DA 4/Dr 5, *Léger to Daladier*, 15 April 1939.
34 For this paragraph see 'French Military Intelligence', p. 196.
35 Cited Pascal Ory, 'L'opinion publique et la "Puissance" française vers 1938: quelques jalons', in René Girault and Robert Frank (eds.), *La Puissance en Europe, 1938–1940* (Paris, 1984), p. 343.
36 Cited 'French Military Intelligence', p. 199.
37 Op. cit., p. 199.
38 Cited *Making of the Second World War*, p. 93.
39 Cited 'Military Intelligence', p. 199.
40 Op. cit., p. 201.

Epilogue

1 Winston S. Churchill, *The Second World War* (London, 1948), II, p. 38; 'A record of visits to France and Belgium in May and June 1940', Brigadier Lund, Liddell Hart Centre for Military Archives, King's College London, *Misc.* XIX.
2 Adamthwaite, *France and the Coming of the Second World War*, p. 351.
3 Adamthwaite, *The Making of the Second World War*, p. 95.
4 Martin S. Alexander, *The Republic in Danger*, p. 310.
5 Jean-Paul Sartre, *Notebooks from the Phony War* (Paris, Gallimard, 1995) reviewed in *The New York Times*, 13 February 1995, pp. B1, B4; *FNSP*, 3 DA 1, Note pour le président du conseil, 30 September 1939; Elisabeth du Réau, *Edouard Daladier* (Paris, 1993), p. 392.
6 *Testament of Experience* (1979), p. 229; *Testament of a Peace Lover: Letters from Vera Brittain*, ed. Winifred and Alan Eden-Green (1988), p. 13.
7 W.N. Medlicott, *The Economic Blockade*, (HMSO, London, 1952), p. 134.
8 *Servir*, II, p. 27.
9 D.W. Brogan in Alexander Werth, *The Twilight of France* (London, 1942), xii.
10 Adamthwaite, 'France and the Coming of War,' p. 252.
11 *Securité d'abord*, pp. 123–4.
12 Adamthwaite, *France and the Coming of the Second World War*, p. 15.
13 Will Brownell and Richard N. Billings, *So Close to Greatness: A Biography of William C. Bullitt* (New York, 1987), p. 203.
14 Adamthwaite, 'France and the Coming of War,' p. 252.

15 Adamthwaite, 'War Origins Again,' *Journal of Modern History*, 56 (1), March 1984, p. 103.
16 Anne Hogenhuis-Seliverstoff, *Les Relations Franco-Soviétiques, 1917–1924* (Paris, 1981), p. 239.
17 William R. Shorrock, *From Ally to Enemy: The Enigma of Fascist Italy in French Diplomacy 1920–1940* (Kent, Ohio, 1988), pp. 292–3.
18 Martin S. Alexander, p. 18.
19 *BDFA*, 21, p. 204.

Guide to further reading

The following is intended as a guide to further reading. It does not include all the books and journals from which material has been drawn. It concentrates on the most recent or definitive studies. An asterisk denotes essential reading.

Periodicals are abbreviated thus:

AHR	American Historical Review
EHQ	European History Quarterly
FHS	French Historical Studies
GMCC	Guerres Mondiales et Conflits Contemporains
HJ	The Historical Journal
INS	Intelligence and National Security
JCH	Journal of Contemporary History
JMH	Journal of Modern History
RI	Relations Internationales

General

There is no up-to-date overview of French foreign policy in this period. J. Néré, *The Foreign Policy of France from 1914 to 1945* (1975) appeared before the new specialist literature of the mid and late 1970s. Good overviews of the international history of the period are:
Sally Marks, *The Illusion of Peace: International Relations in Europe, 1918–1933* (1976).
Ruth Henig, *Versailles and After, 1919–1933* (1984).

Paul Kennedy, *The Rise and Fall of the Great Powers* (1987).
W. R. Keylor, *The Twentieth-Century World: An International History* (1992).
René Girault and Robert Frank, *Turbulente Europe et nouveaux mondes, 1914–1941* (1988).
For overviews of French society see James F. McMillan,* *Twentieth Century France: Politics and Society 1898–1991* (1992).
Maurice Agulhon, *The French Republic 1879–1992* (1993).
Gordon Wright, *France in Modern Times* (4th edn, 1987).
René Rémond, *Notre Siècle de 1918 à 1988* (1988).
Three volumes in the *Nouvelle histoire de la France contemporaine* are indispensable: J.-J. Becker and S. Bernstein,* *Victoire et frustrations (1914–1929)* (1990).
D. Borne and H. Dubief,* *La crise des années trente (1929–1938),* (1989).
J.-P. Azéma,* *From Munich to the Liberation (1938–1944)* (Cambridge, 1984).
The most important specialist journals for French policy are: *Diplomacy and Statecraft, French History, French Historical Studies, The Historical Journal, The International History Review, Relations Internationales and Revue d'Histoire Diplomatique.*
Excerpts from French archival sources are in A. Adamthwaite, *The Making of the Second World War* (Unwin Hyman, 1990). *The Lost Peace: International Relations in Europe, 1918–1939* (Edward Arnold, 1980). Claude Paillat, *Dossiers secrets de la France contemporaine* (5 vols., 1979–84), incorporates important documentary material.

Official publications

France

Documents Diplomatiques Français, 1st Series (1932–5); 2nd Series (1936–9) (Paris, 1963–   ). A new series for the 1920s is in preparation.

Britain

Documents on British Foreign Policy 1919–1939, First, Second, Third Series and Series 1A (HMSO, 1946–); *British Documents on Foreign Affairs,* Part 2, Series F, *Europe 1919–1939: France,* vols. 16–23 (University Publications of America, 1993).

Germany

Documents on German Foreign Policy, 1918–1945, Series C (1933–7); Series D (1937–41) (London, 1949–); *Akten zur deutschen auswärtigen Politik, 1918–1945*; Serie A. 1918–25; Serie B, 1925–33; Serie D, 1937–41 (Göttingen, 1966–).

United States Department of State

Papers Relating to the Foreign Relations of the United States (Washington, 1873–1931); *Foreign Relations of the United States Diplomatic Papers* (Washington, 1948–).

Memoirs and private papers

Politicians

Georges Bonnet, *Défense de la paix*, 2 vols. (1946–8).
J. Caillaux, *Mes mémoires*, 3 vols. (1942–7).
Georges Clemenceau, *Grandeur and Misery of Victory* (1930).
P. E. Flandin, *Politique française*, 1919–40 (1947).
Edouard Herriot, *Jadis*, 3 vols. (1942–7).
Pierre Laval, *The Diary of Pierre Laval* (New York, 1948).
Louis Loucheur, *Carnets secrets 1908–1932* (ed. Jacques de Launay, 1962).
J. Paul-Boncour, *Entre deux guerres* (3 vols., 1945–7).
Raymond Poincaré, *Au Service de la France*, 11 vols. (1928–74).
The Memoirs of Raymond Poincaré, 4 vols. (London, 1926–30).
Paul Reynaud, *La France a sauvé l'Europe*, 2 vols. (1947).
Au Coeur de la mêlée 1930–1945 (1951).
In the Thick of the Fight 1930–1945 (London, 1955).

Diplomats and generals

P. Cambon (ed. H. Cambon) *Correspondance, 1870–1924*, 3 vols. (1940–6).
F. Charles-Roux, *Souvenirs diplomatiques: une grande ambassade à Rome, 1919–1925* (1961).
R. Coulondre, *De Staline à Hitler* (1950).

A. François-Poncet, *Souvenirs d'une ambassade à Berlin* (1946).
The Fateful Years: Memoirs of a French Ambassador in Berlin, 1931–38 (London, 1949).
F. Foch, *Mémoires*, 2 vols. (1931).
M. Gamelin, *Servir*, 3 vols. (1946–7).
J. Laroche, *Au Quai d'Orsay avec Briand et Poincaré, 1914–1926* (1957).
Léon Noel, *L'Aggression allemande contre la Pologne* (1946).
Comte de Saint Aulaire, *Confession d'un vieux diplomate* (1953).
P. de Villelume, *Journal d'une défaite, avril 1939 – juin 1940* (1976).

1914–1918

R. J. W. Evans and H. Pogge von Strandemann (eds.), *The Coming of the First World War* (1988).
James Joll,* *The Origins of the First World War* (2nd edn, 1992).
M. B. Hayne, *The French Foreign Office and the Origins of World War I, 1898–1914* (1993).
John Keiger,* *France and the Origins of the First World War* (1983).
G. Krumeich, *Armaments and Politics in France on the Eve of the First World War: The Introduction of Three Year Conscription, 1913–1914* (1984).
J.-J. Becker,* *1914: Comment les Français sont entrés dans la guerre* (1977).
The Great War and the French People (1986).
J.-B. Duroselle, *La France et les Français, 1914–1920* (1972).
P. J. Flood, *France 1914–18: Public Opinion and the War Effort* (1990).
M. M. Farrar, *Conflict and Compromise: The Strategy, Politics and Diplomacy of the French Blockade* (1974).
B. Hunt and A. Preston (eds.), *War Aims and Strategic Policy in the Great War* (1977).
R. A. Prete, 'French Military War Aims 1914–1916', *HJ* 28 (1985).
David Stevenson,* *French War Aims Against Germany 1914–1919* (1982).
David Stevenson,* *The First World War and International Politics* (1988).
'The Failure of Peace by Negotiation in 1917', *HJ* 34 (1991) 65–86.

Peacemaking, 1919

L. S. Jaffe, *The Decision to Disarm Germany* (1985).
A. Lentin, *Guilt at Versailles: Lloyd George and the Pre-History of Appeasement* (1985).

A. Lentin, *The Versailles Peace Settlement 1919* (1985).
P. Miquel, *La Paix de Versailles et l'opinion publique française* (1972).
Alan Sharp,* *The Versailles Settlement: Peacemaking in Paris, 1919* (1991).
Marc Trachtenberg, 'Versailles after Sixty Years', *JCH* 17 (1982). *JMH* 51 (1979) includes the following articles: Walter A. McDougall, 'Political Economy versus National Sovereignty: French Structures for German Economic Integration after Versailles', 4–23; Marc Trachtenberg, 'Reparation at the Paris Peace Conference', 24–55.
Charles S. Maier, 'The Truth about the Treaties', 56–67. Walter A. McDougall, 'Comment', 78–80.

1920s

Jacques Bariéty, *Les Relations Franco-Allemandes après la première guerre mondiale* (1977).
M. Jabara Carley, *Revolution and Intervention: the French Government and the Russian Civil War 1917–1919* (1983).
Alan Cassels, 'Repairing the Entente Cordiale and the New Diplomacy', *HJ* 23 (1980), 133–53.
Frank Costigliola, *Awkward Dominion: American Political, Economic and Cultural Relations with Europe, 1919–1933* (1984).
Carole Fink, *The Genoa Conference: European Diplomacy 1921–1922* (1981).
Paul Guinn, 'On Throwing Ballast in Foreign Policy: Poincaré, the Entente and the Ruhr Occupation', *EHQ* 18 (1988) 427–37.
Jon Jacobson,* *Locarno Diplomacy: Germany and the West, 1925–1929* (1972).
'Is there a New International History of the 1920s?' *AHR* 88 (1983), 617–45.
'Strategies of French Foreign Policy after World War I', *JMH* 55 (1983) 78–95.
Bruce Kent, *The Spoils of War: The Politics, Economics and Diplomacy of Reparations, 1918–1932* (1989).
Marion Kent (ed.) *The Great Powers and the End of the Ottoman Empire* (1984).
Melvyn P. Leffler, *The Elusive Quest: America's Pursuit of European Stability and French Security, 1919–1933* (1979).
Edward D. Keeton, 'Economics and Politics in Briand's German Policy, 1925–1931', in Carole Fink et al., *German Nationalism and the European Response, 1890–1945* (1985).
Franz Knipping, *Deutschland, Frankreich und das Ende der Locarno-Ara, 1928–1931* (1987).

Stephen S. Schuker,* *The End of French Predominance in Europe: The Financial Crisis of 1924 and the Adoption of the Dawes Plan* (1976).
Dan P. Silverman, *Reconstructing Europe after the Great War* (1982).
Charles S. Maier,* *Recasting Bourgeois Europe: Stabilisation in France and Italy after World War I* (1975).
Walter A. McDougall,* *France's Rhineland Diplomacy, 1914–1924: The Last Bid for a Balance of Power in Europe* (1978).

1930s

Anthony Adamthwaite, *France and the Coming of the Second World War, 1936–1939* (1977).
P. M. H. Bell,* *The Origins of the Second World War in Europe* (1986).
Robert Boyce and Esmonde M. Robertson (eds.),* *Paths to War: New Essays on the Origins of the Second World War* (1989).
John E. Dreifort, *Yvon Delbos at the Quai d'Orsay* (1973).
J.-B. Duroselle,* *La Décadence, 1932–1939.*
J. T. Emmerson, *The Rhineland Crisis* (1977).
René Girault and Robert Frank (eds.), *La Puissance en Europe, 1938–1940* (1984).
Klaus Hildebrand, 'Hitler's Policy towards France until 1936', in *German Foreign Policy from Bismarck to Adenauer: The Limits of Statecraft* (1989).
F. D. Laurens, *France and the Italo-Ethiopian Crisis, 1935–1936* (1967).
Gordon Martel (ed.), *The Origins of the Second World War Reconsidered: The A. J. P. Taylor Debate after Twenty Five Years* (1986).
W. J. Mommsen and L. Kettenacker (eds.), *The Fascist Challenge and the Policy of Appeasement* (1983).
D. Winegate Pike, *Les Français et la guerre d'Espagne* (1975).
Stephen A. Schuker,* 'France and the Remilitarization of the Rhineland, 1936', *FHS* 14 (1986), 299–338.
Maurice Vaïsse,* *Securité d'abord: la politique française en matière de désarmement, 9 dec 1930 – 17 avril 1934* (1981).
Donald Cameron Watt, *How War Came* (1989).
Eugen Weber, *The Hollow Years: France in the 1930s* (1994).

1939–1940

F. Bédarida, *La Strategie secrète de la drôle de guerre: Le Conseil Suprême Interallié, septembre 1939 – avril 1940* (1979).
P. M. H. Bell, *A Certain Eventuality: Britain and the Fall of France* (1974).

J.-L. Crémieux-Brilhac, *Les Français de l'an 40*, 2 vols.: I, *La Guerre oui ou non?*: II *Ouvriers et soldats* (1990).

J.-B. Duroselle,* *L'Abîme 1939–1945* (1982).

Marc Bloch, *L'Etrange Défaite* (1946).

Français et Britanniques dans la drôle de guerre (CNRS Paris, 1979).

Alistair Horne, *To Lose a Battle: France 1940* (1990 edn).

Brian Bond, *France and Belgium 1939–1940* (1975).

Eleanor M. Gates, *End of the Affair: The Collapse of the Anglo-French Alliance, 1939–40* (1981).

John C. Cairns, 'Along the Road Back to France, 1940', *AHR* 64 (1959), 583–603.

Bilateral and regional interests

Central and Eastern Europe

Magda Adám, *The Little Entente and Europe, 1920–1929* (1993).

Anna M. Cienciala and Titus Komarnicki, *From Versailles to Locarno: Keys to Polish Foreign Policy, 1919–1925* (1984).

A. Hogenhuis-Seliverstoff, *Les relations Franco-Soviétiques, 1917–1924* (1981).

K. Hovi, *Cordon sanitaire or barrière de l'est? The Emergence of the New French Eastern European Alliance Policy, 1917–1919* (1975).

Alliances de revers: Stabilisation of France's Alliance Policies in East Central Europe, 1919–1921 (1984).

'Security before Disarmament, or Hegemony? The French Alliance Policy 1917–1927', in R. Ahmann et al., *The Quest for Stability: Problems of West European Security 1918–1957* (1993), pp. 115–26.

Pierre le Goyet, *France–Pologne 1919–1939* (1991).

Nicole Jordan,* *The Popular Front and Central Europe: The Dilemmas of French Impotence, 1918–1940* (1992).

Anthony J. Komjathy, *The Crisis of France's East Central European Policy, 1933–1938* (1976).

W. E. Scott, *Alliance Against Hitler: The Origins of the Franco-Soviet Pact* (1962).

P. S. Wandycz, *France and her Eastern Allies, 1919–1925: French-Czechoslovak-Polish Relations from Paris Peace Conference to Locarno* (1962).

P. S. Wandycz,* *Twilight of French Eastern Alliances, 1926–1936* (1988).

Britain

W. M. Jordan, *Great Britain, France and the German Problem, 1918–1939* (1971).
Nicholas Rostow,* *Anglo-French Relations, 1934–1936* (1984).
Neville Waites (ed.) *Troubled Neighbours: Franco-British Relations in the Twentieth Century* (1971).
Arnold Wolfers, *Britain and France Between Two Wars* (1966).

United States

Henry Blumenthal, *Illusion and Reality in Franco-American Diplomacy, 1914–1945* (1986).
J.-B. Duroselle, *France and the United States* (1978).
Y.-H. Nouailhat, *France et les Etats-Unis, 1914–1917* (1979).
André Kaspi, *Le Temps des Americains: Le Concours Americain à la France en 1917–18* (1976).

Italy

William I. Shorrock,* *From Ally to Enemy: The Enigma of Fascist Italy in French Diplomacy 1920–1940* (1988).

Germany

R. Poidevin, J. Bariéty, *Les Relations Franco-Allemandes 1815–1975* (1977).
E. Jackel, *La France dans l'Europe de Hitler* (1968).

Far East

John E. Dreifort,* *Myopic Grandeur: The Ambivalence of French Foreign Policy toward the Far East, 1919–1945* (1991).

Economics and finance

Denise Artaud, *La Question des dettes interalliés et la reconstruction de l'Europe 1917–1929* (1976).
Hubert Bonin, 'Le Monde de l'argent et les décideurs politiques en France

dans les années 1850–1960', *Etudes et documents (Comité pour l'histoire économique et financière de la France)*, II (1990), 245–79.

L'Argent en France depuis 1880: Banquiers, Financiers, Épargnants (1989).

Barrie Eichengreen, *Golden Fetters: The Gold Standard and the Great Depression 1919–1939* (1992).

Robert Frankenstein,* *Le Prix du Réarmament Français, 1935–1939* (1982); Robert Frank, *La Hontise du éclin* (1994).

John F. Godfrey, *Capitalism at War: Industrial Policy and Bureaucracy in France 1914–1918* (1987).

J.-N. Jeanneney, *François de Wendel en République: l'argent et le pouvoir 1914–1940* (1976).

L'Argent caché: Milieux d'Affaires et Pouvoir Politique dans la France du XXe Siècle (1980).

D. E. Kaiser,* *Economic Diplomacy and the Origins of the Second World War* (1980).

Edward Keeton, *Briand's Locarno Policy, French Economics, Politics and Diplomacy, 1925–1929* (1987).

T. Kemp, *The French Economy 1913–1939* (1972).

R. Kuisel, *Capitalism and the State in Modern France* (1981).

Philippe Marguerat, *Banque et Investissement Industriel, Paribas, le Pétrole Roumain et la Politique Française 1919–1939* (1987).

Kenneth Mouré, *Managing the Franc Poincaré* (1991).

Vincent J. Pitts, *France and the German Problem: Politics and Economics in the Locarno Period, 1924–1919* (1987).

Haim Shamir, *Economic Crisis and French Foreign Policy 1930–1936* (1989).

Alfred Sauvy,* *Histoire économique de la France entre les deux guerres* (3 vols., 1965–72).

Stephen A. Schuker,* *American 'Reparations' to Germany, 1919–1933: Implications for the Third World Debt Crisis* (1988).

Georges Soutou,* *L'Or et le Sang: les Buts de Guerre Économiques de la Première Guerre Mondiale* (1989).

'L'impérialisme du pauvre: la politique économique du gouvernement français en Europe Centrale et Orientale de 1918 à 1929', *RI* 7 (1976) 219–39.

Marc Trachtenberg,* *Reparation in World Politics: France and European Economic Diplomacy 1916–1923* (1980).

Military doctrine and armaments

Martin S. Alexander,* *The Republic in Danger: General Maurice Gamelin and the Politics of French Defence 1933–1940* (1992).

P. C. F. Bankwitz, *Maxime Weygand and Civil-Military Relations in Modern France* (1967).

André Corvisier (ed.), *Histoire Militaire de la France*, 3, Guy Pedroncini, *1871–1940* (1992).

Jean Doise, Maurice Vaïsse, *Diplomatie et outil militaire 1871–1969* (1987).

Robert Alan Doughty, *The Seeds of Disaster: The Development of French Army Doctrine 1919–1939* (1985).

The Breaking Point: Sedan and the Fall of France, 1940 (1990).

Jeffrey A. Gunsberg,* *Divided and Conquered: The French High Command and the Defeat of the West, 1940* (1979).

Alistair Horne, *The French Army and Politics, 1870–1970* (1984).

J. M. Hughes,* *To the Maginot Line* (1971).

A. Kemp, *The Maginot Line: Myth and Reality* (1981).

Paul Kennedy (ed.), *Grand Strategies in War and Peace* (1991).

B. A. Lee, 'Strategy, Arms and the Collapse of France', in R. Langhorne (ed.) *Diplomacy and Intelligence during the Second World War* (1985).

Alan R. Millett and Williamson Murray,* *Military Effectiveness*, vol. 1, *The First World War* (1988), vol. 2, *The Interwar Period* (1988).

B. R. Posen (ed.), *The Sources of Military Doctrine: France, Britain and Germany between the World Wars* (1984).

Williamson Murray and Alan R. Millett (eds.),* *Calculations: Net Assessment and the Coming of World War II* (1992).

Robert J. Young*, *In Command of France: French Foreign Policy and Military Planning 1933–1939* (1978).

Intelligence

Anthony Adamthwaite, 'French Military Intelligence and the Coming of War 1935–1939', in Christopher Andrew and Jeremy Noakes (eds.) *Intelligence and International Relations, 1900–1945,* (1987).

Martin S. Alexander, 'Did the Deuxième Bureau Work? The Role of Intelligence in French Defence Policy and Strategy 1919–39', *INS* 6 (1991), 293–333.

Douglas Porch, 'French Intelligence and the Fall of France 1930–40', *INS* 4 (1989), 28–58.

'Le Renseignement et les relations internationales', *RI* 78 (1994).

Ernest R. May (ed.),* *Knowing One's Enemies: Intelligence Assessment Before the Two World Wars* (1984).

Politics

M. S. Alexander and H. Graham (eds.), *The French and Spanish Popular Fronts: Comparative Perspectives* (1989).
S. Berstein,* *Histoire du parti radical*, 2 vols. (1980–2).
M. Blinkhorn (ed.), *Fascists and Conservatives: The Radical Right and the Establishment in Twentieth Century Europe* (1990).
N. Ingram,* *The Politics of Dissent: Pacifism in France 1919–1939* (1991).
J.-N. Jeanneney, *Leçons d'histoire pour une gauche au pouvoir: la faillite du Cartel, 1924–1926* (1977).
W. D. Irvine, *French Conservatism in Crisis* (1979).
J. Jackson,* *The Politics of Depression in France 1932–36* (1985).
The Popular Front in France (1988).
C. A. Micaud, *The French Right and Nazi Germany* (1972).
Pierre Milza, *Fascisme français: passé et présent* (1987).
E. Mortimer *The Rise of the French Communist Party* (1984).
A. Prost, *Les Anciens Combattants* (1977).
R. Rémond and J. Bourdin (eds.),* *Edouard Daladier, chef de gouvernement* (1977).
La France et les Français (1978).
Jean-François Sirinelli (ed.), *Histoire des droites en France*, 3 vols. (1992).
Robert Soucy, *French Fascism: The First Wave* (1986).
Zeev Sternhell, *Neither Right not Left: Fascist Ideology in France* (1986).
Antonio Costa Pinto,* 'Fascist Ideology Revisited: Zeev Sternhell and his Critics', *EHQ* 16 (1986), 465–83.

Culture and society

John Cruickshank, *Variations on Catastrophe: Some French Responses to the Great War* (1982).
F. Field, *Three French Writers and the Great War* (1975).
F. Field, *British and French Writers of the First World War* (1991).
Herman Lebovics,* *True France: The Wars over Cultural Identity* (1992).
H. Stuart Hughes,* *The Obstructed Path: French Social Thought in the Years of Desperation 1930–1960* (1968).
H. Stuart Hughes,* *Consciousness and Society* (1958).
Herbert R. Lottman, *The Left Bank: Writers, Artists and Politics from the Popular Front to the Cold War* (1982).
Claude Lévi-Strauss, *Tristes Tropiques* (Penguin 1992).

Alice Yaeger Kaplan, *Reproductions of Banality: Fascism, Literature and French Intellectual Life* (1986).
Robert Wohl, *The Generation of 1914* (1979).

Cultural diplomacy and propaganda

Roger Levy, *French Interests and Politics in the Far East* (1941).
Ruth Emily McMurray and Muna Lee, *The Cultural Approach: Another Way in International Relations* (1947).
Reinhart Meyer-Kalkus et al., *Entre Locarno et Vichy: Les Relations culturelles franco-allemandes dans les années trente*, 2 vols. (1993).
'Propagande et conditionnement des esprits au XXe siècle', GMCC 173 (1994), 3–92.
Cecile Méadel, *Histoire de la radio des années trente* (1994).
Christian Brochard, *Histoire générale de la radio et de la television en France*, vol. 1, *1921–1944* (1994).
Pascal Ory,* *La Belle Illusion: la politique culturelle du Front Populaire* (1989).
Daniel R. Headrick, *The Invisible Weapon: Telecommunications and International Politics 1851–1945* (1992).

Political and diplomatic machines

A. Adamthwaite, 'France's Government Machine in the Approach to the Second World War', in H. Shamir (ed.), *France and Germany in an Age of Crisis, 1900–1960: Essays in Honour of Charles Bloch* (1990).
Jean Baillou,* *Les Affaires etrangères et le corps diplomatique français*, vol. 2, *1870–1980* (1984).
Gordon A. Craig and Felix Gilbert (eds.), *The Diplomats 1919–1939* (1994 edn).
Frederick L. Schuman, *War and Diplomacy in the Third Republic* (1931).
Walter Rice Sharp, *The French Civil Service: Bureaucracy in Transition* (1931).
Paul Gordon Lauren, *Diplomats and Bureaucrats: The First Institutional Responses to Twentieth Century Diplomacy in France and Germany* (1976).
Zara Steiner (ed.), *The Times Survey of Foreign Ministries of the World* (1982).

Media, opinion and empire

D. R. Allan, *French Views of America in the 1930s* (1979).

Claude Bellenger, et al., *Histoire générale de la presse française*, vol. 3, *1871–1940* (1975).

Yvon Lacaze,* *L'Opinion publique française et la crise de Munich* (1991).

Ralph Schor, *L'Opinion française et les étrangers en France 1919–1939* (1985).

Christopher M. Andrew and A. S. Kanya-Forstner,* *The Climax of French Imperial Expansion 1914–1924* (1981).

Catherine Hodeir and Michel Pierre, *L'Exposition coloniale* (1991).

Jacques Thobie et al., *Histoire de la France coloniale 1914–1990* (1990).

Jacques Marseille, *Empire colonial et capitalisme français* (1984).

Biographies

Robert J. Young, *Power and Pleasure: Louis Barthou and the Third French Republic* (1991).

Jean-Luc Barré, *Le Seigneur-Chat: Philippe Berthelot 1866–1934* (1988).

Joel Colton,* *Léon Blum: Humanist in Politics* (1966).

J. Lacouture, *Léon Blum* (1977).

J.-C. Allain, *Caillaux*, 2 vols. (1978–81).

D. R. Watson,* *Georges Clemenceau: A Political Biography* (1974).

J.-B. Duroselle, *Georges Clemenceau* (1988).

Bernard Oudin, *Aristide Briand* (1987).

Elizabeth du Réau,* *Edouard Daladier, 1884–1970* (1993).

J. Raphael Leygues et Jean-Luc Barré, *Delcassé* (1981).

B. Ledwidge, *De Gaulle* (1982).

J. Lacouture, *Charles de Gaulle*, 3 vols. (1984–6).

Serge Berstein, *Edouard Herriot ou la République en personne* (1985).

Geoffrey Warner, *Pierre Laval and the Eclipse of France* (1968).

Fred Kupferman, *Laval* (1987).

J.-P. Cointet, *Pierre Laval* (1993).

A. Conte, *Joffre* (1991).

Stephen D. Carls, *Louis Loucheur and the Shaping of Modern France 1916–1937* (1993).

John Sherwood, *Georges Mandel and the Third Republic* (1970).

J.-N. Jeanneney, *Georges Mandel: l'homme qu'on attendait* (1991).

M. M. Farrar, *Principled Pragmatist: The Political Career of Alexandre Millerand* (1991).

Richard Griffiths, *Marshal Pétain* (1970).
M. Ferro, *Pétain* (1987).
P. Miquel, *Raymond Poincaré* (1961).
François Monnet, *Refaire la Republique: André Tardieu* (1993).
R. Binion, *Defeated Leaders: The Political Fates of Caillaux, Jouvenel and Tardieu* (1960).

Reference

Robert J. Young, *French Foreign Policy, 1918–1945: A Guide to Research and Research Materials* (2nd edn, 1991).
David S. Bell et al., *Biographical Dictionary of French Political Leaders since 1870* (1990).
J. A. S. Grenville, *The Major International Treaties 1914–1945: A History and Guide with Texts* (1987).

Index

Joan of Arc, St (1412–1431) 73, 79, 129
Joffre, Marshal Joseph (1852–1931) 21, 23, 27, 32
Joliot-Curie, Irène 22
Joll, James 21
Jordan, Nicole 204
Jouhaux, Léon 69
Jusserand, Jules 86
Jouvenel, Bertrand de 166
Jouvenel, Henri de 128
Jouvenel, Robert de 8

Kayser, Jacques 188
Kemal, Atatürk (1881–1938) 94–5
Kerr, Philip (Lord Lothian) 54
Keynes, John Maynard (1883–1946) 44, 55, 74, 90
Keynes plan 56
Kellogg–Briand pact (Pact of Paris) 125, 128
Klotz, Lucien 48–9
Krupp 19, 99, 205

Lamont, Thomas W. 73, 98, 102
Lansing, Robert (1864–1928) 50–1
Lancken, Baron 36
Laroche, Jules 92
Laski, Harold 79, 112–3
Lausanne conferences (1922) 95, (1932) 192
Laval, Pierre (1883–1945) viii, 82, 131, 134–5, 155, 158, 165, 194–9, 228
Law, Andrew Bonar (1858–1923) 75, 95
Lawrence, T.E. (1888–1935) 50
League for the rights of man 169
League of Nations 53–4, 70, 96, 106–7, 111, 199–200
Lebrun, Albert (1871–1950) 157
Léger, Alexis (Saint John Perse, 1887–1975) 8, 9, 113–5, 132, 156–7, 195, 219
Lévy, Bernard Henri 167
Leygues, Georges 94
Libya 220
Liddell Hart, Basil 152
Liggett, General 58
Lindbergh, Charles 126
Little Entente 97, 118, 207
Litvinov, Maxim 136
Lloyd George, David

(1863–1946) 8–9, 30, 33, 35, 42–62, 71, 76, 83, 86, 93–5
Locarno conference (1925) 120–3
Locarno treaty *see* Treaties
Loizeau, General Lucien 208
London conferences (1919) 114, (1921) 96, (1924) 105–6, (1930 naval), 133–4
Long-Bérenger agreement 71
Lyautey, Marshal Louis-Hubert 64, 69, 74, 81, 119, 153
Lytton commission 184
Luther, Hans 120
Luxemburg 44

MacMahon, Marshal 12
MacDonald, Ramsay (1866–1937) 84, 101, 103–9, 129–30, 192
Madagascar 36
Maginot, André (1877–1932) 117
Maginot Line 117, 144, 151–152, 207
Mainz 42
Maison de la presse 33–4
Mallarmé, Stéphane 113
Malraux, André viii
Malvy, Louis 38
Manchurian crisis 137, 184–6
Mandel, Georges (1885–1944) 38, 43, 148
Mansfield, Katherine 38, 40
Mangin, General Louis 58, 69
Mantoux, Etienne 90
Mantoux, Paul 49
Margerie, Pierre de 22, 23, 48, 62, 83
Marin, Louis 115, 126
Massigli, René 156, 185
Maurin, General Louis 152
Maurois, André 75
Mayence 24
Mayrisch, Emil 118
Marienwerder 57
Marne 30
Mediterranean 2, 6, 24
Mellon-Bérenger accord (1926) 126
Memel 220
Mein Kampf 33, 188
Middle East 61, 74, 76, 93–5
Mitteleuropa 23, 26, 134
Messimy, Adolphe 21
Millerand, Alexandre (1859-1943) 12, 85, 94, 97, 100, 114
Mitterand, François 167
Monaco 51
Monet, Claude 26